CHILDREN'S SERVIC

P9-ECK-918

PARENT-TEACHER COLLECTION

Pride, Mary
The next book of home
learning

THE NEXT ARNING

PTC

ALLEN COUNTY PUBLIC LIBRARY

FORT WAYNE, INDIANA 46802

You may return this book to any agency, branch,
or bookmobile of the Allen County Public Library.

THE NEXT BOOK OF HOME LEARNING

THE NEXT BOOK OF HOME LEARNING

y Pri

tcl

Allen County Public Library
Ft. Wayne, Indiana

The Next Book of Home Learnin
by Mary Pride. Published by C
division of Good News Publis
Illinois 60153.

All rights reserved. No part
be reproduced, stored in a
transmitted in any form b
mechanical, photocopy, r
without the prior permiss
as provided by USA copy

Cover Design by Karen L.
Interior Design by Karen
based on the original cor
Illustration by Guy Wol
Linotronic® Typesettin
Oklahoma 74119

First printing, 19

Printed in the U

Library of Co

ISBN

INTRODUCTION

Quick quiz: just one question.
"Is there life after the Three R's?"
The Trivial Polls Association is now tabulating your answers. Breathless silence, please! The envelope with the results is being handed to the emcee. The answer given by a majority of our sample audience, ladies and gentlemen, is

"After the Three Whats?"

This book is designed to answer that burning question, "Is There Life After the Three Whats?" We're talking about three Three R's . . . Reading, 'Riting, and 'Rithmetic. Is there more to education at home than the basics?

Now, if you bought my first book, *The Big Book of Home Learning*, you know perfectly well that there is lots more to home learning than the basics. That book tried to cover the gamut of home education, from Preschool to Adult and Vocational Education, with some side trips into fun things like Toys and Games.

But a funny thing happened on the way to the second edition. The book exploded!

You see, you can only stuff so much information between two covers. *The Big Book* was already enormous— almost 350 pages long. And here I was staring at a list of 300 more suppli-

ers, all with new products to review.

I had two choices. (1) Change my name and move to Argentina and forget I ever promised to do a second edition; (2) grab all that new information, wrestle it to the floor, and produce *two* books instead of one. My family didn't want to move to Argentina, so here we are with a brand-new set of two books.

The NEW Big Book of Home Learning covers all the basics of getting started in home education and all the basic categories. Over a hundred new reviews went into that book. The other book, the one you are now holding in your hands, covers everything else. All the "extra" and "fun" subjects, like art and foreign languages, and all the new categories that I never thought of before. Plus some hints on managing your home life to make home education even simpler.

Due to the nature of this project— separating one book into two in order to add tons of new material— owners of the original *Big Book of Home Learning* will notice a few familiar reviews and chapter introductions. After all, I didn't want to completely throw out everything I had done before! However, at least 90 percent of *The Next Book of Home Learning* is brand-new material. And all the rest has updated prices, addresses, ordering information, and so on.

I'm really enthusiastic about all the great new products coming out for the home education market. We're going to be able to do things we hardly dreamed about! But before you can start taking off with a great new product you have to find it. More: you need to know if it is right for *you*. That is why, as always, the reviews in this book are as much as possible based on actual observation and use.

Our family tried out most of these products, trying to discover their personality— what about each product would delight or disgruntle what kind of person. With so many items to review, we have become experts at smashing boxes flat and carrying them to the dumpster,

if nothing else! The children (Theodore, Joseph, Sarah, Magdalene Joy, and little Franklin) helped produce mailings, favored us with their official opinions on products, or lay in the crib and looked cute, depending on their ages. And I finally achieved one of my lifetime goals— constructing a home learning program that is both academically excellent and ridiculously simple. We knew the products had to be out there . . . somewhere . . . but now we HAVE them.

So here it is at last, the fruit of many long days and nights, many long-distance phone calls and letters, many hours leafing through catalogs and unpacking packages. Between the covers of this book are the products and methods that have made the difference for us. Go ahead— put your home learning program into overdrive!

HOW TO USE THIS BOOK

You know how to read a resource book. Just turn to the section that interests you and browse through the reviews until something pops out at you from the text.

Well, guess what?

You can do the same thing with this book!

The editors and I have, however, incorporated a few innovative features that, we hope, will make *The Next Book of Home Learning* more useful than the average resource book.

If you'll flip to the Suppliers Index you can see that it is more than just names with addresses attached. We're added all sorts of helpful information: toll-free telephone numbers for ordering, best times of day to call, methods of payment allowed, refund policy, whether or not the supplier has a free brochure or catalog and what it costs if it isn't free, plus a brief description of the supplier's product line. Underneath all this you'll notice a little code that tells you in which chapters the suppliers' products are mentioned.

Because the addresses, telephone numbers and all the rest of it are in the index, not in the text, we were able to include much more information about each supplier, as well as giving you a cross-index to other products that might interest you. For example, say you're looking for art games. In the Art chapter you see that Firm ABC sells these. The catalog sounds good. In the index you see that Firm ABC also carries games to teach classical mythology and music. You're interested in all of these, so you look up those reviews too. Now you have a much fuller picture of the company.

This way it is also easier to find the address of any given company. Instead of searching through a chapter to find the company, as you have to when full addresses are given in the text, just flip to the index.

What all this means is that you can relax and enjoy *The Next Book of Home Learning* without having to write down reams of information about every product that interests you. Just jot down the name of the supplier and the name of the item on a handy index card or whatever. If you think you will want to order it right away, you might also jot down the price. When you get your whole list together, then you can turn to the index and highlight or underline the companies you intend to contact. Stick the card you were taking notes on in the index and go your merry way. When you are

ready to order, all the addresses are in one convenient location and you have all the item names and prices handy, too.

The information in *The Next Book of Home Learning* is as current and up to date as we could possibly make it. The prices listed should be good for a long time (since I asked about possible price increases while preparing the reviews), and the ordering information is current. Even so, it is always wise to write or call the supplier for information before ordering, especially if you're considering an expensive product. These prices are meant to give you an idea of costs, so you can compare products by price as well as content.

Lastly, this book would not have been possible without the active cooperation of many of the companies listed. Those who supplied me with samples and free catalogs bravely ran the risks of review, and I have not hesitated to point out their products' warts. I would like them to feel they gained something besides a critical going-over by their largesse. Both the publisher and I would be grateful if you would mention *The Next Book of Home Learning* if you write to a supplier whose product is mentioned here.

PART I

THE LAZY MOTHER'S GUIDE TO HOME EDUCATION

CHAPTER ONE

METHODS—STREAMLINED TEACHING AND LEARNING

One of the fascinating things that happens to people who write books is that readers write back. On any given day, our old family mailbox is jammed full. Not just with letters— as avid mail-order shoppers we get more than our fair share of catalogs. And even though we never send in a sweepstakes form, practically every day we are informed that we are but an envelope and stamp away from winning a million dollars. Still, I spend at least five hours a week just sorting and reading my personal mail.

After *The Big Book of Home Learning* came out, many mothers and fathers wrote to share about the fantastic time they were having teaching their children at home. Meanwhile, I received a small but significant number of letters with sad stories to tell. Typically, a mother of one or two would tell me she tried home schooling or after schooling and gave it up because it was "too hard" and "wasn't working out."

I really wondered about those last letters for a while. We have five children and a home business, plus I write books and Bill worked until recently as a full-time computer programmer. How come we, and other parents of large families who had written to us, could manage to teach our children at home, while parents with much more time and fewer children were struggling? Why was the question readers most frequently asked, "How do you find time to do it all?"

It could be, of course, that Bill and I are just utterly amazing Superfolks, and I could try and put this explanation over were it not for the large number of people still living who know us personally and know better. (That's why it's better to wait until you're 90 to write your memoirs!) It could also be that we have given birth to five infant prodigies in a row, an explanation their grandparents favor. It's certainly not that we have maids or hired help (don't I wish!).

We do have a secret for our success. It's . . . laziness! Like other survival-oriented parents of a large brood, for many years now we have been searching for easier, simpler ways of doing things. And surprise! There *are* easier, simpler ways to learn at home.

In *The Big Book of Home Learning* and its successor *The NEW Big Book of Home Learning*, we looked at the different styles of home education. Now let's take a look at some shortcuts.

TIME-SHARING

You've heard of "time-sharing." If several terminals are logged onto the same computer at the same time, they are time-sharing— swapping the computer's resources back and forth as needed, while all the programs appear to run at once. Time-sharing means doing more than one thing at the same time. How? By keeping large "background" tasks running while interruptions are handled as efficiently as possible.

Time-sharing was a major leap forward for computing. On large computers, it has permanently replaced the old "one thing at a time" way of handling jobs.

So at home why do we so often get stuck in the rut of "one thing at a time" teaching? We make up little charts with time marked off for phonics, math, science, and so on, and then consider ourselves failures if we don't get through the planned-on material without interruptions. It's time we faced facts. Children *are* interruptions! And wasn't one of our reasons for taking on home schooling or after schooling that we wanted to give our children the individual attention that they need?

One-thing-at-a-time teaching works well for "input" teaching like reading literature aloud or lecturing on science concepts. But when your children range widely in age and abilities and are working independently on a lot of different subjects, time-sharing is a must.

Let me give you an example of how time-sharing works. You are sitting on the couch helping son Fred with his math. As soon as he gets going on a page of problems, you call over little brother John and explain the writing project he is supposed to finish today. Once John gets up to speed, sister Jennifer gets her first five minutes of reading practice. Fred now interrupts with a question. If it's a short one,

you answer it right away and get back to Jenny. If it's not, you ask him to save it for a bit later and work at something else for a while. Meanwhile, baby Jason is playing in his crib. When he needs a diaper change or a nursing, you do that while checking on the other children's work, e.g., "Bring your paper over here to the changing table, Fred, so I can see how you're doing so far."

Does this sound complicated? It isn't, really. The secret of success in time-sharing is *how you handle the interruptions*. In our example above, interruptions which will take a long time are put off until you finish your present task. Only highest priority interruptions (feeding the baby, changing him) are an exception to this rule, and during those interruptions you continue to monitor the children's work. In this way you can keep on top of an amazing amount of different projects at once.

Time-sharing is not easy at first. It requires a mental game plan for each child so you and the child both know what he is supposed to do while you are not hovering over him. But this "teaching" part of the day need not take very long, thanks to the next shortcuts.

ACCESS

The best way to teach is to not have to teach at all. Ideally, our children should learn how to learn and begin to teach themselves.

How can we help our children reach this stage? In part, by giving them access to educational tools.

Let's define what we're talking about here. Access does not mean simply having educational items available somewhere in the house. It means having them ready to hand, right where the child can get them when he wants them or when you want to direct his attention to them. Children blessed with access to the tools of learning will tend to use them on their own much more frequently than those who have to climb stairs, navigate stacks of clutter, or ask you to get out the items in question.

Here is how the access principle works.

FOR A BABY: Alphabet letters, numerals, and educational pictures clutter our homes.

But how often do you have the time to sit down with your little one and help him play with all his educational toys? Instead of all those fancy toys, try taping a simple sheet of paper with the ABC's on it on the wall next to your changing table. You have to spend what seems like hours there every day anyway, so why not give your baby something interesting to look at? You will have plenty of opportunities to point to and say each letter, and your youngster will have lots of time to become familiar with the shape of print. The same can be done with color and shape charts, "touch 'n feel" strips with different fabrics glued to them, numeral strips, and so on.

FOR A TODDLER: Is the piano lid often left rolled back so he can plink away at the keys? Are there lots of hard-to-destroy books around that he can "read"? Even better, have you trained him how to handle *your* books properly so he doesn't have to be shooed away from them? Do you have special places for his toys so he can find one easily when he wants it, or are half of them lost and the rest scattered all over? Have you taught him how to put cassettes in the cassette player or just stuck them up high somewhere? Remember, if a child is taught how to use it, he won't abuse it.

FOR AN OLDER CHILD: Do you leave that expensive pint-size violin out between scheduled practice sessions, or is it carefully put away in some hard-to-reach spot? Is art material a mere drawer pull away, or is it locked up in a cupboard somewhere? Is the encyclopedia in your family room (or whatever favorite reading spot your family has chosen) or displayed under glass in the den?

Human nature being what it is, you can be sure that if it is hard to find, hard to get out, or hard to put away, children will avoid it. But when parents make the materials of learning accessible, amazing things start to happen! I once read the story of a Suzuki mother who decided to hint that her daughter should put her violin away by leaving it out in plain view. The daughter never did put the violin away that day. Instead she practiced for half an hour more than usual. Every time she saw the violin

she picked it up and used it. You can imagine how this astonished the mother, who had been used to meeting resistance to music practice. In exactly the same vein, Maire Mullarney, an Irish home school mother, tells in her book *Anything School Can Do You Can Do Better* (Holt Associates, $5.95 plus $1.50 shipping) how she used to let her children paint all over their ancient kitchen table and walls, serving dinner around the latest masterpieces before wiping them off. Several of her children won national art competitions. This interest in art continued unabated until the family received an inheritance. With the money they bought fancier furniture and redid the house. The unexpected side effect was that the children no longer felt free to paint all over the new, expensive walls and table, and consequently started spending far less time on their art.

In short, if you put it where they can get it and teach them how to use it properly, children will use it. Provided, of course, that you have a good relationship with them and they are not trying to prove something by upsetting you, and also that your home is not loaded with time-wasting distractions that divert them from better pursuits.

The principle of access applies to all subjects, not just art and music. Our children are surrounded by math and science texts, thanks to all the companies that have let me review their wares. It's not at all uncommon to see Ted or Joe browsing through one of these in an odd moment. All our children have free access to crayons, pencils, pens, and paper, and in return we receive a never-ending stream of poems, stories, and art. Three-year-old Sarah writes great sentences like "HA HAL NAO PHH" (someday she'll stop being addicted to the letter H!) and one-year-old Magda will sit for minutes creatively scribbling (if you knew Magda, you'd know getting her to sit for *anything* is a major event!). Everyone bonks on the piano, and with only casual instruction the older ones are becoming quite good at picking out tunes. The knowledge the children pick up entirely on their own by their free foraging through our books helps schoolwork zip along and makes for interesting mealtime discussions. I'll probably never have to teach them art appreciation because of our art books and art cards, and the same goes for laser technology and robotics.

So the secret of making learning accessible is really

- good resources that the children know how to use
- happy children, and
- getting rid of worthless distractions (more on this, later).

CLONE YOURSELF

Wouldn't it be wonderful if you could hire a private tutor for some minimal sum like, say, 5¢ an hour, to drill your children on all those memory facts and to tell them fascinating stories? You want it, you have it. Introducing . . . the Tape Recorder. Faster than a speeding mother! More powerful than a tired father! Able to leap tall buildings on either Fast Forward or Rewind! This remarkable visitor from our own planet has powers and abilities far beyond those of mortal men. Perfect recall of every story. Perfect patience. Perfect manners— talks at mealtimes without ever having its mouth full. Yes, friends, the humble audio cassette recorder can teach you and your children how to sing or play a musical instrument, how to speak a foreign language, or how to win in business. It can give you math drill set to song in stereo or read you the entire Bible. Art instruction, phonics courses, great literature, even sports tips are all available on cassette direct from the famous people who invented them. It's like having an army of tutors! And the best part is that you and your children can learn together or separately as the fancy takes you.

We listen to a lot of cassettes at mealtimes. I reviewed virtually all the cassettes for this book at lunchtime. The children also like them at breakfast, suppertime, and in between. Adults can listen to cassettes while washing dishes, nursing the baby, or driving to work.

Video cassettes are also becoming popular, but will never be as versatile as the audio versions simply because you have to give video your full attention. Try to picture a video Walkman. Ugh.

Audio lets you learn while you do other things— a classic example of time-sharing.

LEARN THE LINGO

Shakespeare was wrong. A rose by any other name definitely does not smell as sweet. If you'd like a dash of quick encouragement, learn how to give fancy names to what you are doing with your children. A walk down the street can be a Science Excursion. Reading *Tintin Goes to Tibet* is Social Studies (your child is being exposed to the culture of Tibet, after all). That half-hour with the paint pot is Artistic Self-Expression. Weeding the walk is a Hands-On Nature Investigation. And don't forget all the time you spend answering their questions (stop thinking of those as "interruptions"— the official term is "teachable moments"). Write it all up in a daily journal and you'll be astonished at how much you are getting done.

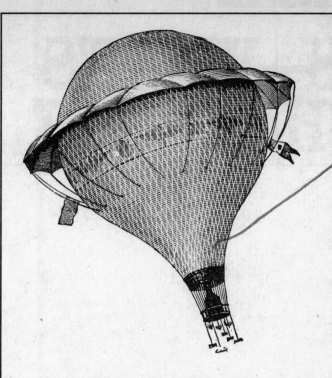

ENCOURAGEMENT AND JOY

As Ruth Beechick points out in her masterful *Biblical Psychology of Learning* (Education Services, $9.70 postpaid), learning is first and foremost a matter of the heart. If your heart isn't in it, you're not going to learn well no matter how wonderful the teacher or material. Conversely, if a student is enthusiastic and determined, he can learn almost anything.

Home education burnout, like all other burnout, comes from too much work and insufficient rewards. Sometimes you gotta do what you gotta do, but when you're hating what you're doing all the time it's time to stop and rethink your position. If you're trying to teach or learn from a resource that you have no fondness for at all, perhaps you should pitch it and try another.

I don't mean that we should expect to play all the time. Learning can be hard work. But it should lead to the pleasure of success and be as pleasurable for our students as we can make it. If it's nothing but unalloyed drudgery, the fault is almost certainly to be found in the teaching materials or method.

When you find yourself working too hard, stop and ask

☞ Am I overdoing it? Am I making a simple subject too fancy? Am I trying to do *all* the suggested activities in the teacher's edition (this will kill any program)?

☞ What can I eliminate? What is essential in this course and what is extra?

☞ Do I need to be doing this at all? Is my child too young for this subject? Am I just trying to show off? Could I or my child live a worthy life in the world without mastering this material?

☞ Should I give it a rest? Are there other worthwhile things we would like to study or do instead of this until we can come back to it later?

Your goal should be to do the essential (teach Johnny to read, clean the kitchen before the Board of Health condemns it) and to get to the rest when you have time. Don't exhaust yourself trying to imitate all the success stories you read in home schooling magazines. Forget the fancy projects and the field trips that need two weeks to plan. You can always get to them later when your children have more enthusiasm for them and you have more time.

At various times I have had to give up piano lessons for the children (too young, not enough interest), art appreciation (overdoing it, neglecting more essential subjects), and French (not enough time, not needed at the moment). In the meantime I have learned a lot more about teaching each of these subjects and located better materials. Art appreciation and piano are now being handled by the children themselves and we have substituted Latin for French. The world did not end because we let some things slip that were giving us no joy for the present.

If it's something basic like reading or math that's giving you headaches you need to check out some of the other resources for these subjects listed in *The NEW Big Book of Home Learning*. But even these subjects can be laid aside for a bit while you all recover.

Let's make learning as simple as we can, and learning will be fun!

CHAPTER TWO

MATERIALS—WHAT'S HOT AND WHAT'S NOT

I have a dream. Or a daydream, actually. It goes like this:

Drums roll. Gorgeous technicolor sweeps onto the screen. Fireworks! Exploding stars! Rainbows zooming into pots of gold! Huge gold letters appear— "Introducing the PERFECT CURRICULUM!" Cut to a deep purple screen with a tiny speck of light in the distance. The speck grows and grows, rushing towards us. As our dazzled eyes focus on the speck, we see it is indeed the Perfect Curriculum. Our long, long search is over. No more a-bit-of-this and a-bit-of-that. No more indecisive shuffling of flyers from dozens of companies. No need to write another resource book, or to buy it!

And what is this Perfect Curriculum, we ask? Why, it's just what educational materials ought to have been all along.

• **The Perfect Curriculum is multilevel.** This means that you can use the same materials with children of all different ages. Actual activities will vary between children, depending on their maturity and attention span. Example: Grandma's Garden Felt Math (reviewed in *The NEW Big Book of Home Learning*) can be used to teach a preschooler how to count and recognize shapes. But it can also teach a kindergartner how to recognize her numerals, a first-grader simple addition and subtraction, and more advanced students simple fractions, multiplication, and division. Another example: *The Drawing Textbook* (reviewed in this book's Art chapter) can be used to teach drawing skills to *anyone* old enough to hold a pencil and follow directions. This means that the whole family can study the same subject at the same time with the same materials, and you won't have to juggle umpteen different books, manipulatives, workbooks, and so on.

• **The Perfect Curriculum is simple.** All the instructions for one job are in the same place. You don't have to go to page 10 of Workbook A for one bit, page 42 in Workbook B for another, and cap it all with a quick jaunt to the graph on page 17 of the accompanying Teacher's Guide and the graph on page 14 of the accompanying handout sheets. The student's work also should follow a sequential order. You do page eight, then page nine, and so on. For "book" courses, ideally no teacher's manual is necessary, since all the instructions are on the page in the student's book.

• **The Perfect Curriculum is efficient.** It zips right along. You only get one lesson on the letter "A" and the exact same format is used to introduce all the other vowels. Enrichment activities and tips for helping slow learners are clearly labeled as such and not built into the basic course. If you want to flap like an albatross or sing a song with lots of "A" words that's fine and dandy, but it's not confused with learning "A."

• **The Perfect Curriculum notes potential difficulties in advance and tells you what to do about them**. For example: Some children have a tendency to write their "2"s and "5"s backwards. A Perfect Curriculum would warn you to expect this and tell you how to overcome it.

• **The Perfect Curriculum is not time-pressured.** You are given lessons to do or projects to complete and allowed to go at your family's own pace. Some of us do need deadlines to function at our best, but even those deadlines should be weighed in months and semesters instead of days or weeks.

• **The Perfect Curriculum has choices within a structure.** If an activity is totally open-ended (e.g., "Do something with an encyclopedia") it breeds confusion and, yes, boredom. If you have to invent your own ideas from scratch, why should you pay for this? Picking from an exciting menu of well-chosen projects can inject energy and enthusiasm while still allowing room for creative individuality.

• **The Perfect Curriculum is easy to handle.** We're talking about basic stuff like spi-

ral-bound Teacher's Manuals with real metal spirals so they will stay open where you want them instead of the pages sliding about, falling out, and getting torn (as with ring binders) or snapping shut just when you're trying to follow some complicated directions (as with regular books). We're also talking about packaging with a place for every item so it can be instantly retrieved. Please don't give us itty-bitty flashcards that kids can't handle or odd-sized materials that won't fit in a normal file cabinet or storage shelf. Don't make it bulky, clunky, slippery, or shreddable.

• **The Perfect Curriculum is durable.** Flashcards should be made out of heavy card stock so they won't bend, fold, spindle, or be mutilated. A hardbound textbook is also much better than a paperback for families who plan to use the text again with younger children. Anything intended for elementary-age children should be waterproof, tear-proof (as in both the act of ripping and the act of crying), and smudge-resistant. Even consumable workbooks should be bound well enough so they can withstand a few seconds of a baby's full attention.

• **The Perfect Curriculum is eye-appealing.** This is the age of desktop publishing. No longer need we put up with Stencil Stupor or Mimeo Muddiness. Even brand-new kitchen-table products can look good after a few hours rented time on a computer. Thanks to laser printing, personal computer output is no longer limited to eye-burning dot-matrix or typewriter quality. We like it big and bold, with a clean layout and lots of graphics. One picture is still worth a thousand words. Just make sure that the picture is artistically correct— following the rules of proportion, at least.

• **The Perfect Curriculum accommodates all learning styles.** It has something for the mover, something for the thinker, something for the listener, and something for the looker.

• **The Perfect Curriculum also accommodates all teaching styles**, from the concept-oriented long-range planner to the Do It Now type who loves memory work and drill.

• **The Perfect Curriculum is not age-graded.** It covers each subject from start to finish. The student can see exactly how much he has to learn from the start in order to launch out on his own. If the curriculum is the spiral sort that covers the same topics again and again, each time they are treated from entirely different angles. Tiresome repetition is omitted.

• **The Perfect Curriculum does not make you feel unnecessarily guilty.** You are not given eight hundred darling enrichment activities and bulletin-board suggestions for each class hour. No way are you going to do all that, so why weigh yourself down with it?

• **The Perfect Curriculum covers everything you and your children need to know, and nothing else.** If you consider Art History a "must," it has it. If Swahili is on your wish list, it's got it. On the other hand, if you consider Art History and Swahili a waste of time, they either aren't there in the first place, or are neatly sequestered in little modules you can just lop off and ignore.

• **The Perfect Curriculum is remarkably inexpensive or even free** (now you know I'm dreaming!).

Fact is, there probably never will be a Perfect Curriculum. We all have different styles and needs. But we can use the above guidelines to greatly reduce our teaching and learning effort.

As home schoolers, we do *not* need resources that are complicated, inefficient, hard to handle, boring, or ugly. With the exception of "ugly," most modern American public school textbooks and programs are all the above. The Teacher's Editions are a veritable

smorgasbord of time-consuming, time-wasting activities. Work that should take days is spun out over weeks, and this inefficiency is disguised by hundreds of little "activities" that wear out both teacher and student. Hours are spent juggling bulletin board brighteners and fooling with useless projects and workbook exercises instead of making real educational progress. The curriculum is spread so thin that twelfth-graders may not know simple fractions, and each grade's work is rigorously and artificially separated from the others.

Home schoolers don't have time or energy to waste, so we are forced to discover resources that really work, and work quickly. So far there has been a tendency to follow the public school curriculum outline, just like most private schools. But as it becomes clear how inefficient this really is, home schoolers are rediscovering simple, elegant solutions to the problems of education today. They are condensing, simplifying, and innovating. They are cutting through the thickets that have grown up in the groves of academe and getting down to the roots.

I really want to see you succeed in your educational dreams. Besides what God has placed in your own heart, you need the right *methods* and the right *resources*. This book is my way of helping you with both of these, while lobbying educational producers to improve the latter!

You can cast a meaningful vote for improved education. How? By spending your money not just on what is cheapest, but on products that really do the job. Believe me, you can't make a better investment than investing in your family's education. Banks may go sour, stocks may falls, and thieves break in and steal, but what you carry in your head and heart is yours forever. Make sure it's the best.

CHAPTER THREE

HOME MANAGEMENT, OR IS THERE HOUSE AFTER LIFEWORK?

Is there house after lifework? What happens to the

- dishes
- laundry
- shopping
- cleaning

while you and the kids are tackling the Three R's?

This is a good question. Reality, for most home schoolers, means a husband who works full-time and kids who make messes full time. Artistic, creative messes are still messes and someone still has to clean them up.

Messes and their removal are even bigger problems for after-schooling families. When you only have a few precious moments with your children every day, you especially don't want to spend that time wrestling vacuum cleaners and scrubbing the bathroom.

We're not down on housework, you understand. We aren't the kind of people who write bitter poems about the slavery of mopping the kitchen floor. We like clean houses, lovely meals, and attractive gardens. We just have other important business, and can't afford to spend four hours every day tidying up.

The first step to earning your Lazy Mother wings is to avoid as much unnecessary housework as possible. Besides the obvious (mopping only half as often, enlisting the kids to help with dishwashing, etc.) there are literally hundreds of ways to rearrange your time, furniture, and cleaning tools so that you simply never have to do as much work in the first place.

I'm not talking about clever little systems for "managing" housework that take as much time to organize and file as the housework itself. No, I'm talking about the Six Steps to Domestic Sanity:

(1) SELF-AWARENESS. Do you have a problem with messiness? The best way to find where you and your housekeeping *really* stand is to read *The Messies Manual* by Sandra Felton. (This, and all the other books mentioned in this chapter, are available in bookstores or from our home business, Home Life. See prices at the end of this chapter.) Sandra defines a dozen different kind of Messies— the Perfectionist Messie, the Spartan Messie, the Rebellious Messie— and offers cures. Her book

Rebellious Messie— and offers cures. Her book has a fairly simple system for organizing your chores, which I will never use, because I don't even *do* most of them yet. How often to wash your baseboards is a moot point for those of us with the attitude, "What baseboards?". However, the book is amply illustrated, cartoon-style, and fun to read.

(2) DE-JUNK! Nothing, but nothing, makes it easier to get things done than getting things gone. If you're like most people, your living space is literally loaded with useless clutter. The problem is we have not been trained to recognize clutter. It's more than crumpled up school papers and worn-out tennis shoes. Clutter is anything that interferes with doing what we are supposed to be doing on this earth— and that could include anything from the TV set to that expensive set of skis gathering dust in the basement. The definitive masterpiece on this subject is Don Aslett's *Clutter's Last Stand.*

(3) LEARN THE TRICKS OF THE TRADE. The best books on *this* subject are *Is There Life After Housework?* and *Do I Dust or Vacuum First?*, both by Don Aslett.

Let me digress for a minute here and tell you about Don Aslett. Here is a man, the father of six, who worked his way through college cleaning houses and office buildings. His cleaning firm grew so profitable that after college he continued in the business.

But Mr. Aslett noticed something interesting. When he was a college kid doing cleaning on the side, people praised him. But when he made cleaning his lifework, people began to look down on him.

Don tells the tale of the time he was working in a bank, cleaning the floor. At this point he was president of his own multimillion-dollar company and a member of the state legislature. A mother with a misbehaving child came in, and to quiet the child, she pointed to Don cleaning the floor and warned, "If you don't cut it out, someday you'll grow up to be like that poor man over there!"

Don decided that enough was enough. Cleaning wasn't a loser's job, it was a profession! He also began to feel a certain amount of sympathy for the embattled American housewife, whose job was treated with the same disdain as his. To make a long story short, he developed a seminar (now on video) to teach housewives the professional shortcuts he had discovered over the years. The seminar went over big, and so did his books.

Is There Life After Housework? is now also available on video, and it's a laugh riot! Don is more than a bit of both an artist (watching him clean an entire picture window in under 10 seconds to the tune of "The Blue Danube Waltz" is a treat!) and a comedian (you'll hate yourself if you miss his "Junk Box" and "Fastest Squeegee in the West" routines). And when you've finished laughing, you'll have gained five years on your life (the time you'll save on your housework chores from now on!).

(4) TEACH YOUR FAMILY THE TRICKS OF THE TRADE. No, I'm not suggesting the old, tired, "50 Sneaky Ways to Get Your Spouse to Help Around the House." But it's only reasonable to expect sentient beings to pick up after themselves. Fact is, though, that whereas the average homeworker today doesn't know how to clean efficiently, her better half and offspring don't know how to clean at all. Once again, Don Aslett comes to the rescue, this time with the provocatively titled *Who Says It's a WOMAN'S Job to Clean?* This book, designed for the dense, is even simpler and easier to understand than *Is There Life After Housework?*, making it a great choice for wedding gifts, baby showers, and welcome-back-from-your-nervous-breakdown parties.

(5) MAKE YOUR HOUSE DO THE HOUSEWORK. This also happens to be the title of a truly fantastic book by, you guessed it, Don

Aslett. America's Number One Cleaning Expert strikes again! This time Don comes up with ways to find out what about your house, apartment, condo, or whatever is making you work too hard, and eliminate it. Buy this book *before* you pick out furniture, wallpaper, carpet, faucets— or keep it around to give you ideas. Some of Don's suggestions involve major remodeling, but most take very little time or effort and can pay major dividends in your free time and comfort thereafter.

(6) DO SOMETHING CREATIVE WITH ALL THAT NEW FREE TIME. This you can manage by yourself without help from Don Aslett or me!

Home Life

All the books reviewed above are available in bookstores. Or you can order them from our home business, Home Life (add 10% shipping).

The Messies Manual— $5.95
Clutter's Last Stand— $8.95
Is There Life After Housework?
    Book, $7.95
    Video, $29.95 (specify VHS or Beta).
Do I Dust or Vacuum First?— $7.95
Who Says It's a WOMAN'S Job to Clean?— $5.95
Make Your House Do the Housework (a BIG book)— $9.95

CHAPTER FOUR

FAMILY MANAGEMENT, OR GETTING YOUR PACK TOGETHER

Lazy Mothers and Fathers need cooperative families. This is simpler to manage than you might think. Love, togetherness, and a healthy skepticism for the opinions of experts are all anyone needs to get started on the right track.

As a mother of five, I know there are days when nothing goes right. The bathtub runneth over, your potty-trained child forgets and waters the new carpet, and the phone and doorbell both ring just as you start shampooing your hair. Nobody can control situations like these, so don't bother to try! And if you feel inadequate, just remember that so does every other adult who ever accepted full-time responsibility for a child.

All the same, we dream dreams. We imagine a family meal with each child politely passing the chicken instead of hovering over the plate and getting his fingers on every piece before thrusting the pawed-over remains at his brother. We think of chores almost magically finished before nine AM because *every* family member helped. We picture evenings spent concocting fudge or reading aloud from the treasures of literature instead of watching tasteless TV commercials.

I will never discourage you by telling you your dreams are unrealistic. You can have high hopes, and by God's grace, you can substantially achieve them. Half of the battle is to believe in what you are aiming for. The other half is to "walk with the wise" by selecting only the family helps that will really uplift your family— in place of those that urge you to lower your expectations, or those that promise you the moon but depend on mind games or faddish gimmicks.

The resources in this chapter are designed to give you a quick overview of what's out there in helps for family life. Some offer a new "way of seeing" that helps you pinpoint family opportunities for growth. Others show how to provide more time for family togetherness. I also included a brief look at the various philosophies of child-training, including those with which I disagree, because confusion on this issue is arguably the Number One cruncher of home learning programs. You don't have to agree with everything I've come up with— after all, I'm just a young mother myself. But this gives us a place to start.

THE HOWS AND WHYS OF CHILD TRAINING

Should we train our children? Double-mindedness about this question probably causes more parental failure than anything else. On the one hand, we don't want them to beat up on their brothers and sisters or trash the house. One the other hand, some people are so convinced that children are "naturally good" that they feel unqualified to put any brakes on their children's behavior.

I've often thought it odd that the same people who insist on the natural goodness of children strongly believe in the natural depravity of adults. Yet, if a typical adult behaved like a typical two-year-old, he would be in the slammer for assault, property destruction, slander, and who knows what inside of 10 minutes. Call it "passion" instead of a temper tantrum; call it "normal frustration" instead of an attack on the baby; but whatever you call it, you know down deep you don't really want it. The Bible says that a child left to himself disgraces his mother, and millennia of experience echo, "Amen."

How, then, shall we train our children? Let's list the three alternatives:

1) We, the parents, control their environment, and trust that in this controlled environment the child will discover self-discipline on his own. This is the Montessori approach in a nutshell. For resources on the Montessori approach, including a taped seminar on child management the Montessori way, contact the International Montessori Society.

2) We, the parents, train the child directly and also take responsibility for managing their environment. This has been the traditional approach in all cultures, and remains the biblical Christian method. *What the Bible Says About . . . Child Training,* published by Aletheia Publishers (a division of Alpha Omega Publications), covers this approach in depth. Subjects include: the need for controlling young children; how and when to use chastisement; devices children use to avoid obeying, and how to respond; and developing self-controlled teenagers. Both video and audio tapes of a seminar based on this book are available. The book is endorsed by Jerry Falwell and Dr. Paul Kienel of the Association of Christian Schools International and costs $5.95.

3) They, the children, run the whole show and we are reduced to negotiating with them. In this setup, exemplified in the best-seller *Parent Effectiveness Training* by Thomas Gordon, parents are forbidden the use of all traditional child-training tools. The children, however, can use physical force, abusive language, disapproval, and the Child Abuse Hotline to get their way.

Is it really worth the effort struggling to raise your children without raising them— to make them do things without making them? According to the books I have read that present this message, it sure isn't any *fun.* One major tactic they employ is to bore the kids into obedience by talking them to death. Another is to turn them over to baby-sitters, day-care, and the public schools, thus craftily evading the problem. A third is to simply ignore unwanted behavior, which can be pretty difficult when the child in question is slashing your clothes with a razor or beating up his baby brother. Perhaps the most popular tactic of this approach is to attribute all misbehavior to psychological problems or learning disorders, thus neatly depositing the problem (and the child) in the hands of professionals.

Raising one child by the strength of one's wit alone can be an exhausting task, and as for three or four, forget it. It's a lot harder to try to trick your children into doing what they ought than it is to simply lay down the law and make sure they follow it. As long as *you yourself* are subject to the same law, this should cause no resentment. In other words, if you want your children to forgive, you must be forgiving; if you don't want them to steal, be careful you are honest yourself. The Bible has lots more to say on this subject of raising children according to absolute rules to which the parents are also accountable. If you're interested, the Ten Commandments (found in Deuteronomy chapter 6) and the book of Proverbs are a wonderful place to start.

WHAT KIDS NEED TO KNOW TO SURVIVE IN A FAMILY

Where can we find help in training our children? We're not talking about character education here, just the simple survival skills that make family life so much more pleasant. Children need to know how to clean up their rooms, how to amuse themselves, how to get along with each other, and so on. You probably know how to teach them all that, but if you feel like you could use some help, look below.

Word Books
Survival Series, $8.80 for each 2 books; 24 volumes in all. Books sent on approval

Since the *Survival Series for Kids* by Joy Wilt Berry has already sold 5,000,000 copies (that's five *million*, folks!), I may not be telling you anything you don't already know. Still, here goes. It's a pile of books that tell kids how to do such things as be kind to guests, get good grades, take care of their clothes, clean their rooms, answer the phone, and so on. The name of each book begins with "What to Do When Your Mom or Dad Says" and that's what they are all about: what to do; how to do it; and why to do it.

The illustrations are a character education in themselves. Kids doing bad or useless things look bummed out; kids behaving properly look cheerful or downright smug.

The books won't do everything the enormous full-color direct mail ad says they

will. No book turns a lazybones into a model of industry all by itself, except the Bible! But they at least provide the how-to to go along with your what-to.

Word is offering the *Survival Series* with one of those send-for-the-first-two-books-and-get-one-free offers. If you are prompt in returning the books you don't like, this offer is a way to look the series over.

FAMILY MAGAZINES

Aren't you a little tired of "family" magazines that assume parents are dolts who need to be ordered about by experts? And what's the use of "baby" magazines that greet the arrival of the newborn with grim articles on sibling rivalry and tips on contraception?

Here are some magazines that march to the tune of a different drummer.

Christian Magazines

Christian Life Workshops
Family Restoration Quarterly, $5.

Our good friend Gregg Harris puts out this very professional-looking newsletter. Areas covered are similar to those you'll find in *HELP* (see below). The difference is that *HELP* is a forum, whereas the Family Restoration Quarterly features articles by leaders in various areas of family restoration. The first issue was fairly philosophical, but we hear future issues will include more practical how-tos.

Family Resources
Subscriptions free to early birds. May charge a small subscription fee later.

One new magazine that promises to be different is *Family Resources*, published by SMS Publications. Right now it is *free*, for one thing! The first issue of *Family Resources*, at press time, was slated to present resources for • Family Music and Worship • Personal Growth and Marriage Enrichment • Home Management • Stuff for Kids • Home Schooling • Film and

Video • Computers • and Church Resources. As a basically advertiser-driven publication, *Family Resources* articles have a how-to and where-to-find-it flavor. Bill and I are consulting editors and hope to influence this new magazine to serve the needs of families who are *not* trying to escape their children.

Home Life.
**   *HELP*, 4 issues, $15. Sample issue, $1. Make out check to Home Life.**

Our own sixteen-page newsletter, *HELP*, is a forum and resource for those serious about enjoying their family and the Lord. Areas covered are home business, pregnancy and childbirth (from the viewpoint of children as a blessing), family growth, age-integration, home management, and so on. People around the world write to share what's happening in the family restoration movement in their countries; readers argue back and forth and share their experiences; Bill and I contribute the occasional article; and a lively time is had by all.

Other Magazines

Family in America

Want to know where your family stands socially? No, I'm not talking about your standing in the community. We're talking politics here. Also economics, culture, philosophy, medicine, law, and so on. What are the experts up to, and how will it affect you and yours?

The first half of each issue of Family in America deals with a particular subject such as, in a recent issue, how the Supreme Court has over the past three decades managed to twine the bureaucracy's fingers around your family. The second half summarizes the latest research in professional journals on how various cultural trends (e.g., family break-up or the birth dearth) affect the family. Scholarly, yes, but also readable, *Family in America* is the single best way for traditional families to understand the impact of social, cultural, political, economic, and judician trends and rulings on the family. For those who really care about the family, this is absolutely essential reading.

Mothering
**   One year (4 issues), $15 USA, $18 Mexico and Canada, $20 elsewhere.**

Mothering is a profamily, non-Christian magazine geared to those currently raising a family. Topics mentioned in the promotional piece include Pregnancy & Birth (from a pro-home birth and other birth alternatives viewpoint), Breastfeeding, Parents as Experts, Midwifery, Immunizations, pro and con, Is Homeschooling for You, Alternatives to Spanking, and Nonsexist Childrearing. As the latter two topics and some portions of the sample issue I received indicate, *Mothering* is more progressive Mother-Earthy than traditional. The writing is honest, earnest, and supportive of those who favor *Mothering's* perspective.

New Families
**   One year (4 issues), $15. Sample copy, $3. Foreign subscribers, add $3.**

A "journal of transitions," geared to those who want to combine career and family without sacrificing the latter. *New Families* explores areas like job-sharing, freelancing, flextime, and home business. Each issue includes book reviews, reader forum, computer literacy, and a bulletin board, plus feature articles written in a big-time magazine style. The latter was a bit of a surprise—I expected a more homey, chatty tone.

Overall, *New Families* is progressive rather than traditional, "dedicated to the exploration of ways to combine parenting and career into an integrated and enjoyable whole." In other words, "We wanna work and have fun with our families."

☐*I*

Parenting
One year (10 issues), $18. Refund of full subscription price if not satisfied.

This magazine is attempting the impossible: helping parents put both themselves and their children first at all times. Geared to yuppies, *Parenting*'s basic premise (that expert advice is just *advice)* is sound, but its execution strongly resembles an updated *Parents* magazine. Articles like "Perfect Vacations— With Child Care" and "Father & Daughter: Changing Rules & Roles," which remind one of the same old *Parents* stuff, are mixed in with *Mothering*-style articles like "Why Hospitals are Pushing Caesareans." Underneath it all is a distressing tone of children-as-pets who are not supposed to interfere with, in the words of a *Parenting* ad, "your own interests, ambitions, needs, and relationships." This *might* be what yuppy couples want, but I suspect a little more diversity in *Parenting*'s editorial content (i.e., some genuinely prochild articles that face the fact that not all kids adore day-care) would be welcome.

Shop Talk
One year (12 issues) $24.

A brand new journal of expert opinion, with only parents as the experts. Great concept! Topics for the first issues included Nursing Toddlers, Tandem Nursing, Homebirth, Homeschooling, Converting to Natural Foods, Family Bed, and Immunizations. Each monthly issue covers one special topic in depth, plus continuing the dialogue from past issues. Had no time to review the actual magazine by press time, but you'll have a fair idea of its philosophy, audience, and style from the above.

FAMILY BUILDING

I quit watching TV back when it was big for characters to sit around and discuss "our marriage" with their spouses. Subsequently the screen characters would get divorced, proving in a strange sort of way that where words are many, sin is not lacking.

You don't want to have to worry about all that what-is-he-thinking-of-me and what-am-I-thinking-of-him and is-our-dog-becoming-neurotic. Personally, I think it's a good sign if you get bored talking about yourself(ves). There's got to be more to life than Us with a capital "U" or Me with a capital "M."

Christian Life Workshops

If you'd like a look at marriage from a Christian viewpoint that is really different, you'll probably get excited about Gregg Harris's tape set, *A Clinic in Christian Household Ministry.* First, the price: it's cheap, just $11.50 for two nicely boxed tapes. Next, the content. Gregg covers what he calls, "The Four Adventures of Household Faith," which are Family Business, Family Evangelism, Home Education, and Civil Influence. The focus here is outside yourself, looking at what your family can accomplish for God in the present and the future— and not just within the four walls of the church.

Gregg's *Home Schooling Workshop* tape set is another great resource for family building. The best part is Gregg's discussions of "how to" do such things as home-style evangelism and hospitality, areas which develop home education into the beginning of a real ministry. Get it from CLW. Gregg is also in process of preparing a Family Restoration workshop, which should be dynamite. Write CLW and ask to be notified when it's available.

Education Services
***Biblical Psychology of Learning,* $9.70 postpaid.**

Greatest book ever written on how children really learn. Unanswerable explanation of why discipline is essential to the learning process. Terrific insights that could turn around the way you relate to your children. For those who are serious about building their family up, not just letting it slide.

F & W Publications
Confessions of a Happily Organized Family, $7.95. Add $2.50 shipping.

Organizational (not discipline) techniques, shared with wit and at length by a Mormon mother. You'll learn how to use a landing/launching pad to keep your house clutter-free, how to sort the laundry in less than a minute, and other useful notions. The sections on how to involve the children in keeping things clean present organizational strategies and incentives that assume you have basically cooperative children. Lots of pages for your money.

Home Life
Family Opportunity Workshop, 6 cassettes plus 50-page illustrated workpacket in a nice binder, $49.95. Sample tape (includes $5 certificate good towards Workshop), $5.

From a Christian perspective comes *The Family Opportunity Workshop*, a six-tape set plus workpacket produced by Bill and Mary Pride (my, those names sound familiar!). Sections include:

• The Biblical Marriage Covenant
• Revival Through Family Restoration
• The Wife Under God
• The Husband Under God
• Parents Under God
• Family Play
• Family Business and Ministry
• Family Worship (i.e., family devotions)
• Extending Your Family's Influence

It comes in a nice binder, with a 50-page work packet loaded with what we think are humorous and helpful illustrations.

This is as good a place as any to mention that our home business, Home Life, was founded specifically to provide family-building and family productivity materials in one convenient location, for people who have difficulty finding this sort of thing elsewhere. If you're interested in home business, home education, home management, family worship, and so on, you might want to send for our free catalog.

NACD
Managing Your Child: Objectives and Rewards, $18. *Miracles of Child Development*, $50. Shipping extra.

Behavior modification with a heart. Bob Doman of NACD spends his life developing at-home programs for severely damaged children and those with extreme behavior problems. His *Miracles of Child Development* six-hour cassette program is positively inspirational in its stress on encouraging your children. This set also gets into Mr. Doman's theories about neurological dominance (see the Special Ed chapter for more details).

Managing Your Child: Objectives and Rewards presents an environmental method for managing your child, including the use of rewards and punishments. Lots of good suggestions (and a few I'd skip), strongly presented from a strictly secular base.

Oak Meadow
Parent Sensitivity Training, 6 tapes plus 200-page manual, $69.95 postpaid.

Based on the Waldorf methods applied in Oak Meadow's home school program, *Parent Sensitivity Training* presents 12 cassette lessons on how to "aid in your child's natural unfoldment." Ages covered are birth through change of teeth (otherwise known as about age seven or eight). *PST* covers

• The creative processes of singing, storytelling, crayon drawing, watercolor painting, and recorder playing;
• Practical applications, including creating the parent-child bond, "the natural approach to toilet training," authority and discipline without tears (one presumes this means without corporal punishment), parents as healers, and schooling and early learning;
• Principles of parenting from the Waldorf perspective: "the fourfold nature of the child, the three major cycles of unfoldment, the

transforming power of unconditional love, polarities in the mother-father relationship, and releasing parent-child patterns."

FEAST AND FROLIC

An important part of family-building is family play. You have doubtlessly seen the bumper sticker, "The Family That Prays Together, Stays Together." Bill and I have adapted this for our new family slogan: The Family That Works, Prays, and Plays Together, Stays Together."

Aside from all the super family games in the Toys and Games section, you might be interested in the following two items designed especially for family togetherness through shared enjoyment.

Raven Images
"Please Pack," $4 in zip-loc bag or $5 in drawstring calico bag. Shipping $1.50, more for orders over $10.

This is a nifty little idea— a bag of 70 little cards, each with activities for a mother or father (or both together) to share with a child. When your little one is due some attention, he picks a "Please" card for you to do together. The cards are color-coded according to the amount of time the "Please" activity requires, so you can make sure he picks a realistic activity by telling him what color card to pick. Some examples: A blue "quick 'n easy" activity might be, "Kiss my nose," or, "Sing me a song." A pink card ("Show me something on a top shelf") or a green card ("Let's draw pictures of each other") take a little longer. The gold cards can fill a whole afternoon ("Help me plant something") or even make for a fun outing ("Take me to a big building and ride the elevators"). All activities are inexpensive or free, and unlike those clever little "activity books" bought by the unsuspecting in bookstores, Please Pack activities need only few and common objects or toys.

Raven Images also sells free-spirited bookmarks, note cards, rubber stamps, and a lovely Advent calendar, all from the talented pen of Claudia Bumgarner-Kirby.

Word Books

Subtitled "Great Ideas for Building Family Traditions and Togetherness," *Let's Make a Memory* by Gloria Gaither and Shirley Dobson is a fantastic treasure trove of ideas for making holidays, birthdays, and ordinary days special. This amply illustrated, highly readable, oversized book also has sections on "Making Memories Through the Seasons, "Making Memories in Special Places," and "Making Memories with Special People." There's even more: a list of resources, including books for the family to read together and sourcebooks for family activities; "Keeping Memories Alive"; "Memorable Memory Makers," in which famous people share their own family traditions; and "Making Memories in God's Word," devices for memorizing and making Scripture meaningful.

Gloria Gaither is a member of the famous Bill Gaither Trio, a Christian singing group, and Shirley Dobson's husband James is the president of Focus on the Family, the most popular Christian family radio show today.

TELEVISION WITHDRAWAL

Remember how I promised in the first chapter that we were going to look at ways to cut down on time waste? Well, here is the all-time time-wasting classic— Number One Then and Number One Now.

You don't have to read this section unless you *really* want to know how it is that some mothers of three or more can find time to write books or make patchwork quilts or run Bed & Breakfast operations while other mothers of fewer don't even get around to making the bed. Those who can, do. Those who watch TV (more than 15 minutes or so a day), can't.

Susan Schaeffer Macaulay (author of *For the Children's Sake*, a wonderful book on education) puts this all in perspective: "I'm not down on television, you understand. I just think it has an abominable effect on our lives!"

Let's list all the good points of having a television:

• It provides a place to put the potted plants.

• It's a free baby-sitter (that is, if we don't mind a baby-sitter who turns our children into zombies and fills them with violence and materialism).

• It keeps the kids off street corners (of course, it also brings the street corners into our living room).

• It helps us unwind after a hard day (as does a friendly massage, a family board game, or a good book).

• It keeps us up on current events (the ones the network considers important).

• It is so *educational!* All those documentaries and public TV offerings (now be honest, how much of that do you watch?)

There's no use in talking about managing our homes and families until we get the television set firmly under control. If we can't handle an inanimate box of electronics, what makes us think we can handle one or more live scaled-down versions of Tarzan?

Much has been written on how to control TV. You can now buy a clever lockout device that prevents the children from seeing anything until you, the parent, materialize with the magic key to unlock the set. People I know who have tried this tend to wimp out after a while by giving the children the key because it becomes too difficult always hopping up down to lock and unlock the set— not to mention finding the key in the first place.

The easiest solution, of course, is to simply pension off the old familiar friend in an attic or sell it to a secondhand dealer and face life without TV. That mere phrase, "life without TV," gets a lot of people asking the same questions Scarlett asked Rhett at the end of *Gone With the Wind* ("Where will I go? Whatever will I do?"), but if you are one of the braver ones, go ahead and join the Society for the Elimination of Television. This somewhat impromptu and free-form group has a newsletter (please send $10 to cover costs), a speaker's bureau, and may just be the support you need to kick the habit for good. Or, if you're fencesitting, try reading *Four Arguments for the Elimination of Television* by Jerry Mander ($10 postpaid from Animal Town Game Company) or Marie Winn's *The Plug-in Drug* ($7.50 postpaid from Home Life). Jerry Mander deals with the physical and social effects of TV, and Marie Winn proves conclusively that it's not only *what* you watch, it's the watching itself that is detrimental, especially to children, who happen to be the main consumers of the stuff.

Now, being realistic, I figure most people aren't ready to give up TV entirely, no matter what the benefits of so doing. Viewers are just used to a certain amount of that kind of visual input— "addicted," if you will. But there is a way you can firmly and completely control your TV-watching and insure that every video image in your house is one you want there. *You can buy a video-cassette player that does not tune in television.* We did just that, and are extremely pleased with both the picture quality (far better than that of a TV set) and our new freedom to mine the riches of video without the need to fear any detrimental programs entering our home. We can study language on video, learn to play musical instruments by watching the best artists, catch up on classic films, and travel around the world in our living room, without constantly worrying if the children are watching raunchy cartoons or if the X-rated cable shows are bleeding onto our home set. Not to mention the best part— *no commercials!*

I searched long and hard before finding the right piece of equipment, and am delighted to announce that TAFHE (Tutorial Aids for Home Educators) will sell you the same kind of quality set that we now own at a sizeable discount. Prices begin in the $500's, so be sure discount. Prices begin in the $500's, so be sure to write for the current brochure.

Now you Have It All— at least all of it that we are in any condition to share with you! I'm writing this between nursing the baby and planning supper, which as usual will feature carrots and broccoli in the starring roles, supported by a cast of eggs (your basic budget dinner). Son Ted is playing *Robot Odyssey* on our Apple computer, the baby is on Daddy's shoulder while he cheers Ted on, and the rest are napping or pretending to nap while they ruin their eyes reading under the covers. Soon will come the scampering of little feet, a few more diapers to change, and a surge of

children into the living room searching for favorite books and art material. We, in our triumphant TV-free condition, will either watch a Walt Disney video tonight or share two new read-aloud books that came in the mail today. Then family worship, washing-up, and more writing if we can stay awake!

As you may have guessed, our idea of a Lazy Mother or Father is just being lazy about what doesn't matter, and not working any harder than you have to at what does matter, so you can spend the most time on what matters the most. May God grant us all wisdom to "number our days aright," so we have time both to pull the weeds and smell the roses.

PART II

BEYOND THE BASICS

CHAPTER FIVE

CHARACTER EDUCATION

He knew which was the right tree at once, partly because it stood in the very centre and partly because the great silver apples with which it was loaded shone so and cast a light of their own down on the shadowy places where the sunlight did not reach. He walked straight across to it, picked an apple, and put it in the breast pocket of his Norfolk jacket. But he couldn't help looking at it and smelling it before he put it away.

It would have been better if he had not. A terrible thirst and hunger came over him and a longing to taste that fruit. He put it hastily into his pocket; but there were plenty of others. Could it be wrong to taste one? . . .

While he was thinking of all this he happened to look up through the branches towards the top of the tree. There, on a branch above his head, a wonderful bird was roosting. I say "roosting" because it seemed almost asleep: perhaps not quite. The tiniest slit of one eye was open. . .

"And it just shows," said Digory afterwards when he was telling the story to the others, "that you can't be too careful in these magical places. You never know what may be watching you." But I think Digory would not have taken an apple for himself in any case. Things like Do not Steal were, I think, hammered into boys' heads a good deal harder in those days than they are now.

(From *The Magician's Nephew* by C.S. Lewis, one of the *Chronicles of Narnia*, published by Collier/Macmillan)

I think most of us agree that C.S. Lewis was right. Do Not Steal and the rest of the Ten Commandments were "hammered into boys' heads a good deal harder" a few generations ago. Assuming that we still cherish these values, which most of us do, the question is, "How can we pass on these values today?"

The Bible's answer is that we should tell our children the Ten Commandments as we "sit at home" and as we "walk along the road," when we lie down and when we get up (Deut. 6:7). Our environment should be permeated with written reminders of the Commandments as well (Deut. 6:8-9).

There was a time in American history when virtually everyone paid at least lip service to the Ten Commandments. It wasn't all that long ago, either. Strangely enough, in those bygone days hardly any children ever committed crimes. As Neal Postman reminds us in *The Disappearance of Childhood* (Delacorte Press, 1982) as short a time ago as 1950, "in all of America, only 170 persons under the age of 15 were arrested for what the FBI calls serious crimes (such as murders, forcible rapes, robbery, and aggravated assault)." That was .0004 percent of the under-15s in the country, or 1 in every 250,000. Since that time, now that the Ten Commandments never appear in classrooms and kids have been trained to do "their own thing," the ugly fruits have emerged. As Postman also notes, "Between 1950 and 1979 the rate of serious crime committed by children increased 11,000 percent!"

The media roam about saying the Ten Commandments are passé and ought to be ignored, and I roam about saying that in this case the media are passé and ought to be ignored. If we're going to get rid of these rules for living and character standards, which at least claim to be divine and I believe *are* so, then what are we going to replace them with? Dr. Spock? The Care Bears? The latest craze along these lines is "character-building books." These are peddled as not only supplements to home character training, but as the character training itself. Supposedly reading these little sermons will make Junior kind, unselfish, courteous, and get him to pick up his room. One kiss from the Care Bears and the frog turns into a prince! Love cures all ills, and the love doesn't even have to come from a family member— cartoon characters can do it all!

It really is hard to build a sturdy foundation for strong character without any absolutes. Without a "Thus saith the Lord," anything adults want kids to do pretty soon looks like tyranny. So secular "character-builders" concentrate on that great character-builder, self-interest. "If you're generous, Johnny, people will like you. If you study hard, Johnny, you will get good grades. If you work hard, Johnny, you'll make lots of money." The problem with this method is that Johnny is never learning to do what is right *in spite of* adverse circumstances. Johnny is also learning to judge every action by its benefits to him. What if he prefers short-term benefits (like a drug "high") to long-term benefits (becoming corporate vice-president)? America is covered with young people who live for *now* and *self*. We need more of this?

Since most Americans profess some kind of belief in God, why be embarrassed at passing down His laws *as* laws? Johnny should not steal because God says, "Thou shalt not steal." He should learn to share because Jesus said, "Do unto others as you would have them do

unto you." As long as the child understands that his parents are also under God's laws, and are not merely using the Bible to tyrannize him, he will readily accept these rules.

There is, of course, more to character building than laying down rules. We lack space here to get into the whole question of discipline and how to raise happy, self-disciplined children. I commend to your attention the products in the Family Management chapter, as a number of them provide good answers to these questions.

The following list, then, contains materials for values education from a number of religions and denominations, including some materials that are purely secular. I have not bothered to include the Care Bears 'n Rainbow Brite 'n Cabbage Patch school of character education, partly because it is in my estimation worthless and partly because you can hardly escape it even if you want to. Nobody needs special instructions on how to order products that line every shop counter and whose main characters star on major cartoon shows. It's hard for me to believe that any adult would rather submit to the preaching of the Care Bears or the Hugga Bunch than to that of Jesus Christ— but if that's what anyone out there wants, he knows where to get it.

CURRICULUM BASED ON CHARACTER TRAITS

Is there more to Bible-based education than the typical school subjects dressed up with Bible verses? Yes, home educators increasingly, reply. Subjects can be studied as they relate to developing a child's character. This approach, odd as it may seem at first, has the advantage of immediately relating all learned material to the child— and not to the child as he is (the fatal mistake of typical affective training), but the child as he can and should be.

The following two character-based curricula represent the leading edge of this new movement. For detailed information about these and other home education programs, see *The NEW Big Book of Home Learning.*

Advanced Training Institute of America

Bill Gothhard's Advanced Training Institute curriculum is based on character traits and strongly emphasizes the father's leadership role in home education. A pilot program available currently only to graduates of Bill Gothard's Advanced Training Seminar, the ATIA curriculum is highly praised by its users.

Konos Character Curriculum

Konos is an integrated academic curriculum in three volumes that covers all subjects for K-6 except phonics and math and that stresses Christian character development. Each volume is good for one or two years of study for an entire family. Units are based on character themes (example: Attentiveness).

MAGAZINES FOR PARENTS WHO WANT TO BUILD CHARACTER

I get the impression looking at a lot of "character-building" material that the manufacturers think parents want a Character Pill. You know, just shove it at the kids and bingo! Character!

Perhaps some parents really feel that way, but they wouldn't be the type to buy this book. So I am safe in assuming *you* are the kind of mother or father who is willing to exert yourself for your children.

Now, the awful truth— character building begins with the parents! You can't give it if you ain't got it. But, frankly, not all of us had a perfect childhood to pass on to our children. We may not know exactly what to teach or how to present it. We may need help getting our own thinking straightened out.

Here are a couple of magazines that can help.

American Reformation Movement

On Teaching is a sprightly newsletter series written by Dr. David Gamble that presents a Christian philosophy of education. Don't get put off by those boring words "philosophy" and "education." It's really fun to read! Recommended for thinking parents who want their chldren to have a truly Christian education, not a baptized secular one.

Evangelizing Today's Child

Child Evangelism Fellowship puts out this very useful, colorful magazine full of teaching tips for Christian education. Intended for Sunday School teachers and the like, it is nonetheless useful for parents. Included are techniques for teaching visuals, parents' tips, info on child development, lots of special departments; and one free visual lesson is bound into every issue! Now how can you go wrong when all this is only $10 a year?

CHILDREN'S MAGAZINES

"Children's Bible Hour"

Cheery Chats, CBH's bimonthly magazine, features poems, a story, a song, and letters from listeners. *Search the Scriptures* is CBH's correspondence course of 10 lessons from the New Testament. *Keys For Kids*, their family devotional booklet, is free, but you'll send $1 to pay for it if you're nice folks! *Keys* contains stories and activities for kids, and non-cynical types are bound to like it.

God's World Publications
God's Big World (K), *Sharing God's World* (grade 1), *Exploring God's World* (grade 2), each $8.50 (includes teacher's guide). *It's God's World* (grades 4-6), *God's World Today* (junior high), $9.50 (includes teacher's guide). *World* (senior high and adult), $18. Bulk orders get discount. Each paper 30 issues, September to May, except *World* (40 issues).

Q: What's black and white and read all over?
A: *God's World* weekly newspapers for Christian schools!
What an intriguing idea— the news for kids from a Christian viewpoint! GWP has papers for all different reading levels from kindergarten to adult. The papers for children are carefully matched to their interests and abilities. Following a newspaper format, you get feature stories, reports on hot news items, editorials, cartoons, and letters-to-the-editor. Papers for the kindergarten through junior high set also include activities for kids. A teacher's guide is included with each edition. No fuzzy-wuzzy copouts here, either; the editors know what the Bible says and aren't ashamed of it.
New in 1987: The God's World Book Club. Write for details.

Happy Times Magazine
One year (10 issues), $18.95. Two years, $35. Free sample issue with trial subscription.

This kids' mag is entirely devoted to character-building. *Happy Times* is colorful and kid-appealing. Each issue has a different theme, such as developing talents, positive self-image, work, integrity, etc. There are games, crafts, activities, stories, and feature articles on famous people like George Washington Carver and Thomas Edison.

Young Companion
$4/year, monthly issues.

Our homeschool group took a field trip to Amish country not long ago. While we were there visiting the harness shop, buying cheese, and so on, I ran across a copy of this magazine for Mennonite young people. The publishers are anxious to preserve virtue in their community, and concerned bout such things as young Mennonites marrying "outside" or picking up worldly habits like playing pool. Ah, lost innocence! It looked charming and certainly represents a different point of view than "Dallas".

Young Pilot
$9/year U.S. $11 Canada.

I had to laugh when I saw the white envelope labeled "North America's Best Kept Secret Inside." *Everyone* is getting into advertising hype these days! Even the solid folks at Prairie Bible Institute! *Young Pilot* is their magazine for Christian children. It's loaded with tear-jerking stories, cartoons and stories about courageous Christians, activity pages, some of those silly riddles kids love, letters to the editor, and even a centerfold (the issue I have displays a kid leading a horse along a wild riverbank).
Young Pilot is a blend of professionalism

and old-fashioned sentimentality. The stories might have been written 100 years ago. The literary quality does not reach the heights of such secular creations as *Cricket* and *Cobblestones* but is workmanlike.

The magazine is organized around a monthly theme, such as stewardship. There also are drive-you-crazy serial stories (remember Flash Gordon?) complete with cliffhangers. Will Sarah's father ever give those worthless Darnley boys their comeuppance? Will Sarah's mother ever get well? I don't know about how well *Young Pilot* will instill other character traits, but readers of their serials are bound to develop great gobs of patience.

BOOKS AND COURSES

Character-training material from a lecture or decision-making approach— that's what you'll find in this section. These materials are less emotive and more intellectual, but not necessarily less valuable, than the story-based materials in the next section. Scripture shows God using both methods: spelling out what is right or wrong with the Ten Commandments and other parts of the Law, and involving us in true stories that show the consequences of good or bad behavior.

Brook Farm Books
Exploring Right and Wrong, **$5.95 US, $7.95 Canadian. Shipping extra.**

Exploring Right and Wrong is a liberal Christian approach to ethics. Not values clarification— children are encouraged to believe in right and wrong— it's not a Thus Saith the Lord approach, either. Followers of John Holt are most likely to appreciate it.

Constructive Playthings
Holiday Puzzles, $16.95 each. Crepe rubber alphabet puzzles, $7.95 for set of 2.

Constructive's free catalog of Jewish educational materials is designed to familiarize children with Jewish traditions, holidays, and beginning Hebrew. It includes such things as Hebrew holiday puzzles (Shabbat, Passover, Purim, and Chanukah), magnetic Hebrew letters, two crepe rubber Hebrew alphabet puzzles, Jewish songs, and Israeli games. Chanukah decorations, a free carnival catalog for your Purim carnival, and more!

Gospel Mission

This non-profit ministry of a small Reformed congregation has blossomed into a large wholesale Christian book outlet. One of their main objectives is to promote childrens' books which encourage traditional values. Gospel Mission has reprinted many charming children's stories written in the nineteenth century. Their total line, over one thousand titles, is offered at generous discounts.

Harvest House Publishers
Christian Charm Course and *Man in Demand*: **teacher's manual for each course is $7.95, and the student manual is $4.95.** *Bible-Time Nursery Rhyme Book*, **$11.95.**

Harvest House carries the best-selling *Christian Charm Course* and *Man in Demand Course*, for teenage girls and boys respectively. These provide methods for improving the outer appearance along with spiritual instructions for developing beautiful inner character, and were written by Wayne and Emily Hunter. Harvest House also now distributes Emily's *Bible-Time Nursery Rhyme Book*. The book includes doctrinal and practical rhymes and Bible stories in verse. The illustrations, also by Emily, are pleasing and innocent, and some are in color.

Jewish Museum Shop
    Individual Member, $35. Associate Member, $30—available only to those living outside a 100-mile radius from New York City. Family Member, $45. Student Member, $20 with copy of ID. Senior Citizen, $25. Lots of expensive memberships for big spenders. Free Museum admission, all members. Mail-order shop.

    All sorts of materials "for preserving and perpetuating the Jewish Experience." Sabbath, holiday, and Passover supplies. Posters, graphics, and Ketuhabs exhibition catalogs. Jewelry. Mezuzahs. Notecards. Children's gifts. Bible and holiday books for children. Art books. Books on Jewish holidays, philosophy, religion, archaeology— children's sections. Hebrew calligraphy. Dictionaries. Fiction. Holocaust books. All available to the general public— 15 percent discount to members.

Sycamore Tree
    ***Character Foundation Curriculum*, $4.95 for student's edition each grade, $8.95 for teacher's manual each grade. *Ladder of Life* series, $18.95, accompanying tapes $26.95. *Let's Talk About* series, each book $3.95.**

    Sycamore Tree, a full-service home school supplier, devoted three letter-sized pages to character development in their most recent catalog. Notable among these are the Christian Charm and Man in Demand courses reviewed above (see the Harvest House listing), Christian family activity books, a series of family devotionals, the *Character Foundation Curriculum* workbook series, the *Ladder of Life* series, and Jo Wilt Berry's *Let's Talk About It* series.
    The *Christian Foundation Curriculum* is, as noted, a workbook curriculum. Children write Bible verses, fill-in-the-blanks, and perform a variety of activities designed to reinforce Biblical character traits. I found the workbook format to be overfussy for a home school situation— too much seatwork. If you use this at home, you might want to pick and choose activities rather than faithfully following the

format. I'd also recommend skipping the self-disclosure questions— you know, the kind of exercises where the student has to write down some pledge of future goodness or some confession of past misbehavior. That sort of thing always makes me squirm with embarrassment for the poor child asked to reveal to a fellow human what is really nobody's business but his own and God's.
    The *Ladder of Life* series, designed for ages three through six, is eight books with a teacher's guide. This lovely, gentle series was produced by the Seventh Day Adventists, but to my untutored eyes seems free of denominational distinctives. Titles include Faith, Virtue, Knowledge, Temperance, Patience, Goodness, Brotherly Kindness, and Love.
    Definitely the zippiest offering from Sycamore Tree is the *Let's Talk About It* series. Colorful, cartooned books present common childhood experiences and explain the difference between the right and wrong way to handle them. Presently numbering 26 books, the series covers such common problems as Being Destructive, Being Lazy, Cheating, Complaining, Disobeying, Fighting, Showing Off, Being Bossy, and Overdoing It. Preachiness is at a minimum, and bad behavior is shown as not only wrong, but foolish.

STORIES ON CASSETTE AND ELSEWHERE

Character-training through stories is as old as stories themselves. Æsop's *Fables*, Homer's *Iliad* and *Odyssey*, and even the Bible itself are all examples of how a story can be used to involve and motivate the listener.
    The current crop of stories, however, leaves something to be desired. Realism, for one thing. Relevance, for another.

Generally, a story touted as character-building will feature either animals, fantastic cartoon creatures, or famous individuals. The last category, famous individuals, is not the problem here. Heros and heroines make good examples, provided they are truly heroic and truly presented in their human dimensions and not as some sort of mystic gods or as people who existed only to provide us an example of some specific virtue. (Actually, even the safe category of human biography is not always handled realistically.) But the real, the glaring problem is the proliferation of cartoon and animal stories.

Fables were initially invented as a political statement— a way to get across a message too dangerous to spell out. A fable stands or falls by its accurate portrayal of human nature: the tyranny of the oppressor, the love of a mother. The sharp edge of the fabulist's wit forces the listener to see conditions as they really are. But the animals in Æsop bear scant resemblance to the cuddly coons and gushy giraffes in today's animal fables. These latter smarmy creatures never come to grips with real evil or even the unpredictableness of real life. They never work for a living or manifest any genuine human or animal characteristics. All-important is the search for friends and self-esteem. Perhaps the most damning thing that can be said about them is that the stories are written as if the peer-group-based life of grade school is the real world.

Even worse are the cartoon characters. It passeth understanding that children could learn anything valuable from the preachments of these creatures. Furthermore, we all know that it is just as easy for a cartoon character to lift the Eiffel Tower as it is for him to lift a straw. Perseverance under stress, the basis of

character development, is impossible for even a *human* cartoon character to present honestly. The strain of trying to make a singing hymn book or talking clock relevant to one's own life guarantees that the effort will never occur.

OUR BEST

Some of my distaste for most of the current crop of character-building stories may reflect my dislike for their values and disbelief in their view of the world. Good and evil never struggle in these stories. In fact, evil scarcely exists; the "bad" characters are only poor lonely souls with unmet needs who immediately blossom into sanctified goodness the first time someone smiles at them. This trivial view of temptation and sin also extends to a trivial view of faith and perseverance. The "character-building" hero immediately succeeds once he learns his "lesson," rather than having to struggle on in faith, believing that in time his faith will be rewarded. I simply don't believe the real world is as superficial as all that, or that distracting children with a sappy fictional world will help them make the tough choices life throws at them. Other people seem to lap up this stuff. But does the booming market in these materials reflect their unquestionably high entertainment value, the public's belief that this stuff really will help children, or simply the lack of any alternatives?

Presented below are all sorts of character-training story series popular with parents. Some in my opinion are good, others not. You be the judge!

Brite Music
Standin' Tall cassette/booklet sets, $7.95 each. *Safety Kids* cassette/booklet sets, $8.95 each. Add $1.95 postage.

Janeen Brady, a Mormon with a knack for musical jingles, started Brite Music in 1977 with her husband Ted. Represented by a network of independent Brite Distributors who demonstrate the products at home shows and other gatherings, the Brite Music line features cartoon children and catchy songs.

Brite's *Standin' Tall* line of story/song cassettes with accompanying coloring booklets includes Obedience, Honesty, Forgiveness, Work, Courage, Happiness, Gratitude, Love, Service, Cleanliness, Self Esteem, and Dependability. The stories have fantasy themes. The characters in Dependability, for example, are two black children transported into a space rocket and into new identities as a Prince and Princess. The evil Professor Un knocks out brave Captain Dependable with Procrastinite gas, placing the children in mortal danger. Oh, how they wish they had listened to their mother when she told them to return those library books right away! Now they have to find out what undependability feels like by being let down by Captain Dependable, who when they most need him disappears to get himself a sandwich. Similarly, the children in the Obedience tape are treated to the contrast between the kingdoms of Obey (a lovely place to visit) and Disobey (you wouldn't want to live there). Entertainment value of this series is high.

The award-winning *Safety Kids* series features a bunch of cartoon schoolchildren who have started a Safety Kids Club. They tackle drug and sexual abuse with catchy songs and analysis of why kids might fall into these traps. For a more detailed review of the *Safety Kids* series see the Safety Education chapter.

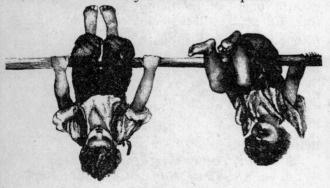

"Children's Bible Hour"

For decades CBH has been on the air with Christian stories aimed at the young. Some stories have an evangelistic emphasis; some concern Christian growth; all are interesting, and available on cassettes as well! CBH tapes are available for $3 each. Also song albums by the Children's Bible Hour Choir, cartooned filmstrip stories ($12 each). The program is aired on over 700 stations— check yours.

CBH, unlike some other Christian groups, isn't afraid to share the *whole* truth— including the reality of hell. All material is of professional quality. Stories are sweet but not sugary. I'd avoid the occasional tale that features Christian kids' misbehavior, because although they always repent, it can be a poor example. Otherwise, recommended.

Christian Character Concepts

Fluffy Tail Home Package (5 tapes and handwork), $38 postpaid. Sample Packet (1 tape and handwork), $9.35 postpaid.

Dr. Karen Evans and her energetic associates are busy these days! They have produced an introductory Spanish program for young learners and are working on a sequel (see the Foreign Languages section) and have also come out with the Fluffy Tail character training series.

Fluffy Tail is a little bunny rabbit. He and his friends eat ice cream, go to preschool, keep fish and cats for pets, and engage in other unbunnylike behavior. Through a series of adventures and misadventures, these thoroughly middle-class bunnies learn various character lessons.

The Fluffy Tail stories are sentimental and appeal to young children. Each store is repeated three times on one side of the tape. On the other side is a Bible story, also repeated three times. Each story has its own catchy song, also thrice repeated, and a Bible verse, ditto.

The Bible stories are not always the most traditional choices for a particular trait. For example, the story of Daniel is used to demonstrate responsibility and faithfulness instead of courage. The important role of parents in teaching character qualities to their children is seen in both the Fluffy Tail and Bible stories.

An Activity Packet accompanies the series, which contains clever exercises for reinforcing the concepts. Color filmstrips of all the stories are also available.

Donut Records
    Cassettes, $6.95 each. Accompanying picture books, $3.95 each. Add $1.25 shipping.

Everybody's gotta have a shtick . . . Robert Evans, a Christian folksinger, one morning stuffed a pastry doughnut hole back into the middle of a doughnut as a joke for his kids. Suddenly realizing what a great object lesson the doughnut hole motif was for how the Word of God fills the emptiness in our lives, he rechristened himself the Donut Man. This smart move immediately made him more memorable, and furthermore prepared audiences for his parable-laden songs and stories.

Let me tell you about these tapes. As we listened to them the first time, we began to notice that every song was done in a different musical style. "All that's missing is some Messianic Jewish music," Bill said jokingly, and sure enough the next song was Messianic Jewish! Irish, Pop, March, Dixie, County & Western, Ragtime, you name it, the Donut Man sings it.

Ah, yes, but what about content? *Bible Tails* and *Bible Friends*, for ages preschool through adult, are collections of parables and Bible stories set to music. *Bible Parables* is for ages 2-12 and features parables of Jesus. Each has an accompanying coloring book with all the words of the songs and with comic-strip pictures drawn by a Marvel Comics artist.

Like most Bible stories, these songs are not exact transcriptions of the Biblical text. You may have to point out to your children that all these details are not found in the original stories. Thus these belong more in the category of Character Education than Bible Study. Scholarly? No. Fun and exciting? Yes. Talented? Definitely.

Legacy
    Pleasant Dreams: Animal, cassette, and book $22; cassette/book only, $9.95. Agapeland records and tapes, $6.98 each. Home Videos, $14.95 each. Character Builders, $4.98 each, $34.95 set of all nine. Shipping extra.

A new company with the motto, "Leaving Something to a Child's Imagination," Legacy carries not only a line of upscale toys but several "character-building" series.

The first, The Land of Pleasant Dreams, features children who go to sleep only to wake up in the Land of Pleasant, an undisclosed location peopled by live stuffed calico animals. Somewhat reminiscent of the Care Bears, the cassette/book stories show children fellowshipping with these critters and "learning important lessons" through either the animals' silliness or their own.

Legacy also carries the Agapeland series, the best-selling inspirational children's series ever recorded. All is sunshine and sweetness in Agapeland, which literally means "The Land of Love." Cartoon children, singing animals, furry fantasy creatures, and "the amazing Music Machine" combine to produce unfailingly upbeat messages. Each record or tape includes a follow-along booklet. The series now includes attractively-priced Home Videos.

Also available from Legacy is Character Builders, a set of nine mini-albums based on the Music Machine concept. "Each package contains a cassette and colorful 'Look, Listen and Learn' book, complete with a page-for-page tone guide in each story helping develop early reading skills for children in the formative years of two through seven," says the brochure. Couldn't have said it like that at all myself. What *is* a tone guide? Am I betraying ignorance here? Titles include *A New Baby in the House* (no, this is not another tape on sibling jealousy, thank heavens), *The Broken Jewel*, *Benny and the Berries*, *The Rabbit Who Lost His Hop*, *Lost In The Woods*, *The Song Without*

A Heart, *Snails In A Hurry*, *The Trouble With Tuffy*, and *What Do You Want to Bee* (no, that is not a typo!).

Living Stories
All titles $2.50 or $2.75.

Could you use 22 colorful, visualized stories designed to present the Gospel message? These are not Bible stories, but stories like "Little Red Hen," "Miss Bump," and "Barney's Barrel." Full instructions for teacher included. Large, durable books.

Majesty Music
All Patch the Pirate super long-play recordings, $9.98 each. Accompaniment tapes: music only, $35; music with complete narration, $45; available in reel or cassette. Music books: Captain's Copy (for choir director), $4.95 each; Sailor's Copy (lyrics and melody line only), $2.95.

You're probably going to think I don't like the Patch the Pirate series because it features cartoon characters and fantasy situations. Well, you're wrong. For every rule there is an exception, and this happens to be the exception.

First, let me describe the series. Patch the Pirate is the invention of pastor Ron Hamilton. After losing an eye to cancer, Pastor Hamilton was forced to wear an eyepatch. Hence the moniker "Patch the Pirate." Making the most of this unhappy situation, Pastor Hamilton decided to dress up as a pirate and tell Christian stories. One thing led to another, and that's how we got the Patch the Pirate series.

Patch, as one would expect from a preacher in disguise, is a very straight-arrow pirate. In fact, he does nothing piratical at all except sail the sea and use sailorly talk.

Instead of a crowd of squirmingly cute stuffed animals or unbelievably adorable children whose adventures resemble nothing on this earth or the next, the Patch adventures are parables of the Christian life. They feature really bad villains who do not roll over and play dead if you just smile sweetly at them. Hence their interest for our family.

Patch, a Real Man, leads the crew— a welcome change from all those series of Worlds Without Adults, Amen.

Kidnapped on I-Land is an action-packed excursion into the kingdom of the nasty King Me-First. Silas Sailor, found floating on a raft by Patch and his crew, succumbs to the blandishments of King Me-First, who promises him a marvelous life on his own if Silas will just determine to always put himself first. With Silas firmly chained to him, King Me-First flies off to I-Land and flings Silas into Pity-Party Pit, a particularly dark corner of the Castle of Despair. Patch and friends set out to rescue Silas, who is slated to become a barbecued sailor steak, courtesy of King Me-First's pet, Torch the Dragon. Silas finally decides to put Jesus first, at which point the castle disappears, Me-First shrinks into nothingness, and all is well. The whole adventure resembles John Bunyan's Pilgrim's Progress (on a somewhat lower literary level), and is characterized by frequent clever jokes and lots of bright, happy music.

The Great American Time Machine has Patch and his crew escorting a delegation of two from Bonkinland back through American history to discover the secret of America's greatness. The Bonkers only understand coercive power (in Bonkinland every higher Bonker gets to bonk everyone lower than him to keep them in line), and the sight of George Washington kneeling in the snow at Valley Forge and Dwight L. Moody preaching in Chicago, among other peeks into American roots, amaze them. Lots of good songs and nice effects, like the Statue of Liberty speaking with a Bronx accent.

The Patch lineup also includes *Patch the Pirate Goes to the Jungle*, *Patch the Pirate Goes West*, *Patch the Pirate Goes to Space*, and *Sing Along with Patch the Pirate*. All the above except *Space* and *Sing Along* come with free 14 page read-along coloring books. Musical accompaniment and music books for choir directors and members are also available, in case your church wants to put one of these adventures on.

Christine Wyrtzen Ministries
The Critter County Musical, $8.98 for record or cassette. Critter County book/cassette packages, $4.95 each. Storytime Books alone, $1.29 each. Stickers, 98¢/set.

Critter County, Christian singer Christine Wyrtzen's invention, is billed as a "fun adventureland where kids learn Bible verses set to music." The critters are cartoon animals and the prices are more than reasonable.

The Critter County Musical has a Bible verse set to music for each letter of the alphabet, sung by Christine together with three children and one Critter County character. The Critter County Storytime Books and Cassettes are stories written by Christine's friend Paula Bussard. Each small hardbound book on the outside has a full-color cover and on the inside is a "delightful application of a Bible verse." Sydney Squirrel and his pals ham it up on the accompanying cassette tapes, with an occasional assist from Mrs. Wyrtzen.

I think I must be reading the prices wrong, because also included in every book/cassette package is a free set of Critter County stickers. Nope, the price list definitely says $4.95. I can't guarantee that the series will enhance your children's character, but with a price like this I'd take a chance and vouch for the character of its producers.

GAMES AND REWARDS

Some people like to make charts and on those charts mark their children's spiritual progress.
Others don't.
Some people like to buy stickers and rewards and hand them out to deserving young lads and lasses.
Others don't.
Some people like to play games, and think a game of moral decisions makes an excellent character training tool.
Others don't.
Some people, who are looking for rewards and incentives for their children and character-building games, will want to read this section.
Others won't (but go ahead, sneak a peek anyway!).

Jonson Specialties

Jonson Specialties has it all: stick-ons, balloons, lollipops, giveaway toys, games, rings, flag picks, pens, pencils, pencil tops, toys animals, treasure chests, and even vending machines and capsules. Any oddball item a teacher might be tempted to buy to hand out to her little flock, they have. Need a dozen yo-yo's, or a package of twist balloons? How about the Success Mix— a bag of 500 (count 'em!) assorted charms, gimmicks, and rings for $7.95? Relive your fond memories of your childhood eraser collection with aminal erasers (72 for $4.95), fruit erasers (36 for $4.95), geometric shape erasers (50 for $3.95), pencil top erasers (72 for $6.95), and on and on.

Not unexpectedly, the lifetime of these toys is short. After a while, they break or disappear. But then, you didn't really want 500 charms and gimmicks around permanently, did you?

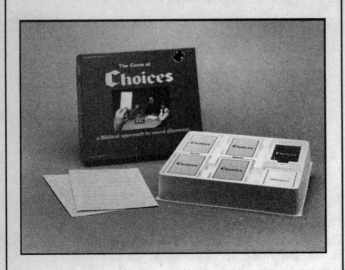

Rainfall Toys (formerly Bible Games, Inc.)
Choices game, $14.99. Not yet released at press time, but expected soon—*Children's Choices*, also $14.99 (comes with gameboard).

Does it help to walk through a situation before facing it in real life? If so, Rainfall Toys' new *Choices* game could be a character-training boon. Designed for teens and adults, *Choices* features three-hundred real-life dilemmas spelled out on sturdy cards, a Scripture Reference Booklet for each of up to four players, an instruction sheet (natch), and a plastic storage tray.

Example of a dilemma: "You get home from the supermarket only to notice that the checkout clerk charged you less than she should have. Do you go back to the store and correct the error?" Other players guess how you will respond, and you try to justify your answer with the Scriptures.

Right and wrong answers are not spelled out but some applicable Scripture verses are included in your Reference Booklet. It's up to you to apply them, or to decide if those verses maybe don't apply! This can make for some lively discussions, especially in games played with more players. You can increase the number of players by simply sharing around the Scripture Reference Booklets.

The game is not too difficult for preteens, but some of the dilemmas focus on painful issues like divorce and abortion and therefore might not be considered suitable for youngsters by some parents.

Choices requires more mental effort than many games, and much more Scriptural knowledge than most. The Scripture Reference Booklet partially saves this situation. Still, people with limited Bible knowledge would do well to use *Choices* more as an attractive springboard for family Bible study than a character training game.

Sycamore Tree
Sycamore Tree Incentive Charts, set of 12 (3 each of 4 designs), $1.95. Motivational Stamp Kits, $6.95. Achievement Awards, package of 30, $1.75. Seals, stickers, stars, 98¢ apiece except for the stick-n-sniffers and the stick-n-flickers.

If you believe in rewards, Sycamore Tree has pages and pages of what you want.

Sycamore Tree's exclusive Incentive Charts cover lessons, chores, manners, and personal habits, with squares sized for mini-stickers or stars.

Motivational Stamp Kits are sets of six goofy stamps that run the gamut from gentle prodding ("Try Again!" says the Apple) to ecstatic ("Wow" exclaims the Cutie Bug). No, I am not making this up. You have your choice of bunnies, robots, kittens, puppies, Cutie Bugs, happy faces, apples, teddy bears, coin tails, and coin heads.

Now, let's talk about stickers. Sycamore Tree has large and small gold stars and stars in assorted colors. Wild Animal seals. Life of Christ seals. Seasonal mini-stickers. Mini-religious stickers. Flip Flap stickers (front layer has a Bible question: lift the flap to reveal the answer). Stick-n-Sniff stickers, Stick-n-Flicker stickers (wiggle the sticker, the picture changes). Sticker albums. More!

CHAPTER SIX

HEALTH EDUCATION

Fifteen men on a dead man's chest
Yo ho ho and a bottle of rum.
Drink and the devil had done for the rest
Yo ho ho and a bottle of rum.
Old English sailor's song

Health is now a required course in the public schools. It is therefore easy to get health textbooks, and any who are content with standard school fare can find a variety of sources in the Textbooks section of *The NEW Big Book of Home Learning*.

Why do I object to standard health texts? Because they spend so much time talking about drugs and drunkenness and venereal disease and so on, and refuse to say that any of these things are *wrong*. All is reduced to "risk-taking." While the general public thinks that Junior is getting a sermon against (for example) drugs, he is actually being taught to play the odds. The text, not being allowed to say hedonistic chemical-pumping is wrong, weakly stutters that Junior is taking a chance with his health by so indulging. Junior, of course, gets the message that he won't necessarily harm himself— there's only a *chance* he will. He's also subtly being conditioned to consider drug abuse a respectable option. So yo, ho, ho, and a bottle of rum.

Most of the "health" subjects really don't belong in a Health course at all. Drug use, or abstention; premarital sex, or chastity; suicide, or life; these are all *ethical*, not strictly medical, choices, and should be taught by the family and church, not the school. Children who know right from wrong don't need to suffer through gruesome units on the physical effects of cocaine or syphilis. Even children who don't know right from wrong fail to profit by what amounts to hours of how-to instruction in breaking the laws of God and man.

Anyone who wants his sons and daughters taught how to commit suicide, or how to masturbate, or how to take drugs, is certainly free to purchase these materials. But if you think public school health materials mainly teach good nutrition and exercise, you're in for a shock.

NUTRITION AND EXERCISE

Jack Sprat could eat no fat.
His wife could eat no lean.
And so, between them both, you see,
They licked the platter clean.
(Mother Goose rhyme)

And speaking of nutrition, don't expect standard school texts to be too much help in this area either. While growing numbers of Americans are baking with whole wheat and sprinkling sesame seeds on their salads, school texts still natter on about the "Four Basic Food Groups." You remember these from your own school days— Meat, Dairy, Breads 'n Grains, Fruits 'n Veggies. You were exhorted to eat one item from each group at every meal, if possible. Very well. So let's have chicken with apple stuffing and vanilla ice cream for breakfast! You can kill yourself with the Four Basic Food Groups, or at least clog up your arteries for good: steak 'n potatoes 'n broccoli with hollandaise sauce 'n chocolate pudding, to name just one meal with all four "essential groups." O.K., it sounds yummy, but is it healthy? Is the perfect meal really a Big Mac with shake and baked apple pie?

While up-to-date nutritionists write about the virtues of complementary protein (combining grains with dairy or legumes to enhance one's protein intake) and vitamin preservation through natural food processing, school texts plod along 20 years behind, informing kids of such earth-shaking concepts as "get plenty of fresh air and exercise." Now you tell me— does it make sense to sit *inside* filling out workbook pages about the virtues of being *outside*? If kids really learn by doing, they'd be better off skipping Health class and playing volleyball in the school yard.

The best nutrition texts to read, in my opinion, are the popular books on this subject written for adults. Since most publishers won't print anything with more than an eighth-grade vocabulary, literate kids can get their nutritional ideas straight from the horse's mouth. And since most books of this ilk include recipes, your kids can learn to press their own cheese and grind their own wheat flour and bake their own all-natural corn chips and do whatever it is that people do with tofu.

I don't claim to agree with all the theories the following books teach. That would be impossible, since they disagree with each other: protein-combining versus skip-the-dairy, megavitamins versus no capsulated vitamins of any dosage. But since nutrition is such a hotly debated field, it makes sense to at least become acquainted with the major practical theories.

Educational Insights
The Nutrition Box, $6.95. Add 10% shipping.

Perhaps the best introduction to public-school nutrition ideas is Educational Insight's *Nutrition Box*. "A complete self-contained kit on nutrition," this low-priced kit consists of 50 cards, each with background info and suggested follow-up activities, neatly stored in a handsome box. Topics include vitamins, minerals, and proteins (a more sensible approach than solely concentrating on the Four Food Groups), nutrition around the world, and proper food preparation. The *Nutrition Box* is suggested for grades four and up, but at home could be used to some extent even with preschoolers.

Herald Press
The More-With-Less Cookbook, **$11.95.**

The *More-With-Less Cookbook* is the simplest, most useful introduction to the doctrine of "protein-combining," i.e., eating combinations of foods for your protein instead of noshing on steak at every meal. The religious group that put this out has a notion that if Americans eat less, somehow hungry folk on the other sides of the world will find more rice in their dinner bowls. You may remember this as the "How can you leave all that food on your plate when there are children starving in India?" school of thought. Anyone who can't read the book through without feeling guilty should read David Chilton's *Productive Christians in an Age of Guilt Manipulators*, available at a great price from Puritan-Reformed. Apart from the guilt, it has a lot of useful nutritional data (tables of protein amounts in various foods, etc.) and some very decent recipes.

Kimbo Educational
Slim Goodbody's Nutrition Edition, $9.95 postpaid.

Slim Goodbody is an actor/singer in a body suit. A real body suit: all the inner organs and veins and such printed in living color on a jumpsuit. Yuk. Naturally, kids love him.

Slim (real name: John Burstein) likes to sing, and what Slim likes to sing about is health. *Slim Goodbody's Nutrition Edition* has Slim going to town with inspirational songs about how neat it is to eat natural foods, along with some educational ditties about Protein Power, the Vitamin ABC's, how food gets digested, and the virtues of water-glugging. Easy to remember, upbeat.

Mother's Bookshelf

Good source of books on natural nutrition, including tracking down wild food (of the vegetable variety), organic gardening, natural food preservation techniques (drying and root cellaring, for starters), and natural cookery. Mother's Bookshelf even has books on how to build your own food dryer, root cellar, apple bins, and so on. Upbeat reading for energetic, self-sufficient types.

Rodale Press

Rodale Press publishes *Prevention*, the world's largest circulation health magazine, and another biggie, *Rodale's Organic Gardening*. While they're at it, the folks at Rodale Press also publish 50 or so new books each year. Cookbooks, gardening books, and health books are their specialty, with the emphasis on fresh food, minimal use of fertilizers and pesticides, and natural management of the soil and one's self.

Harvey and Marilyn Diamond

Warner Books
Fit for Life, $16.50.

Fit for Life, by Harvey and Marilyn Diamond, is your introduction to Natural Hygiene. The grabber is that this is a weight-loss diet as well as a permanent lifestyle. Natural Hygienists are interested in how the body absorbs and eliminates food, and figure that by making the process more efficient excess weight will also be eliminated. Their basic tenet is that the body wants to be healthy, and is always working towards a healthy weight and trying to get rid of toxins.

To accomplish this noble task, the Diamonds recommend abandoning dairy products, eating nothing but fruit before noon, and never consuming meat and starches in the same meal. You can lose weight fairly rapidly this way, if you can stand the change of diet and initial hunger pangs.

Several nutritionists wrote to me condemning this book. Their concern is that people not go overboard and rigidly follow the *Fit for Life* diet. Cheat on it occasionally— sneak a glass of milk or a cup of yogurt— and pump the proteins more than the writers suggest, if you'd like to make the nutritionists happy.

Some New Age thinking is sprinkled

throughout, along with the sesame seeds. You also get a section of reasonably easy recipes.

ANATOMY

There was a young lady from Lynn
Who was so excessively thin
That when she essayed
To drink lemonade
She slipped through the straw and fell in.
(Anonymous)

Now that we know what Jack Sprat and his wife should eat, we can study what their peculiar lifestyle actually does to them. Anatomy uncovers the systems digestive, endocrine, muscular, skeletal, and reproductive, among others. Part of the required Health subject is the study of all these layers of anatomy.

American Map Corporation
    Anatomy Wall Charts, $29.85/set.
Anatomy Atlas, **$1.75. Notebook Anatomy Charts with transparent identifying overlays and index, $17.95**

American Map Corporation's *Anatomy Atlas* is ridiculously cheap, with sixteen pages of full-color labeled drawings and short text for each. Like the publisher says, it's "virtually a complete course in basic anatomy." The same drawings are available in a set of 14 Wall Charts, 29 x 37 inches.

Ideal for self-testing is the new Colorprint-Schick Anatomy Charts notebook. Spiral-bound, it has 30 full-color drawings with transparent nomenclature overlays. This means the part labels are on a separate see-through sheet, so you can first try to identify the parts you are studying and then flip the accompanying transparent page over the drawing to check out your answers.

Carolina Biological Supply Company
    Large price range. Plastic is cheaper. Catalog, $10.95.

Skeletons for sale! Every budding anatomy student sooner or later wants his very own skeleton. Plastic (human) and real (animal) are in stock at Carolina Biological Supply.

Ever want a nice set of shark jaws? The small size is only $13.70, and you can get a single large shark's tooth for $4.75. Fishermen, think twice before throwing away the next catch's bones: a nice fish skeleton, fully articulated and mounted on a Plexiglass plate in a display cabinet, goes for $70. Unmounted bullfrog skeletons can be had for under $35, whereas a rather nifty-looking snake skeleton is between $65 and $155. I should mention that you can generally get just a skull, too: a chicken's skull is under $25. More exotically, there are rattlesnakes, moles, opossums, armadillos, wallabies, and muskrats. Cats and dogs, rabbits and rats, sheep and pigs, and monkeys of all sort are for sale in their bony state. You can get feet and limbs of some of the larger mammals. These all being so plentiful, all items come in natural bone.

Now, on to Man. Most human skeletal preparations come in very realistic plastic, this being one case where art is preferable to nature. You can get all different bones, individually or all together and hanging from a rod.

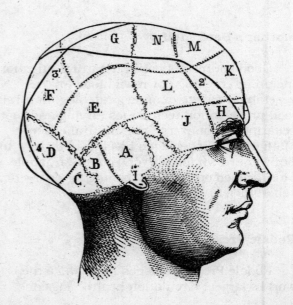

Educational Insights
    Human Body Kit, Pumping Heart Kit, Human Lung Kit, Human Skull, $21.95 each. Brain Kit, Heart Kit (non-pumping), Human Ear Kit, Human Tooth Kit, Human Eye Kit, $19.95 each. Anatomy Apron, $19.95. The Human Body Box, $6.95. Add 10% shipping.

    Other must agree that these kits are good value, since Educational Insights now has twice as many to offer as last year. Each kit contains 25 activity cards, reproducible worksheets, games, student and teacher record sheets, and quizzes. The Human Body kit includes not only a transparent human form with muscles molded inside, but also a small plastic skeleton with some abdominal organs exposed. Most models can be taken at least partially apart. The new Human Tooth model stands on an easel and is hinged to show interior detailing. The Pumping Heart, a rather yukky concept sure to be beloved by preteen boys, is a working model of the heart and circulatory system. Squeeze the bulb and red "blood" wends its ways through veins, arteries, atria, and ventricles. The regular Heart Model is your normal take-apart plastic model. All models look quite attractive, at least as attractive as this sort of thing can. Color is used where appropriate.

    A brand-new, fun idea beloved by schoolteachers is Educational Insight's Anatomy Apron. The teacher puts on this washable vinyl apron pre-printed with outlines of the internal body organs. No big deal so far, you say? What about colorful cutout body organs that attach to the apron with Velcro? Put 'em on, peel 'em off, again and again! The Anatomy Apron is one-size-fits-all, so kiddies can proudly wear it, too.

    Lastly, just as Educational Insight's Nutrition Box is the best deal for public school nutrition, their Human Body Box is the most interesting, least expensive substitute for ye boring anatomy text. Fifty durable cards grouped by body parts give info and suggest practical activities.

Todd Gastaldo
    Information on chairs versus the spine, $1 plus SASE.

    One of my more interesting correspondents since writing *The Big Book of Home Learning* is a California chiropractor, Todd Gastaldo. Mr. Gastaldo spearheads a one-man crusade to abolish "compulsory chair-dwelling" in schools. He has all sorts of evidence, both anatomical and sociological, to demonstrate that long hours in chairs cause spinal deterioration and are responsible for the epidemic of chronic back pain in the Western world. In place of chairs, he suggests sitting cross-legged, reading from a reading desk with one foot on a chair (the pose of orthodox Israeli Jews as they study the Scriptures), and even the tribal squat.
    A brief observation period will confirm the idea that children, left to themselves, seek "natural" positions for reading and work. In school they are often denied this choice. I personally remember how I ached after a day hitting the books at school, and how I much preferred to read or study sitting cross-legged or sprawled on the floor. After years of chair-dwelling Bill and I both find ourselves using Back Chairs (those funny little seats with knee pads on which you kneel). In my case, that's the only way I can bear to hang in for the long hours at the keyboard.
    So, while I have no medical expertise to admit or deny Mr. Gastaldo's hypothesis, he certainly has a plausible point worth looking into. Write to him for his side of the story, if this interests you.

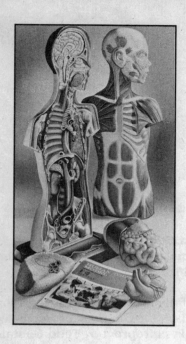

Hubbard

Kits for investigating your own body, including respiratory system, muscles, vision and hearing, personal health, and visual coordination and control. These are mini versions of the classroom-sized kits Hubbard sells and are rather expensive; prices start at $45. Apparatus for the investigation is available separately, and if you just want to do a few of these experiments the price is affordable.

Hubbard's plastic models for anatomy are excellent quality, but might be expensive for a home program. However, you can learn a lot by just looking at the color pictures in Hubbard's free catalog.

Ideal School Supply
Most models under $15.

Calling Dr. Frankenstein! Ever want to build your own . . . thing? Ideal School Supply has unassembled anatomical models. You supply the glue and paint, and Ideal supplies a model of the: eye, ear, heart, brain/skull, body, skeleton, nose/mouth, tooth, lung, and even a pumping heart! Inexpensive, and it makes a

nice change from Sopwith Camel and dragster models.

Milliken
Diagrammatic Prints, $9.95 per package.

For low-cost anatomy studies you might also want to consider Milliken's full-color Diagrammatic Study Prints. *Systems of the Human Body* and *Organs of the Human Body* are each a set of eight poster-size prints with anatomical items clearly labeled. Each comes with four review sheets and a teacher's guide.

Sycamore Tree
Anatomy coloring book, $9.95. Human Body felt set, $25.95.

Sycamore Tree has a great selection of Health and Anatomy materials for home study. Their anatomy coloring book is meant for high school students. Descriptive text accompanies each drawing. Sycamore Tree has several other books on the body and health. Some are Adventist. Skipping over all these, let me tell you about the Betty Lukens felt Human Body Set. When I saw the picture in the brochure I knew this was the teaching tool to get! It is an incredibly beautiful set of felts, containing all the innards and muscle layers, etc. that you'd ever hope to see— even a womb with a little baby inside! Ten talks accompany this set, plus the "I Am Joe's Body" series from *Reader's Digest*, the most popular series ever printed in their history. The Human Body Set is not overly expensive, and with care it will last almost forever. Where else can you get a life-sized *overlayable* model?

HEALTH AND SAFETY COURSE

Jack and Jill went up the hill
To fetch a pail of water
Jack fell down, and broke his crown,
And Jill came tumbling after.
(Mother Goose)

A Beka Books

I'm only going to recommend one series on health and safety. Here it is: A Beka's bright, cheery, colorful *Health, Safety, and Manners* series for grades 1-3.

The books cost around $6 and follow the typical A Beka "programmed" format, where the text talks to the child in the first person (e.g., "I will take care of my body"). I was impressed by the thoroughness of this series, and enjoy the emphasis on manners.

FIRST AID AND MEDICINE

*Up Jack got, and home did trot
As fast as he could caper.
Went to bed, and wrapped his head,
In vinegar and brown paper.*

I find it somewhat ironic that school texts advise children to use alcohol and illegal drugs "responsibly," yet take it for granted that only doctors are wise enough to dispense medicine and medical aid. Kids can get marijuana and cocaine and heroin in the friendly neighborhood schoolyard, but their parents aren't allowed to get their hands on a bottle of penicillin without a doctor's prescription. Strange.

Let me hereby cast my vote for teaching kids *real* medical skills. Unlike such esoteric subjects as the ecology of freshwater marshes and the nomenclature of plants' reproductive systems, both commonly taught in schools and both hardly ever used in the students' real lives, first aid and practical medicine will be needed by almost everybody at some time.

Apprentice Academics

Midwifery Study Course, $700. Discounts for members of ACCORD, NAPSAC, self-check discount, other discounts. Study Guide must be returned at end of course. Course usually takes three years to complete.

A systematic study of midwifery, the Apprentice Academics Midwifery Study Course is designed as an integrated curriculum. As the brochure states, "Although the curriculum is not organized by subject, virtually every related subject is very thoroughly covered." Each section covers every aspect of midwifery, so that throughout the course one subject may be covered in a dozen different ways: diagrams, quizzes, research, reading assignments, and so on. Enrollment includes not only the basic six sections outlined in the Study Guide (terminology, reading record, optional study, required technical study, research topics, and general study), but 12 issues of the *In Touch* newsletter, a Study Pak, individualized course assistance and evaluation, and the certification exam leading to a Certificate of Successful Completion. You will have to purchase books and work hard to finish the course. An incentive program helps with this. You can win an award for outstanding work or win in a drawing for midwifery books and supplies only open to those who submit work during a given quarter, among other things.

Suggested for midwives who want to enhance their education, apprentices, childbirth educators, nurses, CNMs, and future midwives who want to "mommy" their young children now and receive their practical training later, the Apprentice Academics course has garnered testimonials from Dr. Robert Mendelsohn, NAPSAC president David Stewart, and others renowned in the home health movement. Perhaps most importantly, AA's students have written numerous unsolicited testimonials to the course's thoroughness and enjoyableness.

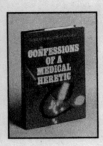

Home Life
Confessions, **hardbound, $9.95.** *How to Raise a Healthy Child*, **$7.95.** *MalePractice*, **$8.95.** *What Every Pregnant Woman Should Know*, **$6.95. Add 10% shipping.**

We have become disturbed lately by the trend to treat doctors as gods whose authority cannot be questioned and whose presence justifies anything, including torturing old people, newborns, and the handicapped to death by starvation and lack of water. If criminals dragged an old lady or newborn babe off to their lair, tied their victim up in a corner, and refused to give her food or water until she died an agonizing death, we'd consider this inhumanely evil and call for severe penalties. If the same, exact thing occurs inside hospital walls, it is "death with dignity." The only difference between the two scenarios is that doctors and nurses were the ones torturing the victim. So why is it that we judge their actions by entirely different rules from those the rest of us must follow?

Western society has come to expect altogether two much from the white-robed fraternity. The result neither benefits doctors (who get sued by patients expecting perfection) or their customers. Yet most medical books simply echo the Doctor-As-God line, featuring "authoritative" pronouncements from On High with never a whisper that today's One True Way may be tomorrow's discredited medical theory.

To meet the glaring need for books analyzing what really goes on behind those closed, sterile doors, our home business now carries a Family Medicine Box line, beginning with *Confessions of a Medical Heretic, How to*

Raise a Healthy Child . . . In Spite of Your Doctor, and *MalePractice: How Doctors Manipulate Women*. These should be required reading for those who believe in required reading. Let me just *suggest* that these three books, written by the eminent Dr. Robert Mendelsohn, will help you see the need for achieving some practical medical skills. If absolute power corrupts, absolute faith in a man doth cause that man to sometimes behave like a ninny. Doctors do much better when we don't encourage them to play God, as Dr. Mendelsohn points out. Both books give strong reasons for becoming more medically self-sufficient, and provide resources for those interested in putting Dr. Mendelsohn's message into practice.

The remaining book on our "must" list is *What Every Woman Should Know: The Truth About Diet and Drugs During Pregnancy*. Good friends forced a copy of this book into my hands when I was pregnant with our second child. Our firstborn was plagued with medical problems, necessitating a five-week stay in neonatal intensive care. After reading *What Every Pregnant Woman Should Know*, written by a husband-doctor and wife-nurse team who have done extensive research into the common practice of making pregnant women restrain their food and salt intake, we saw that poor diet was a likely contributing factor to Ted's problems. I read the book through, took it to heart, and have since had four more entirely healthy children, thus gainsaying the squads of doctors who predicted our future children would be born crippled.

Merck & Company, Inc.
Merck Manual, **$19.75.**

Increase your word power and get a handle on medical procedures with the *Merck Manual of Diagnosis and Therapy*. This is the very same book your doctor uses to help him diagnose and prescribe. The *Merck Manual* is fascinating browsing for those with a large medical vocabulary; extremely helpful in medical emergencies (it's comforting to be able to check out the diagnosis for yourself); and the definitive test of whether Junior really wants to go to med school (can he hardly tear himself away from the *Manual* or does he nod out after reading a paragraph?). Dr. Mendelsohn recommends it.

The *Merck Manual* won't tell you about nonconventional treatments. Nor will you be able, in many cases, to act on its recommendations without a doctor's prescription. But it will educate and inform you about what is going on in the orthodox medical world for every disease known to man.

Medical Self Care
One year subscription, 6 issues, $12. Family Medical Bag, $93. Baby Jogger, $198.

The publishers of *Medical Self Care* magazine, a haven of New Age medical thinking, have assembled a catalog of medical tools 'n stuff for folks who want to keep things medical at home. The Family Medical Bag, for instance, includes a Family Health Record, comprehensive medical handbook, earscope, stethoscope, blood pressure cuff, mercury thermometer, surgical scissors, and surgical splinter forceps, all in a foam padded gray nylon pack. The catalog also contains a long list of at-home medical tests, and comfort, exercise, and food preparation items. Useful stuff (fire extinguishers, home medical emergency kits) is intermingled with condoms, relaxation tapes, gender selection kits, and pricey yuppy trinkets (a Baby Jogger all-terrain carriage).

NAPSAC
Membership, includes *NAPSAC NEWS* and special discounts on books and NAPSAC activities: Individual, $15 USA, $17 other countries; Professional, $35 USA, $37 other countries. *Childbirth Trivia*, $16.96 postpaid. 1986 Summit video "Highlights," $39.95 plus $1 shipping—VHS only.

The organization for those interested in alternative childbirth options. NAPSAC, otherwise known as the InterNational Association of Parents and Professionals for Safe Alternatives in Childbirth, a very professional group with many highly-accredited leaders and advisers, is "an umbrella organization supporting and promoting all enlightened childbirth associations," with chapters of its own all over North America and around the world. NAPSAC issues an excellent quarterly newsletter, NAPSAC NEWS, runs a mail-order bookstore with a wide selection of the best books available on childbirth and mothering (including some NAPSAC productions), and sponsors occasional conferences.

The 1986 Summit Conference was an outstanding affair featuring such notables as Dr. Herbert Ratner of *Child and Family Newsletter*, well-known sociologist Dr. Ashley Montagu, LaLeche League founding mothers Marian Tompson and Mary White, French obstetrician Dr. Michel Odent, Dr. Tom Brewer (author of *What Every Pregnant Woman Should Know*), and Dr. Robert Mendelsohn, among others. At this conference, the last planned for a while, NAPSAC took a prolife stand on abortion, generating heated controversy among some but greatly relieving the minds of others. NAPSAC's position is that, in order to consistently uphold the goal of nurturing babies and providing the best for them— the original impetus for much of the alternative childbirth movement— the baby must be treated as a person regardless of his or her physical comeliness or "wantedness." More info on this is available in the Summer 1986 issue of NAPSAC NEWS (available for $1 postpaid). Video tapes of the keynote conference speeches, plus a tape of conference highlights, may be purchased from NAPSAC. Audio tapes were also made of all the sessions and workshops and can be ordered from NAPSAC.

NAPSAC's *Childbirth Trivia* game, 1152 "thoroughly researched and diverse questions and answers" in "six colorful categories," is a teaching tool designed for consciousness-raising. Most questions will be too difficult for the average uninformed citizen (such as myself!), but you apparently can learn a lot playing the game. Questions range from fairly easy, like "Why should you relax your mouth during birth?" to downright technical ("How accurate is the alpha fetaprotein test?") with some humorous queries thrown in ("What columnist did a Christmas article in which the birth of Christ was disapproved by the AMA?").

Oak Meadow
Free brochure details course contents, price.

Oak Meadow, source of a home school curriculum based on Waldorf principles, has a new home study course for adults entitled Homeopathic Medicine in the Home. The course is written and taught by Jonathan Breslow, N.D., instructor of homeopathy at the California Acupuncture College in Los Angeles. This is a true correspondence course, and you will have to correspond regularly with your instructor. Course includes syllabus, supplementary materials, and correspondence feedback. Send large SASE for details.

Parenting Press
***A Kid's Guide to First Aid: What Would You Do If . . . ?*, $4.95 plus shipping.**

What do you do if . . . Your clothes catch on fire—Your best friend is bitten by a snake while you are hiking together—Your little sister sticks her scissors in the electric socket—Someone eating with you begins to choke? Parenting Press's *A Kid's Guide to First Aid: What Do You Do If . . . ?* book presents children with these, and dozens more, real-life medical emergencies and gives them simple, illustrated rules to follow. A pictorial index helps children quickly find what to do in an emergency. It's a small investment in preparedness that could really pay off.

Your Library
The library is sure to have a number of good books under the headings "First Aid" and "Self Help." Also try "Doctors," "Physicians," "Disease," and "Medicine."

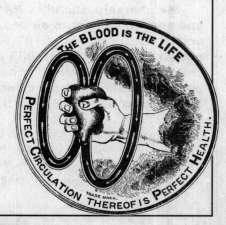

CHAPTER SEVEN

SAFETY EDUCATION

> Two children went sliding on the ice
>   Upon a winter's day.
> As it fell out, they all fell in
>   The rest, they ran away.
>
> Ye parents who have children dear
>   And ye, too, that have none
> If ye would keep them safe abroad
>   Pray keep them safe at home.

Mother Goose

Child safety has received a lot of attention lately. Ever since the social work industry and the networks discovered how saleable child abuse stories are, we have been flooded with materials for paranoid parents and distrustful teachers. In this area, inflated statistics and ignorance abound.

Many books and courses, for instance, stress "Stranger Danger." The figure of a million or more children missing every year is used to scare parents and teachers into training their children to be unfriendly to strangers, and has led to a demand for such privacy-invading programs as mass fingerprinting of children. Yet in a recent year the FBI reported only 67 genuinely missing children. The rest of the "missing million"? Runaways or children

taken by noncustodial parents. And since most children are molested by people who take pains to get chummy with them, not total strangers, children are being made distrustful of new relationships for scant reason.

School child abuse courses also frequently stress the supposed epidemic of child abuse in families. Fathers and male relatives in particular are featured as molesters and abusers in task cards, filmstrips, movies, and live presentations. Children are urged to find a trustworthy adult outside their families in whom to confide, and taught that the Child Abuse Hotline can be used to accuse their parents or any other adult. Almost never are they warned not to make false accusations; instead, courses typically teach them to regard normal family behavior (spanking, scolding, even hugging) as abusive. On top of this, in some areas Child Abuse Prevention teams tour the schools, taking children off alone for interrogations about their family lives. In spite of the known fact that children will tell adult authority figures anything the authority figure clearly wants to hear, especially in a school situation where the entire year is spent attempting to "psyche out" the teacher, every negative comment the investigated children make is treated as gospel. This, because of a belief totally unsubstantiated by statistics, that one in three or four homes is a hotbed of child abuse.

Some "experts" have placed the figure of abusive families as high as 75 or 80 percent! Clearly this includes most of us. Also clear is that child abuse prevention programs designed by such "experts" are not in the best interest of children in general or our children in particular.

Below are some of the better child safety programs, plus a source for the information you need in order to protect your family from the fallout of child abuse hysteria.

Brite Music
Safety Kids Volume 1, *Personal Safety.* **Song book $4.95, cassette and booklet $8.95. Shipping extra.**

Brite's Safety Kids series stars a multiracial group of cartoon schoolkids. Banding together to resist peer pressure, they stand for Truth, Justice, and Self-Esteem. Your child is encouraged by snappy dialogue and show-stopping tunes to identify with the Safety Kids Club, warned against the perils of adult and peer pressure, and given safety rules in song.

Volume 1, *Personal Safety,* deals with child abuse prevention. Most of the rules are quite sensible— like if you're lost, look for a grandma or a mom with happy kids and tell her you are lost.

Like every other curriculum I've seen, *Personal Safety* has trouble defining exactly what kind of behavior children are supposed to resist. In one song a girl draws a huge circle around her and brags that she won't let anyone invade her space. What price hugs or a game of volleyball? Little children can easily be confused by an approach like this.

Better than this is the simple Biblical teaching, "Thou shalt not commit adultery." Children can easily absorb the idea that certain body parts are reserved for their future spouse and that they have no business investigating other people's genitals, nor do others have any business meddling with theirs.

Brite Music's gifted creator, Janeen Brady, could easily whip off a song called, "I'm Saving Me For My Wife," or some similar title that got this message across. Sure hope someday soon she will!

Citizens Against Crime

Keeping Kids Safe comes with a little booklet on how to reinforce the Brite Music Safety Kids program inserted. *Keeping Kids Safe* itself consists of 12 lessons: Personal Safety, Faces (message: you can't tell who has a "sick mind" by looking), Strangers, The Buddy System, Telephone Safety, Lock the Doors, I'm In Charge of My Body, Good Bad and Confusing Touches, Secrets (on not keeping bad secrets), False Accusations, Kidnapping, and Plan to Yell. The appendix has five sections: Indicators of Child Sexual Abuse, Helping a Child to Tell, Reporting Abuse, Helping the Abused Child, Finding a Missing Child.

Keeping Kids Safe, although echoing some misleading figures and policies, conveys a sense of caring and responsibility. This is the only child abuse curriculum I have seen that actually warns children not to place false accusations. Most of the safety rules given are helpful and sensible. The layout and presentation are excellent. Suggestion for improvement: instead of saying offenders are "confused" people with "sick minds," why not just say they are people who indulge their bad side? In its present form, these parts of the text sound like offenders are not really responsible— the very point other sections of the text deny. It would also help if the appendix (1) explained how parents investigating indications of abuse can determine if abuse has *not* occurred, and (2) was more cautious in encouraging parents to turn for help to the child protective agencies. The appendix states that these government agencies can and will help parents whose children have been abused by others, when our research unfortunately shows that the "help" offered sometimes takes the form of seizing control of the family or even custody of the child in exactly the same way as if the parents themselves had committed the abuse.

Home Life
The Child Abuse Industry, $9.95 post-paid.

Over one million North American families were falsely accused of child abuse last year. Next year, one of them could be yours. Yet most people know nothing of the almost unlimited power legislatures have recently granted social workers to enter homes, interrogate children in questionable ways, and remove them from their families without a previous court hearing or indeed any solid evidence that a crime has been committed. Vague child abuse definitions make all parents technically guilty, while basic constitutional rights of both parents and children have been swept under the rug. Social workers and their bosses frequently break even the weak laws regulating them without being called to account, while their victims are faced with huge legal bills and the possible permanent loss of their children.

All this scandalous stuff is thoroughly documented in *The Child Abuse Industry* (Crossway Books, 1986). Unlike other exposé books that frighten without providing solutions, *The Child Abuse Industry* spells out what we can do to protect ourselves now and change the situation for good. Find out what is wrong with statements like, "One out of every four women is sexually abused before age 21," and "The home is the most dangerous place for a child." Discover why school child abuse prevention programs may actually increase child abuse.

The style of *The Child Abuse Industry* is as upbeat as possible with such a subject, so reading it at least should not be a chore. Chapter titles include The Plague That Isn't, Home Horrible Home, "We Just Want to Help," "We Must Err On the Side of the Child," Yours Mine and "Ours" (the history of American child-saving), Bringing in the Thieves (a look at government bureaucrats' plans to exploit children as raw material for bureaucratic empire-building), and If This Be Reason. A book to read if you value your family. I hoped someone else would write it, but they didn't, so my name is on the cover.

DRUG EDUCATION

A hundred bottles of beer on the wall
A hundred bottles of beer
Take one down and pass it around
Ninety-nine bottles of beer on the wall...
(Children's counting-down song)

There's safety of the body, and there's safety of the soul. A drugged escape into limbo endangers both body and soul. Here's some useful information on how to keep your kids out of the clutches of the drug industry (illegal and otherwise).

Brite Music
Safety Kids Volume 2, Play It Smart. Song book $4.95, cassette and booklet $8.95. Shipping extra.

Our favorite of the Brite Music material, *Play It Smart* presents kids with upbeat ways to avoid drug use. The story starts with Gregor, one of the Safety Kids, late at the clubhouse due to a terrible experience. One of his best friends had ganged up on him with a bunch of other kids and tried to force him to take drugs. This leads into a group of dynamic songs. "It's Bad, Bad Stuff" tells kids to forget drug use entirely. "Go for a Natural High" lists exhilarating things kids can do without drugs: swimming, dancing, bike riding, etc. "Designer Genes" warns kids not to mess up their bodies. "You're Not Gonna Get Rich On Me" points out that drug pushers are not your friend. The best song of all, a real show-stopper and our kids' favorite, is "All You Gotta Say Is No." Kids are given ten different ways to say no to drugs: the tough no, the cool no, the bored no . . .

Great graphics, award-winning singing, and a Resource Supplement for parents and teachers bound into the songbook make Play It Smart a fine introduction to real drug use prevention. My only quibble: the song "Everybody Needs to Feel Love" that encourages children to be their own best friends. While it's true that we need to have inner character to resist peer pressure, how much better to look for our strength in God!

Citizens Against Crime
Keeping Kids Safe: A Guide for the Prevention of Alcohol and Drug Abuse,

Like the other *Keeping Kids Safe* program on child abuse, this comes with a folded insert on how to make the most of the Brite Music

Safety Kids program. The Guide itself introduces the problem of substance abuse, presents ten lessons loosely based on the *Safety Kids* format, and closes with Helping the Abusing Child and a Resources appendix.

Unique to this guide are the excellent lessons on Magical Thinking Vs. Reality Thinking and Consequences— Long Term, Short Term. Melody LeBaron, the author, presents some role-playing exercises designed to help children understand the benefits of realistic thinking and delayed gratification. One extremely effective activity she suggests is the M&M's game. The child is allowed to choose whether he wants one M&M now, or 10 M&M's in 10 minutes. Very quickly he learns it's sometimes better to wait for one's enjoyment instead of going for the "quick fix"!

Another excellent section presents situations in which a child might be asked to take drugs. The parent pretends he is the friend offering drugs, and the child practices saying No firmly. He gets two extra points if he says No both firmly and kindly, and two more if he manages to say it in a funny way as well. Later this lesson lists snappy answers to peer pressures. Example: Your friend says, "You've been so sad lately, this will make you happy." Answer: "I'd rather be sad than out of control."

Short, snappy, and easy to use, *Keeping Kids Safe* deserves an A for its clearcut stand on the wrongness of drug abuse and its sensible approach to giving kids the tools to avoid this trap.

Citizens Commission on Human Rights
Free brochures.

While we're talking about drug abuse, let's not forget that the public schools themselves are among the biggest drug pushers. Totally aside from the fact that most street drug transactions take place on or near public school grounds, the schools' increasing practice of drugging normal children in order to cut down their energy or short-circuit their behavior problems deserves a good hard look.

I'm talking, of course, about the massive use of Ritalin, Thorazine, Cylert, Dexedrine, Mellaril, Tofranil, Haldol, and other drugs commonly prescribed for such non-diseases as Attention Deficit Disorder. As the Citizens Commission on Human Rights attractive pamphlet *How Psychiatry is Making Drug Addicts Out of America's School Children* points out, "Under psychiatry's invented criteria, there isn't a single normal childhood behavior which doesn't fall within the broad 'symptoms' which comprise so-called 'mental illness.'" This pamphlet is a veritable treasure trove of information on why and how children are unreasonably put on drugs, and the vested interests behind the 400 percent increase in children in psychiatric hospitals since 1980. Especially alarming is the quote from the American Psychiatric Association "bible," which requires psychiatrists to give more credence to the teacher's report that a child should be drugged than the parents' or even a doctor's observations. (The justification here is that the "symptoms" of Attention Deficit Disorder with Hyperactivity often disappear when the child is not stuck in a large group setting or bored to death.)

CCHR's follow-up pamphlet, *Ritalin: A Warning for Parents*, draws interesting parallels between the increased use of psychiatric drugs on children and the rise in child suicide. Did you know that withdrawing from a "speed-like" substance (which Ritalin is) invariably causes depression, sometimes to the point of suicide?

Did you know that Ritalin can cause an *irreversible* condition resembling demon possession called Tourette's syndrome, where the child develops body ticks and spasms, makes barking sounds, and then passes to a screaming, often obscene, babbling? Did you know Ritalin could bring on epileptic seizures? And that's not the end of the list of fifteen warnings concerning Ritalin in this pamphlet.

CCHR was established by the Church of Scientology in 1969. However, the pamphlets I received contained factual information exclusively— no proselytizing or religious commentary.

Information on other harmful drugs used on children is available through CCHR upon request.

DEATH EDUCATION

Now I lay me down to sleep
I pray the Lord my soul to keep.
And if I die before I wake
I pray the Lord my soul to take.
(Old American rhyme)

As I said, there is safety of the body and safety of the soul. Make sure your soul is safe. Pray the Lord your soul to take.

CHAPTER EIGHT

SEX EDUCATION

Mommy and Daddy, sitting in a tree
K-I-S-S-I-N-G
First comes love
Then comes marriage
Then comes baby in the baby carriage!
Children's rhyme

First comes love. Then comes *marriage*. *Then* comes baby in the baby carriage. See? Who said sex education had to be difficult!

Parents are quite capable of conveying the basic facts of reproduction, whatever the sex ed industry might tell us. "Thou shalt not commit adultery," lays the framework for what kids need to know. In this context of saving sex for marriage, the details of reproduction are interesting, but not threatening. As for the detailed, obsessive how-to's of the sex manuals and some school sex courses, let's just forget it and wish the kids happiness on their wedding night. Sex is supremely a subject for learning by doing.

Below are some resources that teach the facts. Use 'em or not, as it suits you.

AKA Inc.
   AIDS Is Looking For You, $2 plus 75¢ shipping. Quantity discounts.

What you don't know about AIDS can kill you. Endorsed by Dr. William Sears, author of numerous books and consultant to *Baby Talk* magazine, *AIDS Is Looking For You* is a readable exposé of a serious health issue. Designed for parents to share with their children, this cartoon booklet stars Uncle AIDS (a big black germ) and his excitable nephew Li'l Plague.

Uncle AIDS certainly is the biggest, baddest germ on the block, and he's not too shy to tell Li'l Plague all about his career—along the way sharing many little-known facts about the disease, how it is spread, and how it can be avoided. Another production of Dick Hafer, the Comics Commando, *AIDS Is Looking For You* is attractively laid out and pulls no punches.

Committee on the Status of Women
   Student workbook, $7.95. Teacher's Manual (includes student pages), $12.95. Guidebook for parents (includes student pages), $8.95. Preview package, 1 of each above, $28.50. Twelve-minute VHS video program intro, $20. VHS video one-hour teacher training or parent presentation, $50.

You've heard of it from friends, you've seen it written up in the newspaper, you've written to me saying I ought to review it; here at last is the Sex Respect curriculum! Developed by Colleen Mast, an educator concerned about the valueless approach to sex education, Sex Respect teaches teens they have the right and ability to say "No" to premarital sex. Unlike other programs that assume teens are incontinent animals, Sex Respect appeals to their thinking powers, laying out the consequences of premature sexual indulgence and presenting teens with positive ways to refuse temptation and withstand pressure. A bouncy format with games and activities keeps interest high while the message sinks in.

Parents and teens both greet Sex Respect with enthusiasm. Students in classes that used Sex Respect overwhelmingly gave it positive ratings. The course includes materials for parental involvement.

The curriculum does encourage unwed pregnant girls to give up their babies for adoption, with which I personally disagree. From a Biblical standpoint, parents are the God-chosen guardians of their children; nowhere in the Bible does God require or commend a mother turning over her child to others. This easy way out of the problem of unwed pregnancy provides a source of babies for childless couples, but at the expense of the mother and father's growth in responsibility and the natural mother-child bond. My great-grandmother gave birth to her firstborn at age 16; if she could raise 12 successful children with this start, certainly a 15-year-old can learn to be an effective mother. The section on adoption is not central to Sex Respect, so whether you agree or disagree with me you can still use this most useful program.

Concordia Publishing Company
   Sex Ed books, $6.50 each or $39/set of 6 books. Correlated filmstrips available.

Here's a brand-new Christian sex education series, published under the auspices of the Lutheran Church— Missouri Synod. All age groups are covered.

Ages three to five get *Each One Specially.*

This hardbound, colorfully illustrated, over-sized book presents the initial naked facts about sex, e.g., a not-overly-detailed pictures of an undressed little boy and little girl, along with information about different kinds of families (including the church family) and how babies enter a family. All is done in a tasteful, nonthreatening fashion.

For ages six to eight is another oversized hardbound book, *I Wonder Why.* This book has chapters and fewer illustrations. Each chapter is a story about cartoon character Suzanne: her birthday party, her visit to the Miracle of Birth exhibit at a museum, a visit from two boys (one of them wants to be a mommy and has to be enlightened), and so on. She learns about how families grow and get smaller, how babies are conceived, grow, and are born, and how men and women are different. The sexual act is also tastefully explained. The book contains rather unrealistic rib-to-thigh illustrations of naked male and female genitals. It actually took me a second or two to figure out what the illustration was about, mainly because the pubic hair looks more like a Brillo pad placed on the figure and the torsos are ungraced with navels.

Also hardbound, but not quite as oversized, *How You Got to be You,* the book for eight to eleven-year olds, contains quite a bit of detailed information about the sexual organs and the bodily changes of adolescence, combined with devotional material. It is written in an interactive format, where the author speaks for the preteen in italics and then answers those questions. Example:

Lots of people in my class are much taller than I am.
   The most important growing happens inside a person. You'll grow on the outside, too, when

your body is ready . . .
What do you mean?
When you were baptized, God made you a member of His family. Now, as you learn about Jesus, you are growing as a Christian.

When you were a little baby, you needed lots of things and you cried and yelled until you got them . . . Now that you are older, you are able to give as well as take . . .

The New You is for ages 11 to 14. Each chapter starts with a young teen boy and girl sharing their questions about sex with the reader and (somewhat unrealistically) with each other. This book, after dealing with similar questions to those raised in the earlier volumes, provides orthodox answers for some heavy areas: pornography, masturbation, sexual experimentation, birth control, unwed pregnancy, venereal diseases, homosexuality, and guilt feelings.

Lord of Life, Lord of Me, for older teens, deals with the many difficult situations people who date get into. Even more frank than *The New You*, it discusses issues like incest, nymphomania, and types of birth control. Situations teens face are presented, with both positive and negative responses analyzed. Part of this book could be considered premarital counseling.

Not even parents are forgotten; *Sexuality: God's Precious Gift to Parents and Children* covers both adult sexuality and how to present sex to your children at all ages. The book leans heavily on psychological research to emphasize its points.

This entire series is written in spiral fashion, reemphasizing and enlarging on concepts introduced in previous volumes rather than covering entirely different ground at each level. Those for teenagers lighten the subject with an occasional joke; those for younger children are more serious. All books make much of the unisexuality of men and women in the work force, starting with a female truck driver, nurse, banker, and painter and male cook, lion tamer, teacher, and pilot in *Each One Specially*. All are nonjudgmental about divorce and refer to rapists and other sexual offenders as "sick" rather than "bad." All try to meet the reader where he is and suggest ways to overcome bad situations in which the reader may already be

enmeshed. All feature an age-graded vocabulary and such references, illustrations, and study aids as are appropriate to readers of the intended age.

Family Enrichment Bureau
Understanding Our Sexuality, **complete set (3 slipcased cassettes and guidebook) $30 postpaid. Guidebook alone, $4 postpaid. Extra guidebooks available at quantity discounts.**

Understanding Our Sexuality is an easy-to-use, nonthreatening, integrated program for teaching children about sex, featuring Joe and Kathy Connell. The first of the three cassettes, A Guide for Parents and Educators, introduces the program and gives suggestions on how to teach and train children in this area. The next two cassettes contain four talks: Learning to Love, The Girl Grows Up, The Boy Grows Up, and Becoming a Young Adult. The guidebook contains the complete text of all the talks.

Physical changes and emerging desires are explained in the context of love for others and responsibility for one's own actions. The series is very understanding of teens' sexual feelings, and encourages the listener to think of others first. The series ends this way:

Are you going to be a hurting person, a playing person, or a loving person? Only you can decide. Only you can become the person you want to be.

The Family Enrichment Bureau has been around for 22 years. They are happy to work with schools, churches, and parents.

Master Books
Life Before Birth, **hardbound $9.95. Read-along cassette, $5.95.**

Fun! Dr. Gary Parker's *Life Before Birth* follows a father explaining the facts of life to his children. Loaded with cheerful cartoons and helpful illustrations. The book is written like a play, with dialog, instead of a lecture. Nicest looking book on the subject I have ever seen. Christian perspective.

CHAPTER NINE

PHYSICAL EDUCATION

Awright, ya guys! Up-down, up-down, one, two, three, four! Hey, Jergens, yer tryin' ta touch yer toes or just wavin' goodbye to yer girlfriend? Up-down, up-down, and put some muscle into it!"

Such is the melodious song of a football coach in the fall. It is indeed difficult to duplicate this performance at home. For one thing, you need enough players to make at least one complete team. With a little stretching, my brothers and sisters and I made up a baseball team, but most modern families are not blessed with enough members to carry this off. Also, although dads do love to play coach, at home there is not enough incentive to run one's off-spring ragged for months on end, like real coaches do for their teams. We must conclude that serious, all-out, gut-grinding, competitive team sports are not for the home. Shucks.

What *did* kids do for exercise before grown-ups invented Little League, anyway? Girls played hopscotch and jumped rope. Boys shinned up trees and played pick-up games of football, baseball, stickball, and street hockey. Everyone played catch and "It" and "Blind Man's Bluff" and dodgeball. Everyone did somersaults and handstands and drove their par-

ents crazy on rainy days running around the house.

Modern kids are fat and soft compared to their old-time counterparts, thanks to TV and adult-sponsored game leagues which force most children to spend hours waiting for a turn to play. The schools try to remedy this by providing "physical education" classes a few hours a week. These classes often provide very little exercise for the ones who need it most: just more standing around in line watching the athletes perform. We are almost at the point upper-class Americans had arrived at in 1920, not believing children will exercise unless some adult stands around and *makes* them.

There are, then, two kinds of exercise products on the home market. One is exercise furniture. There it sits, the Jungle Gym or climbing rope, trusting that children will hop on it and use it. The other is programmed "movement learning." Children are put through a series of movements and exercises in time to music. The second approach can result in a useful physical skill, such as folk dancing or ballet. But if movement education is used as an compulsory exercise program, it is a waste of time and insulting to children, besides. Just because we adults are obsessed with the shape of our bodies is no reason to dump this trip on a five-year-old!

PLAY AND EXERCISE EQUIPMENT

If you're thinking of making a major investment in play equipment, you might first want to send for Community Plaything's free illustrated booklet, *Criteria for Selecting Play Equipment for Early Childhood Education*. The booklet is more interesting than it sounds, containing numerous candid pix of children playing with (naturally) Community Playthings equipment. The booklet is both philosophical (stressing cooperative play) and a handy guide to what equipment is best for what age, and what features make for superior equipment. There is also a section on the special play needs of handicapped children. You don't have to take all the suggestions as gospel— if you do, you will end up spending your year's wages!

**Childcraft Educational Corporation
Constructive Playthings**

These companies both offer standard playground equipment, plus exercise equipment for indoors such as balance beams and mats.

Child Life Play Specialties
    Sample prices: Jungle End Swing Set, $565. Complete Fireman's Gym, $445. Kinder climber, with platform, knotted rope, and climbing pole, $191. Knotted rope alone, $20 (it's manilla, with large knots). Doorway Gym, $40. Kits are about 20% less. Shipping is extra.

Play equipment is this Massachusetts company's only product. It's durable and distinctive, too, painted with lead-free forest green enamel. Products are all made from Northern hardwoods except for chains and ropes and suchlike. The prices are quite acceptable considering the quality, and you can start with a basic frame and add on accessories, such as swings and ladders. Some products are also available in kit form.

Child Life has quite a few small items, such as their Doorway Gym, their Knotted Rope, a Tree Hanger that attaches a swing to any tree of at least sixteen inches diameter, etc. Many items are clever and innovative. The Doorway Gym, for example, includes a flexible belt swing, a trapeze bar, steel trapeze rings with comfort-grips, and a blocked climbing rope. You just hitch the contraption to your doorframe and let 'er rip. Kids can adjust the height of the paraphernalia themselves.

Do we have a Child Life swing set in our back yard? No, we do not. We bought a Sears set before I ever heard of Child Life, and you don't just toss out something made of steel that took several days of hole-digging and concrete-pouring to install. Do I kick myself every time I look at my Sears set, wishing it were a Child Life? Well . . .

Community Playthings
Sample prices: Variplay Triangle Set, $125. Kiddie Car, $39.75. Scooter, $65.50. Mini Scooter, $45.50. Shipping extra.

Good solid play equipment, originally designed for schools and day-care centers. The Hutterite community makes its living assembling and selling these items. Many are made of solid wood and most have exceptional play value. Example: the five-piece Variplay Triangle Set. It can be a seesaw, a balance beam, a ride-a-plane, a go-cart, a wheelbarrow, a slide with steps, a steering wagon...

I should mention that Community Playthings equipment is quite attractive, in a sensible, solid sort of way. The maple is clear-finished, wheel hubs are painted red, and some wood is stenciled. The catalog is adorned with pictures of Hutterite children enjoying play on the equipment.

All this equipment is designed to *last*. Community Playthings has testimonials from schools that have been using the same piece of equipment for 20 years. This explains why their products cost more— over $90 for a tricycle, for example. The machine in question has a solid wheel (no spokes), and a frame that Superman would get a workout trying to bend. Prices are significantly less than the other institutional suppliers, like Childcraft. It's a real alternative to the tinny, mass-produced items available in standard mail-order catalogs and department stores.

Rifton Equipment for the Handicapped

The Hutterites also manufacture very sturdy and useful exercise items for children and adults who need extra help in these areas. It all is quite attractive, as much as this type of equipment can be, and the prices are not any more outrageous than anyone else's.

MOVEMENT EDUCATION

Kimbo Educational

Kimbo's colorful catalog has more exercise and movement albums for children than any other I've seen. Kids can mess around with folk dancing, bean bags, parachutes, Hawaiian rhythm sticks, and so on. Page after page after page of gymnastic routines (with ribbons or without), preballet and ballet, tap dancing, stunts and tumbling, plus the usual leap-and-stretch stuff we all have seen for years on Romper Room. Many of the recordings feature simple, folk-style music. Some thump about with disco.

Kimbo has movement and exercise albums for adults, too: square dancing, slimnastics, jumpnastics, ethnic dancing, and of course the ever-present Jane Fonda. Kimbo has not forgotten senior citizens, either; they have exercises you can do sitting down and other gentle pulse-persuaders.

Send if you wish for Kimbo's free sample record, which also includes snippets of their children's music.

Montessori Services
  Perceptual-Motor Lesson Plans, **Levels 1 and 2, $7.95 each.** *Step By Step*, **$14.95. Shipping extra.**

Montessori Services devote the entire next-to-last page of their catalog to Movement Education of a "non-competitive, non-threatening" sort. Besides parachute activities, parachutes ($96 and up!), kits with rhythm sticks and bean bags, and a rope ladder, Montessori Services offers several sets of movement education lesson plans.

Perceptual-Motor Lesson Plans is 25 weeks of activities for gross motor skills, plus equipment construction diagrams for such things as a balance beam and a jump box. Level 1 is for ages two and a half to six; Level 2 is for ages seven to nine.

  Step By Step is the output of one Sheila Kogan, a Montessori teacher, dancer, and movement consultant. It has eighty flexible lesson plans and a comprehensive index. The lessons use movement to teach physical concepts and reinforce academic concepts. Most activities require little or no equipment. The rest describe "innovative uses for balls, balloons, scarves, ropes and other inexpensive props." Example: "Throw the scarf in the air and catch it. Catch it with your elbow, head, shoulder, tummy, seat, hip, knee, foot, any-thing but your hands." Just like the rules for that ol' competitive soccer!

Moving & Learning
  First 5 sessions (40 lesson plans, 5 cassettes, imprinted binder), $125. All 10 sessions, $235. Sample lesson and demo tape, $2.

If you really want to get into movement education, Moving & Learning has the stuff. It's programmed. It's complete. It's developmental. It has lesson plans, a teacher's guide, and original music and lyrics. It stresses feelings. It culminates in actual dance steps and improvisation. It requires no special training— but you can get a video tape, or sign up for a workshop, if you wish.

Each of the 10 sessions includes eight lesson plans you can tailor to your personality and needs. In the early sessions your child begins by imitating simple actions like jack-in-the-boxes and popcorn popping and working with easy locomotor and nonlocomotor skills. From here the lessons become progressively more challenging until, in the final units, he or she is learning dance steps and performing complicated imagery— the beginning of miming.

Each of the 10 sessions takes approximately eight weeks to complete in the classroom, and probably less at home. The entire curriculum is nonconsumable and can be used for any number of children.

Pacific Cascade Records
  Each cassette $8.98 plus shipping.

Children's songs on record or cassette are this company's stock in trade. Their material, some of which has won awards, has a folksy feel. It includes several activity albums.

Some popular offerings: Nancy Raven's *Singing In a Circle and Activity Songs* and *Hop, Skip, and Sing*. Children participate along with these live-recorded albums. Another: Mark Weiss's *The Moving, Counting, Rhyming, Feeling, Up-Down, Left-Right, Look What I've Got Album.* Nancy Raven's albums consist of authentic folksongs, while Mr. Weiss's songs are originals.

Pacific Cascade's activity albums are not "movement education" in the strict sense. They foster movement, but do not demand it. The activities are fun and invigorating, but not programmed" with "skill levels." Mellow folks will like it.

Silver Burdett Company
$76 total program. Volumes 1-4, $19.25 each.

This textbook company has "a movement program that teaches music concepts." Entitled *Move Into Music*, it features professional performers, recorded directions, and specially-composed music. The series consists of four volumes, each covering two grades, and including a LP record and teacher's guide.

Sycamore Tree
***Perceptual Motor Development Series*, books 1-5, $4.95 each. *Good-Time Fitness*, $5.95. Shipping 10%.**

Ya gotta shake, rattle, and roll! That's the message of the movement ed series Sycamore Tree carries. Each activity helps you "assess your child's motor strength and weaknesses and provide practice to develop his/her skills." The books can be used for grades K-6. Titles in the series: *Basic Movement Activities*; *Ball, Rope, Hoop Activities*; *Balance Activities*; *Bean Bag, Rhythm Stick Activities*; and *Tire, Parachute Activities*. Sandy Gogel, co-owner of Sycamore Tree, says the tests and tasks require minimal instruction time, and reports much success with them with her own children.

Sycamore Tree is also the exclusive distributor of *Good-Time Fitness for Kids—A Guide for Parents, Coaches and Counselors*. The book is about proper exercise habits and sports conditioning, from birth on up.

PHYSICAL FITNESS PROGRAMS

Alpha Omega Publications
***Dynamic P.E. for Elementary School Students*, $33.95. *Lesson Plans*, $14.95. *Dynamic P.E. for Secondary Students*, $27.95 complete.**

If you want a school-style physical phitness program (everyone should be physically phit, eh what?) this is the only one I know of that sounds like it could work in a home setting and be phun besides.

Dynamic P.E. for Elementary School Students is a resource textbook with hundreds of simple activities for both fitness and recreation. Its how-to directions include rules, diagrams, and instructions. The accompanying resource book, *Lesson Plans for Dynamic P.E.*, details 36 weeks of activities for K-2 and 3-6 levels.

Dynamic P.E. for Secondary Students is the whole ball of wax in one book: lesson plans, instruction units, game rules, and everything else you need except the balls and mats.

Kimbo Educational

As mentioned in the Movement Education section of this chapter, Kimbo has a huge line of physical fitness programs on recordings.

Example: Georgiana Stewart's popular *Good Morning Exercises for Kids* gets sleepyheads moving with first gentle, then more vigorous exercises, followed by a cool-down exercise. This secular album asks children to make a good morning wish that will "last the whole day long." More vigorous stuff is available for older kids and adults, like gymnastics and various types of dance. The elder set can work out in their chairs, if desired, with Kimbo's exercise albums for senior citizens.

Rockport
   Rockport's *Fitness Walking*, $10 postpaid.

There's nothing like jogging, stationery bike riding, weight lifting, rebounding, and fifteen minutes of diligent calisthenics to convince you that walking is a superior exercise. Nothing to it, this walking stuff. No shin splints or nauseous stomachs. No emergency visits to the chiropractor. No department store racks of flirty "walking clothes" that are actually undernourished underwear. No heart attacks. No stale gym air to breath. No boring repetition. In short, almost no sweat.

So why isn't walking the "in" sport? Probably because it's too inexpensive and not conducive to creating fashion empires. You can walk wearing anything but a pair of one-legged trousers, whereas as everyone knows jogging can only properly be done in Nike shoes and fancy sweat suits with a stripe down the sides and aerobic workouts require slinky, sexy leotards even more than the ability to bend into unnatural positions without cracking.

One man, however, could change all that. His name is Robert Sweetgall, and he has accomplished the amazing feat of walking through every state in the USA in one year. No, I didn't forget Alaska and Hawaii. Rockport, the shoemakers who sponsored his cross-country excursion (Aha! Finally the promotion of walking has a profit motive!), flew him to Hawaii and let him tour it a while before flying back stateside. His story forms the nucleus of Rockport's *Fitness Walking*, a fascinating book on the benefits and techniques of fitness walking that well could make a believer out of you.

SPORTS TRAINING

EDC Publishing Company
   Ballet and *Dance*, $5.95 each or $8.95 as a combined volume. *Soccer, Riding and Pony Care*, $4.95 each.

Straight from England, the Usborne sports training books answer the question, "Can you really learn anything about a sport from a book?" *Ballet* and *Dance* both teach simple techniques (and the reasons behind them) as well as presenting the history of these art forms. *Soccer* does an excellent job of explaining technique even to someone like me who knows nothing about these fine points, and so undoubtedly must *Riding and Pony Care*. Like all other Usborne books, these are lavishly, colorfully illustrated with pictures and text carefully designed to impart information with minimum effort and maximum fun.

Jameson Books
   Dennis Van Der Meer's *Complete Book of Tennis*

Staring at you on the first page of this book are these words from tennis player Billie Jean King: "Dennis Van Der Meer is the best tennis teacher in the world." Intriguing enough to keep me reading after midnight, even though I intended to finish this chapter tomorrow!

Laced with humor and based on sound learning strategies, the *Complete Book of*

Tennis covers it *all*. From lobs to groundstroke drills, from how to deliver the perfect low volley to corrective strategies for tennis mistakes, from improving your grip to tennis etiquette and picking the right tennis racket, the author gives you real tools to improve your game.

Dennis Van Der Meer has taught thousands of tennis pros his Standard Method® of tennis instruction. Tennis pros who use his method are certified by the United States Professional Tennis Registry. Based on the principle that simple is best, the method is suitable for anyone old and strong enough to wield a racket.

The book's well-designed combination of photos and interactive text makes you feel like you are receiving those personal tennis lessons yourself. It closes with a sports psychologist's analysis of the Standard Method®. According to this psychologist, who attended one of the author's clinics, the in-person method • establishes the proper learning climate—firm yet friendly • consistently builds from the simple to the complex • emphasizes learning by doing • effectively uses positive reinforcement • provides a steady diet of success • effectively provides visual feedback • encourages perfect practice, and • reconstructs only one mistake at a time, among other things. An excellent formula for tennis success, or success at any learning endeavor, explaining why so many people give Van Der Meer credit for improving their total life outlook.

SyberVision

Al Geiberger *Men's Golf*, Patty Sheehan *Women's Golf*, Stan Smith *Tennis*, Jean-Claude Killy *Skiing*, Jeff Nowak *Cross-country Skiing*, Rod Carew *Baseball*, Holman and Petraglia *Bowling*, Dave Peck *Racquetball*, Men's *Defend Yourself!*, Women's

Defend Yourself!, each $69.96 for a 60-minute video or $89.95 for the complete system that includes video plus training guide and four audiocassettes. Dave Stockton *Precision Putting*, Mike Dunaway *Power Driving*, Hale Irwin *Difficult Shots*, each $49.95 for the video and training guide. All videos available in VHS or BETA.

Those who can, do. Those who can't, watch. At least that's what SyberVision's developers hope. Their programs are based on the learning theory that (1) we learn best from role models— people who are highly successful at performing the desired behavior, and (2) skills are best learned when key fundamentals are isolated, explained, and either visually presented or vividly described. Thus, SyberVision's *Women's Golf* course not only features LPGA champion Patty Sheehan, but shows Patty delivering perfect stroke after perfect stroke in a mesmeric rhythm, alternating views of the stroke from in front, on the side, on top, in slow speed and regular, even with an occasional semi-digitized "skeletal shot" of Patty making the stroke in a special suit with the bones drawn on it in luminescent ink. The same stroke is repeated for a long, long time, and then the video goes on to the next— from tee drives to long fairway drives to bunker shots and so on. Techniques are explained on the accompanying audio cassettes.

All this sounds rather boring, and it is, unless you are passionately hooked on a game and strongly desire to improve yourself. Apparently a lot of people fall in this category. Three of SyberVision's products— *Men's Golf*, *Downhill Skiing*, and *Tennis*— have won the Golden Cassette Award for selling more than a hundred thousand copies. Also, in spite of SyberVision's 60 day money-back guarantee, they are apparently not flooded with returns.

CHAPTER TEN

SPECIAL EDUCATION

As just about everyone knows, "Special Education" is a euphemism for classes for students labeled slow or learning disabled. In most cases, there is nothing "special" about it.

At home, Special Education becomes truly special. For the first time, the labeled child gets a chance to show he or she can achieve. Unlike school teachers, who have been trained to always "blame the child" when his learning does not progress, parents have a stake in discovering a better teaching method. This is *your* child and if he doesn't learn, you can't chalk it up to fate and hope for a better group of students next year.

HELPING YOUR LABELED CHILD

Step one in helping your labeled child is to reject the label. Unless the school, or whoever labeled your child, can demonstrate that an *organic* problem exists, they're just saying, "We don't know why Johnny doesn't learn and we aren't interested in finding out." If Johnny has crossed eyes and can't see the blackboard, or his earwax is the consistency of concrete, then obviously he will have learning problems until his eyes get uncrossed or his ears get cleaned. But if Johnny is labeled "learning disabled" or "retarded" or "developmentally delayed" these so-called diagnoses have no *medical* significance at all.

Albert Einstein's teachers thought he was stupid, and would have called him learning disabled if the term had been around back then. But Mr. Einstein was merely disinterested in their teaching; there was nothing wrong with *his* brain.

So if your child is doing poorly in school, consider the following possibilities:

(1) He is bored.

(2) He has a poor teacher.

(3) He is being taught by a poor method.

(4) He is being taught in a way unsuited to his learning style.

(5) He is very bright and has contempt for his classes.

(6) He is very bright and is trying to "fit in" with the gang by acting stupid.

(7) He is a thorough chap who doesn't like to race on to new items until he has digested the old. (But school leaves no time to digest the old.)

(8) The class is graded subjectively, and the teacher doesn't like him.

(9) He is not well disciplined and rather than dealing with his bad behavior, the school prefers to label him "hyperactive."

These nine possibilities are just the tip of the iceberg. The bottom line, when dealing with physically normal children, is this: shall we give up and blame them, or consider their failures *our* failures, and keep searching for the solution?

DEALING WITH PHYSICAL PROBLEMS

Let's assume that your child has not been labeled, but diagnosed. There is solid medical evidence that something is wrong with his brain and/or body. What then?

Popular prejudice to the contrary, these are the very children who need most to be taught at home. Very few professional therapy programs provide hours of individualized therapy every day, and those that do are prohibitively expensive. In the family, on the other hand, a special child can receive hours of instruction and help, *without* being made to feel abnormal.

The materials you will want to use depend on your child's special problems. Look in the School Supplies and Preschool sections of *The NEW Big Book of Home Learning* and you will find loads of colorful, noisy, hands-on, grabbable learning devices. Many materials designed for early childhood education work well with special children. Make it as much fun as you can for yourself— pick stuff you would enjoy playing with, too! If you are able to take your time and let your child learn at his own pace, this takes off a lot of pressure.

Our first son was born premature and had to spend five weeks in intensive care. Ted was very slow in his physical and muscular development as well. On first diagnosis, one nationally known neurologist predicted that Ted most likely had the fatal disease of spinal muscular atrophy, and if not that, he at least would be handicapped for life. We called in the elders of our church and had them anoint Ted with oil in the name of the Lord. Ted did *not* have spinal muscular atrophy, as it turned out, and neither is he a cripple. Nor is he mentally retarded, another pleasant prospect that was held out to us. When the experts were busy trying to discourage us, my reaction was, "Even if they are right, I bet he *still* can succeed!" Today's "normal" kids are busy retarding themselves, lolling around in front of the TV set and wasting their lives trying to impress their peers. A "retarded" child who worked hard at his studies should be able to beat a "normal" kid who never puts forth any effort. Ditto a "handicapped" child who exercises vs. a "normal" kid who lounges around all day. In fact, when a "handicapped" child really works hard, sometimes he or she even beats the "normal" kids who are trying! They said little Wilma Rudolph would never walk again, but Wilma's mother was determined enough to spend her one weekly day off sitting for hours on the bus, taking Wilma to get therapy. Wilma walked. Then Wilma ran. Then Wilma won the Olympics.

Rifton: Equipment for the Handicapped

As I said, school supply houses and firms that cater to preschoolers are good places to start, especially those that carry Montessori materials. For physical therapy, Rifton Equipment for the Handicapped has the stuff. Exercise chairs, bolsters, wedges, play equipment, and so on— it's all here. Prices are acceptable for the quality, and it's possible that insurance may pay for some of it if you get a doctor's prescription. We've used similar equipment of our own manufacture, and it did Ted a lot of good.

BOOKS AND BOOKLETS ABOUT "LEARNING DISABILITIES"

Education Services
A Biblical Psychology of Learning, $10 postpaid.

How can you prevent learning problems? How can you motivate a labeled child? These are common questions parents and teachers ask. Dr. Ruth Beechick's excellent *Biblical Psychology of Learning* preempts all these questions. Beginning with the importance of first establishing a proper heart attitude through parental discipline and nurture, Dr. Beechick spurns the manipulative trickiness of much modern learning theory. By answering the most important question "Why do children and other people learn or refuse to learn?" she provides a road map for the lesser questions as well. Highly recommended.

Holt Associates
Everyone Is Able—The Myth of Learning Disabilities, $3 plus $1.50 shipping.

If you would like to find out why intelligent people are questioning the whole premise of "learning disability," and why you should fiercely resist your child being branded with this label, this booklet from Holt Associates provides the ammo. Hear from the "other experts"— parents of labeled children (or whose children would be labeled if the mainstream experts got their hands on them), and specialists within the schools who see what the LD label does to children and education. These are real-life stories and articles that first appeared in *Growing Without Schooling*. The quality of the writing as a whole is thoughtful, but not dispassionate. Must reading.

Reading Reform Foundation
The Magic Feather, $16.95 plus $1 shipping.

From the book jacket: "His parents called him bright and curious— his teachers called him hopelessly retarded. A million kids are similarly judged every year. His parents fought the schools and proved the tests wrong. You can too."

Bill and Lori Granger, a prolific husband-wife writing team, have a son, Alec, who at age six could read several years above his grade level. When a routine school test diagnosed Alec as having an IQ of 47, the Grangers at first pooh-poohed it, and then trotted out Alec's precocious reading ability. Unmoved, the school psychologist who gave the test said Alec would have to be deposited in a Special Education class. But, unlike other parents, the Grangers dared to fight the test-worshiping "experts."

The Magic Feather is the story of Alec's narrow escape from the Special Ed net (his parents ended up placing him in a Montessori school), and an exposé of the special ed industry.

Some juicy quotes from the book jacket:

While perhaps 3 percent of all school-age children might benefit from Special Education, nearly 11 percent of the nation's schoolchildren are currently confined in Special Ed programs— *more than four million children.*

In some school districts, racial and ethnic segregation are enforced by using the Special Ed program as a dumping ground for unwanted program as a dumping ground for unwanted students.

For each child successfully captured by a Special Ed program, a school district may receive *four thousand dollars* in government monies.

As the Grangers say, "We learned some startling things. We have found that the process that pins such labels on children is at best expedient and at worst outright fraud . . . Nobody knows what a 'learning disabled' child is, and the difference between him and another called 'emotionally disturbed' or 'retarded' may be nonexistent. What they share is that they did not 'fit in' in a regular classroom . . . Nearly one out of eight kids in school are in Special Education today . . . This is too many and educators know it."

More than an exercise in consciousness-raising, *The Magic Feather* is a resource book for parents who want to fight the system from within, and a list of good reasons for those who want to get out.

Pantheon Books (check your library for this one—it was published in 1975)
The Myth of the Hyperactive Child and Other Means of Child Control. Large book with bibliography, appendix, footnotes, and index.

Here in Missouri we are favored with a early childhood education pilot program enticingly labeled "Parents as First Teachers." Part of this program, beside the group meetings supervised by "experts" and the in-home visits to check on the parents, is a strong emphasis on early screening of children to catch cases of "developmental delay." Its proponents hope that this presently-voluntary program will soon become compulsory in every community in the USA.

In view of this push to force children into early childhood screening, you owe it to yourself to learn why diagnostic screening is *not* helpful and why the "scientific" labeling process is a bunch of self-serving hooey. The book that will do this for you is Peter Schrag and Diane Divoky's scrupulously-researched *The Myth of the Hyperactive Child*.

Authors Schrag and Divoky are serious journalists who regularly write for major national media. Diane Divoky recently contributed the *Encyclopedia Britannica* entry on Home Schooling.

ORGANIZATIONS THAT OFFER HELP

Citizens Commission on Human Rights
Free brochures: *How Psychiatry is Making Drug Addicts Out of America's School Children* and *Ritalin: A Warning for Parents*.

The special education label can become a self-fulfilling prophecy, not only because of how it undermines a child's scholastic confidence but because of the dangerous misuse of drugs on labeled children. CCHR's pamphlet *How Psychiatry is Making Drug Addicts Out of America's School Children* explains why and how healthy children with no organic disorders are unreasonably labeled and put on drugs, and how this sometimes leading to real brain damage or irreversible handicaps.

CCHR's follow-up pamphlet, *Ritalin: A Warning for Parents*, lists 15 little-publicized but important possible side effects of Ritalin use and withdrawal. It also briefly discusses Thorazine, the "chemical lobotomy."

"If a teacher, psychologist psychiatrist or a school employee is trying to force your child or a child of a friend or relative into 'therapy,' CCHR may be able to help," says their brochure. CCHR has chapters in most major American cities and in Mexico, U.K., Canada, Austria, Holland, Norway, Sweden, Denmark, Switzerland, France, Germany, Italy, Australia, and South Africa.
Evangelistic & Faith Enterprises of America,

Evangelistic & Faith Enterprises of America, Inc.

On-site evaluations, $125 to $225 (sliding scale) includes 60-plus page report and individualized program. Talent Development books available separately.

Dr. Paul Cates of Evangelistic & Faith Enterprises crisscrosses the country with his team providing evaluations and individualized programs for special needs children and setting up Talent Development centers in Christian schools.

Based on up-to-date secular learning theory, the Talent Development material is written in normal special education jargon. Terms like "learning disability" and "attention deficit" are freely used, and medication is approved for extreme cases of "hyperactivity." Each child is evaluated individually and a learning program constructed to meet his learning style and particular strengths and needs. The Talent Development approach also revolves around minimizing student distractions, improving diet and exercise, and beefing up the home's spiritual atmosphere.

Home Educators of Special Education Children

A big title for a little organization that could provide a lot of help. Home schooling moms Myrna Vogel and Saunny Scott are looking for others who home school labeled or handicapped children. The idea: pool knowledge and make friends. The goal: less isolation, more confidence.

Latebloomers Educational Consulting Service

Let me quote from the brochure:

LATEBLOOMERS offers a new model for viewing learning disabled children. Just as the buds on the freesia of **LATEBLOOMERS'** logo are in different stages of growth and bloom in their own time, so too, will children who are not flowering academically have their time to bloom. . .
LATEBLOOMERS believes many children

who are experiencing difficulties in learning, overcome these problems and "latebloom" when they are in a trusting, warm, supportive atmosphere which allows them to move at their own pace and according to their own natural patterns of growth. . .

LATEBLOOMERS provides individual academic therapy, educational evaluations which focus on *strengths* and achievement potential, educational materials for both parents and children, workshops, lectures, and consultations, and above all its "growth model" for lateblooming children rather than a "deficiency model."

Thomas Armstrong, the president of **LATEBLOOMERS**, has lots of experience in these areas. You may be interested in his new book, *In Their Own Way: Discovering and Encouraging Your Child's Personal Learning Style* (Jeremy Tarcher, publisher; St. Martin's Press, distributor). It's available in most major bookstores.

Missionary Vision for Special Ministries

Free literature and programs for your group, church, school, neighborhood, or home. Donations welcome.

What does it feel like to be blind . . . or crippled . . . or different-looking? How should you treat someone who is physically different? With games, activities, and songs, blind Christian missionary Ruth Shuman shares ways to break down the walls between "handicapped" and "normal" people.

Materials available from this ministry include: Blindfold Experiments, Children's Book List of recommended reading about handicaps, Teasing Really Hurts, Put Yourself in Their Place, Yes or No — How Would You Respond? and Toppling Stereotypes About the Handicapped. MVSM's materials provide a realistic picture of handicapped life and give guidelines for conducting positive relationships.

National Academy of Child Development
Miracles of Child Development **6 hour cassette program with note outline, developmental profile, and data reporting forms for home use, $50.** *Learning Disabilities: What Do the Labels Really Mean?* **2-tape set, $18. More tapes and books available.**

Founded by Robert Doman, a nephew of the Glenn Doman who runs the Institute for Achievement of Human Potential and who wrote those books on teaching look-say reading to your baby, NACD specializes in home therapy programs for the really hard cases. Children who have suffered severe brain damage, or who have neurological problems, or fits, or physical handicaps, are thoroughly diagnosed by NACD's staff and then presented with a home program tailor-made for them. NACD is expensive (hundreds of dollars a year per child) and many of their methods are severely criticized by the medical establishment. They do have some spectacular success stories, however, and their philosophy of optimism at least keeps them trying to achieve results, whereas medical experts seem to be getting more and more pessimistic these days. We were members of NACD for a while, and Ted just loved his program (all except the knee bends).

NACD programs are a lot of work for the parents and are highly patterned. You do exercise A for two minutes three times a day, and listen to tape B for three minutes twice a week, etc. NACD is also into the "dominance" theory of brain organization, whereby the goal is to be right-handed, right-footed, right-eyed, and right-eared, or conversely left-handed, -footed, -eyed, and -eared. Thus your child may end up wearing an eye patch or ear plug to assist him in "switching over" from right to left, or vice versa. NACD also believes strongly in the stages of development, and enrolled teenagers and even adults sometimes wind up crawling around like babies until they improve their coordination in that stage.

You can order NACD's introductory tape set, *The Miracles of Child Development*, for $50. The tapes are fascinating and inspirational, but take them with a grain of salt. B-mod is not the answer for all childhood discipline problems as Mr. Doman believes, though his suggestions for

motivating children, and especially his stress on praise and encouragement, are well worth hearing.

Learning Disabilities: What Do the Labels Really Mean? challenges parents not to rest until they find out what is *really* wrong with their children. Mr. Doman explores some common sources of children's problems (hearing/sight problems, memory problems, neurological imbalance and so on) and offers practical suggestions for unearthing and remedying these problems.

I really appreciate NACD's philosophy that labeling counts for nothing; it's solving the problem that counts. This is also the only remedial organization I know with the optimism to strive for bringing handicapped and labeled children up to or beyond *normal* (not handicapped) functional levels.

Orton Dyslexia Society

If your son does cute little things like write *Z* backwards and read *saw* for *was*, and if you are teaching him at home, just ignore it. If, however, he is enrolled in school and the pressure is on to *do* something because for heaven's sake this child is *dyslexic*, don't panic. Get in touch with these folks.

True dyslexia is just a different way of processing information and doesn't need to be "cured." Dyslexics are often geniuses who only need the right teaching method to turn them loose on the world. Dr. Samuel Torrey Orton did pioneering work in developing these methods, and the society carries on his work.

It's very likely that your little one is not dyslexic at all, just learning and making normal mistakes. Most so-called dyslexia is actually the fallout from teaching the look-say method of reading in which children are required to memorize the shapes of every word in the language. This type of "dyslexia" can be instantly cured by a good phonics program, of which there are two dozen in the Reading section of *The NEW Big Book of Home Learning*.

In 1975 the Michigan Reading Clinic examined over 30,000 allegedly dyslexic children. These had all been neatly labeled so that their reading failures could be blamed on them, instead of on bad teaching methods. Of all the 30,000 only *two* children were found to be unable to learn to read.

Since the Orton Dyslexia society uses multisensory, intensive phonics, which works equally well with dyslexics and nondyslexics, it can't hurt to send for a list of their materials.

MATERIALS THAT COULD HELP

Academic Therapy Publications
Four free brochures. Send large SASE with 39¢ postage (U.S.) to LEARNING IS FUN at Academic Therapy Publications. Free *Directory of Facilities and Services for the Learning Disabled*, send $2 per copy to cover postage and handling.

Great *free* materials that help parents help their kids. Academic Therapy Publications' motto is "special materials for special needs in today's education." They put feet to this motto with a series of free brochures: *Helping Your Child at Home with Reading*, *Helping Your Child at Home with Arithmetic*, *Helping Your Child at Home with Spelling*, and *Helping Your Child at Home with Handwriting*. Each brochure tells parents the most common reasons a child might have a problem with the subject in question, and gives dozens and dozens of really practical tips for reinforcing these subjects in a fun way using things found in every home.

Also free from Academic Therapy Publications (add $2 for postage and handling) is their yearly *Directory of Facilities and Services for the Learning Disabled*. Now in its twelfth edition, the *Directory* offers a tremendous array of contacts for the parents of labeled children. The body of the *Directory* is state-by-state listings of facilities and services for these children. Each listing contains scads of information besides the standard address and phone number: size of staff, services offered, types of problems handled, ages served, fee type, year established. Also included is a comprehensive listing of companies offering specialized materials for labeled children and their teachers, national organizations and agencies serving this community, educational journals, college guide for LD students, and more. An alphabetical index and index by service provided finish off the book, which closes with an area code map so parents can easily call any interesting references. A terrific resource!

Lastly, Academic Therapy Publications is the publisher of High Noon Books, a line of more than one hundred high interest/low reading level novels. Intended to tempt the older slow reader, these paperback books are designed to look "adult." The plots are grown-up but also clean and wholesome, unlike so much modern reading material for children. I had to read the samples Academic Therapy sent in brief snatches, since my sons kept disappearing with them when I wasn't looking.

Ball-Stick-Bird
Set #1, Books 1-5 with Instructor's Manual, $59.95. Set #2, Books 6-10 with Instructor's Manual, $59.95. Add $3 shipping.

Ball-Stick-Bird, a phonics program invented by research psychologist Dr. Renee Fuller, differs tremendously from every other phonics system. For one thing, it was designed to teach certified, institutionalized retardates to read (people with an IQ of 60 or less). For another thing, it worked. No other phonics program, not one, has ever made its debut under such difficult circumstances.

Dr. Fuller's breakthrough, at first sight, might seem to be her system for breaking down the capital letters into three strokes: the Ball (a circle), the Stick (a line), and the Bird (two lines joined at an angle, like the cartoon of a bird in flight). Color-coding these basic forms to make the difference between the strokes even more dramatic, beginning with capital letters presented in a carefully planned sequence, and requiring the student to "build" each letter out of its forms (thus involving all four sense modalities) Ball-Stick-Bird goes out of its way to make basic phonics mastery painless.

But—and here comes the rub—other phonics programs also feature simplified approaches to reading. Yet nobody dares take them inside institutions for the mentally handicapped and expect success.

Ball-Stick-Bird gets its punch from, of all things, a really different story approach. Dressed up in the cutting-edge formula of a science-fiction story, Dr. Fuller presents some heavy-duty moral applications. Her Good Guys and Bad Guys star in fables about human nature: the lust for power, the foolishness of sloganeering, how experts use their authority to stifle criticism of their actions, and so on.

It is easy to see why "labeled" people—like the "mentally retarded" and "special education" children—lap up these stories. Dr. Fuller tells it like it is. She literally gives them the words that explain their experience as the powerless victims of "experts."

I should mention that Ball-Stick-Bird can be used with any person or child mentally old enough to follow a story. Dr. Fuller's contention is that Story Readiness, not some mystical amount of Motor Skill Readiness, is the real preparation for reading, and that successful reading itself grows out of the basic human desire to understand one's own life as a story.

From a Christian perspective, this makes great sense. If the spirit of a man is truly independent of his physical brain, there is no reason why any human being, however "mentally deficient," should not be reachable through the basically spiritual medium of stories—especially stories that help him make sense of his own life. Like, for example, the original, unbowdlerized Bible stories. Let's start thinking about it . . .

Educators Publishing Service
Parents' Packet, **$6.** *Language Tool Kit*, **$21.** *Teaching Box*, **$92; accompanying storybooks, $14.50.** *A Guide to Teaching Phonics, Orton Phonics Cards*, **$8 each.** *Reading, Writing and Speech Problems*, **$5. Lots more.**

Educators Publishing Service has a nice little brochure offering "Home Use Materials for Students with Learning Difficulties." EPS carries a number of Orton books and packets, plus Orton Phonics Cards and Orton-Gillingham Language Kits. You can also get reference books on learning problems, including Dr. Orton's classic *Reading, Writing and Speech Problems in Children.*

The *Parents' Packet* of articles from the Orton Dyslexia Society Reprint Series tell what dyslexia is, how to diagnose it, and how to remedy it using the Orton-Gillingham method. The booklet ends on an uplifting note, profiling eminent achievers who have had dyslexia.

Language Tool Kit of 119 cards and a teacher's manual can be used by a parent for teaching reading and spelling to a student with a "specific language disability." The *Teaching Box* is a very highly structured, step by step, program for children with severe learning difficulties. You get 69 groups of 3 x 5 cards, separated by dividers. Two accompanying books explain how to use and supplement the cards, and explain dyslexia. One pack of phonogram cards is enclosed, and you can buy a set of 14 storybooks to accompany the program.

There's lots, lots more that I have no room to describe. Hey, why don't you send for the brochure?

Home School Headquarters
Resource Guide, **$10 postpaid.**

The *Resource Guide for Home Education* lists dozens of organizations that serve the handicapped and their families, plus listing magazines, recreation opportunities, and educational resources especially designed for those with physical impairments. Plus the *Guide* lists hundreds of specialized resources for researchers and home school leaders, many of which are not included in my book because of their limited audience. If your child has been

labeled, or has an actual handicap, the *Guide* can help you find people who can help.

Love Publishing Company

If you are looking for standard public school materials for special children, Love Publishing Company has them. See what the schools practice and what they preach, if you're interested.

Patterned Language

Unit 1, home use (includes both teacher and learner materials), $69.51. Unit 2, $169.90. Unit 3, $132.41. Complete Sample Set, $368.67. Add 10% shipping.

Can you teach deaf pupils written language skills? Yes, according to the people at Patterned Language. Their program, based on color-coded instructional materials (nouns, verbs, etc. coded differently), teaches deaf students how to manipulate the words they do know into all basic simple sentences.

Instructor's materials for Unit 1 include a large apron with color-coded pockets and pocket stiffeners, instructional manuals for home and classroom use, 50 large color-coded vinyl word cards to sort into the apron pockets, six color-coding pens, a ruler/pencil set, and a card marker. Learner's materials include a small color-coded apron and 50 small vinyl word cards. Unit 2 materials are built around a slot-chart and tray with eight color-coded card files. Unit 3 graduates to word reference symbol cards and wall charts for the teacher, the Patterned Language paper and a New Vocabulary notebook for the student.

The Patterned Language staff is also available for teacher training workshops around the world at extremely reasonable rates.

CHAPTER ELEVEN

GIFTED EDUCATION

Are the school Gifted and Talented programs a device to provide private schooling for the children of the elite at public expense? Notice all the special attention paid to children in those intellectually segregated classes. Special field trips, more computer access, more motivated teachers, more interesting projects. Every child not in those special classes feels excluded (and he is).

Yet, like the Christian doctrine of election, G&T selection is purely by grace. Some anointed person declares a child gifted, and there he is. The anointed differ sharply among themselves as to who these gifted ones are, but the basic premise is that one is either born gifted or not. Children cannot earn, or learn, their way into these classes. No amount of sprucing up one's study habits or striving to do better will get your child labeled "gifted," only the anointing from On High.

IS THE GIFTED LABEL REALLY A GIFT?

Once in, "gifted" children are drilled rigorously in open-ended— e.g., humanist— thinking. They are trained to consider *all* possibilities: shall we feed Marvin his dinner, or kill Marvin and eat him for dinner? As supposed "future leaders" they are taught to believe in a future one-world Socialist government. They are trained to worship their own intelligence (guaranteed result: unpopularity) and to disdain the collective wisdom of history. Doesn't this smack of some adults' power trip more than a beneficial program for children?

"Gifted" children typically suffer feelings of isolation and rejection. Popularity lingers out of reach, as giftedness equals nerdhood in the eyes of schoolmates. Furthermore, a genuinely gifted child's interest in ersatz subjects and strange pursuits is not likely to be widely shared. And nobody likes a self-ordained Future Leader.

This brings back memories of my own childhood as a snotty smart kid who felt persecuted for my "giftedness," when in reality my problem was the lack of a servant heart. All the grades your child has skipped, all his odd interests like science fiction and classic literature, all his good report cards will cease to bother other kids as soon as he learns to *help* others instead of showing off. It also helps to cultivate wider interests rather than fanatically focusing in on one pet project; to keep one's personal grooming current (nobody likes a smelly genius!); to listen to other people (they know something, too); and to humbly admit that your achievements were the result of sweat as much as talent. But that last point, of course, cuts the feet out from under the rationale of special, segregated programs for gifted kids!

WHAT IS GIFTEDNESS?

Giftedness, insofar as it means anything at all, is really intellectual focusedness. The truly gifted child is not necessarily brighter, just more determined to think things through. When other kids might choose a pick-up game of baseball, he prefers to arrange his butterfly collection in correct taxonomical order. While everyone else is admiring the band parade, she is mentally inventing a new kind of martial music.

The nagging creative inspiration is a spiritual gift—whether from God or elsewhere. Both great men and wicked men have found themselves driven by a focused inner compulsion. Giftedness, then, may imply spiritual sensitivity more than mental acuity.

Is it just a coincidence that school G&T programs focus so heavily on occult and pagan themes? *Dungeons and Dragons* units are common, as are activities in which children roleplay pagan worship. I worry about this. Surely spiritually sensitive children are the *last* ones who should be exposed to occult influences.

GIFTEDNESS AT HOME

If giftedness really is focusedness, then *any* child turned on to learning is gifted. And where better to encourage this enthusiasm than at home? You can enrich your enthusiastic child's education with safety at home, using the same materials the best G&T programs use, or substituting others of your choice. In this way you can insure that creative thinking doesn't become an exercise in lack of compassion (if Marvin is hungry, killing him is *not* a viable option) and that training in political strategies

does not evolve into training in challenging one's parents. You can also avoid the heady arrogance of having your child labeled "gifted," which is just the counterpoint to the pain felt by the child labeled "slow." One can't be Lord of the Roost unless one has lesser beings to lord it over; one can, however, be as excited about learning as one pleases without putting anyone else down. There is enough room in the world for all of us, and enough worthy tasks for us all to work on, even if we all were trained as geniuses.

Enthusiasm for learning was never meant to be the province of an elite. Though your child may not be considered "gifted and talented" by the school district, he *is* gifted and he *is* talented. His natural enthusiasm may have been blunted by passive entertainment and peer dependency, but if you throw a tablecloth over the TV and liberate him at least temporarily from the clutches of his peers, his creativity and intelligence will amaze you.

MAGAZINES FOR PARENTS

Challenge

One year (5 issues, August through April), $20. Single issue, $4.50.

Nicest-looking, easiest to use magazine for teachers of gifted kids. Issue layout is clean, inviting, and enhanced with clip art and occasional touches of color. Articles are intelligently designed, with goals, objectives, resources, and so on easily locatable.

Challenge is not really designed for parents. Although most activities and units could easily be used at home, the editorial content is directed squarely at the classroom teacher.

Each issue contains many teaching units, activities, and teaching tips. Examples: "Native Americans, An Integrated Arts Approach," "Can You Solve a Mystery?" and "The Great Pizza Project."

As in classroom G&T programs, a disproportionate amount of energy goes into children role-playing pagan worship. In just one issue, for example, the Native Americans unit required children to "create and perform a chant appropriate for a Native American corn ceremony." The Mythology unit suggested children could "design a temple for a god/goddess and construct a model." The article, "A Celebration of Life," a report on a death ed unit given to public school eighth graders, displayed a large Yin/Yang symbol at the top of the page. To put this in perspective, I wonder how the ACLU would view a classroom teacher who required children to design and perform a Christian Sunday service, make and display a Cross in the classroom, read Christian literature about the Resurrection, or write prayers to Jesus (four activities that did *not* appear in the magazine).

Challenge is a published by Good Apple, the producers of an array of magazines for teachers, including *Shining Star*, a magazine for Christians.

The Gifted Child Today

New reader subscription price, $17.97. Sample issue, $4. Canadians and foreign subscribers, add $5 per year for postage and pay through U.S. banks or by international money order.

The Gifted Child Today is "The World's Most Popular Magazine for Parents and Teachers of Gifted, Creative, and Talented Children." *GCT* contains practical advice, home and school activities, special columns about computers and so on, reviews of books and resources for "gifted" kids, a calendar of meetings about same, an annual directory of summer camps and programs for same, interviews with "experts," and on and on.

The layout, which resembles a newsletter more than a standard magazine format, consists of densely packed small type flowed into columns, relieved by infrequent graphics. This may suit *GCT*'s more scholarly approach, which is less geared to providing step-by-step classroom units and more directed to the "Why?" and "How?" of educational philosophy.

The company also has its own mail-order bookstore of games 'n stuff for "gifted" kids and their parents. See the Brainstretchers section of this chapter for more details.

MAGAZINES FOR "GIFTED" CHILDREN

Creative Kids

New reader subscription price, $14.97 (8 issues, October through May). Sample copy, $2.50. Canadians and foreign subscribers, add $4/year for postage; pay through U.S. banks or by postal money order.

Magazine by and for "creative students." They are safe in this standard, as dullards by definition do not send in articles for publication. Loaded with all sorts of activities, art, poetry, puzzles, mazes, reviews, and so on, *Creative Kids* is edited by adults, but entirely kid-written. Activities may be reproduced for classroom use.

Gifted Children Monthly

I have never seen this magazine, but Helen Hegener of *Home Education Magazine*, a lady who knows more about home education resources than anyone, swears it's the best she's seen in this category. An endorsement from Helen means it's probably upbeat, fun, takes kids seriously, and has lots of do-able activities.

Prism

One year, six issues, $19.95. Sample copy, $4. U.S. funds only.

Billed as "a nationwide network of communication for the gifted and talented," *Prism* is a forum for gifted kids in grades seven through twelve. The editors hope that by connecting these kids together, some kind of synergy will produce cultural revolution. *Prism* is currently distributed to public school districts and private schools in the USA.

Prism has garnered compliments from Carl Sagan, astronomer Frank D. Drake, Florida Governor Bob Graham, and Phyllis Diller.

The stories, poems, and articles submitted by these "gifted" children often express a spirit of loneliness. "Why does everyone treat me like a nerd? Why do all the girls ignore smart kids and like big stupid jocks? Why doesn't anyone understand me?" To combat this feeling of isolation, *Prism* functions like a mail-order support group, with an extensive Pen Pal section in every issue and editorials on how to handle giftedness.

BRAINSTRETCHERS

EDC

Most Usborne oversized paperback books cost between $2.95 and $6.95. Hardbound versions run from $6.95 on up. Library bindings available for some volumes.

Picture Puzzles, Brain Puzzles, Number Puzzles, $2.95 each. Combined volume, The Usborne Book of Puzzles, hardbound, $10.95.

Every book in EDC's Usborne line is suitable for gifted ed. Stimulating and colorful, Usborne Books sparkle with enthusiasm for learning. The line includes a Young Engineer series (four volumes), New Technology series (five volumes), Computer Applications and Concepts series (ten volumes), Computers series (nine volumes), Electronic World (four volumes), Explainers series (eight volumes), scads of science and math entertainment, natural history by the bushel, the Time Traveller history series (five volumes), and too much more to mention. Just get the catalog.

The Usborne Brainbenders series is three full-color puzzle books for kids aged eight and up— or so they say. Our seven- and six-year-olds like them. Brainteasers of all sorts abound in these high-quality, inexpensive paperbacks. According to *Games and Puzzles* magazine, the series is "This year's perfect present."

Educational Insights

BrainBoosters™, $4.95 each. Decoder (works with all BrainBoosters), $1.50. Set of all 6 books and 3 decoders, $34.

You've never seen anything like this before. Educational Insights' brand new Brain-Boosters™ line is six colorful, spiral-bound 32 page books jam-packed with brainstretching activities. The ad says, "Eye-popping two-page spreads brim with information, extension activities, and ten topic-related questions." The ad has it straight. The books are gorgeous.

But eye-appeal is not the biggest deal here. BrainBoosters™ comes with an amazing self-checking apparatus called the Decoder. Kids twiddle each of the ten dials to a circle, triangle, or square in order to answer the ten questions on the left-hand page. The right-hand page has clues in case you had trouble answering the questions, and also a panel of seemingly random circles, triangles, and squares. Place your Decoder over the panel and the correct answers appear in the Decoder's little see-through boxes.

Most books in this series— *Amazing Animals*, *Inventions and Discoveries*, *Digging into the Past*, *Worldwide Wonders*, and *Outer Space Adventures*— concentrate on teaching children facts in an interesting way. The brain-stretching here comes from following clever clues to find answers. Puzzles and Thinking Games takes the BrainBoosters™ concept one step further with all kinds of colorful picture riddles, analogy puzzles, and other real mind-benders.

The BrainBoosters™ series gets *my* nomination for This Year's Perfect Present. To see it is to buy it.

Kolbe Concepts, Inc.

Kolbe Concepts, Inc. operates a nationwide network of educational consultants who demonstrate and sell the Thinkersize critical and creative thinking materials directly. If you would like to see such a demonstration, call 602/840-9770. They'll be glad to give you the name of their nearest consultant.

Midwest Publications

Public school materials directed at improving thinking skills. They have workbooks on Syllogisms, Word Benders, pattern 'n puzzle Brain Stretchers, and so on. Midwest endeared itself to me by question number fifteen in its *Inductive Thinking Skills* workbook, which begins, "Larry lives in Iowa. He doesn't like school." The problem proceeds with Larry trying to talk his folks into moving to south Texas so that he won't ever have to go to school again (we don't go to school when it's warm, and it's *always* warm in south Texas). If you can't figure out what's wrong with Larry's reasoning, you'd better buy this book.

Midwest's publications seem to really do the job of improving the accuracy of a student's

thinking and exposing him to new possibilities within the confines of logic. See the Midwest reviews in the Logic chapter for more information.

Resources for the Gifted, Inc.

Kathy Kolbe began Resources for the Gifted as a frustrated mother. When regular programs didn't respond to the needs of her two children, Kathy Kolbe decided to create brain-stretching alternatives to standard school fare. After the major publishers told her there was no market for materials specifically designed to teach thinking skills, she started publishing them herself. Mrs. Kolbe soon built her business into the world's largest producer of learning aids for gifted children.

RFG carries a full line of gifted/talented materials in every category. They are all stimulating, entertaining, and expensive. Suitable for kids from prereaders to high-school seniors, they use a light-hearted approach to encourage creativity and emphasize the teaching of problem-solving skills. RFG encourages parents to use the materials with kids of all ability levels.

Timberdoodle

One-stop shopping for the best thinking skills material. Timberdoodle carries Midwest Publications *Figural Mind Benders*, the WFF 'n PROOF games, and probably most of the other worthwhile entries in this section by the time you read this. A Christian home business, Timberdoodle weeds out the iffy stuff and offers the rest at good prices with great service.

Treehouse Publishing Company

Resources for gifted children, much cheaper than Kathy Kolbe's materials. This public school-oriented series has quite a strong emphasis on the future and on options, which means I'd be careful and see if any values-molding is going on here. I haven't had a chance to evaluate Treehouse's products. The catalog to get, if you want to look them over, is called "World of the Gifted."

WFF 'N PROOF Learning Games Company
Games prices vary from $2.75 to $16, with most offerings in the $12 to $16 range.

You want games that raise IQ? You've got it. All WFF 'n PROOF games involve heavy thinking and clever deduction. All follow the rules of logic ("If A is not B, and C is not B, then is A necessarily C?") Children who regularly play these games show measurable increases in IQ. For more info, send for a brochure, order the Timberdoodle catalog, or see the detailed reviews in the Computer, Language, Math, and Science chapters of *The NEW Big Book of Home Learning*.

Zephyr Press
Zephyr Learning Packets, $14.95 each.

A "new wave" educational company, Zephyr Press publishes materials for whole-brain learning, self-directed study, and self-awareness. Their attractive catalog also includes innovative materials from other publishers. Examples: The Capsela electronic series, Steven Caney's *Invention Book*, the David Macaulay architecture books. More controversial offerings include the *Utopia* game (create your ideal world) and *Dilemma* (which virus victims should receive life-giving serum?).

Zephyr's line of 19 reproducible learning packets covers history, anthropology, and science, with such offerings as Middle Ages, Early Japan, Early People, Ecology, Entomology, and Volcanology. Each packet has the same attractive, easy-to-use format and contains two units, one for K-3 and the other for 4-8, plus suggestions on how to adapt the unit to different teaching/learning situations.

Each Zephyr Learning Packet begins with an introduction to the Zephyr approach, a list of suggested readings on the subject of self-directed study, and a page on how to set up an "Interest Development Center" based on the unit. Each unit activity occupies a single one-sided reproducible page and includes eye-pleasing graphics as well as the suggested activity highlighted in large text or large, clear handwriting.

A sample activity from the Entomology unit: "Label the body parts of this insect." The graphic was a large grasshopper, with boxes for body part names and lines pointing to the body parts thoughtfully provided. A more open-ended activity: "Which insects are believed to be friends of man and which insects are believed to be enemies? List at least two of each and tell why."

Sometimes children are given a choice of activities, as in this sample from the Early People packet:

BE AN EARLY ARTIST—choose one
• **Draw or paint** animals of the time of cave people. **Label** them.
• **Make** a cave drawing using chalk, charcoal, ink and sand on a large paper bag. Prepare the paper bag first by wrinkling, then soaking it in water and allowing it to dry Not the meaning of your "drawing."
• **Make** replicas of tools or weapons used by early people. Identify and explain their use.

Although marketed as "gifted" materials, the Learning Packets are not intricate or difficult. For parents who agree with the Zephyr philosophy, they would be ideal for home use. The self-directed study and clear-cut format fit well into a home education situation. Add to this the convenience of learning activities for grades K-8 all contained in the same book, and you've got a good thing going!

CLASSICAL GOODIES

CHAPTER TWELVE

CLASSICAL LANGUAGES

"People who live in a small town know more than an outline of its history; they are themselves woven into the textures of its life. They know whom to respect, whom to despise—and why. They understand the code, they get the jokes. To be familiar with the classics is to be on that same sort of small-town footing with the civilization we have inherited."

Thomas Fleming

Let us now praise famous men, and our mothers who begat us. Specifically, C.S. Lewis, J.R.R. Tolkien, and Dorothy Sayers.

Together these writers produced an impressive amount of the best English fiction of the current century— works that deserve the title "classics." Tolkien's *Lord of the Rings* needs no introduction as the most popular and best-written fantasy trilogy of all time. C.S. Lewis's *Chronicles of Narnia* continues as a bestseller unto this day, while his *Perelandra* trilogy and *Screwtape Letters* are found in every library. Dorothy Sayer's impeccable murder mysteries starring the unflappable Lord Peter Wimsey adorn bookstore and library shelves everywhere. Not to mention the hundreds of other books produced by this prolific trio, many of which are still in print half a century after they were written.

Beyond their obvious excellence as writers, these three all were members of the Inklings, a select literary club. What common link drew them together? What did they share that made this companionship and literary outpouring possible? What was the secret of their success?

THE CASE FOR CLASSICAL EDUCATION

The answer is that this favored three were all Christians with excellent classical educations. Each had been trained in logic and was able to apply it remorselessly to himself and others. Each had a wide knowledge of history and a personal acquaintance with the greatest writings of Western civilization— and its barbaric predecessors. None was stifled by that vague confusion about right and wrong that plagues modern agnostic writers. Each knew what he or she wanted to say and how best to say it.

So why don't we routinely see writers of this caliber emerging from the public schools and the Christian schools? Because modern education, Christian or otherwise, has forgotten the past. The silliest theories of a barely-wet-behind-the-ears PhD. matter more in education today than the collective wisdom of five millennia.

Most children today are processed through increasingly identical school programs. And what is in these programs? Little boxes called "subjects" dispensed in little chunks called "grades." Children in each grade may only study "age-appropriate" bits of the few approved subjects. And even this limited amount of knowledge, captive as it is to the enormous amount of required busywork assigned both in class and out, often contains more propaganda than truth. Thanks to the rabid demands of special interest groups, history cannot be taught as it really happened, but must be refashioned into sermons on women's rights or centrally planned government. Similarly, a simple math class must include compulsory units on "careers," the emphasis here being an attempt to indoctrinate girls into seizing 50 percent of all mathematically-related occupations. Time formerly set aside for grammar is given over to lessons on the horrors of nuclear war, and we find that even the grammar lesson, once we get to it, consists of sentences extolling the brave new socialist world. Meanwhile, children are scrupulously shielded from the real writings of the real people who actually built our civilization.

Do you think I am talking about public schools only? Do Christian schools give children the writings of Augustine, Calvin, Luther, and Wesley to think over? Are Christian schoolchildren trained in Latin, Greek, and Hebrew and given responsibility for wide-ranging studies on their own? The unfortunate truth is that most Christian schools follow the secular agegraded, subject-dependent model. Parents demand it. "What if we have to transfer our child back to public school?" Government presses for it. "If you want to be accredited, you have to follow this state-approved curriculum sequence." The pressure for children to be able to regurgitate a number of state-approved facts in order to get good grades on standardized tests determines the curriculum of both public and private schools.

The Inklings accomplished what they did because they escaped modern education. After learning how to read English, they learned the classical languages. They read the classics. They studied logic and persuasive speech. Thus fortified, they were amply equipped to storm and capture spiritual strongholds.

As Dorothy Sayers points out in her excellent essay, "The Lost Tools of Learning," children who have learned to think and study can learn anything they need. Do not confuse this with modern mislabeled "thinking skills." Socalled "thinking skills" curricula usually consist of a one-sided apologetic for atheism, with all arguments for God and family scrupulously censored out. Real thinking starts with an understanding of the rules of logic, and sufficient honest data on which to build a worldview. This is not accomplished by squeezing all knowledge through a state-approved grid.

LATIN OF THE BRAVE, HOMER OF THE FREE

If the main reason why Latin and classical studies are not standard fare for elementary schoolchildren is that there are no Latin questions on the Iowa Test of Basic Skills, shall we let the bureaucrats who design these tests control our children's future? It's as simple as that.

As it so doth hap, Latin actually increases those sacred test scores. *Chronicles of Culture* editor Thomas Fleming, in his excellent report "The Roots of American Culture: Reforming the Curriculum," points out,

> Studies done in several major American cities reveal an astonishing record of success for Latin programs. What is particularly striking about these experiments is the fact that most of them have been conducted in inner-city schools with a high proportion of disadvantaged and minority students. The best experimental program has been conducted in Philadelphia, where between 1967 and 1976 Latin enrollment in the public schools rose from 490 to 14,000. In 1971 the Philadelphia schools conducted a study in which fifth graders were given fifteen to twenty minutes of Latin a day. The Latin students were matched with a control group selected for both ability and background. At the end of the year, the Latin students were found to be one year ahead of the control group on the vocabulary section of the Iowa Test of Basic Skills. In a sim-

ilar experiment conducted in Washington, D.C., a randomly-selected group of poor students took part in daily Latin instruction. These were students who had been rejected for other foreign language training, because of their below-grade level reading skills. At the end of the year, it was discovered that these students had come "'from behind to achieve above average achievement in vocabulary and total reading." The most impressive aspect to the Washington experiments was the comparison with students given another foreign language. In one study, sixth graders were given Latin instruction for only eight months and succeeded in climbing "'from the lowest level of reading ability to the highest level for the grade, equalling the achievement of pupils who had studied French or Spanish for 38 months."

Similar results were reported in Indianapolis, Boston, and Worcester, Massachusetts . . .

In one case in Colorado, with which I am familiar, a young Spanish teacher was told by her principal that she was going to have to teach Latin. Being a good sport, she gave it a try. The good results she witnessed made her a convert. She proved to be so successful a teacher that in five years Latin enrollments increased from one section to five. This year she sent her best students on a five-year scholarship to Harvard . . .

So, no problem, you just sign your kid up for one of those neat Latin programs at your nearby public school, right? Not so fast . . .

Despite these successes, Latin is not growing as rapidly as ought to be predicted. The program in Washington has been scaled down, and it was only public outcry that prevented a massive budget cut in Philadelphia. Rudolph Masciantonio, who directed the Philadelphia program, comments ruefully that "Decision-makers sometimes tend to ignore the research data . . . for budgetary, political, or other reasons."

Ah, yes. Here come those "decision-makers" again. Let's put them on hold for a minute while we consider Mr. Fleming's synopsis of classical education:

Under the old dispensation, most of what a student learned beyond the three R's were the Bible and the Greek and Latin Classics. Some higher math was taught, and a student might dabble in one or another of the sciences, but what we now call the humanities was at the center. I say what we now call the humanities, because the terms has come to be used so broadly that it includes everything that isn't *science*. It once meant nothing more (nor less) than the languages and literatures of ancient Greece and Rome. It was supremely interdisciplinary, since it included the teaching of grammatical theory, several genres of literature, philosophy, and history. What is more, it relied heavily on comparing two quite dissimilar civilizations. Above all, the long winnowing-out process— a matter of some two millennia— ensured that students were typically exposed to nothing less than the most splendid achievements of the human mind. Finally the old humanities was a central core of learning that could be taken for granted in anyone who had stayed in school to the age of sixteen.

Just makes you drool, doesn't it? Imagine, education with class! No more Blipspeak. No turgid politically-correct textbooks. Back to freedom and dignity, serenity and grace. Forward, if you can stand it, to a truly Christian civilization.

NOW, ABOUT THOSE OLD, DEAD LANGUAGES

The schoolboy who first chanted

> "Latin's a dead language
> As dead as it can be
> It killed the ancient Romans
> And now it's killing me"

obviously never had clapped eyes on the fabulous list of resources you are about to see. Compared to other languages, both Latin and Greek are absurdly simple. Old Testament Hebrew is a bit trickier, because of the verb structure, but still quite learnable.

Now, let me share a secret: learning these languages is *fun*! You and your children can learn them together, or you can learn alone and teach them later. Your vocabulary will grow by leaps and bounds. Good books will make more sense, as you will be able to pick up the literary allusions and decipher the classical quotes. TV fluff will seem less filling when compared to the treasures of the past. Who knows? You or your children might even start writing *new* classics!

MAGAZINES FOR CLASSICAL SCHOLARS

Ares Publishers

The Ancient World, 4 double issues/year, $20. Back issues, $5 each.

"The Scholarly Journal with the Double Issues forming an up-to-date current-research library for the student of Antiquity." They said it! Reports on what's new in ancient history. Some past issue themes: Alexander the Great (the Great One got four issues!), Ancient Games and Athletics, Corruption in Ancient Greek and Roman Politics, Hellenistic Warfare, and Where Was the Cretan Labyrinth?

Ladislaus J. Bolchazy, of Bolchazy-Carducci Publishers, is one of the editors.

Classical Bulletin

Four issues/year, $6 U.S. Single copy, $2.50 U.S.

Another Ares Publishes production. The very muted ad simply announced this bulletin's existence and provided no information whatsoever about its content, other than the names of the editorial committee, here appended: Michael J. Harstad (Editor) and R. Robert Joly (Associate Editor).

Pompeiiana

Memberships: Student, $3 (mailed to home address); Adult, $10; Library, $13; Contributing, $15. Classroom orders, mailed to the teacher at a school address, 6 (minimum) to 50, $2.75, less for larger quantities. Australia, add $15. Canada, add $2. Sweden, add $10. Other countries, write and ask.

Cross *Teen World* with *People*, translate it into Latin, and what do you have? Good heavens, it's *Pompeiiana*! Simple Latin stories highlighting current sports, music, and media idols, Top Ten rock titles in Latin, games, riddles, puzzles, words searches, student articles, self-test quizzes, and a bunch of other "relevant" stuff. Also info directly relating to classical studies. About ten thousand subscribers.

University of Calgary Press

Echos du Monde Classique/Classical Views, 3 issues/year. Subscriptions: individual $11, institution $18. Single copy $7 plus $1.50 shipping (Canada), $3 (outside). Outside Canada prices are in U.S. dollars.

Articles and reviews on classical history, literature, archaeology, and culture. The Canadian classical community is invited to share in the ongoing scholarly discussions, which include the how's and why's of teaching and learning the classics. *Echos du Monde Classique/Classical Views* also has up-to-date archaeological progress reports on sites excavated by Canadian archaeologists. A taste of what *Echos du Monde Classique/Classical Views* has recently offered: Michael Lynn-Goerge on Introductions to Homer, H.D. Jocelyn on Latin Sexual Humor, Paul Murgartroyd on Tibullus, Elaine Fantham on Women in Antiquity, Ian Storey on Old Comedy.

LATIN COURSES

AMSCO

AMSCO has Latin texts, workbooks, and dictionaries. Unlike other publishers, AMSCO has third-year texts for all its languages, and even a fourth-year text for Latin. Texts are inexpensive and sample copies may be obtained by writing on school letterhead.

Audio-Forum

Pronunciation and Reading, Ancient Greek and Classical Latin, each language $19.95.

Audio Forum's *Pronunciation and Reading* guides to ancient Greek and classical Latin each come with a booklet and two cassettes.

Bolchazy-Carducci Publishers
Student Text, Level I, Books 1 (Units 1-15) and 2 (Units 16-30), $15 each. Unit Test Booklet, $8. Graded Reader, $9. Reference Notebook, $4. Teacher's Manual (covers both books in Level I), Teacher's Graded Reader, Guide to Unit Tests, $7 each. Set of 15 coordinated drill cassettes (units 1-30), $11.95 each. Set of 5 *Artes Latinæ* filmstrips, $10.50 each. Set of 5 *Roma Antiqua* filmstrips, $11.50 each. Level II materials also available at similar prices.

Looking for the best Latin course around? Waldo Sweet's *Artes Latinæ* course wins here, hands down. This programmed language Latin course is so easy to follow our seven-year-old uses it by himself.

The course begins with a series of cassette lessons correlated with the attractive programmed text. These teach the student how to use the course. *Artes Latinæ* then proceeds to teach Latin pronunciation and a number of "Basic Sentences." These Basic Sentences are famous quotations from famous classical writers and the Bible. Each Basic Sentence gives the student a grammatical form—like the basic subject-verb-object sentence *Vestus virum reddit.* By adding vocabulary words, the student can create a infinite range of new sentences using the basic models. At the same time he is exposed to Latin thought and introduced to classical literature.

Filmstrips, cassettes, and even Latin buttons featuring the Basic Sentences are available.

Cambridge University Press

Thomas Fleming recommends this Latin course, the same used at English prep schools. At press time, I still had not seen it or heard from the publisher. Sycamore Tree plans to carry it, as well as the Independent School Press materials—write them for details.

Independent School Press
Preparatory Latin, Book I and II, $8.95 each. Many more texts available.

I rejoiced to see ISP's Latin text for junior high students. Bright elementary pupils could use it too, in my estimation, which is a giant step towards providing Latin for suckling infants: my fond dream.

Preparatory Latin was intended to help young preppies prepare for that inevitable moment when they are flung into a sea of Latin translation. As is so often true, in striving to make a text usable by younger students the authors have produced a book that makes their subject accessible to all, not just the young.

Prep Latin is not merely simplified explanations. It incorporates a variety of teaching methods: "the Traditional, the Aural-Oral, the Linguistic, to name a few." Technical terms are not introduced until absolutely necessary. Grammatical elements show up one at a time before being pinned into a framework. Drill consists of 30 brief sentences per lesson that include the elements being drilled. Also, you get the romance of Pauline the Ant called, you guessed it, *Pericula Paulinæ* or *The Perils of Pauline,* complete with cliffhangers.

ISP has a dozen and more other Latin texts, including such gems as the ever-popular *A Latin Crossword Puzzle Book.* (Hey, be honest. It's probably the *only* Latin Crossword Puzzle Book.) Other gems: *Freddus Elephantus,* a Latin elephantasy about pachyderms and show biz. Plus old standbys like *Latin Word Lists* and *Lively Latin* and *Review Latin Grammar* for those made of sterner stuff.

Independent School Press
Phenomenon of Language, $9.95.

What do you get when you cross Latin with an introductory course in linguistics? It sounds awful, like pasta with barbecue sauce, but really it's good enough to deserve a separate review of its own. It's *The Phenomenon of Language,* a sprightly text that uses Latin as a vehicle for giving students a method for learning all languages quickly and efficiently. Besides the charming Roman style cartoons and clever

Besides the charming Roman style cartoons and clever activities, the student spends a lot of time discovering how languages work. The exercises are designed according to the Platonic method: students are gently led to draw the correct conclusions on their own.

I cannot overemphasize the usefulness of a text like this. Competence in handling language is really competence in thinking, and as Dorothy Sayers says the student who masters these processes will reduce by at least 50 percent the amount of effort it takes him to learn future subjects.

Office of Instructional Technology/University of Delaware

You knew it had to happen. Somebody would interface Latin and computers. Well, it's called *Latin Skills*, it's a series of five Apple microcomputer programs with variable skill levels.

According to the ad, *Latin Skills*' 40 hours of instruction can supplement a traditional Latin course, provide enrichment, help the slowpokes, or with some add-on options even work as a standalone self-study course covering the same ground as one year of college-level Latin.

Since we're thinking of home learning here, the option to look into is the *Individualized Latin Curriculum* (Wheelock version). Based on Wheelock's *Latin: An Introductory Course* (Harper & Row), the package contains a syllabus to guide students through their studies, six audio cassettes, and a test generator program so you can evaluate your progress.

CLASSICAL AND BIBLICAL GREEK COURSES

Alpha Omega Publications
$19.50 for complete set of 10 LIFEPACS. Greek Manual, $3.95. *Textus Receptus* (Greek New Testament), $10.95. *Greek/English Lexicon*, $22. Shipping 10%.

AOP has LIFEPAC worktexts for one full year of New Testament Greek. New Testament

Greek covers the essentials of grammar, with plentiful exercises for translating both Greek to English and English to Greek.

Audio-Forum
***Pronunciation and Reading*, Ancient Greek $19.95.**

As I mentioned above in reference to Audio-Forum's classical Latin *Pronunciation and Reading* guide, the ancient Greek program also comes with a booklet and two cassettes.

Bethany House

Subtitled *New Testament Greek for Laymen*, *Basic Greek in 30 Minutes a Day* is a book for people who don't need to be Greek scholars, but do want to study the New Testament in the original. After completing it, you will • feel at home with the Greek alphabet • pronounce Greek words fluently • know the meanings of hundreds of New Testament words • understand theological terms that came from Greek • see connections between Bible words that are not obvious in English translations • be able to use Greek dictionaries and other valuable reference tools, and • understand the basic principles of Greek grammar.

How is this possible in 30 minutes a day? Author Jim Found uses cognates (words that resemble English words of similar meaning), introduces Scripture quotes very early on, and avoids long-winded grammatical explanations and convoluted terminology. The book is laid out like a junior high school workbook and is about as easy to use. Designed for Real People, not scholars who dote on tiny print and footnotes, *Basic Greek in 30 Minutes a Day* can either be used as a standalone introduction to Greek study through reference aids, or the gateway to serious Greek study.

Loyola University Press

A Reading Course in Homeric Greek: Student Text, Book I and II, $14.95 each; Flashcards, Book I and II, $3/set; Teacher's Manual and Key, $14.95.

A colorful revision of the original program introduced over 30 years ago. *A Reading Course in Homeric Greek* helps students quickly tackle selected undoctored passages from Homer's *Odyssey*. Contains "stimulating essays on aspects of Greek art and culture which highlight humanistic values and increase literary appreciation." Includes a special supplement, "Transition to Attic Greek," to help the student read more recent versions of Greek, whether classical or *koine*.

Moody Correspondence School

Correspondence courses in Biblical Greek. Inexpensive, designed for success. Plus, of course, Moody's famous large selection of Bible study courses, Hebrew study, and so on.

Puritan-Reformed Discount Book Service

Huge selection of all kinds of Biblical Greek one-book courses and study aids, including many only sold in seminary bookstores. Directed mostly to seminary students and pastors. Also huge selection of theological works and current Christian books.

BIBLICAL AND PRAYERBOOK HEBREW COURSES

Davka Corporation

Ulpan Davka™, $49.95 (needs 512K). *Hebrew CalendarMarker*, $24.95 (requires 512K and *CalendarMaker* by CE Software). *Learning to Read Hebrew*, $39.95 (requires 512K). *Achbar*™, $249.95. *DavkaGraphics* $34.95. *MacShammes*™, $995. Add $2 shipping for each order.

Does anyone read the ads in *MacUser*? Sure they do. Otherwise, how would I know about all Davka's Judaic software for the Macintosh? *Ulpan Davka*, according to the ads, is a "unique Hebrew vocabulary program" with one thousand words in a "dynamic flashcard format [whatever that is] with built-in sound." Add on whatever words you want to drill with the built-in editor. *Learning to Read Hebrew* sounds like it could be a real help, since coming to grips with the alphabet and pronunciation is enough to flummox many would-be Hebraists, and this is what the program claims to do. Finally, *Achbar* is a Hebrew/English bidirectional word processor, which I assume means it knows enough to change your Hebrew entries to read right to left while retaining your good ol' English left-to-right text around it. For this one you can get laser fonts— hearken, scholars!

The remaining Davka programs have nothing to do with learning Hebrew, but I'll mention them anyway: *DavkaGraphics* is Judaic clip art (menorahs, "Happy Hanukkah," maidens lighting the Sabbath candles, etc.); *Hebrew CalendarMaker* lets you add Hebrew dates, Torah portions, and Jewish holidays to CE Software's *CalendarMaker* (see *CalendarMaker* review in the Supplementary chapter); and *MacShammes*™ is a synagogue management system with membership and Yahrtzeit modules— demo disk available.

Does anyone at Davka read my letters? That's another question. I asked for a review copy of *Learning to Read Hebrew*, 'cause I'd love to extol it— if it works, it would be great— but so far, no show, no go.

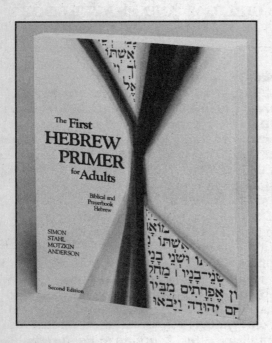

EKS Publishing

Teach Yourself to Read Hebrew: 5 cassettes and book, $29.95; book only, $6.95. *Prayerbook Hebrew the Easy Way*, $14.95; Teacher's Guide, $4.95. *The First Hebrew Primer for Adults*, softbound $16.95, library edition $29.95. *Tall Tales Told and Retold in Biblical Hebrew*, $8.95; Teacher's Guide $4.95. *Giant Hebrew Alphabet Chart* set (4 charts), $9.95. *Handy Hebrew Alphabet*, single alphabet $1. *3-Way Aleph-Bet Lotto*, $7.95. *Sounds of Hebrew Bingo*, $11.95. *Hebrew Grammar Poster Set* (10 posters), $18.95. *Sounds of Hebrew Flashcards*, $5.95. *Verb Flash Charts*, $5.95.

One-stop shopping for all kinds of great Hebrew language gear. *Teach Yourself to Read Hebrew* is a pronunciation/letter recognition guide using Sephardic pronunciation. It does not teach translation skills, just how to make the proper Hebrew sounds associated with the words. Each cassette tape has one lesson per side. You would be smart to get the cassettes. *Prayerbook Hebrew the Easy Way* is designed for those who can already read the Hebrew words in the prayerbook but don't understand their meaning. The 21 chapters provide a simplified introduction to grammar, oral reviews, lists of new vocabulary, and each ends with a prayerbook selection. The Teacher's Guide provides answers to the exercises and teaching tips. *The First Hebrew Primer for Adults* is a complete course of 33 lessons requiring no previous language experience. You get some heavy-duty grammar here— all seven regular conjugations and three of the most common variations on same. Exceptions are presented in the same chapters as the basic rules, making for completeness but somewhat impeding easy learning. No separate teacher's guide is necessary, since exercise answers are in the back of the back. You will have much more success with this course if you first study through *Teach Yourself to Read Hebrew*. *Tall Tales Told and Retold in Biblical Hebrew*, designed to accompany *The First Hebrew Primer for Adults*, expands and supplements the *Primer* with familiar fairy tales translated into the style and vocabulary of Biblical Hebrew. This you gotta see, right?

The remainder of EKS's line is study aids and games. The *Hebrew Alphabet Chart* set of four classroom-sized posters covers the shape, sounds, and English-letter names of Hebrew letters and vowels, and three ways Hebrew is written: printed, block, and handwriting. The *Handy Hebrew Alphabet* is the same information scaled down to one three-hole-punched card designed to fit in a ring binder. *3-Way Aleph-Bet Lotto* is a matching game that teaches recognition of the print, block, and script alphabets. It includes six heavy cardboard playing boards and three sets of 36 cards (one each for print, block, and script). Each set has a differently colored background. The game can be played solitaire or with up to six participants. *Sounds of Hebrew Bingo* takes 104 of the most frequently used letter-vowel combinations and can be played with up to 12 people. The Bingo caller needs to know Hebrew pronunciation. Flashcards are included to teach how the combinations look. These are also sold separately as *Sounds of Hebrew Flashcards*. The *Hebrew Grammar Poster Set* of classroom-sized charts printed on heavy card stock has Hebrew roots in brilliant magenta while the endings and vowel patterns that change are printed in black. English translations appear below each example. *Hebrew Verbs Charts for Beginners* is a set of 20 sturdy cards. Ten each show a complete verb pattern, and 10 have blank charts for student practice.

Moody Correspondence School

Beginning Biblical Hebrew courses for Christians. Write for brochure.

Puritan-Reformed Discount Book Service
Biblical Hebrew Step by Step: Volume 1 book $12.95/$9.32, cassette and book key each $7.95/$6.36; Volume 2 book $13.95/$10.04, cassette and book key each $7.95/$6.36. *Biblia Hebraica Stuttgartensia*, $17.95/$17.05, larger edition $24.95/$23.70. *The New Englishman's Hebrew/Aramaic Concordance to the Old Testament*, $39.95/$23.97. Discount prices for members are listed second. Shipping extra.

Puritan-Reformed has literally dozens of Hebrew courses and study aids, including interlinear Bibles, concordances, lexicons, study charts, grammars, and so on. Let me just mention a few of these that we have found most helpful.

Manahem Mansoor's *Biblical Hebrew Step by Step*, a usable introductory Hebrew course for adults, has just been improved with the addition of cassettes. You still might find the introductory how-to-pronounce-Hebrew sections tough sledding— try EKS or Davka instead for this. Once into the actual lessons, though, the course proceeds briskly. A typical lesson begins with vocabulary words separated into nouns, adjectives, and so on, followed by grammar notes, study hints, and well-designed exercises. I marvel that I ever attempted this course with an answer key; you will be

smarter!

The *Biblia Hebraica Stuttgartensia* is the standard Hebrew Old Testament used worldwide. Thanks to excellent printing and quality paper, you can actually read the type, including all point marks. The *New Englishman's Concordance* (available in both Hebrew and Greek), helps you find all Biblical references of a given word in the original language. Each word is coded to *Strong's Exhaustive Concordance* and several other major language references.

LITERATURE, WORKSHOPS, FLASH-CARDS, AND BUTTONS!

American Classical League
Membership includes *The Classical Outlook*: $15 USA, $17 Canadian and foreign. U.S. funds by international money order only.

Whatever remnants of Oxonian thinking still survive in the American graves of academe find their home at the American Classical League. ACL offers its members *The Classical Outlook* magazine, teaching tips and materials, info on new products, the National Junior Classical League (is it open to home schoolers?), national Latin and Greek exams, teacher and student scholarships, fraternal support, and an annual Institute. The latter mainly concentrates on pedagogical issues, with only a frigid nod to the usual feminist/special issues hype that has overcome most school programs. Lest the attenders be overcome by their mental exertions, the Institute program includes such things as picnics, riverboat rides, sing-alongs, social hours, and tours. Frankly, if I were a Christian schoolteacher, I'd attend it.

Bolchazy-Carducci Publishers
Buttons catalog, $2. Latin Easy Readers, $11 each.

The publishers of *Artes Latinæ* also carry a huge line of classical texts in the original languages. You know, get-down stuff like Euclid, Plutarch, Cicero, Ovid. For those not quite ready for the Big Time, here come the Easy Readers! The first, exotically titled *Elementary Latin Translation Book,* introduces students to Roman history and Greek mythology. The second, a Latin translation of Vergil's *Æneid* by none other than *Artes Latinæ* developer Waldo Sweet, substitutes an easy Latin paraphrase for the usual student notes in English. Lots of other readers are available.

Now, I know you've been waiting to hear about those buttons. Picture your junior egghead proudly sporting a button that declares *Veritas Vos Liberabit* ("The Truth shall Set You Free") or some pithy Greek aphorism. Each of these buttons costs only $1. Unfortunately, you have to order at least $15 worth. How about handing them out as rewards? Covering a T-shirt with buttons and pretending it's armor-plated? Giving them as Christmas presents to your favorite librarians? *Verbum sapienti satis.*

Jeffrey Norton Publishers

The company that owns Audio Forum (see the Adult Language Course review) also has a wide line of spoken-word cassettes, including literature in other languages. Their classical line includes *A Recital of Ancient Greek Poetry* and other classical Greek works, and *Selections from Cicero* in Latin.

Les Editions du Sphinx
Index inversé du vocabulaire botanique des oeuvres hippocratique, $10. *Eduquer au dialogue des civilisations,* $9.95. Etc. All prices in Canadian dollars.

Books on classical studies in French. Medium-sized line of *laboratoire de recherches hippocratiques.* G. Maloney écrit plusiers de ces livres. Alors!

Visual Education Association
Biblical Hebrew, Latin, Biblical or Classical Greek vocabulary flashcards, $4.95 each. Add $1.50 postage (U.S.) or $3.50 (other) for first set.

Bill's constant seminary companion was a box of Vis-Ed vocabulary flashcards. Each set contains 600-1000 1½ x 3½ cards plus a very useful study guide with index. The Biblical Hebrew study guide, for example, shows words in frequency of occurrence and by grammatical categories. Each card has the target language word on the front and both its English meaning and pertinent grammatical info on the back.

CHAPTER THIRTEEN

FOREIGN LANGUAGES

Why learn a foreign language? Here are some intellectual reasons: a desire to broaden your mind through exposure to another culture, the need to communicate with non-English speakers in your business, or just the fun of cracking a strange code. In years past, the man or woman who didn't know at least one language other than English was considered only half-educated. Now that so few American students are even learning to grapple with English successfully, the demand for fluency in another language has considerably abated. Yet it still is true that those who know several languages have an edge on those who do not.

Why learn a foreign language? Here's an economic reason: it can land you a job. I was amazed, during a visit to New York City, to see the many newspaper ads begging for executives who were fluent in German. It also doesn't take a genius to see that we could use a few good men in the computer field who speak Japanese, or that an importer of African artifacts might want to know Swahili. And knowing the languages in which English has its roots, namely French, German, and to a lesser degree Latin, increases your command of our own native tongue. One of the most famous classic texts on preaching recommends that ministers study French and German for this very reason.

Learning another language sharpens not only your speech, but your thinking. The habits of analysis and organization are increased by the study of the multitudinous patterns that make up any language.

You've now heard most of the arguments that foreign language teachers marshall in order to convince someone (*anyone!*) to please enroll in their classes. They really are good arguments. The only reason more students don't act on them is that you can get just as many credits for Basket Weaving I as for Advanced French I and learning a language is, frankly, harder than learning to weave a basket.

You, however, are made of sterner stuff than the average basket-weaver. For you, the question is not so much, "Ought I to learn another language," or "Should my children learn another language?" as "How do I go about it?"

ESCAPING THE TYPICAL TEXTBOOK TRAP

I am well qualified to speak on the subject of foreign languages, having had 10 years of French instruction, two years of German, and one year of intensive Russian. All these classroom courses, none of which resulted in actual fluency, have burned into my soul several basic truths about how not to learn a foreign language.

The first thing you must watch out for is the Typical Language Textbook. It comes in all sizes and colors but only one flavor: boring. You can recognize the Typical Language Textbook by the endless drills and listless dialogues that make up 99 percent of the book. The writers of these books have got it into their heads that you do not want to *speak* the language: rather, you want to *read* it. Furthermore, the stories you want to read all have sentences like "Jean rode his bicyclette to the store. Marie rode her bicyclette to the store. See Rex catch the ball. Run, Spot, run." This Dick-and-Jane approach to foreign languages not only leaves you gaping with boredom, it also leaves you fluency-free, as no normal Frenchman, or Italian, or Bulgarian, talks like that.

Another trap to watch out for is the Cute Language Textbook. This is the Dick-and-Jane-Go-To-The-Disco version. We still get Dick and Jane, or as it may be, Jean and Marie, but now our young friends are doing "contemporary" things. Unless you really just want to read teenybopper magazines in the target language, this approach won't get you much of anywhere either. Furthermore, in their anxiety to be "with it," publishers tend to overstress the negative aspects of youth culture abroad. Life in France isn't an eternal no-adults-allowed camping trip, like some books make it out to be, any more than it is here in the good old U.S.A.

The last all-too-common trap is the language "course" that consists of phrases you're supposed to memorize. My first year of junior high French was larded with dialogues *sans* grammatical explanation, and my classmates unanimously agreed that it was a waste of time. Some adult self-study courses for tourists do this also. Naked phrases go into short-term memory, which they quickly evacuate on the slightest encouragement. Pattern drills, on the other, whether or not they incorporate overt grammar, lock the language into place.

THE BASIC TOOLS OF FLUENCY

Obviously, the best way to learn another language is the way that already has worked for you once. You know English: how did you learn it?

First, people talked to you a lot. Your mother grabbed your chubby little foot and said, "Foot. Foot." Or perhaps she said, "My little baby has a cutesy itty-bitty footsie," in which case it took a while longer to catch on to what she was talking about. In any case, you heard the word "Foot" a lot in many different contexts ("Yike! I hurt my foot!" "Stick your foot in the shoe.") until finally you made the connection. This was the intake, or data-gathering, stage.

Then one day you tried to say, "Foot." If you were really successful it came out sounding like "Foo." If you weren't so successful, it might have been "Doof" or "Voob." Why did you try to say "Foot?" It wasn't because you needed to pass a test! No, you needed someone to do something and do it *right then*. Perhaps your foot hurt or you wanted to put on your shoes. If your father or mother caught on to what you were trying to say, you all were happy. If not, you tried again. "Boof? Foob?" Sooner or later you made a noise that was close enough and everyone was ecstatic! "Our baby is talking!" Take note of this: they did *not* try to make you feel like a fool for your mispronunciations.

Instead, they encouraged you. If they didn't do this, it's a fairly sure thing that you were slow in learning to talk.

You also developed a pattern of asking for data in a certain way, and your parents responded predictably. "What dat?" "That's the saltshaker, Johnny. Saltshaker. Saltshaker. No, don't grab it, dear." You also became accustomed to the rhythms and patterns of English through hearing thousands of simple sentences. "Give Mommy the spoon." "Lift up your arms." "Swallow the nice medicine." You heard additional thousands of sentences not addressed to you, that you were under no pressure to translate but were curious to understand. "Little Johnny spat out all his medicine all over his shirt this morning and I had to feed it to him four times before I got any down him."

So kids learn to talk by seeing and feeling objects and asking other people to do things for them and doing the things that other people ask them to do and hearing sentences that nobody even wants them to understand. But how do we ask kids to learn foreign languages in school? Too often, it's by filling out workbook pages. They only get to hear the language spoken an hour or so a week in Language Lab, and even if the classroom teacher is a native speaker of the language, he or she only has the students for another few hours.

If you or your children really want to learn to *speak*, not just read, another language, at the minimum you will need:

• Cassettes or records of the language as it is spoken. (Video is great!)
• Transcripts of the above, so you can make some sense out of it.
• Translations of the above, so you don't get stuck forever wondering what *izquierda* or *wiederkommen* means.
• Plus a reasonable framework for the language's patterns, which may or may not need to resemble a conventional grammar.

You will also desperately need some manageable memory devices to help you keep track of the thousands of slippery little words you will be learning.

If you only have a few hours a week to learn a language, it makes sense to spend as much of the time listening to it as possible. At home you can listen to a cassette again and again until you have it memorized from sheer repetition. More and more publishers are adding songs to their material, making use of the musical part of the brain to help you retain your lessons. One publisher that I know of uses pictures in all his courses to help you associate the spoken word with a visual image. With the advent of the VCR, we are just beginning to see courses developed featuring sound-sight association. The new computers can (in theory at least— I'm waiting to see the software) go even farther, with interactive oral language drill. These are all steps forward in foreign language instruction.

I don't know of one course that does it all— gives you extensive hearing practice, action practice, sight-sound association, and pattern drills. Still, you can learn quite a bit from some of the select programs following. For children, look especially for songs, action practice, and pictures, as if all these features are lacking in a program few children will bother with it. For adults, look for a clean, logical framework coupled with lots of data. We adults can make up our own action practices and drill ourselves, being more accustomed to self-discipline.

LANGUAGE COURSES FOR YOUNG CHILDREN

Audio Forum
Springboard to **French, German, or Spanish: $19.95 each plus $2 shipping, USA ($8 overseas). Includes 40-page booklet and 2 1-hour cassettes.**

A play-oriented introduction to the target language for very young children (preschool-early grades) based on the Total Physical Response method. Children learn by acting out commands given by the teacher ("*Levante los brazos, uno, dos. Tome la banana. Corte la banana en dos pedazos.*"— i.e., "Lift your arms, one, two. Take the banana. Cut the banana in two pieces.") Activities include songs, coloring, cutting with scissors, and games. Content includes basic body movements (standing, sitting, walking, running, etc.), parts of the body, colors, counting from one to fifteen, clothes and dressing, members of the family, eating, playing, and everyday activities.

Like the other language materials for very young children reviewed in this section, each *Springboard to . . .* language course follows an identical format, making the transition to additional languages easy.

Neither teacher nor student need previous foreign language experience. Pronunciation is handled on the two included cassettes. Each command is repeated in the target language, then in English, then again in the target language. You then get a few seconds to act out the command. Once you have done this, the section is repeated in the target language only, with time to act out every command.

Every foreign phrase or sentence in the 40-page booklet is translated into English. The booklet also includes cutout shapes for the games.

Christian Character Concepts
Conversational Spanish I, $13.75
postpaid.

Sing, play a board game, make paper bag puppets, and flip flashcards with Christian Character Concepts' new Spanish I and II programs for young Christian children. The songs are really cute (if anything, *too* cute!) and the activities are fun. The lessons don't include very much vocabulary and some of the speakers have a Texas accent, but the music is professional and kids will like it. (Shucks, *I* wander around the house singing the songs!)

EDC
The First Thousand Words in . . .
English, French, German, Spanish, Italian, Russian, and Hebrew, $10.95 each. *Round the World* **in English, French or Spanish, also $10.95 each. Oversized hardbound book.**

Foreign language vocabulary books for young children with a consistent user interface. Each book has the same pictures on each page as the others in the series, making it at least theoretically possible to add on new languages with little effort. Each page illustrates an environment (the kitchen, a street corner . . .) full of labeled objects. Even the margins contain more labeled pictures. (Those familiar with Richard Scarry's word books will recognize this format.) In the back of each book is a foreign language/English dictionary.

On every page of *The First Thousand Words* a little yellow duck is hiding. Finding this duck fascinates my children, more than learning the target words, to be frank.

Round the World carries on where *The First Thousand Words* left off. More vocabulary, more colorful, amusing illustrations by the same illustrator.

Though each book has a pronunciation guide in the back you really should not count on achieving perfect pronunciation with it. A matching set of cassette tapes would greatly enhance this colorful, clever series' usefulness.

Family Discovery Center
Richard Scarry's *Word Book*, **German or French, oversized hardbound, $14.95 each.** *Picture Dictionary* **in German, French, or Spanish, $9.48.** *Sign Language Fun*, **$8.50. All prices postpaid. Mail-order lending library option—see review at end of chapter. Tons more available, all major languages.**

Formerly known as Foreign Language through Song and Story, this home business for home schoolers still emphasizes learning through stories and activities. The huge selection of language materials includes Japanese, Hebrew, and Portuguese along with more commonly-available languages.

Some selections that caught our eye and ended up in our home library:

• Richard Scarry's colorful *Best Word Book Ever* in German and French gives you two languages for the price of one, and tempts preschoolers just as much as the originals in English. Each illustration is identified with the name and article in German, English, and French. The text is in German and is not difficult to figure out. You can quickly increase your vocabulary as you look at this book with a youngster who wants to know, "What's that?"

• The *Picture Dictionary* has several unusual but extremely useful features. Words are listed alphabetically in English with German translation. Each word is then used in a German sentence with English translation. A colorful illustration accompanies each word and sentence. The characters in the illustrations reappear again and again throughout the book, giving it the feel of a story.

• *Sign Language Fun* stars Linda Bove of Sesame Street fame. She shows the signs and the Muppets show the meanings. A really fun book to go through with children because signing is not talking but *action!* The first thing ours learned was how to say, "I love you." Write for Family Discovery Center's list of video and other sign language books— including some with religious signs.

Hear An' Tell
   Cassettes, $7.95 each. Flash Cards, $4.95 each. Game Boards, $7.95 each.

Teaching manual $4.95. Little Lamb wooly puppet, $14.95. Add $1 per item for shipping.

A new idea in French and Spanish study based on the Suzuki approach, Hear An' Tell believes that children can and will learn the basics of a new language long before they learn to read or are ready for formal language study. Through a series of well-known stories (*Goldilocks*; *Simon, James, and John*; *Little Lamb*; *Noah's Ark*; and a nonmagical version of *Cinderella*), Hear An' Tell introduces children to the basics of a new language. Careful phrasing, controlled vocabulary, and repetition (like that found in other programs) is mixed with games, flashcards, puppets, and other active materials.

Hear An' Tell's cassette story tapes have the story in the target language translated phrase by phrase. The Teacher's Manual suggests pantomiming the story with hand motions while you listen and adding props to illustrate the words. The correlated flash cards illustrate words from each story, with the picture and English on one side and the foreign words on the other. The game boards come in sets of four (Picture Tic Tac Toe, Four Word Ho, Tengo, and Lotto). Up to four children may play at once. Workbooks and story books are being prepared for each tape.

At press time, Hear An' Tell was just coming out with several new items, including a story text for *Cinderella* in Spanish and French and a phonetic Spanish coloring book (*The ABC's of Spanish)* based on Bible words. Send an SASE for the latest developments from this energetic new company.

International Linguistics Corp.
   Courses in English, Spanish, French, German, Chinese (new!), and Russian. Four books, each with accompanying set of 5 cassettes. Each book $5, each cassette set $30 except for the set for Book 2 which contains 6 cassettes and is $36. Intermediate series in English and German only, another 4 books plus cassettes, same

prices. Ten % discount and free postage on prepaid orders. Sample cassette and text, $1.

International Linguistics invented the first language program designed especially for very young children. Unlike other programs, which stress repeated sentences, grammar, and drill, International Linguistics teaches language through word-picture association. Cassettes accompany picture books; each sentence or phrase goes with a picture. This results in "natural" learning the way a baby learns. No written words are in the text, either English or in the other language. International Linguistics is insistent that you must learn through sounds only. It is possible to get a transcript of the tapes, but International Linguistics does not sell translations. This is an unnecessary hindrance, and the only feature to which I object.

Pictures are in amusing but understandable cartoon style. The stories are clever. Our sons love the sequence with the baby throwing eggs at the window and the harried mother rushing about looking for a paper towel to wipe up the mess. Every language uses the same picture book, so subsequent languages can build on the first one learned.

Book 1 has one thousand sentences, as does Book 2. Stories begin in Book 2, and you are introduced to prepositions and pronouns. Book 3 has more complex stories and gets into verb tenses. Book 4 has complex sentences. The Beginner Series of all four books contains a total of three thousand basic words and grammatical constructions. The Intermediate series, available only in English and German, teaches 1,500 words and advanced grammatical structures.

When you buy a whole series (Beginner or Intermediate) International Linguistics throws in a vinyl cassette case. You can buy a little at a time, and easily branch out into new languages.

I recommend that you buy a separate picture book for each learner (they are not expensive), as otherwise squabbles develop over who gets to hold the book. We found that mealtimes are a good time to turn on the cassette player and learn a little French, and you might try it too, if you don't mind getting the pages greasy!

R.S. Publications
Learning Spanish Through Spanish, **$27.50 complete program. Extra student manuals, $4.75 each.**

You don't have to know Spanish to introduce your children to it with this program. Designed for elementary school aged children, it includes a teacher's manual with detailed lesson plans and lots of suggested activities, a student's manual, a tape of Spanish folk songs, and two tapes to accompany the book exercises. Children sing the folk songs (which are not just played but taught on the tape), dance, do some Hispanic arts and crafts, and learn a little about Hispanic culture. The pronunciation is authentic and the language is introduced in a natural way. You get a medium amount of vocabulary, sufficient to prepare youngsters for more advanced Spanish courses.

Learning Spanish Through Spanish is a really fun, comfortable program that younger children should respond well to.

Regents Publishing Company
First Steps in French, **$3.25.** *First Steps in Spanish,* **$3.50.**

Regents, besides its voluminous language materials for teens and adults, also carries Margarita Madrigal's *First Steps* and *Open Door* materials. *First Steps* (in French and Spanish) introduces little kids to the target language through pictures and cognates. A cognate is a word that is very much alike in English and the target language, and Madrigal's genius lies in using these extensively to build much larger vocabularies than would otherwise be possible. It takes no effort at all to learn a cognate. I'll teach you some right now. English words ending in "or" are often the same in Spanish, with the difference that Spaniards put the accent on the last syllable. So color is *colór*, doctor is *doctór*, and so on. See how easy it is? *Open Door* is Madrigal's approach dressed up with classroom exercises and language cassettes.

LANGUAGE COURSES FOR OLDER CHILDREN

Alpha Omega Publications
$19.50 for complete set of 10 LIFEPACS. Spanish Instruction and Testing Tapes, $10 for each LIFEPAC unit ($100 in all). Shipping 10%.

AOP has LIFEPAC worktexts for both Spanish and New Testament Greek, one full year of each. The Spanish course comes with a set of two cassette tapes, one for practice and one for testing. Along with the dialogs and grammar, each LIFEPAC in the series of 10 Spanish worktexts has sections on Cultural Activities, The World of Music, and a What Does the Bible Say? translation exercise.

AMSCO

AMSCO has texts, workbooks, and dictionaries for French, German, Italian, Latin, and Spanish. Texts are inexpensive and sample copies may be obtained by writing on school letterhead.

Family Discovery Center

Full line of language products for all ages. See other reviews in this chapter.

Regents Publishing Company

Tune in to English and *O, Susanne*, **$5.25 each text, $25 accompanying**

cassettes. *Everyday Spanish Idioms*, **$5.95 Hundreds more inexpensive ESL, Spanish, French, German, and Chinese materials.**

Let me say right off that anyone who is seriously interested in teaching languages to young people, or in learning a number of languages, should get Regents' catalog. I don't have space to list all the fascinating methods Regents' texts use: but here are some of the humdingers.

Uwe Kind (that's the author's name) thinks you can learn English through music. Take a song like "This Old Man." Change it to teach a specific language function. Put it in songbook form and on cassette, add nineteen more songs, throw in games, puzzles, and other activities to review the language, and presto! You've got *Tune In to English*. Not content with English, Uwe Kind got together with Ursula Meyer to produce the same sort of "Audio-Singual" method in German. It's called— are you ready?— *O Susanne, Ja Konjugier Fur Mich!* which according to my faulty memory of German is something like *Oh, Susannah, Conjugate For Me!* The title song, roughly translated, goes,

> I work from one to two
> You work until three
> She works the whole day long
> And Sundays she has free.
> Oh, Susannah, you work too hard [all day]
> [Oh, yes] you work from dawn to dusk
> You have no time to play.

In this way, each verse conjugates a verb such as "work" and you couldn't forget the conjugation form even if you wanted to.

One great stumblingblock when learning languages is mastering the idioms. For immigrants, Regents has several books of American idioms. I like the title of this one: *Colloquial English: How to Shoot the Breeze and Knock 'em for a Loop While Having a Ball.* And for Americans, Regents has books of idioms in other languages. *Everyday Spanish Idioms* is a treasure house of idioms, proverbs, proverbial comparisons, and riddles. This kind of book is a peek into the soul of another nation, and worth reading even if you have no intention of learning the language.

I could go on and on. Regents' catalog is full of enticing titles like *Do's and Don'ts for the Japanese Businessman Abroad* and *Word Games in English*. There are dozens of different programs and hundreds of texts and thousands of cassettes. Don't miss this catalog.

LANGUAGE COURSES FOR TEENS AND ADULTS

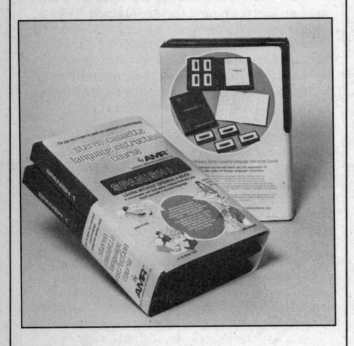

AMR Educational Systems
French, German, Italian, Latin American Spanish: same format for all. Level I, $110. Level II, $130 (Italian not available). *Strictly Vocabulary*, Levels I and II, $49.50 each. *Practical Spanish*, $79.50. Also available: Medical and Law Spanish. Japanese and Mandarin Chinese, $135.

What kind of foreign language courses would two Wheaton college professors design? Believe it or not, the profs don't want you to hit the books. In fact, AMR lets you learn the language right off the cassettes. Courses are recorded in stereo, with the foreign language and the English translation on separate levels. Thus you can fade out one or the other, and test yourself. This method, unique to AMR, is protected by a U.S. Patent.

All Western languages follow the same format (your choice of French, German, Italian, and Latin American Spanish). You hear a short, useful dialog with very soft mood music in the background. Each sentence has the English translation. Next, individual words and phrases are repeated with their translations. Finally, the dialog is repeated without translation, so you can try pronouncing the phrases and see if you understand it. Each dialog introduces new grammar; for example, the "I" form of the verb might be used for the first time.

After several dialogs, AMR has a short section on how to expand your speaking power by adding extra vocabulary words and phrases to what you have already learned. This section also includes very simple explanations of some essential grammatical features.

AMR uses native speakers, both male and female, carefully chosen from different regions of the target country so you get a cross-section of the different regional accents.

AMR's accompanying manual contains a complete transcript of every cassette, plus informative cultural notes.

AMR's approach would be suitable for anyone except young children. They, not seeing the need for learning the language, would be bored by the adult dialogs. For the traveller, AMR is excellent. Not only do you learn the essential vocabulary for coping with life overseas, but AMR includes cultural notes in its accompanying manual. These notes are obviously written by someone who has been there and who understands that Americans need to know if French hotel rooms have a bathroom (most do not: in fact, you're lucky to have a bathroom on your floor) and other vital facts.

Japanese and Mandarin Chinese are available in Level I only, and are different from the others in that they have been adapted to include significant features of Chinese and Japanese culture. Each course teaches a phonetic form of the language using the English alphabet. The Japanese and Chinese written characters are also provided as they correspond to each dialog.

Each course contains eight one-hour stereo cassettes, a manual with cultural notes and the transcript of the recordings, and a dictionary listing words used, all bound in two very impressive gold-stamped vinyl-leather cases.

AMR also has *Practical Spanish* courses for medical workers, policemen, and firemen. These are less expensive than the foreign language courses, probably because nobody had to fly overseas and locate native speakers. You get six high quality C-60 cassettes, and all the other gear included in the regular language courses.

Also from AMR: a *Strictly Vocabulary* series using its patented Bilingual Stereo Self-Test method. This series, available in all the languages mentioned above, is arranged in topics and supplements the Level 1 and Level 2 programs. The price is quite reasonable, for a memory and pronunciation tool covering about two thousand words. Those using a standard language text might want to consider getting AMR's *Strictly Vocabulary* program to help them with pronunciation. In this way you could create a total language program for around $60. (It will, of course, be more work than if you got the total AMR language course.) Contents: four cassettes, dictionary of words used, and vinyl-leather case.

AMR's program is among the best for those who want to learn a foreign language with reasonable fluency but do not plan on permanently moving to the country in question. It is not boring, the recordings are excellent, and you can test your progress as you go.

American Map Corporation
$13.95, 2-cassette courses: French, German, Greek, Italian, Spanish.

Langenscheidt, "the world's foremost publisher of bilingual dictionaries and foreign language instruction for more than 125 years," is distributed by AMC.

Two LP cassettes plus a 96-page text with the foreign language and English side-by-side

are what you get with Langenscheidt's Quick and Easy language series. Langenscheidt also puts out a series of dictionaries: see mention at end of this chapter.

Audio-Forum
Individual courses all have different prices. Price range from about $100 to over $200 for FSI courses. Languages: Many Spanish courses, including Business, Medical, Spanish for Policemen and Firemen, Spanish for Health Professionals, and Household Spanish for Home Managers, plus FSI Spanish (several levels). FSI French, plus Basic Haitian Creole and several dialog series. German. Italian. Modern Hebrew. Arabic (several dialects). Chinese (several dialects). Portuguese. Japanese. Polish. Russian. Modern and Classical Greek. Classical Latin. Scandinavian languages. Eastern European languages. Turkish. Urdu. Thai. Vietnamese. Khmer (Cambodian). Trade languages of Africa. Survival English. Living Language® Videos: French, German, Spanish, $39.95 each; Sign Language Video, $34.95. In all, more than 100 courses in more than 40 languages. Less expensive courses available.

Audio-Forum does not develop their own courses. As they say, "We have drawn on the expertise of our academic advisory board to help us identify and locate the most effective courses in use anywhere in the United States or abroad. We then obtained the rights to offer these by mail throughout the English-speaking world."

Most Audio-Forum courses are duplicates

of the Foreign Service Institute courses used to train U.S. diplomats and overseas personnel. These are the full-length, in-depth courses. Unlike others' language programs, Audio-Forum FSI courses do not all follow the same basic format. They do, however, offer a wider variety of languages than anyone else, including Arabic, Cantonese, Hungarian, Hebrew, and Vietnamese, to name just a few. If you want to dig down to your family's "roots" and learn the language of your non-English ancestors, Audio-Forum probably has it.

How does it work? Repetition, repetition, repetition, repetition . . . FSI students normally memorize the dialogs, and one can understand why, since you hear the same one over and over and over. I was surprised to hear the street French of the French I series: *Juizreux* or some such mangled remnant for *Je suis hereux.* That may be the way they talk in France, but it puts a stumbling block before beginners to not hear extremely distinct pronunciation. We don't mumble at babies, after all!

FSI courses come with culture notes and big, fat textbooks. Make no mistake about it, FSI is the heavy artillery of language instruction.

New from Audio Forum are the Living Language® video courses. These consist of real-life tourist situations— hotel, airport, restaurant, store. A friendly emcee explains what's happening in between the adventures of our totally-fluent tourist couple. Phrases and words are introduced at conversational speed, then repeated slowly with English subtitles. The emcee then shows how to use the sentence structures you just used to create more new sentences. You're learning to speak, not to read, since the target language never appears on screen. A booklet with additional vocabulary and dialog transcripts would add a lot to this program.

Berlitz Publications
   One-hour course, $9.95: Arabic, Chinese, Dutch, Finnish, French, German, Greek, Hebrew, Italian, Danish, Japanese, Norwegian, Portuguese, Russian, Serbo-Croatian, Spanish (Castillian and Latin American), and Swedish. Basic Home Study Cassette Course, $59.95: French, German, Italian, Spanish. Comprehensive Cassette course, $140: same 4 languages. Berlitz also has travel guides and phrase books for almost everywhere—get these at bookstores.

Berlitz is now, according to itself, "the world's leading publisher of books for travellers . . . plus Cassettes and Self-teaching courses." Berlitz, as you may recall, started as a you-attend-the-classes language school. The company has wisely decided to put together inexpensive courses using the Berlitz method. These are aimed mostly at the tourist market.

The bottom of the line is Berlitz's one-hour cassette course. You get basic phrases spoken in four voices and a little booklet with the text of the recordings, plus translation. I don't think much of these phrasebooks as a serious learning tool. If all you want is a taste of the language, that's all you'll get.

The Berlitz Cassette Course looks more promising. You get a 90-minute "zero" or beginner's cassette with ten basic lessons in four voices. These are not just random phrases, but follow a grammatical plan. This is followed by two more 60-minute cassettes. You also get two illustrated books with the text of all lessons plus helpful notes, a rotating verb finder, a Berlitz phrase book, and a pocket dictionary.

The Berlitz Comprehensive Cassette Course includes all the above, plus two more C-60 cassettes and four more illustrated manuals.

I believe in "baby-talk"— slow, exaggerated pronunciation— for beginners, and Berlitz apparently does not. The Spanish cassette I heard didn't quite race along at Puerto Rican speed, but was pretty brisk nonetheless.

Conversa-Phone Institute, Inc.

"Round-the-world" courses, $7.98: Indonesian, Serbo-Croatian, Chinese (Mandarin and Cantonese), Hindi, Arabic, Czech, Ukranian, Eastern European and Scandinavian language courses, Turkish, Malay, Irish Gaelic, Korean, Yiddish, Thai, Afrikaans, and Tagalog, plus all the standard European and Asian languages. "Modern Method" courses, $17.98: French, German, Italian, Spanish, Portuguese, Swedish, Russian, Modern Greek, Mandarin Chinese, Advanced Spanish. Many courses available on cassette and 8-track. New Compact Disc courses in French and Spanish, $29.95 each. Also "English for Foreigners" series, $17.98: 20 courses, including European, Asian, and Scandinavian languages plus Arabic and Greek. $2 shipping for the first course, 50¢ additionals.

Let me skip quickly over Conversa-Phone's "Round-the-World" courses. These are one record plus text. You can get the standard courses on cassette or 8-track as well, and the "exotic" languages on cassette. In the latter case, the price goes up to $11.98.

I'm skipping over these little courses because I am anxious to extol the "Modern Method" courses. These come boxed, with your choice of four LP records or 2 C-60 cassettes, plus a 100-lesson illustrated instruction manual. In my estimation, as one who has suffered under many language teachers, these courses are the cheapest, most effective means of brushing up a previously-studied language around. You not only get the recorded text plus translation— all companies provide this—but a number of lists and simplified grammar lessons, plus pictures of hundreds of subjects. The text is even witty in spots, and since the text goes beyond the cassettes you are not limited in your learning to what can be said in two hours of recording time. The whole thing course comes conveniently boxed.

To this line Conversa-Phone has just added the first spoken word language compact disc courses. These include two compact discs and a fully illustrated instruction manual. Presently available in French and Spanish, the compact disc quality should make it easier to pick up on the nuances of correct pronunciation.

ESP

ESP has the very cheapest language instruction around. For eight dollars you can get a cassette with 60 minutes of instruction, plus a student workbook and tests. I have not tried one, but for a low-risk taste of another language it sounds reasonable. Available in Beginning, Intermediate and Tourist Spanish and Tourist French.

SyberVision

SyberVision, a purveyor of sports, exercise, and self-improvement videos, has a winner in their Speak, Read, and Think foreign language series. Based on Dr. Paul Pimsleur's language learning techniques, SyberVision courses feature anticipation, recall, and the use of basic sentences as a model for creating new sentences—just like *Artes Latinae*, reviewed above.

First, you hear a dialog in foreign speech. It sounds like gibberish! Were you foolish to buy this course? Don't despair. Help is on its way. The cassette instructor breaks down the sentences into words and the words into syllables. You are asked to repeat these words and syllables. Then, using what you have learned, you are asked questions in the target language. The correct response is then given, so you can see if you answered correctly. The course also repeats previous matter at scientifically-determined intervals to reinforce your memory. By this means, you actually learn to think in the target language.

The SyberVision courses are not cheap— $245 apiece for Spanish, French, German, and Modern Hebrew, and $229 each for Modern Greek and Russian. But if you can't pass the built-in test at the end of the course at the 1+ level— that required for the diplomatic corps— you can return the course for a complete refund.

Visual Education Association
Think . . . **French, German, Spanish: Level 1 or 2 of each, cards plus records or cassettes, $11.95 each. Shipping extra.**

Vis Ed's Think Language sets are billed as "a whole new concept for learning to speak and understand spoken foreign languages." Illustrated cards match questions and answers on the cassettes or records. No English is included. Through this word-picture approach, you are supposed to learn to think the language the way its natives do. Like the rest of Vis Ed's flashcard sets, the price is right.

GENERAL LANGUAGE STUDIES

Audio-Forum
Most Exeter tapes, $12.95 each. Shipping extra. Complete Exeter Tape Catalog of over 450 cassettes available on request.

The people at Audio-Forum believe "the audio cassette is the ideal medium for presenting linguistic material," so no wonder that their new catalog contains dozens of tapes on linguistics and language usage. Prepared at the Language Centre of the University of Exeter in merry England, the tapes cover such topics as *The Development of the English language*

(two tape set and booklet, $27.95), *Etymology and the English Vocabulary, The Sounds in English, Comparing Sound Systems*, and *Rhythms and Tunes of English* (thank heavens they don't mean Michael Jackson!). If you like this, there's more: the complete Exeter Tape Catalog includes hundreds of cassettes covering French, German, Russian, and Spanish literature and linguistics.

Independent School Press
Phenomenon of Language, **$9.95.**

An introductory course in linguistics based on elementary Latin. Good stuff. See review in the Classical Languages chapter.

Summer Institute of Linguistics

S.I.L., an affiliate of Wycliffe Bible Translators, is where it's at in modern real-world linguistics. Christian missionaries sweat in the jungle and freeze in the tundra in order to learn, from scratch, the languages of their fellowmen and translate the Bible into them. Thus Christian missionaries have become the world's foremost linguistic experts, and S.I.L. publishes their scholarly works: dictionaries, grammars, linguistic treatises, and so on. If you're looking for uncommon works like an introduction to Cheyenne literature or a trilingual thesaurus in Sedang, Vietnamese, and English, S.I.L. is the place. The huge collection of beginning grammars in non-Western languages, such as *Saramaccan for Beginners*, will light up any linguaphile. If you'd like your son to grow up to be a missionary and to accomplish something really worthwhile in that capacity, try to interest him in S.I.L.'s catalog.

WFF 'n PROOF Learning Games Associates
Queries 'n Theories, **$16.**

Delving now into the realm of the arcane and abstract, we come to what might be the ultimate game for eggheads. *Queries 'n Theories* pits a Native against one or more

Querists. The Native invents basic sentence structures represented by colored chips, and rules for legitimate constructions, also represented with chips. The Querist tries to figure out the "language" by asking questions with chips. From here it gets complicated, so don't expect me to explain it in a paragraph. It all has something to do with linguistic theory, and resembles the setup of the LISP computer language, which I know makes it all clear to a select few computer buffs and even foggier to the rest. Linguistics aside, the game stretches your thinker and is really fun to play. It comes nicely packaged, with small vinyl mats and lots of colored chips, plus an instruction booklet and carrying case.

BIBLES, DICTIONARIES, LITERATURE, CULTURE, &C.

American Bible Society

ABS has Bibles in many languages. I remember when I was a child reading a novel whose main character learned new languages by studying a Bible in the target language. This method could work well if you (1) know the Bible very well and (2) only want to read the new language, or (3) also have cassettes to help you with pronunciation. If you're a Christian and want to talk about Jesus in a foreign country, it wouldn't hurt to have some Scripture memorized in that language. Avoid the "classical" translations that correspond to our King James Version; nobody overseas understands these any better than we understand Elizabethan English today.

ABS's "Scripture Resources in Many Languages" catalog lists Scripture publications in the forty most popular languages, about half of the languages they normally have available. Many Scriptures can be specially ordered even if they are in a language ABS does not normally offer for sale.

All ABS materials are inexpensive.

American Map Corporation

$39.95 Languageware, $49.95 Travelware. (Each available for Apple II family, DOS 3.3, 48K, 1 disk drive.) *Lilliput Dictionary*, $1.75: English/ Danish, Dutch, French, German, Italian, Latin, Portuguese, Spanish, or Turkish. Also Danish, Dutch, French, German, Italian, Modern Greek, Portuguese, Spanish, and Turkish/English. *Pocket Dictionary*, $6.95: French, German, Classical Greek, Classical Hebrew, Latin, Portuguese, Russian, and Spanish. Polish Pocket Dictionary, $8.95. Translator 8000, $69.95: French/English, German/English, Spanish/English. Other helps available.

Words, words, words in these dictionaries from the matchbox-sized *Lilliput* with 10,000 entries to standard and college dictionaries. The most useful dictionary for most purposes is the pocket-size. It's $3\frac{3}{4}$ x 6 with between 33,000 and 58,000 entries.

For high-tech types who eschew dictionaries, AMC has the Translator 8000 Pocket Electronic Translation Machine. Type in the word you want in either English or the target language and if it's in the eight thousand word memory, you'll see it on the little screen. It comes equipped with a calculator and, one presumes, batteries.

Now for something new: *Languageware*. Arcade-style computerized vocab and comprehension development programs are available for Spanish, French, German, Latin, and English. And to go along with this, you can get *Travelware* from Baedeker's. "Unique programs with amusing situations, graphics, sound effects, and folk music present cultural differences and help travelers avoid social blunders." Hm. *Correct Behavior Travelware* comes in either English or the language of the country for France, Germany, and Mexico. The Japanese version is only available in English.

Caedmon Tapes

Caedmon has recordings of literature in several languages. The Caedmon catalog is immense and you're bound to find something you want in it, whether in English or not.

Family Discovery Center

Children's literature and songs in foreign languages. Lending library option: membership of $30 allows you to borrow up to $30 of books and tapes for 6 weeks at a time; $10 membership you pay 10% of purchase price each time order placed. Minimum postage, either plan, $1. Excess postage added to order. Details with SASE.

Tons of supplementary material for language buffs young or old. Dictionaries, word books, cassettes, literature, songs, peel 'n play figures, coloring books, Bibles, etc. Some examples: *Culturegrams*, four-page briefings covering customs and manners of a given country, are 35¢ each. Folk song albums (mostly LP's, some cassettes) are generally in the $10 price range. *Little House in the Big Woods* in German or French. Richard Scarry's *Best Word Book Ever* in German or French (we bought this one!). Fairy tales in foreign languages. Verb charts, grammar aids. Most major languages. Items are chosen to fit a home schooling lifestyle. This is a home business, so don't forget to specify your language of interest and enclose an SASE!

Hammond

***Qu'est-ce Que C'est?* $34 for schools.**

Hammond has come out with something that every French enthusiast will want: a visual dictionary! Thousands of pictures and photos show familiar objects, with all the parts labeled in both the target language and English. Now you won't have to stumble around wondering what the French word for "wheel" or "shin" is anymore. It's called *Qu'est-ce que C'est*, which

is French for "What's What?", the name of the original English visual dictionary. Although *Qu'est-ce Que C'est?* isn't really a language course, I put it in this section because it looks like a fine addition to a language course.

Jeffrey Norton Publishers

The company that owns Audio Forum (see the Adult Language Courses review) also has a wide line of spoken-word cassettes, including literature in other languages. You can get stories in Chinese, songs from Israel, an Italian interview with Frederico Fellini, or Alexander Solzhenitsyn reading *One Day in the Life of Ivan Denisovich* in Russian. J-N also has the complete New Testament on cassette in Spanish, French, Arabic, Hindi, Mandarin, Italian, Portuguese, English, Urdu, German, and Korean. Plus classical Greek and Latin works (see the Classical Languages chapter).

Regents Publishing Company

Classics of Spanish and French literature, reasonably priced, some abridged. Don't miss Regents' wacky but effective language programs, reviewed above.

Visual Education Association

***Vocabulary Flashcards*, $4.95/language. *Compact Facts*: Conversation, Grammar, Verbs—$2.95 each in English, French, German, Russian, and Spanish. Shipping extra.**

Vis Ed is your premier source for flashcards. *Vocabulary Flashcards* are 600 to 1,000 small cards plus study guide with index: available also in classical languages. *Compact Facts* are prime ideas, rules, and grammatical formulas in plain speech on 60 pocket-sized cards.

CHAPTER FOURTEEN

LOGIC AND THINKING SKILLS

"Like all other arts, the Science of Deduction and Analysis is one which can only be acquired by long and patient study ... Let the inquirer begin by mastering more elementary problems."
Sherlock Holmes

Did you know there really once was a live, breathing Sherlock Holmes? Sir Arthur Conan Doyle, the man who invented the keen-minded Holmes, was himself the prototype of his own creation. His son, Adrian Conan Doyle, in a fascinating introduction to the International Collectors Library edition of *A Treasury of Sherlock Holmes*, lays the matter before us:

Holmes was to a large extent Conan Doyle himself. Incidentally, and it stands to their credit in view of my father's reticence, this fact was recognized almost from the very first by the police chiefs of the world who, speaking or writing from America, France, Germany, China, India, or Egypt, paid him tribute. The exception was, of course, Scotland Yard, whose silence put to shame even that of the immortal Colonel Bramble. Scotland Yard owed too much to Conan Doyle and it is always painful to acknowledge large debts.

The use of plaster of Paris for preserving marks; the examination of dust in a man's clothing to establish his occupation or locality; the differentiation between tobacco ashes; all these were introduced into the science of criminal detection by my father through the mask of Sherlock Holmes. Far above all else, his own work in the famous Edalji case resulted in the introduction of the Court of Criminal Appeal into the British legal system. And to change the British legal system is almost equivalent to bailing out the English Channel with a teaspoon. The facts are there for all to read, including some noteworthy instances of my father rescuing the innocent from the clutches of the police by using the very methods which he had invented for his man in Baker Street.

It appears, then, that Sir Arthur Conan Doyle knew something about how to think, and that the advice of Holmes at the beginning of this chapter can be taken seriously.

"But why should we even care about logic? Everything's relative, anyway. Let's just emote!

Let it all hang out! Have a positive mental attitude!" John Robbins, in the introduction to Gordon Clark's *Logic*, has the sufficient answer to these notions:

> Logic does not describe what people think about or how they usually reach conclusions; it describes how they *ought* to think if they wish to reason correctly . . . Logic concerns all thought; it is fundamental to all disciplines . . . Anyone who disparages or belittles logic must use logic in his attack, thus undercutting his own argument . . . If one abandons logic, as many people in this century have, than one cannot distinguish good from evil— and everything is permitted . . . The rejection of logic has led— and must lead— to the abandonment of morality . . . Once logic is gone, truth is also.

Well, there it is. Would you rather be a lightweight or a heavy hitter? Would you rather be a logical Holmes or a doltish Watson? (Actually, even Watson was a heavy hitter compared to most of us today!) Would you rather be a hammer or a nail? Logic makes the difference!

LOGIC COURSES

Midwest Publications

Midwest's *Critical Thinking Skills* series, designed for senior high, includes two texts. A teacher's manual is available for each book. Between them the books cover: formal and informal logic, inferences and implications, advertising and propaganda techniques, and debate and problem solving. Written at a fifth-grade reading level, it is also used in public school junior high gifted programs. Since the series exercises draw on newspaper articles, letters to editors, advertisement, conversations, and the like, some might be controversial.

Building Thinking Skills, a four-book-plus-teacher's-manuals course, covers both mathematical and verbal logic. Book 1 uses an extremely limited vocabulary, and Book 2's vocabulary is only slightly more advanced. The series has two Book 3's— *Book 3 Figural* and *Book 3 Verbal*. *Book 3 Figural* is based strictly on mathematical figures. You're not learning math or geometry— let me make that clear.

What you are learning is how to predict patterns, produce accurate analogies, identify sequences, and recognize similarities. Content is quite similar to the separate *Figural* series reviewed under Logic Exercises. *Book 3 Verbal* is full of pencil-and-paper exercises in very basic formal logic.

Midwest also offers a *Logic In Easy Steps* series of fourteen books. Starting with "AND" and 'OR," it proceeds through arguments and proofs to universal statements and all sorts of other heavy stuff.

Trinity Foundation
   Logic, $8.95 each copy, $5.37 each for ten or more. Professor's examination copy, $5, will be credited to any bulk order.

We have something here. The late Gordon Clark, professor extraordinaire and evangelical gadfly, took time to write his logic textbook (aptly named *Logic*) because he believed Christian children were growing up ignorant of the same. The book is logically laid out and covers a lot of ground: unfortunately, not in the most organized way. The student is expected to already know, for example, that NaCl is table salt and how to prove the theorem that in an isosceles triangle the angles opposite the equal sides are equal. Information is densely packed and unformatted. It gets better towards the end, but this is a textbook that needs multiple readings.
   John Robbins' introduction, "Why Study Logic?," is excellent.
   Dr. Clark's erudition is apparent throughout, as is his somewhat caustic humor.

If the Trinity Foundation develops a workbook to accompany and expand on Clark's opus, this could be one good little course.

LOGIC AND THINKING EXERCISES

Midwest Publications

Terrific lineup of thinking skills workbooks using both word problems and mathematical figures. *Figural Analogies* shows you three figures. You have to figure out the relationship between A and B, and then draw a figure with the same relationship to C. Example: If A is a circle and B a semicircle, then if C is a square, what should D be? The questions rapidly get more difficult, so be glad an answer key is included in the book. Others in this series include *Figural Similarities*, *Figural Sequences*, and *Figural Classifications*. Except for *Figural Similarities*, a series of four workbooks, each of these comes in a series of three book (titled A-1, B-1, and C-1).

Mind Benders is a series of 12 workbooks featuring deductive thinking skills. You might want to invest in the *Mind Benders Instructions and Detailed Solutions* for this series. Books are labeled A-1 through A-4, B-1 through B-4, and C-1 through C-3. For novices, look into the first series book, *Warm Up Mind Benders*. Mind Benders sets A-1 through A-3 is also available as Apple II family or TRS-80 software.

The word problems series includes: *Verbal Similarities*, *Verbal Sequences*, *Verbal Classifications*, and *Verbal Analogies*. And this just begins to scrape the surface of Midwest's more than hundred-book line. What about the Visual Logic series? Or the five books of Syllogisms? Brain Stretchers (two books)? Classroom Quickies (three books)? Etc.

The virtue of Midwest's *Figural* series is that the problems are strictly logical, involving no particular political or religious presuppositions. Word problems, in contrast, reflect the particular background of their designer. For this reason, some parents have found the "critical thinking" exercises in some publishers' Gifted & Talented programs unacceptable.

Timberdoodle

Source for Midwest Figural workbooks, WFF 'n PROOF games, and other brainstretching paraphernalia. A home business run by home schoolers for home schoolers. Good prices, great service.

Tin Man Press
"Discover" packs, $1.95. Series 1 or 2 (12 titles each), $23.40. Add $1 shipping on orders $6 or less, $1.50 on orders $6 to $15, 10% shipping on orders over $15.

These really neat little card packs each feature twenty observation and thinking activities centering on common household items. In "Discover Aluminum Foil," for example, one card asks the child to look carefully at both sides of the foil and write about what he notices. Another card asks him to drop a square of foil and a ball of foil at the same time and see which falls faster.

"Discover!" Series 1 looks at • a comb • paper bag • spoon • table knife • egg carton • handkerchief • paper clip • tape dispenser • pencil • crackers • scissors, and • popcorn. Series 2 investigates • buttons • a peanut • shoelace • key • toothbrush • crayon • paper plate • milk carton • envelope • notebook • paper • aluminum foil, and • your hand. Each card pack covers all learning styles (visual, conceptual, tactile, etc.) and is really FUN! Sherlock Holmes would have loved it.

WFF 'n PROOF Learning Games Associates
Propaganda, $13. *Queries 'N Theories*, $16. *Equations*, $13. *Real Numbers*, $2.75. *Wff 'n Proof*, $16. All prices postpaid.

Coauthored by Lorne Greene (remember "Bonanza"?), *Propaganda* defines propaganda devices and provides sample exercises. Players challenge or go along with group consensus as to which statement contains what illogic. The game can be played alone: check yourself with the answer key.

Queries 'n Theories is a logic workout. You create and test hypotheses, trying to break your opponent's code. The code is produced with cute little colored chips. In theory, this game is similar to Midwest's Figural series. In practice, it is more colorful and visual and interactive.

All the other games are reviewed at length in *The NEW Big Book of Home Learning*. Suffice it to say that these are indisputably among the most challenging logic games ever invented. *Wff 'n Proof*, for example, has been shown to raise IQ up to 20 points in dedicated players.

LOGICWARE

Let the reader remember that Sir Arthur Conan Doyle did not possess a personal computer; it is possible to have the sharpness of Holmes without the help of RAM. However— and it's a big "however"— in some ways educational software is ideal for developing thinking skills.

Computers are innately logical; each bit is either yes or no, on or off. Their very architecture favors yes/no, right/wrong, if/then structure. Humans might be susceptible to flattery or emotional appeals: the computer, never.

A software package can propose problems adorned with graphics and let you see your solutions or failures in living color. Immediate, interactive feedback can tell you what you did wrong and help you back on the track.

Though none of the software here reviewed helps you analyze a politician's speech or boss's memo for logical errors, they do all contribute in some way to the habit of orderly thinking.

The Learning Company
All programs reviewed run on Apple II family, IBM PC family and PCjr, and Commodore 64/128, except *Robot Odyssey* and *Think Quick!*, which do not have a Commodore version. *Rocky's Boots* and the *Gertrude* series come for Compaq. For Tandy 1000 you can get *Rocky's Boots*. *Rocky's Boots* and *Robot Odyssey* are available for Tandy Color Computer. Color monitor recommended; required for *Rocky's Boots*, *Gertrude*, and *Moptown*.

Prices: *Moptown* series $39.95 each. *Gertrude* series $44.95 each ($29.95 for C-64 version). *Rocky's Boots* $49.95 ($34.95 C-64). *Robot Odyssey*, *Think Quick!*, $49.95 each. Add $3 shipping if ordering directly.

Moptown Parade is a matching and sequencing game. The user needs to know how to find a specific key on the keyboard and match it with a code, placing *Moptown Parade* beyond the range of babyware, but the tasks themselves are simple. The graphics characters are Bibbits and Gribbits, who may be fat or thin, tall or short, red or blue. The seven games included on this disk include making a twin to the displayed character, recognizing differences, making opposites (for the game's purpose, a Gribbit is the opposite of a Bibbit), creating the character who should come next in a sequence, creating a character who differs by a chosen number of traits from the previous character in the parade, and discovering the rule that selects which characters may enter a clubhouse. A child who can master the first game may take quite a while to learn to play the last, making *Moptown Parade* worth its price. *Moptown Hotel* carries these skills (analogies, sequences, pattern recognition, and hypotheses) further, being aimed at the eight- to twelve-year old.

Gertrude's Secrets has to be the most enabling educational software for the just-barely-school-age child. The game consists of a series of rooms. You zap about from room to room by means of cursors or a joystick. When you enter the game, a friendly tutorial shows you how to move around, how to pick up and drop objects, and explains the game options. There are three official logic games— loop puzzles, train puzzles, and array puzzles, each with multiple levels of difficulty— but the geniuses who designed this game also included a room where you can edit the shapes of the pieces used in the games, and it is to the Shape-Edit Room that my two sons fly like homing pigeons the minute the game is turned on.

If you play *Gertrude's Secrets* in the orthodox way, you carry Gertrude the goose to the puzzle room of your choice and drop her there. She then will fly back with puzzle pieces for you, and once you solve the puzzle she will return bearing a treasure for you, which is kept in the Treasure Room. If you play it like my sons, you edit the shape of not only the game pieces kept in the storeroom, but the treasures and even Gertrude herself. "What's that funny little house sitting in Gertrude's room?" I asked Ted yesterday. "Oh, that's Gertrude," he explained. "Ha, ha."

Children really are in control with *Gertrude's Secrets* and with its sequel, *Gertrude's Puzzles* (which is on my wish list). They can leave puzzle pieces scattered everywhere, change them at will, or even solve a puzzle if the fit takes them. It's a rewarding way to learn about learning without making any real-world messes, and you will not regret buying it.

The last Learning Company programs that belong in this section are three software classics that are possibly the greatest learning software ever invented. These are *Rocky's Boots* (for grades four and up), *Robot Odyssey* (for grades seven to adult), and the brand-new *Think Quick!*.

Rocky's Boots and *Robot Odyssey* are reviewed at length in the Engineering chapter.

For now, let's concentrate on *Think Quick!*

Think Quick!, a game designed specifically to teach problem-solving and logical thinking skills, has you prowling through the Castle of Mystikar solving puzzles, avoiding Slime Worms and the nefarious Dragon, and collecting oddments. Some oddments (keys and flowers) are helpful in problem-solving or simply maintaining your existence. Pop other oddments in a cauldron and out comes a piece of the Knight. When the Knight is totally assembled, he stalks and slays the Dragon.

In order to traverse the ever-more-difficult maze and collect your oddments, you need to solve puzzles and open doors. Typically, you might be faced with several doors that must be opened in a specific sequence for you to enter and collect your prize. But wait! First check the Owl's clue to see if you want what's behind the door. The clue consists of a simple figural analogy. Time might be running out (if you set the clock), so Think Quick!

Best of all, Learning Company has left in the Castle Creator software they used to create the game. You can create your own mazes and puzzles and then play them (or stump Mom and Dad). This makes *Think Quick!* truly open-ended.

Think Quick!'s symbolism could be improved. In this day of increased parental awareness, occult imagery is meeting with disfavor. Occultism is not central to the plot, though, and could be easily deleted. Instead of a knight "created" in a magical cauldron, all the Learning Co. staff would have to do would be substitute pieces of a robot knight for the magical oddments. These could then be assembled in the already-existing workshop. This aside, the program is a wow! When the brochure promises, "Endless hours of fun," they aren't kidding. Since the day it arrived I've hardly been able to pry my sons' figures off the joystick.

Learning Technologies

All programs $19.95; includes certificate for free Learning Kit. Apple II family and Commodore 64/128.

Is it worth $20 for a piece of thinkware and a learning kit? Learning Technologies has cracked the price barrier with this outrageous offer, which we hope other companies will emulate.

I have a shelf full of LT programs. Although LT's schoolware is decent for the price, their thinkware is better than a bargain.

Speedy Delivery requires you to help the postman deliver his packages to all the houses in the randomly-generated maze without ever visiting the same house twice. This is a challenging game that requires planning ahead.

For classic problem-solving skills, Learning Technologies has a computerized version of the game known as King Tut's Pyramid or the Hindu Pyramid. Called *Monkey Business*, it asks the user to move a stack of monkeys from one location to two others. He can only put a smaller monkey on a larger. I spent more hours than I'd care to admit in eighth grade figuring out how the puzzle worked, and I can still remember the rush of satisfaction when I understood the trick of how to do the puzzle in the least amount of moves. *Monkey Business* has three levels, with a stack of three, four, and five monkeys respectively, so if you don't already know how this puzzle works you can spend some time finding out.

And now for Learning Technologies' two best thinking programs.

Scrambled Eggs presents you with an expectant hen and four eggs. You deduce which number is in which egg by making guesses and analyzing the computer's response. It tells you (1) how many of your guessed numbers were in the eggs but not in the position you guessed and (2) how many numbers were in the right position. You'll be doing some heavy-duty thinking by the time you get these chicks hatched.

Alpine Tram Ride is the same sort of puzzle as Scrambled Eggs, featuring a menagerie of animals rather than a brood of chicks. Of the two, *Alpine Tram Ride* is more colorful and also somewhat harder to use, since instead of displaying the numbers you selected, as in *Scrambled Eggs*, the screen shows you the animals corresponding to each number code. The accompanying learning kits for these two games were really fun to work through.

I'm not afraid to recommend Learning Technologies programs, because of their excellent refund policy. If you try it and don't like it, you get your money back.

Sunburst Communications

Most programs in the $65-$75 range. Everything runs on Apple. Most programs also run on Atari, Commodore, TRS-80, and IBM PC or PCjr. Something for everyone. Send for Sunburst's catalog.

First, let's look at a few of Sunburst's Home Programs. (You can order a color brochure describing them, by the way.) *The Pond* is a game of logic, pattern-recognition, and experimentation. Your frog wants to gaily leap from lily pad to lily pad until he reaches "home." Only one pattern will get him there. Can you recognize it? It sounds easy, but since you only see part of the pond at a time, you have to carefully hoard your test jumps. *Pond* isn't quite as much fun as some others, but if you like this kind of mental challenge, its six levels of difficulty will keep you hopping.

The Incredible Laboratory is an analysis/deduction game. I had doubts about *The Incredible Laboratory* before I saw it, mainly because I try to shun products that stress monsters and horror. The monsters that you invent just stand there, though, since the program's emphasis is on deducing how they are made. Briefly, you have to figure out which chemicals produce what results. In the Novice level, the same chemical always does the same thing. In higher levels, you're looking for combinations that react together to produce the monsters' characteristic (high heels or cowboy boots, three eyes or two eyes or cat eyes, etc.). You'll be grabbing for pencil and paper before you're through. As an introduction to scientific deduction, *Incredible Lab* is cheerfully motivating.

Now, on to the School program designed just for logical thinking. Unlike other math games, *The King's Rule* was designed to help learners develop unobvious hypotheses. In order to progress to the throne, you must recognize the pattern which defines three numbers. But watch out! The simplest answer is not always right! For the numbers "1, 2, 3" for example, the rule may be "All numbers under 10" instead of "Whole numbers in counting sequence." You test your hypotheses on new number sets until you think you have it down. Then you challenge the computer and see if you're right. With six levels of play, it can get plenty tricky!

CHAPTER FIFTEEN

CLASSICAL LITERATURE

It is true that children (and adults) can read for hours armed with nothing more than Spiderman comics and the backs of cereal boxes. If you want your children to fit right in with the current literary trend, this is indeed the best training they could get. For some time American comic books have been getting better— not in a moral sense but in the quality of the stories and art— and novels have been getting worse in both morals and quality. Instead, however, of blowing the whistle on the gutter-loving writers who are so busily foisting off their deviant fantasies as literature, our Literary Moguls are actually celebrating the disaster! Indeed, *The New York Times Book Review* has gone so far as to inquire if we are living "in a Golden Age of the American Novel." But, as literary observer Bryan Griffin points out,

> Now, it goes without saying that people who are living in a Golden Age of anything do not spend their afternoons asking one another if they are really living in a Golden Age, but the stragglers of 1980 didn't know this, and the response to the questionnaire was almost touching in its fevered loyalty to the dead faith. Yes, yes, they were living in a Golden Age, said everybody

tearfully, and it was going to get better and better, and everything was going to be All Right.

The point nowadays is to be shocking: film flies crawling around on your nude wife as per John Lennon, make giant soup cans, a project any fifth-grader could have mastered (Andy Warhol— the shock here is at the pettiness of the "art"), or flash your fanny at the screen á là Frank Ripploh. To be a modern literary great, go and do ye likewise. Advocate child-molesting (Vladimir Nabokov was only the first), marital infidelity (Gay Talese), torture, especially of women and children (William Goldman), or ceaseless "creative" fornication (Henry Miller, followed by too many other "greats" to mention). If possible, wrap the sex and sadism in a mélange of disconnected and absurd scenes. Even better, put it all in the first person and ramble on interminably about yourself. If you do this, the critics will fall all over themselves praising your boldness and creativity. As Bryan Griffin also notes,

> Perhaps the lowest of many low points came when a "blue-ribbon commission" charged with supplying the White House with "great recordings reflecting the wide range of American

cultural interests" decided to fulfill their 1980 responsibilities by awarding the President of their nation a copy of a new recording called *Never Mind the Bullocks*, by those great reflectors of the wide range of American cultural interests, the Sex Pistols. But the laugh was on the beribboned authorities, because the Sex Pistols weren't really monuments to the American culture at all; they were monuments to the culture of the United Kingdom.

SEPARATING THE GOOD, THE BAD, AND THE UGLY

Home Life
Panic Among the Philistines, $6.95. *Abolition of Man*, $4.95. *Addicted to Mediocrity*, $4.95. Also by Franky Schaeffer: *Bad News for Modern Man* ($8.95) and *A Time for Anger* ($7.95). All prices postpaid.

What to do? The very first step to take if you want to improve your own or your children's literary sensibilities is to read Bryan Griffin's *Panic Among the Philistines*, quoted above. Mr. Griffin's book exposes the spiritual, literary, and literal nakedness of the present Cultural Establishment. It's the bracing tonic we all need, and is good for a few hearty laughs beside— for the real problem in many cases is that we have been taking the laughable seriously. Expanded from an article published in *Harper's* in the summer of 1981, this book is the literary "Shot Heard Round the World." Regnery Gateway publishes it. No serious reader should miss it.

While you're at it, you might also pick up a copy of C.S. Lewis's *The Abolition of Man*, published by Macmillan and now in its zillionth printing. In delightful prose, *Abolition* uncovers

the termites who even back in the forties were gnawing steadily away at our cultural heritage. Further, Lewis explains why great art can't exist without classical values, and why an easy toleration of the obscene and ugly results inevitably in unfreedom.

What more remains but to rediscover the genuine literary treasures of the past? Here those of us who are Christian immediately run smack dab into a problem. Those great old books weren't all evangelistic tracts. And certain folk in our own small version of the Cultural Establishment would have us totally ignore anything that doesn't arrive embossed with the Praying Hands.

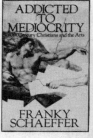
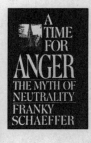

If you're all tied up in knots over this problem, I suggest that you read Franky Schaeffer's award-winning *Addicted to Mediocrity*, published by Crossway Books. Written in Franky's inimitable vivid style and lavishly illustrated, its premise is essentially correct: reality is God's world, and you don't need to plaster Bible verses all over art to make it edifying or Christian.

Home Life also carries Franky Schaeffer's other books. Combined, they present a brilliant exposé of both secular and church hypocrisy and clear directions for reclaiming our culture from the literary (and other) vandals.

"WHAT IS TRUE, NOBLE, RIGHT . . ."

In Philippians, Christians are told to seek after what is true, noble, right, pure, lovely, and admirable. I believe that as this applies to art we are to look for what is *true to life*. God does not condemn fiction, for Jesus himself told parables. The point is that evil should not be glamorized, or even explicitly described. God tells us, for example, that the men of Sodom were sinners. The Bible does not glamorize their sin, though, or give us details about how to sodomize strangers. Thus stories of heroism, true or fictional, are usable by Christians even if the protagonists do not spend their entire time preaching, and scenes of evil that show its ugliness without dwelling on how it is perpetrated are also usable.

Classical literature shows good and evil in their true lights; most modern literature, sadly, does not.

MAGAZINES

Chronicles of Culture
$14.97/year (12 issues); two years, $27.97.

Every issue of this independent, slick journal simply reeks of wit. The editor is Thomas Fleming, whose cultural acumen we already noted in the Classical Languages chapter. *Chronicles of Culture* covers all the same cultural areas as *Time*, *Newsweek*, and the rest, only with insight and reason instead of perverse dogmatism and full-color spreads.

I do this day confess my faults. I do not understand everything in this magazine. Some of the literati they praise or condemn are total strangers to me. (Perhaps it's just as well). It's obvious that the editor and writers had a classical education, and I haven't. But the writing is vivid and involved, and the content uplifting. Recommended.

Classical Calliope
One year (4 issues) for $12. Quantity prices and back issue sets (1985-86 only) available.

Homer is looking for a few good men. Well, a few good boys and girls, anyway. The optimistic folks at Cobblestone Publishing actually believe there are American children

who are interested in such things as the temple of Artemis at Ephesus, Greek and Roman coinage, and other trivia surrounding the vast amount of Greek and Roman writing known as "the classics." Myth and fable are cunningly resurrected, illustrated, and explained in hopes that American youth will show some slight interest in this part of our Western cultural heritage. Picture now the bespectacled hordes of Homer-lovers invading our libraries in search of an authentic rendering of the *Iliad!*

Besides myths retold and articles about classical society, *Classical Calliope* contains games, a section on English abbreviations that arise from classical language, a section on word origins, and another on the history of language. Even the page numbers are in Roman numerals! All is done with finesse, including the illustrations.

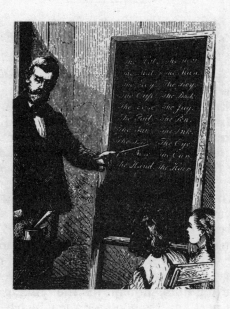

St. Paul's Family Magazine
$10/year (four issues). Single issue/ $2.75. Back issues, $2.75 each. Boxed set of back issues, $14/year (Volumes I and II available). Outside USA add $3.

So here I am, reading back issues of *St. Paul's Family Magazine* when I am supposed to be writing a review. Shame, shame! But if I don't read them all right now, son Ted might see them and snake them away, and then where would I be?

What a gorgeous, elegant feast! Here are *real* children's classics like the story of Bearskin by Howard Pyle and "The Race" from *Hans Brinker or The Silver Skates.* Shakespeare, Chaucer, Cervantes, Aesop, Grimm, and many more all grace these pages, paired with illustrations that match the timeless text. Poetry, prose, and art masterpieces are all presented reverently and without condescension to children. Even the activity pages, uncomplicated as they are, take the child's maturity and interest in enduring beauty for granted. The activities are actually valuable (how to make a book, or bread, or pretzels) instead of the typical hokey make-it-for-the-sake-of-making-it that so infests much children's activities. The stories are not sentimentalized— evil is allowed to be evil so it can be conquered.

Departments include: St. Paul's Gallery (children's artistic and written contributions) • Color This Page • Puzzles and Fun • Games • Art (how to do it) • Cooking (how to make something) • Handicraft (ditto) • Star Gazing • Natural Science • History and Geography (history as a story!) • Stories From the Bible • Art Masterpieces (one each issue) • Poetry • God's Heroes • Music • and The Principal's List (reviews of "the thousand good books" as opposed to the ten thousand trashy ones). And joy of joys, you can order the "good books" with a handy form in the back!

St. Paul's Family Magazine has the same flavor as the works of G.K. Chesterton (who would have loved it)— Catholic and cultured.

CLASSICS MADE SIMPLE

Aristoplay
By Jove! $20

It can't be any simpler or more enjoyable than this. "What can't be simpler than what?" asks Bill. "Learning Greek and Roman mythology, which happens to be the background knowledge necessary to understand all classical literature," I explain patiently, "is usually a bit of a chore. Jason, the Minotaur, Odysseus, Hera, Athena, and all the rest get jumbled up. What you really need," I continue, "is a fun way to remember all those stories." "So?" interjects Bill. "*By Jove!*" I exclaim. "Step on your foot?" Bill asks solicitously. "No, I mean *By Jove!*, the board game from Aristoplay. It's a beautiful board game simulation of one of the bigger and better myths— Jason and the Golden Fleece. You, a Mere Mortal, voyage about the board contending with Oracles and the whimsical, ever-foolish gods and goddesses. It all comes with: • the invaluable, award-winning *By Jove Stories* • eight hero cards with stands • one game board • one pair dice • 16 potluck cards • 12 minotaur/labyrinth awards • 50 VAP cards (I'll explain those later) • 60 gold coins • and 40 oracle cards. Up to six players can play at a time . . . Hey! Where are you going?" I hear Bill hallooing in the next room, "Boys! Want to play one of the new games that came today!" Shucks. Didn't even get to explain the VAP cards . . .

DIDAX
Ladybird books, $2.50 each.

If you're looking for classics recast in Dick-and-Jane vocabulary, DIDAX has the stuff! From England DIDAX imports the Ladybird books, brightly colored and lavishly illustrated redoings of classics and fables. This grew, as you can guess, out of the "sight word" approach. Ladybird also sells a sight word reader series of 36 (count 'em) little books plus two picture dictionaries and workbooks, very aptly titled "The Key Words Reading Scheme." (Not that they aren't cute and clever little books— it's just that any program which persuades teachers and parents that they must buy 36 readers deserves to be called a "scheme.")

But we digress. The Ladybird books are inexpensive (singly) and will provide a diluted taste of the real thing for very young readers or those whose progress has been temporarily crippled by look-say.

Ladybird also has a clever little series for beginning readers featuring huge print and instruction about numbers, time, the alphabet, and so on.

EDC
Greek Myths and Legends, $6.95. Norse Myths and Legends, $5.95. Aesop's Fables, $2.95. Picture classics, World Legends $2.95 each paperback, $6.95 each hardbound, $11.96 library-bound, or $10.95 for hardbound combination volumes.

You won't find a less expensive, more colorful, more sprightly intro to the classics anywhere than right here. Top-quality art combines with vibrant illustrations as is usual with EDC series.

Usborne's World Legends series covers *Hercules*, *Jason*, and *Ulysses*. Designed for the seven-to-eleven year old set, the illustrations are absolutely charming, somewhat belying the gory stories. Animal Stories, for a similar age group, covers *Aesop's Fables*, *Animal Legends*, and *Magical Animals*. Picture Classics, for seven-to-nine year olds, includes *King Arthur*, *Robinson Crusoe*, *Treasure Island*, and

Gulliver's Travels. The Myths and Legends series for 11- to 15-year olds features grotesque fantasy art suitable to the actual gloomy myths themselves.

Educational Insights
Each set of 12 cartoon books, 12 spirit masters, and teacher's guide, $19.95. Accompanying read-along cassettes for each set, $40. Thirty-six-booklet sets, $50. *Read-Along* cassettes, $110.

What do you get when you cross Spiderman with Edgar Allan Poe? Something I wouldn't want to meet in a dark alley— or the Educational Insights literature comics. Yes, you read that right! Educational Insights has compiled several boxes of four-page comics. Each comic tells, in compact form, one classic tale. And there's more! For the really hard-to-motivate literary dilettante, you can also purchase read-along cassettes to accompany the comics!

Each box also contains a number of spirit masters equal to the number of comics, and a teacher's guide. The spirit masters, one presumes, are for testing the carefree readers to see if they were really reading or just had a schoolbook propped open inside the comic.

Sets are: American Short Stories, which has 36 different comics by 35 different authors; Short Stories Around the World, which has 12 stories each at second, third, and fourth grade reading levels; three series of Adventure Stories (Ghost and Monsters, Adventures in Mystery, and Adventures in Science Fiction) each featuring 12 tales; and three series of Classic Tales (Tales of Robin Hood, Tales of King Arthur, and Tales from Shakespeare— the latter "in modern dialog"), each likewise containing twelve tales. Oh, yes, I almost forgot the set of Great Sports Stories, perhaps because it doesn't really count as literature in the finest, truest sense of the word.

Your learner will not discover great writing by reading comics, but he will at least become aware of the main plot of many masterpieces and perhaps become interested in the masterpieces themselves. I read several of these comics, or something like them, when I was in pigtails and it didn't cripple me for life. (What almost did turn me off to the classics was trying to read the agonizingly long *Lorna Doone* in an unabridged version at the age of eight.) We do not scoff, then, at Educational Insights' humble efforts to bring the classics to the people.

CLASSICS MADE AFFORDABLE

AMSCO School Publications, Inc.
   Paperback classics, $3-$4 range.
Hardbacks, $5-$6.

These incredibly inexpensive, library-quality paperbacks and hardbacks run the gamut of old and new classics. Some come with a "Reader's Guide" that "focuses the reader's attention on the humanistic and aesthetic elements of a specific literary work." These teacher-written Guides looks at such things as

plot, character, and literary devices, as well as exploring unfamiliar vocabulary. If you would rather face literature without a teacher holding your hand, 57 of the titles come without a Reader's Guide.

AMSCO offers discount prices to schools, so if you are a school be sure to mention this. The selection includes classics like *Wuthering Heights*, *Vanity Fair*, *Huckleberry Finn* and *Tom Sawyer*, plus Dickens, Hawthorne, Shakespeare and so on, as well as some modern works like *Flowers for Algernon*, a genuine science fiction classic. All books are complete and unabridged, and most are under $4 (for schools).

Bluestocking Press
   How to Stock a Quality Home Library
***Inexpensively*, $4 postpaid.**

You think you know how to shop for book bargains? Well, think again. Do you know how to make your home library pay for itself? How to get a complete set of *The Great Books of the Western World* (retail: $1500) for $100? How to find free or almost-free books that you really want? How to avoid duplications in your book shopping? Author Jane Williams, a lady whose home library I'd like to visit, spells out all this and more in a book that itself is a price bargain.

Publishers Central Bureau

Most of PCB's huge stock is remaindered current books. Classics do pop up from time to time amid the other bargains, and when they do, the price is right. Example: $4.98 for a Shakespeare play in fancy mock-leather binding with gilt-edged pages. Another time we got a one-book edition of Shakespeare's Complete Plays for under $10. Drawback: The catalog is only semi-organized. You may have to spend an hour with it to be sure you don't want anything this time. Also, PCB sprinkles its porn offerings throughout instead of leaving them all on one easy-to-rip-out page, thus making browsing an iffy proposition for those of us who care about this.

Silver Burdett
Hardbound classics, $3.25 each.

I couldn't believe the price when I first saw it, and I still find it hard to believe. Where else can you get a complete, unabridged, hardbound classic for under $4? The selection is not very large, but all are genuine classics. Each includes a Study Guide with "short-answer questions, background information, composition skills practice, research topics, creative activities, a bibliography, and an audiovisual list of resources."

CLASSICS ON CASSETTE

Mind's Eye
Most cassettes $5.95 each, including *Color Book Theater*. Sets are less per cassette.

This gorgeous, easy-to-use catalog contains mystery, intrigue, horror (those I skip) and set after set of classic tales that I drool over and hope to buy someday. For only $5.95 each you can get fairy tales (fully dramatized), classic children's stories, Mark Twain, Charles Dickens, Tolkien, dramatized biography, radio classics, "far-fetched pets" series, Greek classics, American novels, and more!

Of interest to parents is *Color Book Theater*,

for children ages three to eight. Each *Color Book Theater* pack contains a cassette, a coloring/story book, and a box of crayons. A special "act-with" feature allows child to become the hero, as Side 2 contains the same story without the hero's lines. By reading the appropriate lines in the accompanying book (which are printed in boldface) your child can become the main character! Twelve children's classics are in this format. We bought several and the children loved them.

Jeffrey Norton Publishers

Jeffrey Norton has a smallish selection of famous writers reading their own works.

Recorded Books
Thirty-day rental or sale. Prices start at $14.95, which includes a "durable bookshelf album with color cover art and contents information."

"Cover to cover studio recordings of the very best in current and classic fiction brought to life on standard-play cassettes by professional narrators." Rental available. Some "adult" cassettes. RB has lots of good stuff, too: P.G. Wodehouse, Tolkien, Jane Austen, James Hamilton narrating the New Testament, Gilbert and Sullivan operas with libretto, and Solzhenitsyn, among others.

SBI Publishers in Sound
Children's classics cassette library, $5.75 each, $65 for a set of 12. Slow-playback cassette recorders start at $120 (with discount).

Parents magazine recommended SBI's Children's Classics Library. SBI offers adult classics as well. Some material is substandard from a Christian viewpoint; all is superbly read. All titles are unabridged.

SBI offers slow-playback titles also (80 in all). The advantage of slow-playback is that much more material can be recorded per cassette, thus bringing the price down and sparing you unnecessary trips to flip the cassettte. SBI also sells slow-playback cassette players.

SBI's 45-day rental plan is the longest in the industry.

I'm really tempted by the slow-play machine. Imagine taping an entire three-hour meeting on one C-90 cassette! SBI thinks the industry will move this way because it is so much more economical. If you're looking for economy and/or innovation, you might send for this catalog.

LITERARY CRITICISM

Everett/Edwards Cassette Curriculum
Each cassette, $12.50 postpaid.

What you hear is what you get: Hundreds of critics on cassette.

Everett/Edwards says "The true purpose of a "critic" . . . is to aid and enlighten the student . . ." Strong in this noble purpose, E/E has assembled a veritable army of critics and turned them loose on the literary giants. E/E believes that by listening to the critics criticize, the student will learn to analyze and ultimately to think for himself. It does help, of course, if the student reads the work in question, and E/E is the first to point this out.

E/E has an American Folklore series which includes lectures on all the principal genres as well as such ersatz themes as "The Military in Folklore" and "The Folklore of Social Elites." If I were a schoolteacher spending department money I might look into it; having only our own money to spend, I shall wait. E/E also has a Women's Studies series (intended for schools, mind you) which includes such objects as *Was Jesus a Feminist?*, *Women, Witches, and Worship*, *Open Marriage* (a euphemism for consenting adultery), and *The Prejudice of Parents*. Ironically, E/E suggests we should "Give Cassettes for Christmas." We would be happy to consider this if E/E would kindly get rid of the portions of its curriculum that knock Christ and Christianity.

Jeffrey Norton Publishers
Most cassettes are $12.45 postpaid.

This company, which also owns Audio-Forum and Video-Forum, has a catalog entitled Sound Seminars. Captured on cassette are a host of critics dissecting the works of other people. If this sounds like a good idea to you, Jeffrey Norton has, besides individual cassettes of individual critics, a series by Heywood Hale Broun and another by Gilbert Highet, both of which have been hailed as provocative, intelligent, and, in Mr. Highet's case, charming. You can also get Norman Mailer talking about existentialism, Stephen Spender talking about everybody, and Shakespeare talked about by everybody. Auden discusses poetry and Frost reads his own poems.

CLASSICS MADE CLASSY

Britannica

You want to spend some real money on books? Lots of books? Big, fancy, important books? Britannica has them. *The Great Books of the Western World*, a fifty-four volume set with very fancy bindings, brings you "443 undisputed masterpieces from 74 of the greatest thinkers the world has ever known." You know, home folks like Plato and Aristotle and Copernicus and Thomas Aquinas, plus all the popular trendsetters of our age— Darwin, Marx, Hegel, Freud. It all comes with "the amazing Synopticon," a one-volume index to 163,000 topics covered in the books (a sure giveaway that Britannica does not actually expect you to *read* them).

Another good reason for not actually reading all these admittedly influential works is the ten-volume Great Books Reading Plan— "your guide to reading and profiting from The Great Books." I've seen thinner encyclopedias, but not sold by Britannica, at least not since 1768 when the original three-volume *Encyclopædia Britannica* made its debut.

We all have our own favorites, of course, but I do wonder: why does Kant make it in, but not Luther or Wesley? Why Marx, but not Washington or Jefferson? The further back you go, the better the selections become. Few would quibble over the inclusion of Plutarch, or Chaucer, or Shakespeare. But from Adam Smith (volume 39) on, and in spots before him, the *Great Books* do most solemnly tread the anti-classical party line.

Eaton Press

The 100 Greatest Books Ever Written, monthly plan. $34/month for 4 titles on 8 cassettes. Thirty-day replacement or refund of any volume of 8 cassettes. Subscription cancellable at any time. Shipping extra.

Here's an idea for the busy exec— classics on cassette! "Oh, that's been done before." "Not like this, it hasn't. See, the cassettes come in sets of eight, housed in quarterbound leather cases. They look like books, see? You get one set a month, so they aren't all dumped on you at once. Then you just slip 'em in the 'ol cassette player and let 'er rip!"

"But . . . " "But what? I thought I explained all that." "But do I want these cassettes? I mean, are they real classics?" "Not to worry. I checked out the titles in the ad and they are for real. True, the selections are kinda haphazardly grouped— like *Grimm's Fairy Tales* with *Tragedies of Shakespeare*, *Canterbury Tales*, and the *Odyssey*— but these things happen. And listen, they've got real actors doing the performances! Guys like Charlton Heston, Richard Burton, and Sir John Gielgud. Gals like Julie Harris and Vanessa Redgrave."

And it all costs money, real money, lots of real money . . . so I asked for a review copy. No reply. Frustrating. How much can I praise a great idea when I never saw the product?

CLASSICS MADE TO LAST

Perma-Bound

Source for jillions of classics and others with an unusual binding that (the ads claim) makes ordinary paperbacks last dozens of times longer. The size of the catalog indicates the process must work.

Reade Books

Make New Friends But Keep the Old Department: In these crazed modernistic days when crusading librarians routinely trash whole libraries full of classics to replace them with the latest and greatest Gothic novels and sleazeball celebrity biographies, it makes sense to hold on to your oldie but goodie, unlikely-to-be-reprinted-in-the-near-future books.

Here's a hand bookbinder who specializes in book repairs of all kinds. Namely, Doug Reade.

Mr. Reade says he can handle anything from "a page repair to a full rebind." We enjoyed his column in the *Stay-Homish Trading Post* very much, while that worthy magazine lasted. Mr. Reade seems to know his stuff, and like it, too, which counts for something if you care about an old-fashioned thing like craftsmanship.

Now, do librarians really throw out great old books? In Middletown, New York, the head librarian even threw out (get ready to shudder) most of the P.G. Wodehouse books. Yes! Even Jeeves, the Perfect Butler, was not spared!

Remember, what one librarian can order, another can trash. It's time to hop down to your local library and make some bids at their yard sales before all the good books fall victim to some radical activist.

THOSE FAMOUS *McGUFFEY* READERS

One last word: McGuffey. No discussion of literature would be complete without some mention of the famous *McGuffey Readers* used by millions of American children. McGuffeys are coming back "in" for sure. You can find them in the strangest places— like a catalog mostly devoted to Jack Daniel whisky paraphernalia.

The question is not, "Should we get a set of *McGuffeys?*" You either love McGuffey's Christian emphasis and moralizing or you don't. The question really is, "Which set of *McGuffeys* is the best?"

There are, you see, McGuffeys and McGuffeys. Mott Media prides itself on offering the *original McGuffeys*, á là the 1836-37 version compiled by Rev. McGuffey himself. (Eight volumes: hardback with teacher's guide $89.95, paperback without teacher's guide $49.95). Others are quick to point out that Mott's version is not an exact reproduction; words have been changed, the grammar has been amended, and the layout has been revised. The only completely authentic McGuffey's around is the facsimile edition of the *Pictorial Eclectic Primer* sold by Buck Hill Associates. Buck Hill also has a version they call a "faithful reproduction" of the originals, seven illustrated hardbound volumes for $32.50. Is it a facsimile edition also? I don't know.

Now that we've settled (or confused) the issue of authenticity, several contenders still remain in the field. Thoburn Press has published a very successful Christian School Edition of the revised edition of 1880. Lacking Rev. McGuffey's strong Presbyterian bent, these readers moralize more and evangelize less. The Primers in this version are much more useful for actually teaching reading than the originals, following a more phonetic plan. The price is right, too ($42.75 for seven hardback readers or $24.95 for all seven paperback volumes in an attractive slipcase).

Hewitt Research Foundation has gone all the field one better and put out the *Moore-McGuffey Readers* with new illustrations in color. Unafraid to tackle the venerated script, Hewitt has edited McGuffey with an eye to practicality in teaching reading. The grammar has been updated and some stories rewritten to remove spiritual teaching Hewitt considers misleading or offensive. Condensed into four volumes, Hewitt's entry is popular in spite of its expense ($55 for the set of four hardbound books: $14 apiece).

I am not much help in picking out *McGuffeys*. Although we have owned three different sets over the years, when friends ask my advice about McGuffeys I suggest that they forgo the use of "readers" entirely and patronize the library. For its moral character McGuffey's is worthwhile, as are a host of other books written at the time. As an introduction to hearty American and English literature McGuffey has its uses. But the point of studying literature is to study *literature*— the actual books themselves. It takes more than a passing handshake to get to know Shakespeare, or Longfellow, or Donne, or Dryden. Reverend McGuffey kindly offers to introduce us to the greats, but if we knew what we were doing we could introduce ourselves.

HIGH TECH GOODIES

CHAPTER SIXTEEN

DESKTOP LEARNING— WHAT'S HOT IN COMPUTERS

Computers— the biggest thing to hit education since ditto masters, right? That's what everyone is saying, but I'm not sure I agree. After all, kids can ruin their eyesight just as well in the traditional way, reading under the bedsheets with a flashlight, as by sitting for hours mesmerized by the tiny flickering lights on a computer screen. And as for the great educational benefits, most of the "educational" software on the market now is just glorified flash card drill, with a little animated song-and-dance to reward the student for getting the answer right.

For millennia the human race has learned its needed academic skills without the benefit of computers. The average eighth grader of the last century could read and write better than most of our modern college graduates, even though he never sat at a keyboard or twiddled a joystick.

So what's educational software's big selling point? *Motivation!* Any device that can get a normal kid to spend hours drilling himself on school subjects without an adult standing over him is bound to have audience appeal. Software can make drillwork more interesting. And a few rare programs actually use the computer's power by allowing students to create and discover instead of merely regurgitating facts.

When it comes to writing, computers are much more friendly than typewriters and much faster than the well-chewed #2 yellow pencils we struggled with in our youth. Today's kids can invent and print out endless letters, stories, reports, and so on with a tithe of the effort required in years past. Learning to type is easier and more interesting when the screen "talks back" to you, and editing is a snap.

Computers are also a fun way to get kids involved in the world of business: balancing the family checkbook, keeping inventory for the family business.

If you don't have a computer, relax. Your children don't need one, despite all the ballyhoo about "computer literacy." The hardware field is changing so rapidly that anything a child learns about computers in second grade will be out of date in sixth, let alone when he graduates from high school. Furthermore, any child who has been given the "tools of learning" can learn what he needs to know about computers when and if he needs to know it.

ERIC AND SAMANTHA MEET THE COMPUTER

Having said all that, let's suppose the Smith family is in the market for a computer. Father Eric hopes to organize the family finances, mother Samantha wants to automate the mailing list for her women's organization, and kiddies Ignatz and Ermintrude are all agog to play some games on it. Where should the Smiths begin?

Ten Speed Press
Computer Wimp, $9.95 postpaid.

Far and away the best place to begin is with this book: *Computer Wimp* by John Bear. Dr. Bear warns you about every horrible mistake you can make in buying computers and their accessory "stuff" (peripherals, supplies, software etc.) and explains how to do it right with such wit that the book is worth buying even if you're not in the market for an electronic beast of burden. The book deals mostly with basics of computer buying and setup, such as the 99 percent rule and the only-buy-it-if-you-can-lift-it rule, so it isn't likely to become outdated.

Larson Publications
Complete Home Educator, $10.95 postpaid.

If you want to go beyond store-bought software and learn to program, or if you have a son or daughter who's frantic to get into BASIC, your best bet is Mario Pagnoni's *The Complete Home Educator*. The title is misleading, because although Mr. Pagnoni has a lot to say about education and home schooling (and I don't agree with all of it!), his strong suit is the extended discussion of home computing. Written specifically for the home schooler, Mr. Pagnoni's book will ease you into these troubled waters.

IGNATZ AND ERMINTRUDE AS DESKTOP STUDENTS

Ignatz and Ermintrude, after playing a few computer games, both decide they want to do some real programming. Yikes! Panicked parents! "I don't know this stuff myself. How'm I supposed to teach it to the kids?"

Take it easy, Smiths. The following sources have what any motivated preteen (or adult) needs to become a grade-A Computer Whiz.

Computer Literacy Bookshop

Are you an adult or precocious hacker anxious to load up on computer knowledge? A good place to start might be Computer Literacy Bookshops, the world's largest store devoted to computer and electronics books. Located in Silicon Valley, Computer Literacy carries every title recommended in the *Whole Earth Software Catalog* and nearly ten thousand others. They publish a bi-monthly newsletter (free upon request). Computer Literacy says they will gladly answer any book questions you may have.

EDC Publishing Company

Computer Fun, Computers: A simple and Colorful introduction for beginners, Usborne Guide to Computer Games, Computer Battlegames, Computer Spacegames, Understanding the Micro, $2.95 each. *Understanding Computer Graphics, Practical Things to Do with a Microcomputer, Inside the Chip,* $2.95 each. *Better Basic, Computer Jargon, Machine Code for Beginners, Practise Your Basic, Intro to Computer Programming,* $2.95 or combined volume, *The Beginner's Programming Handbook,* $6.95.

From England, the Usborne Computer Books are aimed at beginners aged 11 and up. Straightforward text, innovative page layout, and colorful graphics make these books superb values. A Best Buy.

Learning Systems Corporation

People who like to pinch a penny until it bleeds will be happy with LSC's introduction to BASIC. At just 79¢ it's a friendly handshake to Apple, Atari, Pet, and TRS-80 programming. Miniworkbook, 16 hand-sized pages.

Love Publishing Company

Books on computing for beginners, kids, and teachers. Love's selection seems good.

MAGAZINES AND CLUBS

For obvious budgetary reasons, I haven't subscribed to every computer magazine or joined every club. Thus, the following list is skewed slightly towards Apple and Mac.

A+
Year's subscription, $24.97 (12 issues). Canadians, add $5 postage, other countries add $10.

A good choice for the Apple user or potential Apple user. Slick, color magazine. Software and hardware reviews keep you up to date. Something for hackers too. Read the ads if you can't understand the text yet. Not quite as fresh and readable as *MacUser*, but now that Ziff-Davis, *A+*'s publisher, has bought *MacUser*, maybe some of *MacUser* will rub off on it.

Christian Computer News
$20/year for membership in the Christian Computer Users Association includes this bi-monthly newsletter. *Christian Computer Users Sourcebook*, **$25 (updated continually).**

Newsprint magazine dedicated to "expanding the Kingdom of God through the use of computers and related technologies." You have to fill out a largish membership form (one page full of print).
The Christian Computer Users Sourcebook is billed as "the most up to date source for Christian software you will ever find." It contains close to 200 vendors for church software, Christian educational software, computerized Bibles, and such.

Christian Educational Computing
One year (10 issues): individuals, $15 US (US funds), $26 Canadian (Canadian funds); institutions $25 US, $36 Canadian. Make check out to MVP Software. Also, free catalog of MS-DOS educational software.

As is its name, so is its nature. Magazine about issues in educational computing from a Christian perspective. Plus reviews, letters to the editor, news notes, and the like. Output is IBM-laser-printer-style, e.g. somewhat clunky but readable. Most Valuable Section: "On the Market: What's New in Educational Computing." Good generalized coverage of what's new for a variety of machines. The editor is a Calvin College philosophy prof and the content has intellectual appeal.

Learning Advantage
Mighty Micro, Fast Track, Competitive Edge, **$39.95 for each monthly 2-disk issue, sent on approval.** *Boot!*, **$19.95 per selection. Service available for Apple II and MS-DOS machines.**

The Software™ of the Month Club, billed as a "monthly magazine on disk," is here, in versions for all ages.

Boot!, for children aged three to six, is a monthly software selection for children of this age. The promotional material I received had *Stickybear Numbers* as the first selection, to be followed by *Stickybear Reading*.

Mighty Micro, for seven to 10-year-olds, includes two program disks, the *Mighty Micro* 32 page magazine filled with tips, articles, and activities centered on this month's software, a Disk Wallet to protect your disks, the *Bank Street Software Newsletter* for Mom and Dad, and a "really great poster." Here the initial selection were *Mr. Pixel's Programming Paint Set* and *Creative Contraptions*.

Fast Track, for the junior high and early high school set, has the same setup as Mighty Micro: two disks, *Fast Track* magazine, full-color poster, disk wallet, and the *Bank Street Software Newsletter*. First selections were the classic *Rocky's Boots* (reviewed in the Engineering chapter) and Tom Snyder Production's world peace game, *The Other Side*. Future selections looked good.

Competitive Edge, for those college-bound young sharks, provides one new software package per month, plus the *Future Tech* newspaper for computing students and, of course, the *Bank Street Software Newsletter* for

parents. Selections here run about half the retail cost and focus on college readiness.

For adults, the Software Selection Service each month provides a new program chosen by the editors, for approximately half the list price.

All programs are sent on approval and may be returned if you don't like them. All are first-quality, top brand products.

MacUser
One year (12 issues), theoretically $27, but really $19.95 if you send in one of the little cards tucked into the magazine or get their promo in the mail. Canadians add $2. Other countries, add $12 for surface mail, $50 (ouch!) for airmail. Single issue $3.95 US, $4.95 Canada. U.S. funds only.

World's best computer magazine. Zippy writing, honest reviews, upbeat graphics, clever layout, useful MiniFinders section with reviews of hundreds of products you need to know about. Anti-editor John Dvorak tries to keep it all from degenerating into rank flattery of Apple and all its software hangers-on. Doug Clapp writes great sentence fragments. Like this. Easy to read. Some hate him for that; I don't. Sharon Zardetto Aker writes like me, or vice versa. I'm trying hard not to covet her job. More, lots more, all helpful.

Not one pompous word or incomprehensible article in this magazine, yet they cover everything available for the Macintosh. Amazing!

All *MacUser* needs to be perfect is an advertiser index that lists both companies AND products. I can't be the only one who forgets which company makes SuperDuperLaserPaint or the 500 meg Dodo Drive.

MacWorld
One year (12 issues) $30 US (really $24 with the subscription card). Add $6 for Canada and Mexico. Other countries, add $12 surface mail or $80 airmail.

Bland computer magazine written mainly by nonenthusiasts. Lots of arty white space. One issue featured an editorial that asked readers to protest Georgia's anti-sodomy law, because "many programmers are homosexuals" and thus sodomy innately must be an important computing cause. Mixed causes, mixed logic. Put out by the *PC World* crowd. Good ads, but save your subscription money, the same folks advertise in *MacUser*.

Microzine
$179 for school year postpaid includes 8 school-year issues and 4 programs per issue. Apple II family.

Scholastic Software, *Microzine's publisher*, says *Microzine* is "today's best-selling (by far!) instructional software." In other words, these programs-of-the-month are topnotch award-winners with a high wow factor.

Scholastic not only guarantees *Microzine*, but the promotional piece I received offered a free four-program Back to School disk.

Microzine boils down to four programs per issue for less than the price of one. The catch is, you have to pay up front. The good news is, you can cancel after receiving the first issue and still keep the freebies (presuming that promotion offer still stands).

Each issue of *Microzine* includes two disks (one main disk and one backup), a Student Handbook to get kids using the software right away and a Training Guide with reproducible activity sheets and other stuff beloved by teachers.

Microzine is specially designed to present thinking and computer skills along with curricular basics.

Teaching and Computers
New subscriber price, $17.95/6 issues.

Can you dig a magazine that calls itself "Electronic Lesson Plans"? (See, someone *does* read those card deck cards!) Scholastic, the big-time book and software people, put out this glossy magazine for K-8 classroom teachers. *Teaching and Computers* is designed to be *used,* if you can believe the card: pullout Activity Posters, punchout Task Cards, holiday and seasonal activities, lesson plans for all sorts of subjects, even classroom management ideas (you'd think it would be pretty easy to manage a classroom full of kids in front of video tubes). Plus, of course, software reviews and recommendations. Scholastic would like to reach out to parents; don't be intimidated by the classroom atmosphere. You get a 30-day cancellation privilege, so it won't hurt to check this one out.

DISCOUNT SOURCES AND CATALOGS

Business Computers of Peterborough

Good source for Apple software cheap. They advertise in *A+*.

Horne Book

Horne Book's prez asked me to mention that, along with Christian Reconstruction books and Mott's Classic Curriculum, he sells Lateral Technology's IBM clones. According to *PC Week* magazine, "Overall, [the LTX's] are very impressive technical achievements that have pushed the limits of XT architecture further than any product we've seen."

Long Associates

New venture plans to pool hardware and software orders from home schoolers and offer co-op pricing. In other words, deep discounts. We're looking at Apple hardware here, with software to follow. Write for info.

Mac Connection

Best source for discount hardware/software for the Macintosh. After enduring late shipments and nonshipments from other dealers (who first charge your credit card and then only ship when they feel like it), we believe Mac Connection is definitely worth the extra buck or two.

TAFHE
$5 membership fee.

Like Long Associates, TAFHE is a discount buyer of hardware and software for home schoolers. Unlike Long, TAFHE (which stands for Tutorial Aids for Home Educators) is a membership organization. You join, you get the price list and newsletter, you buy what you want.

TAFHE has buying contracts with virtually every major software publisher in the country, including the famous MECC (Minnesota Educational Computer Consortium), and several major hardware suppliers. A recent letter offered the Laser 128, an Apple compatible, for $395, a Zenith IBM clone, the Model 148-2 with two disk drives and monitor, for $949, and another IBM clone for $749.

COMPLETE SOFTWARE CATALOGS (MANY MACHINES)

Manna Computing Concepts

One-stop shopping for a huge variety of Christian computer products. Bible concordances and study tools. Bible computer games. Church accounting programs. Etc.

Scholastic, Inc.

Enormous color catalog of educational software for the classroom. Scholastic carries both their own software and other software that they recommend. These include all the best-known educational programs from such companies as The Learning Company, Random House, MECC, and Brøderbund. Terrific 30-day preview guarantee: you try it for 30 days with no risk. Every program comes with a backup disk and a replacement warranty.

Every program is reviewed at reasonable length; many have color screen shots. Programs are available for a variety of computers, not just Apple or IBM. Programs are not discounted, but with your order you receive a $20 certificate good on your next order.

Microzine back issues are available here at discount: $39.95 each versus the list price of $49.95.

A large, color Scope and Sequence Chart shows which programs are meant to cover which curricular areas.

Software Shuttle

If you already know what you want, you can get it at discount from Software Shuttle. Software Shuttle carries Apple, Atari, Commodore, and IBM software all in one catalog. Programs are listed by name, with retail price and Software Shuttle's list price. Some hardware and accessories also available.

AN APPLE TODAY . . . OR A LASER . . . OR AN IBM . . . ?

It wouldn't really be fair to put in all this info about educational computing without at least hinting which system we think is best value. The market changes constantly, so your best bet is to stay on top of it by subscribing to a few choice computer magazines. Even so, you can narrow down your hardware options by looking at some major differences between computer families (a family being the "original" computer and its clones).

The most essential thing for the average parent to consider when buying a computer is what software runs on it? Hackers who can write their own compilers and assemblers and read hex code dumps don't have to worry about software support, but the normal American who doesn't know what a compiler or assembler is and who thinks hex code is something Amish farmers put on their barns has to face facts and realize that any software he uses he will have to buy.

This being so, the field of sensible choices narrows down to the Big Five:

Apple or Laser 128 clone (forget the Franklin)
Commodore
IBM or clones
Atari
TRS-80 (Radio Shack)

These are the computers for which most educational software is written, in order of how much runs on each.

You can pick up some small-time computer (say a Texas Instruments model) for a rock-bottom price. This computer will have maybe twenty to fifty programs that run on it. So far it looks good. But what if you want a different kind of program that is not offered, or if you don't like the ones that are? It's just too bad. Big software companies don't put out versions for small-time computers. All the really excellent programs reviewed in the following chapters are only offered for the computers listed above.

If you're serious about using your computer for educational purposes, you had better stick with the Big Five.

But how do you choose which of the Big Five to buy?

At this point many people start thinking price. This can be a serious mistake. A computer is more than a toy; it is an expandable piece of equipment. Used rightly it can be one of your most powerful home tools or even launch you into an independent home business. If you are sure you will never want to write a book on your computer, or prepare tax returns, or hook into an electronic information service, or do any heavy statistical work, or use it for mass mailings, or any of a thousand other possible uses, then go ahead: buy cheap. But if you would like to keep your options open, there are other matters besides price to consider.

Atari and Commodore are the cheapest all-purpose computers for which a decent amount of educational software has been written. The reason we do not consider Atari and Commodore as good options for the home computer is that they are not very powerful or expandable. These computers are slow, compared to Apple or IBM clones. If you try to use them for serious number-crunching or word processing, you will see what we mean. Both Atari and Commodore were originally developed for playing arcade-style games, and although these companies have struggled to adapt their equipment to wider use, they are still just not a professional's choice. Also in the case of Commodore we have heard complaints about the hardware's reliability. A computer that keeps breaking down is not worth buying.

Eliminating Commodore and Atari leaves Apple, Mac, and IBM as the contenders. Among IBM clones, the Radio Shack computers are overpriced for their quality. They also have far less software support than either IBM or Apple.

So it's IBM clones or Apple. You can forget about the IBM PCjr. It was immediately labeled a dog upon its first entry into the market. We're talking about the IBM PC or clones versus an Apple //c, IIe, IIGS, or Macintosh (or any expanded version of these that might have appeared by the time you read this).

The IBM PC is a good business machine, and if you're primarily looking for business hardware and only secondarily considering it as an educational machine it's an OK investment. This also goes for the Apple Macintosh, a computer that really appeals to us for its ease of use and excellent graphics capabilities.

But if you're looking for an educational computer for your *young* children now, and only thinking about expanding into other applications sometime in the future, the Apple //c, IIe, or IIGS or a clone is your machine.

*(**NEWSFLASH!** At press time, Central Point Software had just unveiled the Laser 128EX, a machine three times faster than the Apple IIe or //c. Built-in 192K Ram (128K - User and 64K - Video) expandable to over one megabyte with its fully socketed AppleWorks-compatible RAM board. Built-in disk drive and interfaces for all normal peripherals, including serial and parallel printers, modem, mouse, joysticks, external 3 1/2 and 5 1/4" drives, and color RGB or monochrome monitor. Like other Laser products, it "performs like a top-of-the-line Apple, but is priced like a Commodore." Price: Just $499 (add $20 shipping and handling). Remember, this just buys you the CPU and internal disk drive. You'll have to purchase a monitor and the rest of your peripherals separately. Call Central Point Software at (503) 244-5782 for more info.)*

Almost everything educational for the elementary grades runs on Apple. Apple has sold more personal computers to the elementary school market than anyone else, and the software companies are aware of this.

The only reasonable Apple clone is the Laser 128 (and now, 128EX), sold by Central Point Software. At about half the price of an Apple IIe, it runs all Apple software and interfaces with most peripherals and add-ons.

The Apple //c is a non-expandable version of the IIe with adequate power to meet all normal applications. Its virtue has been a lower price and that it comes already set up. You don't have to know anything about what hardware cards you want to start running your //c. I wrote *The Big Book of Home Learning* on a //c.

The Apple IIe is expandable. The reason this computer is still around after so many years is that its farsighted inventors designed it to accommodate endless hardware updates. Our little IIe, which came with 128K of RAM (128,000+ bytes of usable memory), can as of this writing be upgraded to hold more than three million bytes of RAM. We could add on cards to make it run ten times faster, to produce stereo-quality synthesized voice or music, or to turn our home appliances on and off. In addition, we could add on external memory devices that hold an extra ten million bytes, and there's talk of mass memory in the trillions of bytes being soon available. It seems there is no limit to the speed and size of a little Apple.

Just out, the Apple IIGS (for Graphics and Sound) has zippy color, marvelous sound, and insufficient software. The latter will change as soon as developers get used to its Mac-like interface. This machine has real potential for some serious foreign language and music software, and will run most existing Apple software (so they say). You'll really want software specifically written for the GS, though, that makes use of its rich color and faster speed.

What about older children? Bill Bailey of TAFHE tells me that IBM clones are taking over in the high school market. The reason? Clone salesmen approach the schools with the notion that their students are going to have to use MS-DOS (the IBM operating system) in the real world, anyway, so how about some half-price IBM-compatible equipment for the office and a rebate on their classroom Apples? This argument is knocking the stuffing out of both IBM and Apple.

Meanwhile, back on the campus, Apple is wiping out college town dealers by offering huge discounts to colleges who buy Macs for their students. (So much for MS-DOS in the real world. Unless college doesn't count as the real world.) This strategy is supposed to prepare the students to keep using Macs in the business world. Our local Apple dealer tells me that his new Mac II's are being snapped up by large corporations, proving that now that Mac has the speed and memory as well as its superior desktop publishing capability, businesses will use it.

I love my Mac, like my Apple, and wish they were as cheap as the IBM clones. We currently run our home business and lay out catalogs, newspapers, and books on a Mac Plus and Mac II. The Mac also has great potential as an educational machine because of its pictorial interface (you point to what you want and click a button instead of typing in lines and code).

Unfortunately, the lovable Mac is not a clear pick, mainly because of higher price and less software. At the moment, Mac educational software is slim pickings, primarily because of the machine's smaller customer base. (I do review some of the best of it in this book and *The NEW Big Book*— see if you like what exists enough to live with a smaller selection.) Parents won't buy a Mac for the kids; they'll buy one for themselves and maybe let the kids play with it now and then. The lack of Mac clones prevents the price from dropping like IBM's.

So our advice to you is to

1) Choose your machine. Pick up some back issues of single-computer magazines: *PC World, MacUser, A+,* and so on. These will acquaint with what's new in hardware and software for the machines in question. You will get a feel for the machine's personality (like: IBM=pompous, Mac=innovative and brash). You will know what you want when you go shopping so the dealers can't put anything over on you. Most magazines are also loaded with ads from hungry discount dealers, who sell both hardware and software at bargain prices. You can then play these dealers against your local computer dealer. You want to buy hardware locally if possible, since you can then expect better support, but you don't want to pay outrageously large sums for the privilege of buying locally. Know the prices you can get at discount and haggle your local dealer down.

2) Choose your system. For games a color monitor is very nice, although many games can be played without one. Two disk drives are almost essential if you do any writing or number-crunching. A printer is necessary if you want to write on your computer (and you will). Don't buy a clunky, noisy letter-quality printer if you can possibly get by with one that delivers near-letter-quality print and speedy drafts and also prints graphics. Add-on memory is a luxury needed only by those who use their computer as a business tool and you can always pick it up later. (Note: If you get a Mac, though, you want at least a Mac Plus, since much new Mac software won't run, or runs like molasses, on the smaller machines.)

3) Know what you want.

• For an El Cheapo machine compatible with the most "serious" (e.g. boring) business software, and some educational stuff as well— Buy your IBM compatible.

• For the cheapest, faster machine that runs the most early grades software— Buy your Apple or LaserEX.

• For the most creative art, music, and writing programs (plus the possibility of serious desktop publishing and/or home business)— Buy your Mac.

CHAPTER SEVENTEEN

ENGINEERING AND INDUSTRIAL ARTS

E to the X, DY, DX
E to the X, DY
Secant, tangent, cosine, sine
Three point one four one five nine
Square root, cube root, log of PI
DisINTEGRATE them, RPI
Official school cheer of
Rensselaer Polytechnic Institute

I went to Rensselaer Polytechnic Institute, a school immortalized on the cover of *Sports Illustrated* when our football squad finally won their first game after the longest non-winning streak in USA history, and Bill went to MIT, a school justly proud of its world-class tiddlywinks team.

Obviously, engineering school is more than Big Football and dorm parties. First of all prospective students must cope with the (often well-deserved) nerd image. "I'm going to Whoopie Tech!" often translates as "Check me out for buck teeth and glasses." Plus there is the lack of big-time sports and a relatively lackluster social climate. Oh, and let's not forget the insane amount of homework assigned by sadistic profs whose attitude is, "If I can do it in an hour (after 30 years of practice), so can you."

Why does anyone go through this torture?

ENGINEERING FOR THE REST OF US

Good question. Future physicists and others who need multimillion-dollar lab equipment might see some reason to embed themselves for four or more years in engineering school. But today's seven-year-old has access to more lab and computing power than the average sixties E.E. grad. Heath/Zenith and Radio Shack, to name just two sources, have more hands-on engineering stuff than a university lab of twenty years ago.

Most of the time in engineering class the prof just ends up reading you the textbook, anyway. You should wait until you're 18 and pay $10,000 a year for this? Why not just amble down to the college bookstore, buy the books, and save $9,500 or so (plus meals, lodging, and student activity fees) a year?

O.K., not everyone can learn all he needs to know without the peer pressure of a classroom. But what about those who will never make it into the classroom in the first place? What about all those schoolkids, supersaturated with half-baked science and underdeveloped logic, left to stumble about in the real world without the faintest idea of how anything works? Why should All-American Know-How be reserved for a few with the money, time, and boredom-bearing ability to graduate from engineering school?

We think a basic understanding of engineering is

(1) Necessary for self-reliant daily life. Daily life is an endless succession of design problems— where to put a light, should we terrace the lawn before it all drops into the street, how can we figure out what is making that awful rattle in the washing machine, how to keep the neighborhood dogs out of our new veggie garden.

(2) Fun! Kids just naturally love to invent and build things. Why should we assume they outgrow this when they pass the tower-out-of-wood-blocks stage? Why should we assume *we* outgrew it?

ENGINEERING MEANS SOLVING PROBLEMS

Engineering is:

1) Defining your inputs— what goes into this device?

2) Defining the desired outputs— what is it supposed to do?

3) Listing your assumptions— what are your variables? What can go wrong, and what are you assuming will not go wrong? (Hint: Expect everything to go wrong!)

4) Designing the "black box" that turns your inputs into the outputs.

5) Finally, testing out the design to see if it works. This includes designing the tests.

As a mindset, engineering is the ability to look at a problem, dissect it without sentimentalism, concentrate on the desired result, and make allowances for real-world constraints. The boy who, wanting to play

Indian, whittles a tree branch into a bow and tests out different strings to see which works best, is really playing engineer. Other women had dreamed of an easier way to cook, but Lillian Gailbraith, the engineer, invented the efficiency kitchen because she broke down the problem into a series of questions and then answered those questions. People who simply fantasize about what they'd like to see someday, or whose proposed solutions would only work in some nonexistent Utopia, are not engineers.

INDUSTRIAL ARTS MAKES IT HAPPEN

Industrial arts is the conglomeration of skills necessary to make the engineer's designs happen. The carpenter swings his hammer, the mason his trowel and chisel, the welder his torch, the electrician his wire crimpers, and the plumber his wrench, and without them nothing would get built.

Robots neither build houses nor make house calls. Well into our foreseeable future, men and women will still need and want to put up their own curtain rods, make their own bookshelves, and fix their own or others' faucets. The industrial arts are really home arts that happen to be useful in other people's homes as well as your own.

OK, we know how to break it (a chair, a door, a light switch), but do we know how to make it? Following is a selection of the most useful books, projects, games, and tools for families who dare to learn how to make it on their own.

BOOKS ON ENGINEERING AND INDUSTRIAL ARTS

EDC

Usborne's Electronic World series: *Films & Special Effects, Audio and Radio, TV and Video,* $4.95 each or $12.95 for the combined hardbound *Usborne World of Electronics* volume. New Technology series: *Satellites & Space Stations, Robotics, Lasers, Information Revolution,* $5.95 each

or $12.96 for the combined hardbound *The New Technology* volume. Young Engineers series: *Superbikes, Supertrains, Supercars*, $4.95 each or $12.95 for the combined *Book of Speed* volume. *How Machines Work, How Things Began, Introduction to Electronics*, $5.95 each.

Absolutely terrific introductions to basic engineering and its applications, for preteens and up. Usborne, an English company represented in the USA by EDC, has the best, most colorful books around on almost any subject. Each page is artistically laid out with color pictures, diagrams, cutaway illustrations, captions, cartoons, and text to illustrate the principles discussed on that page. All is done with humor, and the information conveyed is actually interesting. The overall effect is that of a series of topnotch magazine pieces crossed with a comic book.

For the younger set, Usborne's *How Machines Work* and *How Things Began* are excellent. I should mention that *How Things Began* is a look at the history of inventions, not a treatise on origins!

Our sons, at the ages of five and six respectively, chose of their own free will to spend hours with the Usborne Electronic World series. After, that is, I had sneaked a peek at them myself. We hand out these books as prizes to our children for special accomplishments. 'Nuff said!

Mother's Bookshelf

How to and project books, all kinds. Books on how to make wooden toys for the tykes and how to build an earth-sheltered house for the whole family. Build your own tractor, rowing machine, family-sized storm shelter, wood-gas generator, wind-driven electrical generator, and on and on. *The Mother Earth News*, the magazine that runs this bookshelf, also carries lots of articles on how to do-it-yourself. They assume you know how to use tools and how to follow plans.

Owner Builder Publications
The Work Book, The Owner-Builder and the Code. Write for latest prices.

Hear now my confession. Long, long ago—maybe two years ago—I wrote to some publishers asking for review copies of their books for a book I was writing about how to do everything at home. That book contained one chapter on home education. The chapter grew and grew. It swallowed the book. It became *The Big Book of Home Learning*.

Problem was, not every book I had asked for fit into *The Big Book*. Some, in short, got left out. My conscience bothered me about this, all the more since I had lost my list of publisher addresses and couldn't even return some of the books. But, aha, there was a solution! Stick 'em all in *The Next Book*. Oh, dear, depression again: I still didn't have those publisher addresses!

I was especially sorry that I would not be able to review Ken Kern's book, *The Owner-Builder and the Code*, sent to me way back when by his wife. Ken and his coauthors, members of a hippie community in (where else?) southern California, had run up against the local building code bureaucracy as they attempted to provide themselves with houses built by their own sweat on their own land. The book not only traces this struggle, but raises some valid questions about to what extent the codes help us and to what extent they simply prevent human beings from living in houses. Ken and his fellow authors also detail ways some of their more imaginative friends around the USA have outwitted or avoided the codes. (And before you condemn them for putting an unapproved roof over their heads—do *you* rush to inform City Hall every time you slap up a partition in your basement?)

The good news is that today I found the address of Owner Builder Publications tucked into a Ten Speed Press book. Jubilation! Now I can also mention Kern and Turner's *The Work Book: The Politics of Building Your Own Home.* Unique among home construction books, this one gets into the psychology and politics of building. Avoid alienating your spouse, kids, and neighbors by reading it first. I never got a review copy of this one but do remember its writeup in an old edition of *The Whole Earth Catalog.* So now I wrote one more review than I had to. Are we even, Ken?

Rodale Press

Another source for how to and project books galore. Rodale Press, the publisher of *Rodale's Organic Gardening* and a magazine on house design and construction, among other ventures, has a friendly, back-to-nature style. Their books are user-friendly; the authors generally lead you by the hand rather than assume you already are a technical whiz. Rodale also publishes numerous books just for how-to beginners.

Ten Speed Press
Before You Build, Build Your Own House.

For someone who has never built a house, I surely spend enough time reading books about how to do it! There's something satisfying about imagining one's dream house: digging the foundation, pouring the cement, choosing and rechoosing the style and shape, raising the structure and clothing it graciously, and adding the finishing touches.

Perhaps the best introduction to the homebuilding arts is Ten Speed Press's *Before You Build* and *Build Your Own House,* two oversized, illustrated quality paperbacks.

Before You Build helps you plan realistically. A combination of text and workbook, Before You Build covers buying the land or lot, choosing the site, solar heating and cooling, water systems, power and phone, driveways, roads, and bridges, waste systems, permits, codes and inspections, insurance, financing, estimating, inner resources, tools, and types of construction. The introduction is by Ken Kern, author of *The Work Book* and *The Owner-Builder and the Code.* Ken knows the ins and outs of trying to build oneself a dwelling in the face of bureaucrats whose mission is to discourage the poor from building at all. The rest of the book carries out this innovative, mother-earthy flavor, with both useful and far-out suggestions. Example: the caption under a really strange photo reads, "A house I built from a large wine barrel. Six inches of wine was left in it to create a wine cellar." Caught me by surprise, resting as it did amid pix of log and stone houses and A-frames.

Build Your Own House leads you through the building process, copiously illustrating and explaining each step. This is a real course on house construction, complete with photos, worksheets, instructions, and resource lists. You'll appreciate what goes into producing the family castle a whole lot more after living a while with these books.

Time Life Books

Source for many series of "how-to" books sold on the easy payment plan. How to Fix Appliances, for example. Blow-by-blow descriptions of the innards of our household friends. "No, thanks," I told the friendly saleslady, "we have Sears three-year warranties on our refrigerator, washer, and dryer." It's not that we disdain fixing things with our own hands, but sad experience teaches that you spend five minutes fixing and five hours visiting every hardware store in town searching for that one essential little part. The series might be useful if you live over a hardware store. Time-Life also has/had a series on how to redesign your house room-by-room, and lots of others.

CONSTRUCTION KITS AND GAMES

You remember the hours of fun you had with your good ol' Erector set. How dazzled you were when the Christmas wrappings were torn off and it sat revealed in all its glory! The little wheels you could stick onto axles would really turn. Imagine! And although the cheap little tin all-purpose widget that came with the set was quickly lost, Dad's tools were quickly found to work even better. The happy hours flew by as you built racing cars and space robots.

Or perhaps you were a Lincoln Logs fan. How you pestered for more kits so you could build bigger and better log houses and bigger and better log villages! You hated having to take them apart and zealously guarded your creations from your kid brothers and sisters.

These classic toys of our youth have been joined by an array of proto-engineering devices that would have made Leonardo da Vinci green with envy. No longer must the space robot suffer the indignations of hand-propulsion; it has a motor. Today's construction kit can walk and soon will talk. Some get chummy with your computer. This is serious design material, folks!

Ampersand Press
AC/DC, $7.95. Add $1.50 shipping.

The neatest introduction to the study of electricity that I've seen, Ampersand's *AC/DC Electric Circuit Game* is played with a deck of special cards. Cards depict energy sources, wires, switches, energy users, and fuses. The object of the game is to construct workable circuits. Players may get "shocked" or "shorted," so watch out! You can't help but learn the rudiments of electricity playing *AC/DC*. I wish someone had given me this game before I went to engineering school (but then, it probably hadn't been invented way back then!).

fishertechnik

No, that's not a typo; fishertechnik is spelled with a small "f." This German company has the highest quality serious engineering construction kits around. See the Timberdoodle review.

Legos

Lego's new Technick kits strongly resemble a fishertechnik knockoff. Each item nestles in its own styrofoam niche in the cardboard box. You get the usual gears, axles, caterpillar tread, and other widgets necessary to make the helicopters and planes (they don't really fly, but the propellers spin), cars, cranes, and so on pictured in the wordless instruction book.

OWI Inc.

While walking in the Heath/Zenith shop one day, in the merry, muggy month of August, we saw to our surprise a display of robot kits. Not just any old robot kits, mind you, but "educational electronic robot kits." Curiosity piqued, I borrowed the Heath/Zenith folks' one and only brochure, from which even now here come the pertinent facts.

OWI's line of MOVIT kits is a series of computerized, logic-controlled battery robot kits designed to teach the basic principles of robotic sensing and locomotion. Each comes with preassembled PC boards, hardware, and mechanical-drive systems. You only need basic hand tools to put these little critters together, and most little human critters over the age of ten are supposed to be able to handle the job. Each robot uses a different type of movement or has a different sensor. Mr. Bootsman, for example, has six insectlike legs, two-speed movement, and a control box. He can run or walk forward or backwards, or even turn in circles. You can program him, or use the wired control to make him play slow-mo soccer, etc. The kits are cute as all getout, that is, not cuddly-fuzzy-animal cute but neat-little-buckets-of-gears cute. Only problem is you will want to collect them all.

Play-Jour

The Capsela kits from Play-Jour feature little see-through capsules containing the gears, motors, et. al. You attach the capsules in various configurations to produce motorcars, cranes, and all sorts of other devices that really move. With care, you can also make floating devices that paddle around in the bathtub, since the capsules are more or less waterproof.

For classroom teachers, Play-Jour now offers a 25 lesson illustrated teacher manual based on the Capsela system and written by Dr. Clifford Swartz. You get teacher overviews, notes, student hand-out masters, classroom management suggestions, and additional projects.

Timberdoodle

fishertechnik sets go beyond Capsela in the variety of widgets you can make and the variety of sets available. fishertechnik is definitely the Rolls Royce. You can build *anything* with enough of these interconnectable sets. The pieces are scaled-down versions of those used in actual industry production lines, which fishertechnik also happens to make. The good folks at Timberdoodle carry the entire fishertechnik line at the best prices around— even the robotics kit that hooks up to your trusty Apple computer.

Bill and the boys spent an enthralled couple of weeks testing out one of fishertechnik's robotics kits. The interface to the Apple IIE hooks into the game port on the motherboard. The kit we were testing had four on/off switched inputs, two rheostat inputs, and three on/off switched outputs— enough to run two motors and an electromagnet for picking up objects. The software provided with the set uses a Basic-like language to program your robot. The model they built solved King Tut's pyramid. Watching the model work was well worth the time it took to build it.

You'll hate yourself if you don't send for their brochure!

TOOLS AND WIDGETS

Global Specialties

Breadboards and electronic testing stuff. Not exciting, but essential if you're into serious electronics.

Jerryco

A course in how to write witty copy crossed with an enormous selection of surplus tools, leftover electronic parts, and lab supplies only an inventor could love. Jerryco's catalog suggests zany uses for the surplus stuff that is their stock in trade, but most (well, let's be honest, some) of their goods find a natural home in the tinkerer's lab.

Learning Things, Inc.
Classroom tool kit, $149.50. Kit items available separately.

Lots and lots of tools, accessories, and construction kits for children. The classroom kit includes a 20-inch hand saw, 13 ounce hammer, hand drill with three drill bits, small saw, four-texture file, wire cutter, blade screwdriver, Phillips screwdriver, slip-joint pliers, two C-clamps, two spring clamps, a six-foot tape measure, heavy duty extension cord, three-hole electrical adapter, sharpening stone, plastic bottle of white glue, roll of twine, and a wooden tool box. Also power tools and industrial arts text books. Plus lots of other goodies, mentioned in the next section.

Toad's Tools

Kid-sized but serious tools. Prices are "reasonable," e.g., $15 for a ten-ounce hammer and $4.40 for a set of three screwdrivers. This is not your typical made-in-Taiwan tinware.

The Toad's Tools basic set, which includes anything a young carpenter could ever need except power tools, presently goes for $135 plus shipping. All items are available separately. All items, except normal replacement parts like saw blades, carry an unconditional lifetime replacement guarantee.

PROJECTS

AIMS Educational Foundation
Project SETUP books, $10.95 each.

AIMS stands for Activities Integrating Math and Science. SETUP is the acronym for Software Evaluation and Testing Utilities. Are you asleep yet? Forgive me for this boring introduction. I wanted to be sure we knew what we were talking about.

All right. The AIMS Education Foundation wants to help you make full use of your best educational software. Integrate it into the real world. Put it into practice. Project SETUP is about developing supplemental classroom materials that play off the best software packages. Like *Rocky's Boots, Robot Odyssey* (both reviewed below), *The Seven Cities of Gold,* and *Agent USA.* These last two programs have nothing to do with engineering, so we'll skip them for now (but remember them when you're looking at history and geography!).

Project SETUP's *Rocky's Circuits* lets students construct the logic gates used in *Rocky's Boots,* using inexpensive and easy-to-locate materials; provides needed background info for the teacher; and includes lots of follow-up activities.

SETUP's *Robot Odyssey* book gives solutions for the program's problems, maze maps, and elementary chip construction techniques, plus other classroom fare.

Burt Harrison & Company, Inc.
Batteries and Bulbs Mini Kit **with activity book, $24.95. Book alone, $6.50. $3 shipping and handling.**

Burt has lots of scientific and engineerish stuff. Innovative, creative stuff. Best of all is the *Batteries and Bulbs Mini Kit* (a larger kit is available for schools). Suggested for children aged eight to twelve, but also usable for impatient four- to seven-year-olds with parental supervision, the kit is a whole pile of materials including (believe it or not) four batteries! Now when's the last time you ever saw a suppler include batteries with *anything*? Kids not only perform experiments, but come to understand the basic principles of electricity and magnetism while making a flashlight, galvanometer, electromagnet, telegraph key, and buzzer. The activity book reveals all, and if our children's reaction means anything, yours would love it, too. Small fry need adult help, of course.

Fiberfab, International

I know you just can't live without your own racing car body to upgrade your basic VW or Ford chassis. Talk about family projects! Fiberfab doesn't think I would really review their product, and I know they are right, which is why I didn't ask for a sample. Thought you'd like to know about it all the same.

Heathkit

For the novice hobbyist or serious student of electronics, Heathkit has both home-study courses and of course its famous kits. Build your own oscilloscope, or TV, or IBM PC-compatible computer (Heath swears it's faster than the original). You won't save all that much money, but it's great experience.

Learning Things, Inc.

This is it—your definitive source for engineering and science gear, projects, and experiments. The black and white catalog has all the usual stuff: fiber optics, gyroscopes, mineral collections, scales, microscopes, etc. But how about the kits for building models of molecular, atomic, and crystal structures (from $5 to $17.50)? Tetrahedral clusters? Rhomblocks? The papermaking kit and book? Now, the topper. Cardboard carpentry! Yes, you heard it here first. Learning Things, Inc. has two whole pages of cardboard carpentry tool kits, projects, accessories, and of course the cardboard.

COMPUTER GAMES

Learning Company
Rocky's Boots, Robot Odyssey, Think Quick!, $49.95 each. Apple II family, IBM. *Rocky's Boots* also runs on Commodore 64K.

These programs have the same universe-of-rooms format as the *Gertrude* series reviewed in the Logic chapter. They also let you pick up and carry around items on your screen. But with these programs, you are not only solving problems, but designing and building.

Rocky's Boots, after guiding you through an excellent tutorial, has you building machines with AND, NOT, and OR gates, plus assorted flipflops, clackers, clocks, and delays. These are elements of computer circuit design that allow you to turn electricity on and off depending on what kind of input you give them. For example, a NOT gate connected in the program to a blue sensor will be off if a blue object touches the sensor and on if no blue object is touching it. This may sound like *Rocky's Boots* gets into electrical engineering, which it does. But these logical design strategies are useful in all kinds of reasoning. You can practically feel your brain growing as you think through these problems.

Such arcane concepts aside, *Rocky's Boots* is fun to play. You get to drag components around, hook them up, and disconnect them. You turn on machines and turn them off. The intellectual challenge is stimulating, and the process itself is enjoyable. "Let's see. I need to select blue diamonds and crosses. Let's get a blue sensor and some AND gates . . . "

Robot Odyssey takes *Rocky's Boots* one step further. You are not only designing little circuits, but programming robots to help you escape from the devious maze of Robotropolis. You can test robots out in the Innovation Lab and save your spot in the game. Each level requires more complex programming, and eventually you'll be burning chips that contain chips that contain chips full of your original circuits. Figure on several months of steady play to get out of Robotropolis. You won't outgrow this program in a hurry.

Think Quick!, reviewed at length in the Logic chapter, lets you create your own castle mazes, construct simple logic puzzles, and tackle the original Castle of Mystikar. Of the three, *Think Quick!* has the greatest play value. You can believe the ads that say it will become a child's favorite program.

Learning Technologies
All programs $19.95; includes certificate for free Learning Kit. Apple II family and Commodore 64/128.

Learning Technologies has several fine programs that develop spatial skills. *Sliding Block* is based on those puzzles our Aunt Rosies gave us when we were young. They came with one empty spot and little interlocking pieces that you slid around until the correct picture or pattern emerged. The computer version includes much tougher levels

(I don't think I will ever solve the 25-piece puzzles) and several different puzzles. Our childhood hand-held versions didn't have color graphics or rocket ships that blasted off when put together, either, both of which features enhance the computer game.

Pipeline is another spatial skills game. You hook together different types of pipe to feed water to objects that need it. The game has three levels of play and you can set yourself a time deadline, making it challenging enough for any age. This game is a favorite at our house.

Sunburst

The Factory, Super Factory, $59 each for school edition or $177 for 10-disk Lab Pack. Apple II family, IBM PC, PCjr, Tandy 1000. Factory also available for Commodore and TRS-80 Color Computer. *Factory Workbook* (170 pages), $25.

The Factory is one of my favorites. You are in charge of a factory with three types of machine. They can rotate, drill, or draw a stripe down a piece of stock. Each of these operations has variations (round or square holes to drill, rotations of different angles, different numbers of stripes of different widths). You can create an assembly line of up to eight machines. Put in the stock and see what you made. Then let a friend try to duplicate it! You can ask the computer for a finished piece of stock, and try to duplicate it yourself. This is a great workout for spatial skills which would be impossible to practice on paper.

Sunburst also has a new *Super Factory* program that processes a cube instead of a flat disk.

The School Editions of these programs come with teacher's guides. In addition, Sunburst has developed a *Factory Workbook* with exercises based on the *Factory* program.

World Book Discovery
How Things Work

How Things Work is supposed to introduce your kids to the four basic machines: wheel and axle, lever and fulcrum, pulley, and inclined plane. The program presents simple problems and asks what machine you would use to solve the problem. The tutorial explains how to use each machine. Good concept, bad execution. Example: the program shows a man trying to lift another man. Sweat, strain, poop out. The man then uses a lever to lift the man easily. But, the lever has the fulcrum right in the middle! This means that its mechanical advantage is one, and that it takes exactly as much force to lift a weight with that lever as if you were lifting it directly. The same thing happens with the pulley setup. The accompanying user's info and activity guide takes the edge off this problem, explaining the concepts more accurately. The activities in this booklet are more kid-appealing than those on the screen, which move too slowly, according to our kid testers.

HOME BUSINESS

CHAPTER EIGHTEEN

HOME SKILLS

Home economics has fallen on hard times. You remember our junior high school courses on housecleaning, nutrition, cooking, and sewing. Well, some people have decided that children should not be "forced" to perform "distasteful chores" such as taking out the trash or doing the dishes. To them, life at home until age 18 should be an idyllic time to lounge on the furniture while Dad does 100 percent of the cooking and cleaning and picks up all the toys and lugs out 100 percent of the trash— since Mom shouldn't be "forced" to do those "distasteful chores" either. If Junior gets a sweaty job in the supermarket hauling boxes that's OK, but at home nobody should expect him to lift a finger.

This attitude that household work is *bad* for children is ultimately both unrealistic and unhelpful. Unrealistic, because children, just like adults, truly enjoy the feeling of success that can only be obtained from a job well done that needed doing, and nothing needs doing as much as fixing up one's daily environment. Unhelpful, because sooner or later these children will be "forced" by life itself to take care of a home of their own.

The character and skills gained by children who know how to cook, clean, and sew will not only make the home a more pleasant place, but enrich their future homes as well.

MAKING CHORES PLEASANT

Having said all that, let us share a few of our family's Home Ec tips with you. If you want your children to actually enjoy and become expert at their home duties, it helps to

1) Carefully explain each step of the job. Then let your youngster try it with you helping on the tough spots.

2) Repeat step one again.

3) And again.

4) In short, don't expect a one-time-lecture to do it all.

5) Count on inspecting their work forever. Everyone loves praise for a job well done, and everyone profits from immediate feedback and suggestions on how to improve a less-than-perfect job.

6) Also count on helping out every now and then, just to show that you're not dumping an unwanted job on the child.

7) Some people give allowances regardless of what the child does. We consider it smarter to pay a child for his work at a reasonable rate (assuming the family can afford it). As the Bible says, "The worker is worthy of his hire." What would it cost you to hire an outsider to do the floors weekly, or wash the dishes, or mow the lawn? Pay less than market wage at first (after all, you are training your youngster for free) and try to work up to market rate. This allows the child to take real pride in his work, since you value it highly yourself.

8) Important Tip: *Give a bonus for work done with a cheerful attitude.* I promise you, this will make a real difference!

Children pick up their parents' attitudes towards work. It really pays to avoid negative comments and grumbling about your own chores. Instead, try to concentrate on the results. Take time to enjoy the clean floor, the scent of the freshly-baked bread, the line of clean damp sheets snapping in the breeze. Share with your children this artistic way of looking at the domestic arts. It worked for Tom Sawyer and it can work for you!

HOUSEWORK FOR KIDS

Home Life
Who Says It's a Woman's Job to Clean, **$5.95. Don Aslett's** *Is There Life After Housework?* **video seminar, $29.95. Add 10% shipping.**

You want your kids excited about cleaning and doing a professional job? Think it can never happen? Think again! Don Aslett, the cleaning man profiled in Chapter 3, has produced a series of books on housecleaning that both educate and motivate. Of these, the most suitable for children is *Who Says It's a Woman's Job to Clean:* not because of the title but because this book, designed to ease recalcitrant hubbies into the cleaning force, is so simple and so well illustrated with numerous clever cartoons that even a child can understand it. Believe it or not, we frequently find our son Joseph reading it. And the whole

family will enjoy Don Aslett's video, in which he combines comic patter with classy cleaning skills. If you think cleaning lacks style, watch this video and learn better! Our kids love the toilet humor (really, it's *clean* toilet humor), and they can't wait to clean windows, vacuum, and wash walls just like Don.

Housework, Inc.

You're going to love me for this one. At last, a source for professional cleaning tools and supplies! Everything from squeegees for your windows and floors to concentrated cleaning supplies (you only need four kinds to do everything in your house). Mops, buckets, sponges, lambswool dusters, dusting cloths, and even the stuff you need to seal your concrete basement floor are all covered in this catalog put out by (who else?) Don Aslett. Save time and aggravation— get what you need to do it right. Speedy service, good prices.

Montessori Services

And for the two- to seven-year-old set: Montessori Services carries kid-sized household tools. Mops, brooms, dustpans, baking equipment, and so on, all sized for little hands. Good quality, not like that discount store stuff. Montessori schools shop from this catalog, so if it will hold up for their classes of kids, it should hold up for yours.

COOKBOOKS FOR KIDS

EDC
First Cookbook series, $5.95 each.

A team of truly little cooks (about teaspoon size) lead your children through the basics of cookery with this series of first cookbooks from England. *Hot Things* covers simple meals like omelets along with a few more challenging adventures. *Sweet Things* is for sugar fiends, and *Party Things*, even more so. The illustrations are colorful, instructive, and charming. The books are printed on easy-wipe laminated card stock with stay-open spiral bindings. Fun!

Alfred A. Knopf, Inc.

If you're looking for an introduction to grown-up cooking, the classic *Fanny Farmer Cookbook,* while not intended for children, does include a sizeable amount of explanations of cooking terminology and techniques. The recipes, often introduced (one might even say "reviewed") with little comments, leave nothing to chance and are generally not complex. The book even explains how to cook hot dogs three ways. How's that for complete?

R & E Publishers

If you really want to get fancy with *educational* cooking— *Learning With Cooking: A Cooking Program for Children Two to Ten* is for you. This large, spiral-bound book covers how to teach concepts through cooking, four different approaches to a cooking program, how to organize and finance a cooking program (no problem for you at home!), recipes for different age groups, "parent-initiated cooking experiences," and all sorts of recipes. The book is salted with humor and experience:

> Try to overcome your own feelings of personal likes and dislikes and present the food in a matter-of-fact way. If a child says, "I don't want to eat it," or, "I don't like that," you can say, "You don't have to eat it, just help us fix it for someone else. I like it." . . . You might be amazed when a child who has already committed himself to, "I can't stand it!" will then eat the repulsive food as he sits at the eating table watching other children and the adult eat this "awful stuff." He might taste, even eat three helpings of this terrible food *when he has the choice.*

You might call *Learning Through Cooking* a child psychology of cooking mixed with teaching techniques and a lot of info. With six

(count 'em) indexes and a bibliography, there's a whole lot of bakin' going on.

Sycamore Tree

Sycamore Tree's catalog has a decent little section on Cooking and Nutrition. Selections: *The Science Cookbook* ($8.95 for cooking experiences with an emphasis on the underlying scientific principles), *Good For Me* ($7.95), *Super Snacks* ($3.95— see below), *The Super Food Cookbook for Kids* ($3.95), *Children's Cookery Naturally* ($4.50), *Food for Your Health and Efficiency* ($10.95), *The Vegetarian Child* ($12), and *Little Workers in the Kitchen* ($3.95). As you can see, Sycamore Tree emphasizes sugarless and meatless cooking as well as simple recipes.

Warren Publishing Company/Totline Press
Super Snacks, $4.50.

You might be wondering about kid's cookbooks that concentrate on sugary goo. "Isn't there more to life than dental decay?" Yes, Virginia, there is. One sure antidote to the gloppy goo set is *Super Snacks* by Jean Warren, a compendium of seasonal, sugarless snacks that also contain no honey or sweeteners of any kind. Designed primarily for daycare centers, the book is laid out month-by-month, with easy recipes and inviting graphics on each page. Fruit is the stand-in for other sweeteners in the sweet recipes like Egg Nog and Rice Pudding. You get almost 60 pages of popular recipes, and an index. No spiral binding, unfortunately.

DRESSMAKING AND SEWING

EDC
Knitting, Making Clothes, $4.95 each. Beginner's Guide to Sewing and Knitting, $2.95.

The Usborne series from England, published in the USA by EDC, has recently added a guide to knitting and a guide to making clothes. Like other Usborne books, these colorful, large (but not thick) glossy paperbacks teach technical terms and techniques in an inventive cartoon style. Each book contains several projects so the novice sewer or knitter can put theory into practice. The *Guide to Knitting* and *Guide to Making Clothes* are designed for young teens on up.

Even more simply, the *Beginner's Guide to Sewing and Knitting* presents the basics for 10-year-olds and above.

ORGANIZATIONAL HELPS

Household work is important. But the tendency has been to give the homeworker no tools and tell her, "Do a good job!" Housewives are expected to keep track of library books, important telephone calls, major maintenance needs, and their children's education on little slips of paper or notes scribbled on the backs of envelopes. No wonder we feel disorganized and unrespected!

A professional job requires professional tools, and one of those tools is an organizational system. If you have to manage a physical plant (your home), train other people (your children), serve the community (volunteer work and hospitality), and perhaps on top of these even conduct a business operation, however small, in your home, you'd better be organized.

Children who grow up accustomed to organization will be more productive as adults. As you get organized, keep in mind that your children, ultimately, should learn to keep and be accountable for their own organizing system. Now all we need is for some enterprising soul out there to come out with a children's organizer!

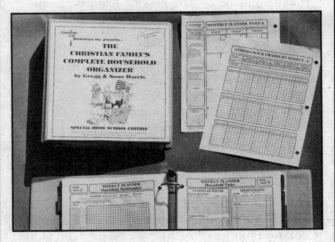

Christian Life Workshops, Inc.
The Home School Family's Complete Household Organizer by Gregg and Sono Harris. **250 pages, with divider tabs in 3-ring binder. $29.50 postpaid.**

CLW's extremely complete organizer has a system of major and minor planning keys that allows you to jot only key references on the month-at-a-glance or weekly planner sections. Details are recorded only once, on the Planning/Record sheets.

Now, what do you get? After an inspiring introductory article on the adventure of family ministry, there are 11 tabbed sections. Each section includes blue Master Copies (you're supposed to store and save these), and where applicable some white copies for your first year's use.

Let's look at these one by one.

1) The Monthly Planner. Each month covers two sides of the sheet: Sunday through Tuesday, plus a column listing the Planning Keys, on one side, and the rest of each week on the other. There's also a section for Notes and Events to Plan. At the end of this section are five Notes to Remember pages, cross-keyed

back to the Monthly Planner pages.

2) The Weekly Planner. Fifty-two sheets. One side covers Phone Calls to Make and Letters to Write, Things To Do (broken down by personal, home school, business, hospitality, and civil influence), Appointments (by day: includes a space for a Bible text), a very complete Household Maintenance chart that gives you an open-ended list of possible maintenance activities for each location plus codes that tell you at a glance whether the job is assigned or done, Projects to Complete, Items to Obtain, and Projects to Plan.

3) Personal Records. This includes master sheets only for personal/family Bible Study, sermon recording, personal study recording, an Idea Keeper, reading list, and Reading Review sheet. The latter would be quite helpful to any budding author or speaker, since it gives you room to record strong passages to remember, quotable quotes, and bibliographic references, plus your thoughts about the book. You photocopy as many of each of these as you find helpful.

4) Household Management. Again, master sheets only. The Household Profile Sheet is a place to write down important facts like your passport numbers; vehicle make, ID, and license numbers; children's birthdates, blood types, social security and driver's license numbers; where to find your insurance policies, what each policy number is and who your agent is; bank information; and emergency contacts. The Daily Checklist holds kids accountable for their hygiene, devotions, and personal and family chores. You're going to want to make a lot of copies of this sheet! You also get a Weekly Menu Planner with a clip-off shopping list, a very complete Babysitting Instructions sheet, a Recreation Planner (this sheet is my idea of being overorganized!), Lending Library Book Marks sheet, and Borrowing/Lending Record.

5) Home Schooling Plans and Records. Forty pages of Weekly Lesson Plan sheets. Each has room for basic comments, six subjects (you could squeeze in seven kids under each subject), and lesson planning codes down the side so you can condense your info into the smallest possible space. This section also includes eight Quarterly Attendance and Grades by Subject sheets.

6) Home School Helps. Another section with Master Pages only. Some of these sheets are helpful, some are more work than they are worth. Quite helpful is the Weekly Assignments sheet— copy up bunches of these and use them to help your children form independent study habits.

7) Hospitality. Master Pages only. The Bed & Breakfast Planning Record is the most useful of these six planning sheets.

8) Family Restoration International. Three Master Pages planning sheets.

9) Family Business. Six Master Pages. One page records names, addresses, and phone numbers of advisors and professionals. There is also an Estate Net Worth Worksheet (find out the sorry truth!), a Household Budget Planner, Auto Maintenance Record, and a Record of Generosity. The Home Business Venture Planning/Report Sheet works better as a take-off point than a sheet to fill out.

10) Civil Influence. Five Master Pages. The most useful ones here are the Prayer List for Those in Authority and the sheet for you to fill out with political and media contacts.

11) The Directory. Two Master Pages. Your basic name/address/phone number sheets.

The organizer comes in a three-ring binder, complete with a full year's worth of materials. You can use it practically forever, because every buyer has permission to reproduce the entire organizer for personal use only for the rest of his life. At year's end, just pop the entire year's organizer in an envelope and there are your school records for the year in easy-to-find order. Use your Copy Masters to reproduce the new year's sheets, click them into your binder, and you're ready to roll again.

Notice that the CLW organizer does provide schedule and chore sheets for the children, making it a true household (not just parent) organizer. Also, because it is reproducible, large families will have enough sheets for everyone.

This organizing system takes some time to master— learning the codes for the planning keys and what goes where. Frankly, some parts are overorganized, but if you just toss those sheets you don't need you won't be overwhelmed with guilt for not filling them out.

I also wouldn't kill myself cross-indexing *everything* to the schedule sheets.

Once you cut the organizer down to size this way you wind up with a useful planning tool that covers many areas others don't. CLW promises you will like it or you get your money back.

Reliable Corporation

Reliable is the office supply company with whom we do most of our business. Besides a terrific assortment of inexpensive time-minding equipment (average price of a monthly planner ranges from $2-$5) and project planning charts (we have one on our study wall), Reliable also carries all the paper, pencils, lamps, desks, chairs, file cabinets, index cards, flip-top files, and so on, that you are ever likely to need— all at deep discounts. If you'd like to *really* get organized, Reliable has the stuff.

Marilyn Rockett
Complete Time Minder™ kit, includes binder, $24.95. Refill package, $17.95, only available to kit buyers.

Probably the easiest-to-use organizer for home schooling families who like to keep it simple is Marilyn Rockett's Time Minder™. Alpha Omega Publications is already carrying this attractive organizer, so you can see it's no amateur effort.

The Time Minder™ includes four sections, all tabbed on the side for easy reference. Section 1, Long-Range Planning, includes the year-at-a-glance calendar, on which you can mark your school year and holidays using the little codes at the bottom of the page. On the back of the calendar is a place to mark special occasions. The second form, the Year Beginning Evaluation, includes four pages for four individual family members. On the flip side of this form is the Year Ending Evaluation. Next come the goal-setting pages, four sheets with room for four goals on each. Last in this

section is the Curriculum Plan and Info sheet. Just as in CLW's organizer, this is a place to make notes and write addresses of suppliers you are thinking of using.

Section 2, Schedule, is your home organizer. On the first form you write down everything you need to schedule, broken down into daily, weekly, semimonthly, monthly, quarterly, and annual. On the flip side is your weekly schedule form. Next comes the Monthly Planner: 12 sides of paper marked with days but not dates. To Do Today, perhaps the most useful form of all, has one unnamed column and one for meals. One sheet covers one week, and you get enough pages for a year. You get a priority column and a check-off column as well. A handy snap-out ruler/tab can be used to mark your place. Last comes four pages of Holiday Planning sheets.

Section 3, School, has a flexible weekly lesson planner (you define the squares however best suits you), Grade Summary pages, Testing forms, Books Read pages, Field Trip Plans, and Special Projects pages.

The last section is a combination address and phone directory and four-year Christmas card record, plus a People and Resources section.

My one big complaint is the four-children-or-less-per-family assumed throughout the Time Minder™. Home schoolers tend to have larger families than the general population, and forms for us should be designed with this in mind. This suggestion most affects the Weekly Lesson Planner (only enough sheets for four children) and the Goal/Evaluation sheets. Could extra sets of these perhaps be sold separately? Also, there ought to be more basic scheduling sheets (at least 10 of the Things to Schedule/Weekly Schedule form) to allow you to regroup frequently during the year. No way in the world would a single weekly schedule last us year-round. Vacation periods and summertime follow different schedules than our school year. Special family projects also require much reshuffling and rescheduling.

All that aside, this planner is easy to use and easy to customize, for the limited areas it covers.

CHAPTER NINETEEN

BUSINESS SKILLS

At present, business magazines and the business culture heavily promote business-as-war. Their hero is the man (it's usually a man) who succeeds in wiping out the competition and swallowing as many other companies as possible. You might call this outlook, "Bloated Is Beautiful." In contrast, the home business movement is largely made up of people (women and men) who just want to make their family a living and supply some fellow beings' needs. These agree with the Bible when it says, "Woe to those who add house to house and field to field until they dwell alone in the midst of the land." Home business owners might compete with others on the basis of quality or service, but have no cutthroat yearnings after an empire of their own.

Does modern education prepare each of us for the opportunity to have our own business? Sadly, no. We are treated to units on "careers" which promote the idea of lifelong servitude. Working for oneself is never covered as even an option, let alone as the desirable outcome of years of training under others. We are not taught how to price products, how to design displays, how to buy or how to sell. Children in public school are shown how to fill out welfare applications; are they told how to file a Fictitious Name Statement or incorporation papers? They are given lessons on How to Apply For a Job; are they taught how to interview prospective employees for their own company?

Perhaps the greatest lesson I have learned from our own home business is appreciation for the amount of work and dedication that goes into even the smallest business. Whenever we go for a ride in the car I am almost overwhelmed, as I look out at the rows of shops, by the thought of how much hope and work went into even the smallest storefront.

You *can* start your own business. But you need training. The reason small businesses fail is, more often than not, a lack of business savvy coupled with unjustified debt. The debt you can avoid by growing a bit slower; the savvy you can find below.

HOME BUSINESS BOOKS

EDC
 The Usborne Introduction to Business,
$5.95.

The best one-book introduction to for-real business around. Designed for English children, the *Usborne Introduction to Business* covers all the basics and quite a few more advanced topics, like import/export. The brightly colored cartoons not only entertain, but explain. If you've never understood how a business worked before, or what goes into starting one, you will after reading this inexpensive book. Very highly recommended.

F & W Publications
 Extra Cash for Kids, *$5.95. Extra Cash for Women,* *$8.95. Internships,* *$18.95.*
Summer Employment Directory of the USA,
$9.95.

Extra Cash for Kids is the most useful and most entertaining job-ideas-and-how-to's book I have seen. One hundred mini-chapters on kid-sized jobs. Some unusual but workable ideas are tucked in with the usual Car Wash, Snow Removal, and Party for Little Kids lineup. The authors not only suggest business ideas and explain why each one is a possible moneymaker, but provide How to Do It and Special Notes sections. The Special Notes tips include ideas on how to expand some of the businesses into other areas. *SuperIdeas*, a

mini-menu of general business tips like how to keep records or how to clean up on school fads, are scattered throughout the book, along with inviting cartoons and graphics.

Extra Cash for Women (by different authors than *Extra Cash for Kids,* above) purports to be more of the same on an adult-sized level.

For those needing to break into the job market but not ready to go it on their own, the annual *Internships* and *Summer Employment Directory of the U.S.* books are a terrific resource. *Internships* lists more than 38,000 on-the-job training opportunities for college students and adults. Sections include:

• Arts (art, museums and cultural organizations, music, dance, and theatre)
• Communications (advertising, PR, film, audio, video, magazine and book publishing, newspapers and journalism, radio, and TV)
• Human Services (career counseling, education, health services, and social service organizations)
• International (see also the international employment directories in the Travel chapter)
• Public Affairs (government, public administration, law, criminal justice, public interest, public service)
• Regional/National Clearinghouses, and
• Science/Industry (architecture, engineering, business, computer science, environment, retail, science, and research).

Each listing includes the duration and season of the position, pay rates, desired qualifications, duties and training involved, availability of college credit, and application procedures and deadlines, plus helpful quotes from recent interns and articles on career trends written by professionals.

The *Summer Employment Directory,* which like *Internships* is revised yearly, lists 50,000 summer jobs along with whom to contact and where, pay rates and fringes, qualifications required, number of openings, and whether or not you can get college credit for the job, plus articles on how to apply successfully for a summer job. The only drawback to these fine books is the listed companies' continuous discrimination against non-college applicants, who more than anyone else need an initial employment opportunity.

F & W Publications also offers a tremendous line of how-to books for hopeful writers, poets, songwriters, photographers, and artists. These include not only books on how to improve your craft, but quite a few on how to sell it. Note that, unlike the internships and summer employment opportunities above, writing and the other arts you perform at home do not require college enrollment or graduation. Recommended.

Home Life
Homemade Money, $14.95. Family Business and Ministry, $9.95. Add 10% shipping.

The best book for home business details is Barbara Brabec's *Homemade Money.* An oversized quality paperback, it contains not only the usual lists of business ideas, but tax info, time management helps, pricing and packaging tips, and a tremendous array of publicity and advertising ideas. The book's strongest point is the extensive resource lists at the back of the book. This information is unavailable anywhere else.

Family Business and Ministry is one of our Family Opportunity Workshop tapes. It covers small business ethics and how to determine your particular calling, and outlines what we feel is a biblical growth strategy for home business, including common errors to avoid.

We also carry *Extra Cash for Kids* and the annual *Internships* directory, reviewed above.

Mother's Bookshelf

Source for home business books and other self-help material from a variety of publishers. A recent catalog included *How to Find and Buy Your Business in the Country, Temporary Employment: The Flexible Alternative,* and *The Mother Earth News Handbook of Home Business Ideas and Plans* (on sale at the time for 67¢!). I have bought 10 or so home business books from this source in the past. Stock changes, so write for the current catalog.

CASSETTE AND VIDEO BUSINESS COURSES

Achievement Basics
Do Your Best, Where's the Wall, and *You Can Lead, $7.95 each postpaid or $19.95 for all 3 Up and On, $7.50. Parent/Teacher Guide included free. Communications Commercials, $10.50.*

Achievement Basics offers something unique: a Junior Business Basics series designed to teach entrepreneurial skills to kids from fourth grade on up. The series is correlated with an optional Junior Business newsletter for inspiration. It comes with a Parent/Teacher Guide with cartoon pages.

The cassettes for younger children are dramatized stories of lovable Uncle Hersh and his nephew Dow and niece Joan. *Do Your Best* teaches kids about productivity and setting standards. In *Where's the Wall on Wall Street?*, Dow and Joan go to the stock exchange. You also get a wall poster and sample stock certificate. *You Can Lead a Horse to Water, But . . .* is about incentive, profit, and loss and includes the Junior Business File Folder that teaches bookkeeping and budgeting.

Up and On With Productivity is a motivational cassette for teens stressing the free-enterprise message. It includes tips on how to be productive and successful without obsessive hype.

Communications Commercials are a cassette or record set for training communications skills through an ad format. Clever!

All cassettes are done by professional actors or announcers and designed for home use.

Audio Editions

Catalog of self-help and business tapes. Largish selection. Now, where did I put the catalog?

Audio Forum

Much wider selection of business self-help courses than I've found elsewhere, tucked among a potpourri of New Age teaching and pop psychology. Once you've fought your way past *Romantic Love and Sexuality*, *Power of Self-Esteem*, and *Self-Transformation Through the New Hypnosis*, you find some truly interesting stuff. Audio Forum has *Listen Your Way to Success*, *Effective Speaking for Managers*, and all the *Speed Learning* modules. Now hear this: *Please Come to Order* (on the art of managing meetings), *Giving a Good Speech/The Art of Conversation* (only $10.95), the *Forbes Stock Market Course* (by the editors of *Forbes* magazine), *Learning from the World's Worst Salesman* (sounds like fun!), Steve Allen's *How to Make a Speech* (this I've heard: it's a good tape), *How to Deal with Difficult People* (who doesn't need that one?), and *Make Time Work for You.*

OK, that was just for starters.

Successful Entrepreneurship, by A. David Silver ($69.50), includes a 200-page book and six cassettes on the following subjects: Characteristics of Successful Entrepreneurs, The Entrepreneurial Process, Survival Plans for

Entrepreneurs, Financing Strategies for the New Business, What Kind of New Business to Start, and Entrepreneurial Growth Techniques. If you're not playing in this league, *How to Start a Home Business* by Gary Null is only $10.95 for one cassette. *Great Home Businesses*, by the same author at the same price, includes case histories. Richard Berman also has several tapes. His *Teenage Business Opportunities* might interest you. According to the blurb "this cassette is packed with solid, practical information about how teenagers can make as much as $200 a week after school and during vacations."

Also for entrepreneurs: *How to Start and Manage Your Own Business* ($79.50), *Public Relations: Do It Yourself* ($59.50), *Advertising: Do It Yourself* ($59.50), *Profitable Spare-Time Hours* ($10.95), and the *Tax-Saver Accounting System* ($79.50). You want more? Then ask for their Business Catalog.

Fast Track

Subscription is $9.95/month "billed on an annual basis," which adds up to almost $120/year paid in one advance chunk.

Business book summaries on cassette. Two each month. From some really good books, like *A Passion for Excellence*, Peter Drucker's *The Effective Executive*, and Steve Allen's *How to Make a Speech.* You also get a free cassette storage case that holds a year's worth of cassettes. The promotional message for Fast Track on each side of each cassette quickly becomes tiresome. Otherwise, good presentation.

Learn, Inc.

Top Selling, Listen Your Way to Success, **$59.95 each.** *Effective Speaking for Managers*, **$69.95.** *Speed Learning*, **$125 for each of these modules: Medical, Data Processing, Science/Engineering, Management, and Finance/Accounting.** *Speed Learning* **video (VHS or Beta), $275 for each module listed above. Standard Edition of** *Speed Learning*, **$99.95 audio, $250 video.**

Another catalog of self-help and business tapes, with a slant toward language usage training (including foreign languages) and learning techniques.

Speed Learning, billed as "much more than speed reading," is supposed to help you understand, remember, and use more of what you read. Not a rehash of the eye-training exercises and speed drills offered by other programs, *Speed Learning* concentrates (according to the ad) on improving your thinking skills. Special modules are available containing an additional workbook with reading material and exercises from particular professional fields. Two hundred thousand people have taken this course.

Listen Your Way to Success focuses on listening skills for managers. It comes with three cassettes, guidebook, listening test, and workbook and a promise that it will "improve your comprehension and retention by at least 100 percent!"

Top Selling, yet another Learn, Inc. product, is directly geared to salesmen. The ad says, "People hate to be sold— but love to buy! They buy because they think we understand them, not because they understand our products or services!" All the same, the course tells you how to professionally handle an interview as well as how to psyche out the prospect.

Effective Speaking for Managers is just one of Learn, Inc.'s product aimed at corporate dundermouths. Mainly focusing on public speaking, it also covers telephone technique and one-to-one conversations.

Learn, Inc. has lots more, some mentioned elsewhere in this book and some not.

Soundview Executive Business Summaries
One year subscription, $59.50.

Who reads those thick business books? Do you? Do I? If you'd like the info in the books, but don't have time to struggle through 500 pages to get to the choice stuff, here's a possible solution. Executive Business Summaries is a subscription service of eight-page book summaries. They pick what they think are the best books and assign each to a professional writer who prepares a summary.

"*Not* a review (someone's opinion). *Not* a digest (book excerpts strung together). A skillful distillation that preserves the content and spirit of the *entire* book." So says the promo piece.

You receive a minimum of thirty summaries— two or three a month. You can also purchase "back issues" to catch up on what's not quite new but still is relevant. Back issues are only available to subscribers.

Books summarized in the past include *Successful Direct Marketing Methods, Getting to Yes, How to Become a Successful Consultant in Your Own Field, Entrepreneurial Management, How to Succeed in Your Own Business, The Organized Executive, The Art of Managing People, In Search of Excellence, Service America, Robert Half on Hiring* . . .

SyberVision
Role Model videos, $49.95 each. *Achievement, Self-Discipline, Leaders,* $69.95 each for 8 audiocassettes and study guide.

SyberVision's philosophy is to find the winners and let them tell and model how they did it. Their Role Models series of 45 minute videos includes Henry Johnson, Kemmons Wilson, Curt Carlson, Norman Brinker, John Teets, Oleg Cassini, and Rocky Aoki. Each of these men is a super achiever who overcame great odds to succeed in business. The blurb for Meet Oleg Cassini, for example, says,

> Starting out as an immigrant in America, Oleg Cassini has become one of the world's foremost fashion leaders. But he is more than a trend-setting designer; he is also a marketing genius. Cassini was the first designer to realize the value of his own name and to license products for large-volume distribution. Watch Cassini in action and you'll realize that there's opportunity everywhere.

Only slightly less glitzy, the *Achievement, Self-Discipline,* and *Leaders* tape sets are all based on Stanford University studies of those who excel in these attributes. Each includes "a fascinating series of exercises that will teach you to saturate your own nervous system with sensory-rich images of success." Hm. It's true that if you can't even imagine where you are going, you are unlikely to get there. On the other hand, I suspect that the parts of these tapes that deal with the nitty-gritties of actually doing something, as opposed to just thinking about it, however fiercely, are what really provides any success on the part of the user. "If wishes were horses, beggars would ride."

Visual Education Association
Business Compact Facts, **sets of about 60 cards: Accounting, Insurance, Investments, Marketing, $2.95 each. Shipping extra.**

Basic stuff about each of these business areas presented in plain talk on pocket-sized cards. Ideas, rules, formulas. At the price, you can't really lose.

TYPING, THE BASIC BUSINESS SKILL

Typing is rapidly becoming the one nonnegotiable business skill. Computer-eager children need it; housewives with aching fingers from writing the family correspondence by hand need it; executives need it. Typing can free your children right now from the drudgery of handwriting, making them much more likely to produce creative stories and letters. And in the future, typing can help secure that first job, whether at home or abroad.

A young child will need to learn on either an electric typewriter or computer keyboard. Manual typewriters are difficult for small, weak fingers, and as for typing practice on a piece of paper marked like a keyboard, forget it. Kids in public school only put up with this because they have no choice. It's not interactive or useful or fun.

You can find inexpensive used electric typewriters, or even whole computers, in the classified section of the newspaper or your area's equivalent of *Trading Times*. A heavy-duty IBM Selectric that can take anything a child dishes out can now be had for as little as

$100, and less-prominent brands may range as low as $25 or less. Consider it an investment in your child's productivity.

Audio Forum
Touch-Typing: Do It Yourself, **$29.50.** *Improve Your Typing*, **$21.95. Both courses, $47.50. Shipping extra.**

Touch Typing: Do It Yourself is designed to teach you to touch type in only four hours. This beginning-level program consists of three cassettes, an "exercise book" (really, a few stapled sheets), and round red "dots" to temporarily conceal the keys while you're taking the course. *Improve Your Typing*, with two cassettes and an exercise book, provides warm-up, accuracy, speed, and speed-accuracy drills, plus score-sheets for recording your progress. The accuracy drills use the 500 most misspelled words.

Educators Publishing Service
Keyboarding Skills, **$6. Shipping extra.**

Here's an innovative new touch-typing system developed for dyslexics but usable by anyone. *Keyboarding Skills* starts with the alphabet in its normal sequence, rather than the usual "home row" approach of *ASDF* and *JKL;*. By saying the name of a letter and pressing its key— a motor process with kinesthetic reinforcement— most students master the alphabet on a typewriter in less than an hour. Next come words of increasing length, phrases, capital letters, and sentences. Numbers, symbols, and punctuation marks complete the course.

Keyboarding Skills is designed for rapid success and ease of use. The spiral-bound top and heavy covers let you stand *Keyboarding Skills* up like an easel, with the copy then in an easy-to-read position. On top of each page is an illustration of the keyboard parts corresponding to the letters freshly introduced. Younger students can use it as soon as their hands are big enough, and the method, though simple, is not too babyish for older students or adults. And note the price! A bargain!

Play 'n Talk
Complete phonics course, $210. Components not available separately.

This complete phonics program, besides the dozen-plus phonics records, lesson books, spelling bingo games, riddle records, and slide rule word construction kit, also contains a typing program. You get three sets of color-coded rings (small, medium, and large) and two sets of color-coded dots with the keyboard letters printed on them. The finger with red belongs on the red row, and so on. The accompanying lesson book begins immediately with simple words. A very motivational method, and worth throwing into the equation when you are thinking about phonics programs.

TYPING SOFTWARE

Brøderbund
Type! is $39.95 for the Commodore 64/128, $44.95 for Apple II family, and $49.95 for IBM PC.

First distinctive of this program: using real words and sentences instead of boring random letters. Next: advanced diagnostics that measure speed and accuracy of each finger, hand, and letter. More: customizable drills, an arcade game, and the program automatically adjusts to your skill level.

You pick a lesson. The top of the screen is a keyboard graphic and a diagnostic setup that tells you your speed, accuracy, errors, and weak letters, as well as your speed and accuracy goals. The rest of the screen has the text to be typed. As you type, the keyboard displays the letters used. Your typed text does not appear, since you are following the screen text. If you make an error in typing, a caret appears under the letter you missed. When you feel ready, you can take a timed typing test.

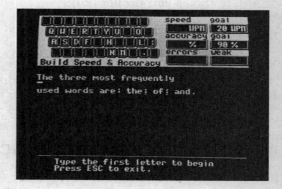

The game is a hurdles race with your typing goal represented as one runner and you as the other. As you type, it keeps track of whether you are ahead of or behind your goal. This is much less distracting than the letters-flashing-at-you-from-all-over-the-screen typing games.

Brøderbund is usually way out front with their programs, and *Type!* is no exception. No wonder they made the Top Ten of the *INC.* 500 last year.

Mindscape

Mindscape

Mastertype, Apple II family, 48K; Atari, 32K; Commodore 64; IBM PC, $39.95 each. $49.95 for the Macintosh version. *Keyboard Cadet*, Apple II or IBM, $14.95; Amiga $39.95.

Mastertype is for learning to type, and for improving your speed and accuracy. You select the keyboard row you want to drill, or ask for a free-for-all. Select the rate, and zap the letters or words zipping at you from all sides of the screen by typing them correctly before they hit your world and destroy it. Everyone agrees this program is more fun and more stressful than the very professional *Typing Tutor III*, which calculates your speed to the tenth of a word per minute and which I have never had the courage to try. Complaint: the practice words are not randomly generated. You have to input your own practice words if you want a change of pace. Another complaint: my seven-year-old can't keep up with even the slowest pace, although he is strongly motivated to learn.

Keyboard Cadet, also available from Mindscape, teaches you to touch type using either the standard QWERTY or Dvorak keyboard. It shows you proper hand positioning and follows the standard typing approach used in schools. The ad says, "An onscreen keyboard helps prevent hunt-and-peck typing, and the arcade game format keeps the typist involved." The benefit here: low price for the Apple II and IBM versions.

SOFTWARE BUSINESS AND FINANCE SIMULATIONS

Blue Chip Software

Millionaire, Baron, Squire, Tycoon, $59.95 each for IBM PC/PCjr and Macintosh, $49.94 Apple II series, $29.95 Commodore 64/128. *Tycoon* also available for Atari 800/XL/XE (48K), $19.95. *Managing for Success* (IBM only), $59.95. *Millionaire, Tycoon,* and *Baron* also available as part of a classroom curriculum packet, *The Economics Challenge.*

The most realistic line of investment and business simulation software anywhere.

Millionaire, the stock market simulation, starts you off with $10,000. Your goal: to parley it into a million. Over a period of 77 simulated weeks, you decide which stocks to buy and sell. The program teaches you about the stock market as you go, including such things as the differences between *puts* and *calls*, the importance of *margins*, and how to measure your portfolio's *net worth*. As in real life, the market is affected by political, social, and economic events.

Tycoon, the commodity market simulation, also teaches both terms and strategies. You trade, trying to get ahead, while the market reacts to seasonal patterns, unusual weather and other world events. Ugly reality department: the program even charges you brokerage fees and taxes!

Baron, the real estate simulation, starts you off with $35,000 and give you five years to invest in residential, commercial, and undeveloped properties. You can take out second mortgages and options, and watch your progress on screen. The mortgage and property appreciation rates are based on real life historical models of the real estate market. As in the other games, real world events impact your net worth and you are charged fees and your net worth and you are charged fees and taxes appropriate to this market.

Squire, the financial planning simulation, gives you a taste of all the above. Here you can choose from an array of investments, including stocks and bonds, commodities, real estate, annuities, and so on. Set your own real life goals, if you wish, by using your actual income and other personal info. The program takes into account taxes, inflation (a rigid eight percent in this program), educational expenses, insurance, and medical bills, as well as the normal bare necessities. *Squire* shows you your net worth broken down by category, and provided you don't go bankrupt, you can keep on for simulated year after simulated year.

All these programs come in a classy gold-stamped vinyl binder and feature an instruction book. If you're like me, you're going to need the book.

Managing for Success, which unlike the others is available only in an IBM version, is tempting me to buy an IBM coprocessor for my Mac. This is the for-real business simulation to get if it does even one-tenth of what the ad claims. You start out as the CEO of a hundred-million-dollar corporation. You are challenged to make all kinds of business decisions, in the course of which you learn to read all kinds of financial statements (including graphs) and reports as well as discovering basic business strategies. Decisions cover the areas of sales and marketing, finance, R&D, manufacturing, production, scheduling, and inventory management. You can even personalize your fictional company to look and feel like your own (assuming you work for a hundred-million-dollar company).

Blue Chip games reward you for financial wizardry by promoting you a level. Each level gives you more prerogatives than the one below. In *Millionaire*, for example, you gain the right to take out loans, buy on margin, and use call and put options. News headlines periodically flash on screen. Some portend serious changes in the market environment; some have no effect. Your reward is strictly monetary: no dancing rabbits or animated screens.

Brøderbund
On Balance, **Apple II family, 128K, $99.95.**

Brøderbund's new *On Balance* is not, strictly speaking, a business simulation. It's a very easy to use personal finance program. But insofar as every home is a little business, the organizational skills gained from this program can be expanded to bigger and better ventures.

On Balance's entry screen looks and works like a checkbook register. You can create up to 175 different accounts—from cash, checking, savings, and credit cards to groceries, auto, and mortgage. You can change the name and type of each account. Each account is defined as an asset, liability, income, or expense. Tax-related items can be flagged for easy tax reporting.

Each month you can enter up to 800 transactions. If this is enough (it will be for most people), a whole year's worth will fit on one floppy diskette. The program reconciles balances and keeps track of those transactions that pop up each month like mortgages and automatic deposits. It helps you set up budgets and lets you know how close you are to your goals.

On Balance will also print any screen or series of screens (it will print your checks if desired), plus your net worth, net income, transactions, and account lists. If this is not enough, all your *On Balance* data can be loaded into Apple's *Appleworks* spreadsheet for further calculations.

If, as the Bible says, "He who is faithful in little shall be faithful with much," getting your home finances under control just might be the best first step towards that business of your own.

PART VI

FINE ARTS

CHAPTER TWENTY

ARTS AND CRAFTS

Scribble, scribble, scribble. Grab a chunk of crayon and splotch on some color. Snip, snip with the scissors. Glop on some glue. Oh, boy! Junior just created another masterpiece!

Little kids all love art— making it, that is— and that is just as well, because what would sustain them through fifth period English if they couldn't scribble cartoons on the margins of their workbooks? Dr. Seuss started this way! But somewhere along the line, most of us learn that we are "not talented" and that we should leave art to those chaps with the berets and the Paris fellowships.

Most of us have a lot more talent than we suspect. Why, then, can so few Americans turn out a workmanlike piece of art? Our training is to blame. Somehow the idea has taken hold in art instruction circles that the way for people to learn art is for them to make "five thousand mistakes" on their own. Then, after making all these mistakes, the talented will emerge and the rest will sink into the dregs. This is the way the schools teach reading, and it of course produces the same sorry results.

Contrast this with the ancient and honorable apprenticeship system, where the eager would-be artist worked under the direction of a master in his craft. At first the apprentice spent most of his time doing menial things: rehairing brushes, mixing paints, and so on. This phase gave him great intimacy with the physical tools of his art. Then the master would let him try some small exercises, and if he was successful he would perhaps get to contribute a minor part to one of the master's own projects. In time, he would learn most of the master's techniques (canny masters kept some back!) and would be ready to try something new on his own.

At each step the apprentice was taught the skills he needed. He saw all the stages artwork goes through; he saw the finished result; he heard the master criticize his efforts, and make suggestions for improvement. He did *not* blunder about making five thousand mistakes, as the master wanted a productive apprentice, not a nitwit.

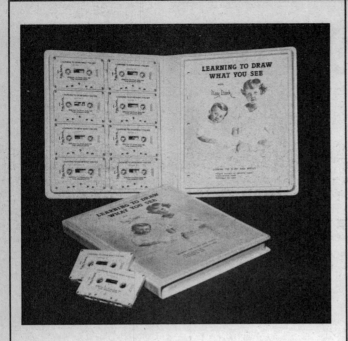

INTRODUCTION TO ART VIA DRAWING

Mary Brock
Learning to Draw What You See, **regularly $69.96: mention** *The Next Book of Home Learning* **and you can have it for $49.95.**

Mary Brock's *Learning to Draw What You See* is a systematic approach to learning to draw, based on a similar approach to that used in *Drawing on the Right Side of the Brain* (see review under Holt Associates below), but minus that book's New Age speculations. This eight-cassette course leads you step by step through the drawing process. You also get an instruction book and the opportunity to interact with Mary herself thought the mail-in critique service.

Learning to Draw What You See covers Understanding the Brain in Creativity (six projects), Your Art History, Introduction to Line Drawings, Portrait/The Profile, Portrait/The Full Face, Portrait/The Three-Quarter View, Still Life, and Landscapes. Figure drawing (bodies) is not included.

Each lesson begins with a supply list of all the materials you will need. The project steps are both on the tape and in the manual; philosophy is confined to the tape.

As an educational tool, this is an excellent course. The recordings pleasantly and systematically lead you through the projects, without overburdening you with philosophy. The course is attractively presented in a handsome cassette binder.

Holt Associates
Drawing on the Right Side of the Brain, **$9.95. Shipping extra. Lots of other books on art, art supplies, and intellectually worthwhile materials for home schoolers in a host of areas.**

For a complete drawing course intermixed with New Age philosophy and neurological speculation, I'd better not skip over *Drawing on the Right Side of the Brain* by Betty Edwards. After a lengthy introduction about right and left brains and artistic states of consciousness, the author gets down to brass tacks with a number of exercises to help you become aware of shapes, perspective, and proportion, with particular attention to drawing the human face. The book is full of before-and-after examples done by the author's students, and these are a powerful commentary on the effectiveness of her teaching methods.

Hugh O'Neill and Associates
Big Yellow Drawing Book, **$3.75 USA, $4.75 Canadians. Great book: buy 10 for Christmas and birthday presents.**

And while we're concentrating on drawing as the foundation of all art, don't miss *The Big Yellow Drawing Book,* a product of the O'Neill clan. Dan O'Neill is a cartoonist of some repute in flower child circles. His Odd Bodkins comic strip gained quite a following in the sixties and seventies. His father Hugh (a genuine Ed.D.) helped by insisting that his wife Marian, an accomplished artist, and son Dan, the cartoonist, adhere to the known principles of learning. The end result of their labors is an extremely charming, simple introduction to drawing (in general) and cartooning (in particular) that has been proved 99 percent successful in teaching people of all ages to draw. You start by adding expressions, per the directions, to cartoon faces, and go on to practice six principles of perspective. A mere $3.75 for American customers or $4.75 for Canadians (postpaid!) to Hugh O'Neill & Associates gets you the book, which includes room for your practice exercises. Anyone four or five years old can tackle the beginning exercises. We got one for each member of our family. *The Big Yellow Drawing Book* makes a great stocking-stuffer (as long as you wear tights— the book is 8½ x 11).

Shekinah Curriculum Cellar
   Drawing Textbook, **$5.50. By the same author:** *Big Easel II,* **$3.50;** *Cute Animals, Things for Sports, Scenery, Flowers and Trees,* **$5.50 each;** *Freehand Sketching,* **$7.50. Add 10% shipping ($2 minimum). Many more art books and supplies, plus home school programs in every subject area.**

It is being overly generous to say that 5 percent of our college graduates know how to draw. There is no successful drawing program in our public schools and educators know it . . .

   If you will evaluate our public-school art program, do not ask the art supervisor. The reply would probably sound much like the weavers' description of their goods in the tale, *The Emperor's New Clothes.* Instead, ask yourselves and your neighbors because you are the products of the public-school art program and NO EDUCATIONAL PROGRAM IS BETTER THAN THE PRODUCT IT TURNS OUT . . .

   Many art supervisors and teachers maintain that there is no "right" and "wrong" in drawing . . . In a drawing program where there is no right and wrong and no rules, the children have nothing tangible to grasp and nothing to take home. They do not learn the right way; they do not learn the wrong way; they do not learn . . .

   One of the main objectives of today's public-school art program is "Free Expression (creative self expression)." We know that people who do not know how to draw cannot express themselves freely . . .

Thus speaks Bruce McIntyre, a veteran public school art instructor who also put in a

decade as a a Walt Disney artist in the era when Disney's art was really something. His book, aptly named *Drawing Textbook,* explains in crystalline detail why public school (and most private school) art programs fail to produce students who can draw. His analysis of what went wrong is combined with a stirring call to achieve drawing literacy in our day, and takes up the first 13 pages of the book. Find out why the ability to communicate visually makes such a difference, and the one approach to art instruction that provides it. Then you and your children can tackle the 222 graduated exercises that make up the rest of the book! These start with simple stuff— a birthday cake, a TV set— and progress along merrily introducing the Seven Laws of Perspective and other goodies until by lesson 58 you're drawing realistic skyscrapers, by lesson 94 you're getting down on paper a twisted candle that would make the Hildebrandt brothers proud, and by the last lesson you can draw *anything!* From here on in, it's merely a matter of adding to your visual vocabulary with his supplementary books, *Cute Animals, Things for Sports, Scenery,* and *Flowers and Trees.* Each of these shows how to apply the seven elements of drawing to a particular class of objects.

   For younger children, *Big Easel* is similar to, but simpler than, *Drawing Textbook.* For high school through adult, *Freehand Sketching* takes it all a bit further.

ART SUPPLIES: STANDARD

ABC School Supply
Chasselle, Inc.
Hoover Brothers
Lakeshore Curriculum Material Center

   These school supply houses all have a wide selection of arts and crafts materials at very attractive prices. I like the Lakeshore catalog best, although they all are good, because Lakeshore offers some crazy items the others don't: wiggly eyes for freaky collages and a device that makes innocent clay into stringy "spaghetti" suitable for providing a clay model with hair, for instance. All the catalogs sell glitter, paints, pens, markers, clay, glue, and dozens of varieties of art paper: everything a young artist needs.

Dick Blick
Five mail order addresses. Send order to the one closest to you.

Blick has a complete selection of art, craft, and related materials for all ages and skill levels. Blick's special emphasis is on fine and graphic arts: many supplies geared to the working artist. You name the art medium or craft, from spinning to sign-making, from oil painting to light tables, they've got it. No serious artist, young or old, should miss this catalog. Worth the $2.

Pearl Paint

"World's Largest Art & Graphic Discount Center." Everything for the serious artist, all at discount. The nononsense newsprint catalog includes heavy-duty equipment like airbrushes, compressors, and easels as well as the usual artistic media (pencils, paper, gouache, oils, brushes, canvas, etc.). Items are listed by category (e.g., Oil Colors) and manufacturer (e.g., Grumbacher). Little or no description of items is offered; it's up to you to know what you want. Less than 2 percent of Pearl's stock is mentioned in the catalog, so if you don't see it, ask.

Toys to Grow On

If you're looking for fancy art supplies for elementary-age kids, this is the place. Every glitzy art material your little heart could desire— stickers, puff paints, colored paper in rolls, foil, doilies, collage kits, fabric kits— this just scratches the surface! Great birthday presents. Ask for the special Art Supplies catalog.

ART SUPPLIES: PROGRESSIVE

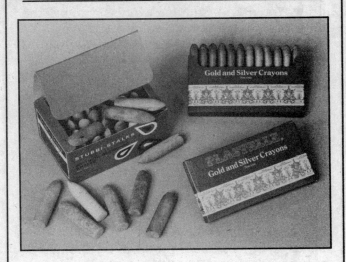

DIDAX, Inc.

Rubber stamps, crayons, and other fun stuff for kids. Small art selection, but nice. DIDAX also sells all sorts of manipulative learning devices for other subjects, especially math and phonics. If you like the hands-on approach to learning, you'll drool over this colorful catalog

HearthSong

Superb quality art and craft supplies, small but well-chosen selection, not cheap. Hearth Song emphasizes natural fabrics and materials, e.g., their wool-stuffed dolls. New Age flavor.

KidsArt
See representative prices below. Shipping extra.

Creative art activities and materials abound in KidsArt's "All Time Great Art Products" catalog. Their Creative Art Bag collections include a Giant Wood Art Bag of interesting wood shapes, supplies to make them into whatever your little heart desires, and an illustrated booklet with easy-to-follow ideas, all in its own burlap storage bag for $15. The rest in its own burlap storage bag for $15. The rest of the burlap bag collection includes Giant Fabric Art Bag ($15), Finger Puppets ($9), Fuzzy Hand Puppet Bag ($9), and Clothespin People ($9). Castles to cut out and put together ($3.50). A Sculpture Poster from the Smithsonian that includes shapes you can cut out and assemble into your own sculptures ($10). How-to books on pottery, carpenter's lace, collage, and more. Fancy coloring books. The O'Neill clan's *Big Yellow Drawing Book*. KidPrints study guides. Seashell sponge stamps ($16). Famous art study prints. Paint and paper supplies. Drawing Kit ($9).

The KidsArt philosophy is to carefully teach the techniques of art, from drawing to sculpture to photography, then turn kids loose to experiment and create on their own, with open-ended assignments and lots of fun and success. Good stuff; you'll like it.

Sycamore Tree
Strokums, 10 for $1.25, 15 for $1.75. Plasti-Tak $1.95. O'Glue $1.45. Fimo modeling set $9.95. *Drawing Textbook* $5.95. *Freehand Sketching* $8.95. Lots more.

Sycamore Tree, along with their thousands of curriculum resources for all subjects, offers a good-sized selection of some of the most progressive art supplies.

Strokums plastic crayons are non-toxic, washable, non-smearing, melt-resistant, beautiful, and *erasable.* That is, almost completely erasable. Some colors are more persistent than others. Still, at last young artists can more or less erase those erratic marks that wandered outside the lines.

Plasti-Tak looks and feels like putty, but it comes off walls and papers. Use it to tack that priceless artwork up without marring surfaces.

O'Glue is a long transparent squeezable tube of glue with a neat applicator. Works on just about anything. Non-toxic, non-flammable, water soluble. No mess!

Imported from West Germany, the Fimo Modeling Set contains eight colors of special Fimo material, a work pad, lacquer, and a modeling tool. Fimo is a brilliantly colored,

nontoxic, odorless modeling compound you can harden in your oven. Used by some professional sculptors.

Drawing Textbook was reviewed in the introduction to this chapter. By the same author, *Freehand Sketching* teaches the next steps.

This only touches the surface of the hundred or more art books, supplies, and projects Sycamore Tree carries. Watercolors, brushes, Bible coloring books and models (build your own Tabernacle!), paint-with-water, Funthinkers™, scissors, coloring markers, lots more.

CRAFT AND SPECIALTY SUPPLIES

Curriculum Resources, Inc.
Price sampling: 12-inch bookshelf for $1.75, birdhouse for $1.60.

This company offers a large variety of craft kits for children and adults. Excellent prices, simple projects. Some unusual crafts: wheat weaving, quilling, smocking— plus basketry, latch hook, and dozens of other "standards." Some crafts come in bulk packs for group projects, and these are often used in schools.

Dover Publications
Publishers of over 3,000 paperbacks in all fields of interest, including many specially suited for home study and instruction. Most priced between $2 and $5.

Tons of economical art and craft books. Dover has a large Clip Art section, consisting of copyright-free designs and illustrations you can paste on to your own productions before duplicating for that professional look. Just for fun, Dover has paper models— you can cut and assemble the Emerald City or a Western Frontier Town, among others. I bet you'll get excited over their unique coloring book series (human anatomy: favorite birds: American Revolution uniforms: Bible stories: make your own calendar . . .) Also books on origami, books about art, books on "how to" almost anything.

The prices are great because the books are reprints. Dover has books in all categories: look for the reviews throughout this book.

Educational Insights
Sticky Things, Beautiful Things, $4.95 each. Make-A-Mask Kit, $7.95. Extra gauze, $3.95. Add 10% shipping.

You want something unusual? This is unusual, all right! Educational Insight's Make-A-Mask Kit includes one face form, one roll Plastergauze, six colors of tempera, paintbrush, and 16 page full-color instruction guide with some project suggestions. Add a little yarn, feathers, or fake fur and you've got . . . something. One model mask project strongly resembles Miss Piggy, another a horrible monster. Kid-pleasing for sure (but skip the monsters!).

Also from Ed Insights, the Fun With Art and Science Series is recipes and art projects with scientific explanations. Illustrated booklets explain why the glop hardens or the ingredients mix, as well as providing projects. The series includes *Sticky Things* and *Beautiful Things,* and if you're a wise and discerning parent I bet I know which you'll pick first!

Harrisville Designs
Twenty-four-inch Personal Loom, $76; 36-inch Personal Loom, $88; 60-inch classroom Friendly Loom $128 (school price). Starter Kit, $25. Shipping extra.

Our children have always been fascinated with weaving. One of son Ted's first independent purchases was a potholder weaving kit, and both he and Joe have turned out at least a dozen of these between them. Sarah and Magda would gladly join in, too, if their little fingers could manage it.

But potholders rather limit the scope of one's imagination, and a real loom is exorbitantly expensive and space-wasting. Not to mention the way the kids would fight over it.

Our kids now are all weaving serious projects, all at once, without squabbling. How did this happen? The Friendly Loom™ from Harrisville Designs. You get a pegged frame that you can adjust up and down, depending on how long you want your finished piece. This rests on a floor stand. You set up the loom quickly by running cotton warp back and forth over the pegs, then select whatever you want to weave through it and weave! Patterns and materials can be as wild or wooly as you wish: feathers, cloth or rag strips, grass bundles, plants, seaweed, twigs, vines, leather or fur strips, plastic bread bags, rolled or twisted paper bags, bead strings, bias tape, ribbons, ric rac, or even yarn! The accompanying booklet tells you how to set up and weave, and gives ideas for patterns. And because the Friendly Loom is so wide, several children can work side by side on individual projects.

The Friendly Loom comes in three sizes: two Personal Models (a two-foot and three-foot model), or the five-foot-wide school model. Each fits flat along a wall when not in use. Harrisville Designs also sells the supplies you will need to get started weaving in the form of a Starter Kit. The Kit contains eight wooden maple shed sticks and eight wooden maple stick shuttles, eight brightly colored balls of Friendly Loom 100 percent wool yarn (different colors), and one 440 yard cone of cotton warp.

Instructor Books

Selection of craft and project books for elementary school teachers, some published by *Instructor* magazine, some not. Nice format, good value for money, easy to use, not expensive. Also all sorts of supplementary/enrichment project books for all school subjects. More books added constantly, so write for current brochure.

Living Word Curriculum
Backpack of Crafts and *Treasure Chest of Crafts,* $15.90 for both plus shipping.

For use at church, VBS, day camp, clubs, school, or home, here are two craft books each containing 101 creative crafts. Conversation suggestions in the books illustrate Bible truths. The card deck ad says the crafts are "simple for teachers to plan and prepare" and "use materials found in every home and church."

S & S Arts & Crafts

Large catalog of all kinds of arts and crafts projects, many sold in classroom-sized packs. In bulk, these projects cost almost nothing apiece. Tons of neat stuff unavailable elsewhere. Golden Foil projects make fancy pictures for 16¢ and up. Mobiles. Kaleidoscopes (make your own). Wind wheels. Phillipine Wind Chimes. Rhinestone studding sets. Japanese Fish Kites. Southwestern Indian Sand Painting (enough supplies for 50 projects, $13.75). Plastic Weaving Baskets. Color-n-Throw Boomerangs. Rainbow Tops. Clothespin art, a page of projects and supplies. Craftsticks in bulk ($1.95/1,000), with projects and accessories.Pop-It Beads, $3.88/one pound bag (approximately 800). Mosaic Tiles at low prices— all kinds (I *loved* making mosaics as a child). Paper projects. Leather projects. Copper and metal tooling. Paper and posterboard supplies and projects. Wood projects ($8.95 for one of those fancy wooden trains in kit form). Holiday crafts. Beadcraft with fusible beads. Classroom art supplies (scissors, glue, etc.).

Sculpture Associates Ltd., Inc.

Everything for the sculptor. SA is growing; it recently bought out Sculpture Services. The catalog offers "fine tools, accessories and materials for the sculptor and artist," including books. *Sculptworld News,* SA's house publication, lists sculpture exhibits across the country. Some books feature nude models, but the catalog itself is pretty restrained.

Warren Publishing House/Totline Press
"Cut & Tell" Scissor Stories, $5.95 each (Fall, Winter, Spring). Shipping extra.

Three seasonal collections of scissor stories, with eight stories each. You've never heard of scissor stories? All right, I'll tell you about scissor stories. What they are, is a paper plate. You take the plate. You begin to cut the plate as you tell the story. At each stage of the story, the plate turns into a different prop. For example: In "The Spirit of Christmas," one paper plate becomes first two mice, next two pieces of cheese, and then the rest of the plate becomes a fancy candle. Or how about the Chanukah basket that becomes a dreidl that becomes a menorah? No kidding! Jean Warren, the author, stayed up nights thinking of these crazy scissor stunts. Full directions and stories are included.

Jean Warren has produced *"Cut & Tell" Scissor Stories* for Fall, Winter, and Spring. In theory, you, the adult, perform these to an admiring group of children at a daycare center. In practice, you, the adult, can try your luck at home and possibly flub the story, but it won't matter, because your kids will be ready and able to take over and show you how it ought to be done. With a little help from you in figuring out the directions, *"Cut & Tell" Scissor Stories* could be the ultimate cut-paste-'n-color kids' books.

ART COURSES

Children need to see good art if they are to produce good art. It's true that when freshly introduced to a new form of art we need to be free to mess about and familiarize themselves with the art media. But this play phase should be followed by real instruction, or frustration results. Any serious artist, whether five or fifty, appreciates teaching that helps him produce better work.

Below are courses that will help you avoid some of those five thousand mistakes.

Alpha Omega Publications

Art I, 1-year course, 10 LIFEPACs plus 2 (optional) answer keys and 1 (optional) test pac, $1.95 each LIFEPAC. Two resource items, Art-A-Color Plates ($5.95) and Construction Paper Packet ($1.50) are also required.

It is my policy never to endorse a product I haven't personally seen, and that is the only reason I am hesitant about piling on the superlatives for AOP's introductory art course for seventh-graders on up. First of all, the price is right. Secondly, the course hits *all* the bases: fine art, applied art, commercial art, and art appreciation. The course layout, which I have seen, maintains Alpha Omega's usual standards of logic and thoroughness, so each of these areas gets a real workout rather than a passing nod. Thirdly, and this is the part I like the best, the course is designed to provide *practical* art skills, giving the student the tools to use the artistic media (graphics, lettering, layout, cartooning, photography, and printmaking) as well as tools to analyze and improve his personal environment.

AOP says that the fine arts portion of the course can be personalized to fit the student's interests and opportunities.

Center for Applied Research in Education

"Let's Discover" art series covers crayon, mobiles, paper, tempera, tissue, and watercolor with over 30 step-by-step activities for each.

Designed for K-6. I wish I could get my hands on a review copy, because it does sound good.

Covenant Home Curriculum

Sample prices below. Add 8% shipping. Full line includes complete home school curriculum, testing, and literature.

Art coloring books, at prices from $2.50 through $6.95. Some sample titles: *The Story of Glass, Geometrical Design, Visual Illusions, Prismatic Design* (all $2.50 each), *Isometric Perspective Designs, Create Your Own Picture* ($2.75 each), and *Favorite American Birds and Wildflowers* ($4.50). History coloring books ($2.50 each), like *Everyday Dress of American Colonial Period* and the *Victorian House Coloring Book*. Literature coloring books (mainly Beatrix Potter). Also art books like *The Notebooks of Leonardo da Vinci* (two volumes) and *Drawings of Rembrandt* (also two volumes). *Complete Book of Silk Screen Printing* ($3.75). *Linoleum Block Printing* ($3.25). *Easy to Make Candles* ($2.50). More, all chosen for artistic interest and excellence.

Dover Publications

Dover, as I mentioned above, has lots and lots of art instruction books, as well as their make-it-yourself projects.

EDC

Usborne Guide to Painting, Guide to Drawing, Guide to Technical Drawing, Guide to Lettering and Typography, $4.95 each. *The Usborne Young Cartoonist,* $7.95.

Inexpensive step-by-step guides to media and techniques. Full color, copiously illustrated. As with all Usborne books, the illustrations and layout teach as much or more than the text. This highly visual approach is ideal for visual subjects.

Drawing covers pencil, pen, charcoal,

crayon, and pastels, as well as techniques of perspective, measuring and proportion, shading and texture, coloring, and just about anything else you'd like to know. Choosing supplies. Composition. Still life. Portraits. Figure drawing. Animals. Drawing from imagination. How to mount your drawings. How to fix mistakes. Plus an index! An amazing amount of information packed into 32 8½ x 11" pages.

Painting, in a similar format, covers oils, watercolors, gouache, and acrylics, plus basic information about painting preparation and supplies as well as techniques. Brushes. Easels. Cleaning materials. How to make your own painting surfaces. Cleanup. Composition, with or without viewfinders. Perspective, measurement, and proportion are just touched on; for detailed instructions in these areas you should consult the *Guide to Drawing.* Like *Drawing, Painting* also covers how to paint people, still life, outdoor scenes, painting from imagination, and how to frame and mount your art. A final section on abstract painting is a bonus. The entirely unnecessary picture on page thirteen of a young man painting a technically modest nude (arms and legs arranged to cover the essentials) may cause some to skip this otherwise fine book.

Finally, the *Usborne Young Cartoonist* is a sassy introduction to the art named. Lots of tips and techniques are crammed into less pages than you would expect. The boffo drawings are a bit too uncontrolled for my liking, themselves resembling kid art (perhaps intentionally). The second half of this book, "How to Draw Monsters and Other Creatures," speaks for itself.

Growing Without Schooling

This very fine home school magazine consistently has articles on art. Readers write in to share their ideas and experiences, and the staff contribute their own. As a forum for creativity, *GWS* is unsurpassed. You'll get more ideas per column inch about teaching and learning art here than anywhere else.

IRIS
How to do Wet-On-Wet Watercolor Painting, $9.95 plus 69¢ postage. Make check payable to Rauld Russell.

Watercolor instruction from a Waldorf school perspective. The Color lessons in *How to do Wet-on-Wet Watercolor Painting and Teach it to Children* start with Yellow and The Rainbow and proceed through Blue, Red, Green, Sunrise, Sunset, and Blue-Violet. Lesson 9, The Suffering of Light, is followed by Lesson 10, The Deed of Light, and then the traditional color circle and color combinations. Part III gives suggestions for teaching children in grades preschool through eight.

The Foreword warns you should plan to commit at least three hours a week "to immerse yourself in the color and to develop brushing dexterity."

Now, the text. Interspersed with quotes from the likes of Goethe and Chagall are a mixture of careful instruction and emotive philosophy. The author, Rauld Russell, tries to inspire a sense of wonder and oneness with your art. For the children he includes Color Stories, with the colors metamorphosed into human beings with (forgive me) colorful personalities. As the promotional letter states,

Wet-on-wet watercolor painting is the most natural style of painting that anyone could possibly begin with. It is a "play of fantasy with flowing color" that springs loose the imagination enhancing one's feeling for just being alive.

You could call this approach, "The Inner Game of Watercolor."

KidsArt
KidPrints Special Introductory Unit, $5. Full Three-Month Unit, $10. Eight Months of Art, $6. Shipping extra.

Fine arts demystified, for kids everywhere. The Special Introductory Unit is designed to introduce you to the activities and methods of the regular KidsArt units. A complete six-week course in fine art printmaking, it contains simple activities with collage prints, eraser stamps, and monoprints taken from the Three-Month KidsArt Unit. It also contains famous art study prints, an artist biography (Mary Cassatt), lesson plans, and teaching guide. All activities are presented with great respect for children. KidsArt provides the techniques and just enough open-ended project suggestions to launch your family into joyous artistic adventures.

Kim Solga, KidsArt director, really knows her stuff. Great tips in these art units, like how to keep stamp pad colors clean, how to make a sturdy portfolio for your kids' art. Graphically-pleasing layout reinforces the lessons. The monthly lesson plans are supersimple and really useful. We're looking forward to her projected KidsDraw and KidSculpt units, and hope many more will follow.

David S. Lake Publishers

Papercraft series and Craft Workshop series are inexpensive books designed for home art and craft projects. Grades preschool through 8.

Learning at Home
Nourishing Creativity Through Art, $18.

Art experiences for your whole family. No lesson requires talent or previous experience. You will learn art terminology, art techniques, and to internalize and express your artistic feelings.

The primary author, Gwen Brennick, treats the reader, no matter how young, as an emerging professional entitled to professional tools and professional respect. Exercises begin with color play, movement of color and line, defining space, and clay sculpture. This level is suitable for the youngest artist. Level 2, for ages starting at six or seven, begin with creating secondary colors from the primaries and discovering colors as they occur in nature, and moves rapidly to using shapes in a composition (through printing, collage, and mosaic with "found" articles) and mobile-making, among other activities. Level 3 explores self-expression; Level 4, observation and expression; Level 5, working with nature (including geometrics in nature, which moves into abstract design); and Level 6 gets into perspective, portrait, and even pottery (clay sculpture).

Every lesson describes the concept covered, lists materials, and carefully leads you through the exercises.

More: appendices. The first appendix, The Language of Art, not only defines art terminology but explains how to "see" in an artistic way. Next, The Organizing Principles of Art, looks at movement, balance, rhythm, space, perspective, proportion, and art's universal qualities: completeness, appropriateness, and unity. Beyond this is another appendix with examples of possible results to the exercises in each unit.

As I said, these are *beginning* art experiences, created for people with little or no artistic background. If you've missed out on all the art your soul craves, or are looking for a place to start with your children, *Nourishing Creativity Through Art* looks excellent. Learning at Home also carries high quality art supplies to go with this course— ask them for info about art supplies.

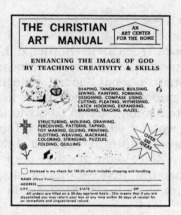

THE CHRISTIAN ART MANUAL

AN ART CENTER FOR THE HOME

ENHANCING THE IMAGE OF GOD BY TEACHING CREATIVITY & SKILLS

SHAPING, TANGRAMS, BUILDING, SEWING, PAINTING, FORMING, DESIGNING, COMPASS USING, CUTTING, PLEATING, WITNESSING, LATCH HOOKING, EXPANDING, BRAIDING, TRACING, MAZES.

STRUCTURING, MOLDING, DRAWING, PERCEIVING, PATTERNS, TAPING, TOY MAKING, GLUING, PRINTING, SLOTTING, WEAVING, MACRAME, COLORING, STRINGING, PUZZLES, FOLDING, QUILLING

OVER 250 IDEAS

☐ Enclosed is my check for $30.00 which includes shipping and handling.

NAME (Please Print)
ADDRESS
CITY   STATE   ZIP
All orders are filled on a 30-day approval basis. This means that if you are dissatisfied you may return your box at any time within 30 days of receipt for an immediate and unquestioned refund.

Motivational Art Training
   Christian Art Manual, **$25 plus $5 shipping and handling.**

Here's a complete art curriculum for Christian kids. The *Manual* is truly Christian, as the exercises are designed to teach Christian truth by allowing the student to develop visual demonstrations of each concept. Example: Make a 3-D model to represent "me" as body, soul, and spirit. The art instruction itself is also excellent and covers most major areas of creativity: lettering, painting, modeling, etc. Each project has ideas for expansion, so the skill taught can be applied to other projects. Lists of easy-to-obtain materials are included.

The *Manual* is usable for all ages, including Mom and Dad, who are encouraged to have some artistic fun along with the kids. Projects can be self-instructional for older children, but younger ones will need some guidance.

Originally sold to Christian schools as a motivational tool to reward good behavior, the *Manual* now comes in a home version at the lower price listed above.

Optasia Fine Art Designs
   Ten coloring postalettes for $5. Includes 10 of one design on a variety of paper stocks and colors, plus gold stickers.

The SCHOOL • MASTER • PIECES Guideline Series of cards takes coloring practice to its artistic limits. These very lovely cards come on a variety of colored, high-quality papers to encourage experimentation with various artistic tools and techniques. The publishers suggest that children use fine line felt tip pens, pastels, wax pencils, and thick water colors (too much water wrinkles the paper).

It can be a great disappointment to a child to create a "masterpiece" on shoddy coloring book paper, which promptly tears or is otherwise destroyed. By using SCHOOL • MASTER • PIECES coloring cards, your youngster's best work can both really look good and be preserved. The cards make lovely gifts, too, thus solving the problem of what your child can do with excess artwork. I am also amazed at the price, which is less than you'd pay for many cheap mass-produced occasion cards.

SCHOOL • MASTER • PIECES crisp card stock is a treat for the fingertips and the designs are a delight for the eyes. It's a way to both introduce your child to quality art and enable him to participate in creating at the same time.

Pecci Publications
   Color Words, **$8.95 postpaid.**

What do you do when it's been raining for two solid weeks and the kids are about to eat the living room drapes from sheer frustration? I smile sweetly and say, "Go get Mary Pecci's *Color Words* book." Now you know that you don't need one hundred pages of assignments to teach those little color words— red, orange, yellow, and so on— so what are all those pages about? Aha! Good question! What we have here is the niftiest bunch of primary art assignments that I have ever seen. All you need are scissors, crayons, glue, and a brad or two and you can: Build a (paper) log cabin! Make an Easter egg which opens up to hatch a chick! Make Thanksgiving napkin rings featuring a Pilgrim girl and boy! Put together a 3-D circus parade! The activities are seasonal, which is great for emphasizing holidays, and the results are so charming that I have our boys glue them onto cardboard to make them last longer.

Share-A-Care

Art With a Purpose: Art Pac for each level, $2.95 each book (two books per level). Teacher's Manual, 2 per level, $1.95 each, 4 levels in all (levels 0 through 3). Add 10% shipping ($2.50 minimum). Postage outside USA will be billed.

Simple, really sweet, step-by-step art courses for grades 1-10 that teach drawing, coloring, lettering, painting, and paper cutting. The art has a Mennonite flavor: simple dress, gentle little girls with braids, Christian messages.

Art With A Purpose comes in two-grade levels. Level O, for grades one and two, covers • simple drawing, including drawing with grids • tracing • craft projects • simple one-point perspective. Level 1, for grades three and four, is considerably more advanced. It covers • more complex drawing • tracing • crafts projects • simple perspective • balance (using stick figures). Level 2, for grades five and six, includes • drawing and shading • lettering • layout and design • Perspective I • drawing children in balance and proportion. Level 3, for grades seven and eight, has • Old English calligraphy • pen and ink sketching • layout and design • Perspective II • more advanced drawing exercises, again with fully-clothed child models.

Each Art Pac has a corresponding Teacher's Manual which presents the lessons' goals and provides teaching guidelines.

Art With A Purpose was designed

specifically to lighten the teacher's workload and to provide truly Christian art instruction. It succeeds at both. For these reasons, it may become the core art course of choice among Christian home schoolers.

Sycamore Tree

Sycamore Tree carries hordes of home schooling resources, including some of the finest art instructional books I've seen. *Drawing Textbook*, reviewed above, features an approach to art instruction so obviously right that you'll wonder why you didn't think of it yourself— guaranteed to teach *all* children to draw! If you don't want to waste your time shopping around, just get this catalog for all your beginning art instruction needs.

Timberdoodle

Creating Line Design books, $4.75 each or $18/set of 4. Add 10% shipping ($4 minimum). Write for shipping costs outside continental U.S.

Learn pre-drafting skills through this series that trains a child's visual perception and memory. OK, that sounds pretty fancy. What are we talking about here? We're talking about the Creating Line Design series. You use a straightedge to connect numbers ranged along the sides of a box. Simple, right? Well, at first it is. In book one, designed for kindergartners, you just connect numbers. This produces a variety of designs. Check yourself with the inset completed design to see if you did it right. In book two, you have to connect pairs of letters as well as numbers in order to produce more complicated designs. Book three designs require you to lift your pencil occasionally while connecting dots, since the square now contains different shapes around which you must maneuver. Book four (intended for grades seven through nine) designs are very challenging, but even young children can complete them after finishing the first three books.

Making the designs is fun. You can color the finished product and display it. Some of the designs could be pasted on cardboard and made into puzzles. Whatever— the Creating Line Design series takes no teacherly effort; kids like it; why not get it?

Warren Publishing Company/Totline Press
1•2•3 Art, $12.95. Add $2 shipping.

You've been tossing and turning at nights wondering what to do with your leftover deodorant bottles, crumpled paper, and wallpaper scraps, right? Your problem is solved. Warren Publishing House's *1•2•3 Art: Open-Ended Art Activities for Young Children* is possibly the biggest and best collection ever of wacky art activities using common household objects.

I've seen lots of art-with-simple-things books, but this one has special features. For one thing, the layout. All the "Painting With . . . " activities, like Painting With shaving cream or food coloring or ice or Q-Tips and so on, are all in the same section. Ditto for the • Painting On . . . • Gluing • Glue Substitutes (can you did peanut butter as a glue substitute?) • Printing With . . . • Prints of . . . • Modeling With . . . • Marking With . . . • Tearing or Cutting • Lacing • and Miscellaneous Art. A Seasonal Index directs you to activities appropriate to that season and its holidays (e.g., forget painting on snow in June). Every page lists materials needed, preparation required, hints, and variations on the activity, plus there is a cute

cartoon of a bear doing the activity. These activities are suggestions submitted by teachers from all around the country, and represent true creative thinking. Gonna get us some squeeze bottles, spray bottles, and tongue depressors and paint us up a storm.

ART APPRECIATION & HISTORY

Aristoplay
Artdeck, $25. *Main Street*, $12. *Good Old Houses* coloring book, $4. *Good Old Houses*, $12.

First, *Artdeck*. Subtitled "The Game of Modern Masters," this beautiful card game is a mini collection of 52 major works of modern art by 13 of the most famous artists. The game involves collecting "suits" of cards in a fashion similar to rummy. All the Aces, for example, are paintings by Joan Miro. The Artist Card for each suit gives pertinent facts about the artist, including a brief overview of his style and the titles of the works on the other cards. The cards are top quality. Shiny and colorful. No wonder art museums carry this game. Now, the $10,000 question: *Why only modern masters?* The same game format would work with medieval art, or Renaissance art, or traditional

English art . . . This could be done by either enclosing a flyer offering additional card sets, or by producing "new" games with different cards but otherwise the same format. Would you be interested in this? I would!

Let me mention in passing that exposure to real art, even on this small scale, has sparked an interest in looking up the artists in our encyclopedia. One little thing leads to another.

Now, two games I have not seen but that look interesting. *Main Street*, billed as "a puzzle/game of historical commercial architecture" is on one level a puzzle for small children and on another a crazy-eight recognition game for older kids and adults. Each puzzle is cut into card-shaped pieces; put 'em together and you have a building. You get a fact sheet with historical and architectural info on styles from Federal to Art Deco-Moderne. *Good Old Houses* is more of the same, only residential properties instead of commercial ones. Each contains eight house puzzles, instructions for play on the possible four levels, and a fact sheet, all in a spiffy box.

You can also purchase a *Good Old Houses* cut-out and coloring book separately. This comes with 12 historical houses, some large to color (with factual text below) and some small to cut out and put together. Presto, your own unzoned neighborhood! Added benefit of these architectural resources: educational walks in the city.

Art Extension Press
Large (7 x 9 or 8 x 10) prints $1.50 each. Small (3 x 4) prints, $1.50 for packet of 10. Accompanying text, $7.50. Two hundred mini-prints (20 packs), $25. Add $3 shipping.

Learn art history and appreciation through a graded series of fine art prints. The text, *Learning More About Pictures*, includes background on each artistic school represented as well as a small version of each print for cross-reference with the actual print. All major schools of Western art are covered, from Primitive to Renaissance to Modern, including each country's distinctive contribution. This is an excellent concept, marred somewhat by

poor lithography, especially apparent on the smaller prints.

Arts in Residence
One year, $18 (12 issues).

A monthly eight-page mini art introduction in the guise of a newsletter. That's *Arts In Residence*, the brainchild of Anne Campbell of Tustin, California. Each issue includes Time Line information (for this reason, you may want to buy the back issues), an About the Artist biographical sketch, in-depth articles about instruments, theatre, definitions of artistic terms, drawing tips, news of upcoming art contests, student work samples, and step by step how-to projects for both younger and older children. The projects are designed to be cut up and pasted on 3 x 5 cards so you can create your own art file.

Arts in Residence covers the fine arts (drawing, painting, and so on), the Performing Arts (music, drama, etc.), and the literary arts. Performance is good: easy to read, useful info. Perspective is gently Christian.

Dover Publications

And while you're thinking of Art Appreciation, try Dover first for those gaudy coffee table books full of paintings. If they have it, it will cost next to nothing compared to the price from other publishers.

EDC
Usborne Story of Painting, $4.95. Also available in a hardbound volume combined with the Story of Music, called Music &

Painting, **$12.95.**

Colorful, copiously illustrated introduction to art through the ages. Includes information on how artists lived and materials they used, as well as introducing several important artists. Starts with cave painting, ends with modern art. Suggested for ages ten and up, but children of any age will enjoy looking at the pictures and listening to the text.

KidsArt News
$8/year (4 issues), 16 pages/issue.

Extremely helpful newsletter that really helps you teach art. You get • easy-to-follow activity pages (different topics each issue, like sculpture or photography) • nationwide artistic events • art teaching tips • interviews with artists, both home schoolers and pros • art product reviews • *and* a fine art print of a famous artwork in every issue. *KidsArt News* looks like it was produced on an Apple Macintosh™ computer, which means that if you like the way this book looks, you will probably like the clean, bold feel of *KidsArt News.*

KONOS
Artists and Composers Timeline, $25.
Timeline lines, $9.95. Add 4% shipping.

Timelines are one of the best ways to learn history. Now your child can get a real feel for art and music history, with the *Konos Artists and Composers Timeline.* You get five laminated blue sheets of figures to cut out and attach to a time line. Each painter holds a major work; each composer holds a major composition. Artists included range from Renaissance to modern, with most concentrated in between. A fun, hands-on way to study art history, and a natural taking-off point for study of individual artists and schools of art.

Parent-Child Press
Mommy, It's a Renoir!, Child-Size
Masterpieces, $10.95 each. Time Lines:
Prehistoric to Present, $19.95; Picasso,

$6.95. Art postcard series for time lines:
Men, Women, Musicians, Mothers with
Children, Picasso, $12.25 each. Animals in
Early Art postcards, $2.95 each or 2 for $5.

A terrific innovation in teaching art appreciation. *Mommy, It's a Renoir!* outlines a course of study based on Montessori principles and using art postcards. First, very young children practice matching identical postcards. They then try pairing two different paintings by the same artist and grouping four paintings by the same artist, eventually progressing to recognizing any studied artist's style in any context. Control cards teach the names of well-known artists and their famous paintings. The book does not include any of these cards, but does contain renditions of 71 works of art.

Child-Size Masterpieces is the first in a projected series of art postcard books to be used with *Mommy, It's a Renoir!* You cut out the cards on the dotted lines and file them in folders. An extra, smaller card is included for each step, to be attached to the outside of the folder. Artists included are mostly impressionists and moderns. This covers only the first three steps (matching identical paintings, pairing companion paintings, and grouping four paintings by one artist). The reproduction is excellent.

Also from Parent-Child Press, the timelines are just that—long strips of paper with dates on them to lay on the floor. The Prehistoric to Present time line takes up a good-sized living room plus some. The idea here is to practice laying the accompanying set of cards down on the time line, so you can see how artistic styles have changed through the ages. I found this impractical. The sheer amount of walking involved tired my children. Also, several time line sections were crammed with cards, while others were completely bare. An improvement here would be to condense the size of the time line to six or ten feet—no more—and choose only one or two card for each time period, spacing them out more evenly.

Publishers' Central Bureau

PCB is another source for low-cost coffee table art books. They sell closeouts, and you can get lavish art books at decent prices. PCB also carries books in many other categories, unfortunately including what is euphemistically termed "erotica."

SOFTART

We have probably a dozen computer art programs scattered around here. We also avidly read the reviews of new computer art programs. So we certainly are willing to try mixing art and computers. But the news is, so far computers are not too good at art.

"How can you say computers are not good at art? Don't they generate all those neat graphics we see on TV and those fancy presentations?" That's right. Computer-aided art is for real. What it is not is fast and easy to control.

Consider what you go through to draw a tree by hand. You grab your pencil or pen, quickly sketch a trunk, some branches, suggest leaves, and that is that. On the computer, you first have to pick up your drawing tool on screen (choice of pen, brush, paintcan, whatever). You drag it to where you want it. Make a line or drop a circle. Size it. Let it go. Go pick up another tool. Drag it where you want it. Use it. Let it go. Pick another starting spot. Make another line. So far, you've just made the tree trunk.

Once you've made a computer drawing, the theory is that you can quickly manipulate it. Sometimes yes, sometimes no. First you have to grab it, which can be difficult if you have lots of lines and shapes on top of each other, as is common in all but the simplest drawings. A break in the line of a drawing will cause your "fill" pattern (another computer benefit) to spread all over the place. Tweaking your drawing can take longer than making another by hand.

The reason most "computer artists" use computer clip art, and the reason computer clip art costs so much, is that producing art onscreen is such a long, long chore. And then,

the finished product's quality leaves something to be desired. Blurry dots are not the same as clean pen lines.

The new generation of art programs (on the Macintosh, at least) get around some of these difficulties. Adobe's *Illustrator*, for example (available for $495!) lets you draw Bezier curves— real lines like in real art, not dot-matrix approximations. It can also select, rotate, skew, resize, and otherwise twiddle your drawings about. But again, for every line you draw, you have to select a beginning point, drag to your ending point, click, select a new beginning point, drag to a new ending point . . . not to mention time spent switching between the line tool, the polygon, the Bezier curve tool, and so on. It will still take you 10 minutes to crosshatch an area you could finish in 10 seconds by hand.

Ah, but you can buy a scanner! This marvelous device will, in sometime between a minute and half an hour, take a page of art and read it into your computer. Just scan in a photo of a building or cat or your mother, touch it up a bit, and you have art! Quickly! And it only cost an additional *$2,000* or more. Ouch!

What we really need are computer tools that let us draw onscreen the same way we do in real life. Graphics tablets that you draw on with a special "pen" claim to approximate this, but have problems coordinating the onscreen cursor with the pen placement when you remove the pen from the tablet. In the meantime, serious computer art is prohibitively expensive for most of us.

The biggest disappointment of all is that there are no good popular computer art tutorials. Why doesn't someone invent a *Learn to Draw* program— perhaps based on Bruce McIntyre's *Drawing Textbook* (and with Mr. McIntyre's cooperation, of course).

Playing with computer art is lots of fun— don't get me wrong. My two-year-old loves to scribble on screen, and her older siblings like to fool with the special effects like airbrushing and design patterns. But this is no way to learn to draw, or to efficiently produce anything but straight geometric art. Not yet.

CHAPTER TWENTY-ONE

MUSIC

Some of us have suffered at the hands of piano teachers, and consequently cast a jaded eye on the prospect of teaching or learning music at home, or anywhere else. Fear not. This section is pretty much free from the sort of musical exercises Miss Grump used to try to force your sweaty fingers through. Yes, some music teachers still make scale exercises and theory the meat of their diet, but they happily are few and far between.

Let me explain that I'm not down on playing scales or learning music theory. Scales and finger exercises are good for developing agility and music theory provides one sort of framework for the art. It's just that people take music lessons to learn to play an instrument, not to learn *about* playing an instrument. I myself quit taking piano lessons when my teacher refused to let me attempt Tchaikovsky's Nutcracker Suite, condemning me instead to more weary months of Bartok piano exercises. I liked Tchaikovsky; I was familiar with the music (unlike Bartok, which always sounded to my youthful ears like a mistake). So why didn't my teacher let me try it?

That question propels us into a burning debate among music teachers. Do people learn music best by proceeding step by cautious step and not being allowed to even try advanced pieces until they have been "taught" how to play them? Another issue: Is it a good idea to concentrate on learning pieces you have never heard? One more question: Is it best to learn theory before, during, or after having mastered the elementary playing techniques?

According to the theory developed in *The NEW Big Book of Home Learning*, it would be a good idea to become familiar with how a particular piece sounds before trying to play it yourself. Listening to music builds up your "data" on which your musical knowledge will be based. It would also be a good idea to mess about on the instrument before settling down to serious learning. "Playing" provides tactile data—you discover what movement makes what sound. Sight reading, a highly refined skill, would follow playing by ear in this view. You'd want to get a "feel" for the instrument and for music in general before attempting to delve into the complexities of music notation and theory.

It just so happens that part of the musical approach outlined above is the famous Suzuki method. Shinichi Suzuki, a Japanese man, developed a method of music instruction that begins by exposing the student to lots of good music— in fact, the very pieces he will learn to play. Once he has become thoroughly familiar with these pieces, he is allowed to begin lessons. Music theory is only introduced after the student has already been playing for some time.

Mr. Suzuki has added some other touches as well. Children's parents are at least present for all lessons, and are encouraged to learn along with the children. Students also spend some time in group lessons and recitals, where they get to hear musicians of various ages and skill levels play. This gives them a taste of what they can look forward to accomplishing, as well as getting them used to playing before a friendly audience. All is done in a spirit of helping and comradeship (at least ideally). Using this method, very young children have demonstrated amazing musicianship.

Suzuki has not confined his thinking to music instruction alone. He is the founder of the "Talent Education" school of thought, which shares some of the spirit of the Human Potential movement. True, Suzuki follows the "mastery learning" approach of forbidding children to tackle anything new until the old is thoroughly learned. And controversy swirls about the questions of how much and if and when parents should make children practice, an issue over which Suzuki teachers have split. But access to an instrument of the right size; a wide mental library of good music; the support of other musicians and the encouragement of one's family; putting off academic studies until the student can see the need for them; these ideas are gaining ground.

Another big name in music instruction is Zoltan Kodaly, a Hungarian man. Kodaly was vitally interested in singing as the best introduction to music of all kinds. As Laszlo Eosze relates in *Zoltan Kodaly: His Life and Work* (Crescendo Publishing Company, 1962),

> "That the teaching of music is best begun with singing," he writes, "that it is through singing, and before ever touching an instrument, that the child should learn to read music, are

recognized as truths by a good many people . . . Mechanical training in instrumental playing, without corresponding theoretical education; music-making with the fingers instead of the soul; the omission of any thorough musical grounding; and neglect of solfeggio— these are the direct causes of the present decadence of singing and of the increasing number of second-rate professional musicians . . ."

Kodaly's great crusade was to revive solfeggio, the ear training of being able to recognize notes and intervals in any key and sing them. We are familiar with this as Do-Re-Mi-Fa-So-La-Te-Do style singing. In this way, the student would be able to pick up a score of music, once trained in sight reading, and hear it in his head. He would also be able to translate music into staff notation, and duplicate it by ear in his instrument.

Kodaly was also a champion of Early Childhood Music Education. He deplored the use of the piano in teaching songs and choral music as a (possibly untuned) crutch that prevented children from appreciating pure, virginal melody. Kodaly also was active in encouraging music societies and choral singing, writing a number of volumes of choral exercises for young people. He then turned to popularizing the pentatonic scale, in an attempt to revive a national Hungarian musical consciousness. This was followed by the publication of *24 Little Canons of the Black Keys.*

> They spring from the idea that, as in the case of singing, instrumental studies should start with pentatonic melodies . . . The first sixteen pieces are transcribed in solmization signs [e.g. do-re-mi style], and only the last eight are scored conventionally . . . Two other points of interest here are, firstly, that the two parts are recorded on the same line; and, secondly, that the eight conventionally scored canons are intended to be played a semitone higher than the score indicates. The purpose of this is to develop musical thinking and a facility for transposition.

At the time *Zoltan Kodaly: His Life and Work* was written, its Hungarian author says, "The principles embodied in this, and in the previously discussed works, have to-day become the basis both for musical training and for the teaching of singing in schools . . . " That was back in 1962. However, Kodaly's methods are by no means dead. Silver Burdett Company, a major textbook publisher, has a line of classroom music instruction based on Kodaly's methods, and Kodaly's name is familiar to students of music.

Suzuki and Kodaly are not, of course, the only names in music instruction today. But they are two you will keep running across, most likely. Between the two of them— Kodaly with his interest in solfeggio and in making the black keys and pentatonic tones accessible, and Suzuki with his stress on exposing the student to lots of good music and allowing him to learn in a supportive atmosphere— you will find plenty of good ideas to start with.

LEARNING TO READ MUSIC

Christian Education Music Publishers
   K workbook $3.75, grades 1-4 $4.75, teacher's guide $3. Shipping $3 extra per order for workbooks only (USA and Canada). Sample set includes all above for $21.50 postpaid. You need *all* **workbooks for the complete program.**

The *Your Musical Friends* workbook series is a music reading program for K-4. Each musical symbol is carried by a cartoon animal. Quacker Treble Clef, for example, has a body made of the treble clef, a tail like a bass clef, and quarter notes for feet! There's Crescendo Whale and Forte Lion and Sixteenth Note Bird and Ritard Turtle— 29 animals in all.

The kindergarten book introduces the characters in the form of a coloring book. The first grade book, *Fun With Your Musical Friends*, gets into the two staffs and notes and rests. The second grade book, *Enjoying Music With Your Musical Friends*, looks at line and space note values and the loud and soft signs. The third grade book, *Learning More With Your Musical Friends*, includes sharps, flats, tempo, repeats, and accents. Finally, the fourth grade book, *Reading Music With Your Musical Friends*, covers the last details of dotted notes

and so on, and launches into actual sight reading.

Each book begins with a review of the previous book. The exercises and stories are fun and colorful and *very* Christian. An example: a fill-in-the-blanks-with-the-note-name exercise in the fourth grade book about how Isaac Watts' mother had to spank him for continuing to drive her crazy by always speaking in rhyme gives Isaac's reply: "Mother, do some pity take. I will no more verses make!" Because the publisher strives to keep costs low and therefore uses medium-grade paper, the art is muddy, but that is my only quibble. If your children want to know what all those funny little squiggles in the hymnbook mean, this is a series for you.

Jeffrey Norton
   Learning to Read Music, **80-minute cassette and booklet, $14.95. Shipping extra.**

A self-instructional course. *Learning to Read Music* covers all the basics in only an hour and a half. Pitch. Duration. Rhythm. Note heads. Rests. Dotted notes. Clefs. Sharps and flats. Key signatures. Naturals. Repeats. Other musical symbols and terms. The little booklet *shows* what the cassette *describes*, plus providing some reinforcement exercises. A total beginner would want to listen through several times; a rusty adult wanting to brush up might only need to go through this once. Any wide-awake and motivated person, no matter how young, could pick up a lot of musical notation through this inexpensive course.

Praise Hymn
   God Made Music **Student Book, each grade, $4.98 retail/$2.98 wholesale. Teacher's Manual, each grade, $9.98/$5.98, except Kindermusic Teacher's Manual, which is $14.98/$8.98. Student Songbook, each grade, $4.98/$2.98.** *Sing-A-Long Cassette*, **each grade, $9.98/$5.98. Home schoolers who prepay are eligible for wholesale rates. Shipping and handling billed separately.**

Christian music-reading instruction. Praise Hymn's bag of tricks includes:

• The *God Made Music* series (K-7), with accompanying Teacher's Manuals for K-6 (the grade 7 book can be studied alone or with an instructor). For K-2, the instructor may have only a limited musical background; for grades 3-7, the instructor needs to understand basic music concepts. This is a much more complete musical program than *Your Musical Friends*, covering band instrument recognition, songs to be learned by heart, classical music introduction (with the recommended selections available on correlated records and cassettes), music styles, Old and New Testament music, and lots more. Of course, this also requires a deeper commitment on the part of both parent and child.

• *We Sing Music* songbooks and cassettes are a collection of American heritage and fun songs to be used with *God Made Music* or alone. This is a completely different series than the *Wee Sing* series from Price/Stern/Sloan, in spite of the similar format and name.

• The *Christian School Band Method, Music Invaders,* and the *Hymnplayer* series, reviewed below under Music Instruction.

• Plus correlated filmstrips, classical records and cassettes, felt board and music symbols, and an Instruments Picture Poster.

Rainfall Toys
Piano Play-Book, **$14.99.**

Really cute way to introduce single-note keyboard playing. Rainfall's *Piano Play-Book* combines a color-coded electronic keyboard that really plays with a hardbound book of 11 best-loved Bible songs. Each song is laid out with both traditional music notation and color codes, so even a three-year-old could play the tunes, if so inclined. Happy pictures and words to every tune round this out. Batteries are replaceable and the book is surprisingly tough. A real bargain at the price.

Reformed Presbyterian Church of North America
Book of Psalms for Singing, **$10.95.** *Praise Him!,* **$6.95. Psalm cassettes, write for brochure. Order individual copies of** *Book of Psalms* **and** *Praise Him!* **from Home Life—add 10% shipping. Bulk orders, send to the RPCNA. Why not buy enough psalmbooks for your whole church to enjoy?**

Testimony time: I learned to read music and sing harmony with *The Book of Psalms for Singing.* This is a hymnbook consisting solely of arrangements of every Psalm in the Bible, mostly set to familiar hymn tunes. *Praise Him!* is a attractive smaller selection of the same (162 arrangements as opposed to 425 in the *Book of Psalms for Singing*), wire-bound, with a leatherette cover.

Singing the Psalms is such a marvelous spiritual blessing that it was worth struggling to learn to read music even without a teacher's guide. (Basically, I practiced singing intervals until I could more-or-less figure out what note went where.) But the RPCNA is at work on a video to teach four-part singing from the Psalter and also a cassette with one verse from every psalm in the Psalter. These two teaching tools, due out soon, will make learning to sing harmony much easier. And right now you can order a number of four-part Psalmody teaching tapes: soprano, alto, tenor, and bass parts sung together, then separately. The songs on these latter tapes are not in sequential order, that is, you don't get Psalm 1 followed by Psalm

2 and Psalm 3, etc., so you will still need the new tape of all arrangements if you want to learn all the psalms.

MUSIC INSTRUCTION

This section is about instruction on specific instruments, not general theory or music-reading. But before we go any further, let me share with you what a reader (Colleen Story) shared with me.

> *The Right Instrument for Your Child,* by Atarah Ben-Tovim and Douglas Boyd (Quill imprint of William Morrow, Inc., 1985), a $12.95 paperback, is a must for anyone considering starting a child on a musical instrument. The authors did 10 years of research and concluded choosing the wrong instrument was the most common factor in musical failure— not lack of "musicality" or music potential. The second most common factor was starting at the wrong time— too early. They felt their research indicated that, for 95 percent of children, the best time to begin an instrument is between eight to eleven years old. The book is designed to help you determine, through questionnaires and profiles of musicians who like specific instruments, which instrument(s) are best suited to your child's temperament, physical characteristics, and readiness. The one instrument suggested for six to eight year olds is the recorder . . .

Thanks, Colleen. I suspected as much. In spite of all the frantic rush to get nurslings involved with a musical instrument, *spiritual* readiness (the ability to persevere and the desire to create a work of art) still seems a logical prerequisite to serious musical instruction.

Play around with music all you like; expose your children to great music and let them fool with instruments, by all means. But if you want to nurture a lifelong love of music, you might be better off telling your youngsters to wait until they've demonstrated the maturity to make good use of official music lessons.

Ability Development

"The Suzuki Place." Violins, accessories, books, music, flutes, strings, cassettes, metronomes, novelties. Ability Development stocks an outstanding array of books about music, including of course all of Suzuki's books and many books about the Suzuki method. I found about a hundred dollars' worth of books I wanted just by glancing through their catalog.

To make your shopping easier, Ability Development has prepared several "Panda Packs" for Suzuki beginners. These include essential books for understanding Suzuki, cassettes of the music your children will be learning, and the music sheets to go along with them.

Ability Development has Suzuki series for violin, viola, cello, and flute, plus the instruments themselves and all necessary accessories. Also classical recordings, a wide selection of the best.

If you're serious about music, this is a catalog not to miss.

Birch Tree Group Ltd.

Suzuki Method International, a division of Birch Tree Group Ltd., is the sole publisher of the Suzuki Method for the world outside Japan. They distribute the core music books and recordings for the Suzuki Piano School, Violin School, Viola School, Cello School, Flute School, and Harp School. In addition they carry supplementary material (both music and texts) for the Suzuki Method. Ability Development, Shar, Kentuckiana, and Southwestern Stringed Instruments carry most of their line, or your local music dealer can order direct from Birch Tree Group Ltd.

Summy-Birchard Music, another division of Birch Tree Group Ltd., carries other educational music methods/texts (e.g., Frances Clark® Piano Method).

Folkways Records/Smithsonian Institute, another division, handles the entire Folkways catalog. This is considered the most extensive collection of international, ethnic, and folk recordings in the world.

Holt Associates

John Holt was not only a major voice in the home school movement, but also an amateur musician of some dedication. Unlike many others, he believed that it's *Never Too Late* to begin learning music, and he published his musical biography under that title. Holt Associates sells the book, which contains valuable insights on the subject of music instruction from the viewpoint of an empirical thinker. Holt Associates also carries a select line of what can only be described as music counterculture: books like *How To Learn the Piano Despite Years of Lessons* and *Mrs. Stewart's Piano Method*. The latter encourages beginners to roam over the entire keyboard by applying solfeggio principles to instrument playing. Holt Associates also sells instruments, some standard and some not. Here's a different view of music: music for the people instead of music for the snobs.

Homespun Tapes

Each 1-hour audio casette comes with printed matter. Single tape, $12.95. Three-tape series, $32.50. Six-tape series, $65. Sixty-minute video cassettes, $49.95 each. Ninety-minute video cassettes, $59.95 each. These also come with printed matter. Shipping extra.

If I told you how much I like Homespun Tapes, you'd think I was exaggerating. So let's stick to bare facts. Here is a company run by professional musicians that sells music instruction tapes produced by themselves and other professional musicians. Styles covered are folk, blues, rock, bluegrass, country, and jazz. The instruction is mellow and familiar and you can rerun the tape any time you want. Along with the tapes come printed matter giving the music scores and perhaps some explanatory notes. It's like having a private lesson with one of the best musicians in the country, and you can repeat the lesson as many times as you like!

Who teaches the courses? Here's some examples: Livingston Taylor on "Hit Guitar Styles", Amos Garrett (several series, including "Electric Guitar"), John Sebastian and Paul Butterfield on "Blues Harmonica" and Lorraine Lee on "Appalachian Dulcimer." These are top musicians, folks, and you couldn't get a private lesson of this quality if you signed up and waited for a year, let alone one that cost less than $7.

Before I start listing some of the "fun" courses, please note this: Homespun Tapes sells an excellent series on Ear Training that teaches the principles of solfeggio. Matt Glaser does the honors, and I can't think of a better introduction to real musicianship for anyone mature enough to do the exercises. In other words, most five-year-olds won't dig it, but Mozart would have.

Homespun Tapes, besides its essential series on guitar, harmonica, bass, banjo, fiddle, autoharp, and piano, has a potpourri of courses on unusual instruments and techniques. We finally moved out of a two-family building with very near neighbors, and I bought the *Learn to Yodel* two-cassette series. It's a great way to call the kids (or the hogs!) home. You can get a pennywhistle (not for a penny, unhappily) to go with the *Irish Pennywhistle* three-tape set. Folksy types can latch on to a selection of Dulcimer courses, and weird ones can tackle something called "Dawg Mandolin." Some of the best courses are now on video, such as *Contest Fiddling* with Mark O'Connor, *Learning to Fingerpick* with Happy Traum, and *Basic Guitar Set-Up and Repair*, a course that is only offered by video, for obvious reasons.

In all, there are 66 different series as of this writing, most consisting of more than one tape. Any musician can learn something with Homespun tapes, and aspiring musicians will find Homespun a feast.

International Montessori Society
The Making of Music, Child's Book $12, Teacher's Manual $18. Shipping extra.

IMS isn't really in the music business, strictly speaking. However, I noticed that some of the Montessori materials they sell feature an innovative approach to music instruction. One in particular caught my eye: *The Making of Music* by Hestia Abeyesekera. Modestly subtitled, "Breakthrough in Music Education," this book can be used with or without a piano in the home. It "covers the entire keyboard through a series of 30 songs, specially designed for transposing on all the major keys and their minors, including their inversions." I don't exactly know how it works, but it's supposed to integrate "the educational philosophies of Montessori, Orff, Kodaly and Laban." The testimonials say *The Making of Music* is very good in its rhythmic training and that it helps children explore the keyboard freely.

Mandolin Brothers, Ltd.

Instruction books for every fretted instrument you can think of: dulcimer, fiddle, cello, acoustic bass, violin, mandolin, autoharp, banjo, guitar, and bass guitar. Large selection. Not to mention the huge selection of instruments, accessories, and songbooks mentioned in the next section.

Jeffrey Norton
Key to the Keys: Volume 1 (one cassette and instruction book), $15.95; Volume 2 (two cassettes and instruction book), $21.95. Both volumes, $35. Shipping extra.

Key to the Keys is a self-taught piano method that begins with chords and gets you playing before you learn to read notes. You start with short familiar melodies and advance to more complex songs and musical compositions. So says the brochure.

Praise Hymn
Christian School Band Method: Flute, Clarinet, Trumpet, Trombone, $3.98 retail/$2.48 wholesale; Saxophone, Bass, $4.98/$2.98; Band Director, $14.98/$8.98. Music Invaders: Student Book $4.98/$2.98; Teacher's Manual, $9.98/$5.98. Hymnplayer series, each book $4.98/$2.98. Home school parents may receive the wholesale discount if order paid in advance. Shipping and handling billed separately.

For those of us who get behind the idea of a Home school Marching Band, the *Christian School Band Method* series has children learning to play hymns and gospel songs while they learn to play their: flutes, clarinets, alto saxes, trumpets, trombones, and basses.

Music Invaders, designed for junior high choir students (but usable by motivated elementary-age home schoolers), is 24 20-minute lessons designed to teach vocal music reading with a "space invaders" theme. You will need the accompanying Teacher's Manual.

The *Hymnplayer* series teaches how to play hymns (surprise!) on the piano. The series has three books for each section: Beginning Hymnplayer, Primary Hymnplayer, Intermediate Hymnplayer, and Advanced Hymnplayer.

Rhythm Band

Educational games for teaching music concepts— pages and pages of these. Flash cards, staff liners, and all that good stuff. Instructional materials geared to elementary-age children. Plus, of course, Rhythm Band's terrific selection of musical instruments. See the Musical Instruments section for further information.

Shar Products

Shar sells the Children's Music Series by Evelyn Bedient Avsharian. This contains workbooks and games for teaching music reading by several innovative methods, plus fun and easy songs. Example: the *Mississippi Hot Dog Lonely Hamburger Band* is said to include "exciting pieces on A alone (!!!), E alone, and both strings. Duets and rounds in two basic Twinkle rhythms." I'd be interested in seeing anything that made playing one note exciting.

Shar's listing of sheet music for string players and records and cassettes of string music is as complete as you can reasonably expect. Plus a large selection of hard-to-find videocassettes of • great string players and teachers • writers • artists • opera • and ballet. You will probably want to send for this no-frills catalog.

Silver Burdett

Silver Burdett, a public school textbook company, has *Listen, Look, and Sing,* a complete elementary Kodaly curriculum. They also sell *Silver Burdett Music,* "the most popular music program in America" for public schools.

MUSICAL INSTRUMENTS

Ability Development
Violin prices range from the low $200's to almost $400. Several different brands stocked. Ten-day money-back guarantee.

Child-sized violins and *all* the accessories (bows, bridges, mutes, shoulder pads, string adjusters, strings . . . even polishing cloths). Plus metronomes, folding music stands, tuning forks, and those other oddments so necessary to the pursuit of musical perfection.

Holt Associates

Several fun 'n simple instruments: pianica, recorder, child-sized violins. Holt Associates stresses playability, believing in the making of music more than endless practice in hopes of someday sounding good. Good prices.

The Instrument Workshop

If you'd like to make your own old-fashioned keyboard instrument, this company is the source. You have to buy their catalogs of tools, parts and plans, replacement parts and accessories, kits, and plan sources. They also have a *List of Recordings of Historical Keyboard Instruments* that has about 150 listings of pre-1850 instruments with artist, record title and content, record company, and record number.

Lark in the Morning

I don't know if these people really exist or not, since they did not respond to my letter. The description of their catalog made my tongue hang out. Here is (if they exist) a purveyor of rare and unusual instruments, including medieval music-makers like the crumhorn and sackbut. Is this for real? I love medieval music!

Mandolin Brothers, Ltd.

If you're a music-lover don't you dare send for this catalog unless you have at least several hundred dollars in hand. Mandolin Brothers specializes in new and vintage guitars, mandolins, and banjos, and the selection will knock your eyeballs out. The brothers are recognized authorities on vintage fretted instruments, and they offer goodies in their catalog such as a 1946 Martin D-28 Herringbone. "We don't know one player who wouldn't like to own this guitar," the brothers say. Too true. The lovely creation goes for $4975. Another Martin D-28 made in 1950 was advertised as "You be the judge— we can ship this guitar to you, on approval. $1800."

If, like me, you can't play in this league, Mandolin Brothers carries an outstanding

Stan Jay

assortment of fretted instruments for small-timers. Plus every fretted instrument accessory known to man, songbooks for dulcimer, fiddle, cello, acoustic bass, violin, mandolin, autoharp, and banjo. Plus instruction books in all the above plus guitar and bass guitar.

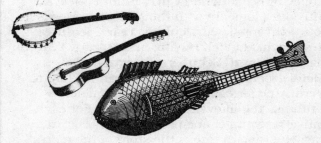

Music for Little People
Sample prices below. Shipping extra.

Definite New Age flavor to this graceful, imaginative catalog of music and instruments for little people. The emphasis here is on folk instruments from around the world. Something for everyone, from the $16 Pan Pipes to the $149 21 chord Chromaharp. Kallisti Marimba, $99. Irish Bohdran Drum, $59. Handcrafted Heartsong Dolphin Drum Miba (slit drum), $75. Ukelele, $22.50. Gianinni Little Guitar, $59.95. Fantasy Flute, $25. Eight String Black Mountain Lyre, $46. Mbira (African Thumb Piano), $38. Mbira Kit that "children over eight can put together," $19. Various models and all sizes of Suzuki and Chinese violins available for purchase or rent-to-buy. Various chime sets. All items chosen for beauty of appearance and tone.

Rhythm Band

If you've got kids, and the kids like music, and you're willing that they should, you'll really like this catalog. Rhythm Band is one of those entrepreneurial success stories that public school economics courses keep forgetting to mention. Started with two employees and a borrowed $6,000, Rhythm Band has grown to be one of the largest conglomerates in the music industry, employing over 3,000 people. The reason for this outstanding success will become obvious the minute you open RB's catalog. It's something for everybody, at prices anyone can afford, and covering 99 percent of the field of kids' music.

Rhythm Band has pages and pages of instruments for sale. You can get rhythm band sets (but of course!), in sizes for small families and for large institutions. Low-priced folk instruments from many countries. Beginning instruments for young players. Fun instruments even a baby can fool around with (you've probably noticed these in the tonier baby catalogs). High-tech instruments. Chromaharps. Pianicas. Metronomes. Orff instruments. Bells.

Rhythm Band also has instructional materials: pitchpipes, staff liners, musical notation flash cards, and books on music instruction. More, they sell educational games for teaching music concepts. The catalog has several pages of these, enough to make any music teacher lose control of her pocketbook. There's a page of Hap Palmer records and a page about Andre Previn's *Guide to Music*. Plus supplementary items like full-color prints of orchestra instruments and composers.

Rhythm Band's prices are outstanding. You can get an Aulos Soprano Recorder for only $2.50. We have one of these and it's no Cracker Jacks job. No wonder schools, with their strapped music budgets, patronize Rhythm Band so freely.

The catalog is full-color and easy to use. Many school suppliers sell Rhythm Band instruments, but if you have a music-lovin' kid, why not go to the source?

Shar Products

Shar is really two companies in one. On one level, they're a heavy-duty supplier of violins, cellos, basses and all the paraphernalia that professional players of the same require. On the other level, they're a big-time Suzuki supplier, with a comprehensive listing of books about Suzuki, Suzuki recordings, and instrument outfits for little players. For more information, see the Music Instruction section above.

MUSIC HISTORY AND APPRECIATION

Aristoplay
Music Maestro, $25.

As a game, I personally haven't found Music Maestro to be all that thrilling, but it is a good overview of musical instruments and their functions and sounds. You get an audio cassette with the sounds of over twenty instruments, a game board, several decks of cards, and rules to play five games of increasing difficulty. Instruments included are classical 'n medieval, bluegrass, rock, and jazz. We have decided the medieval is our favorite period, and our favorite instrument is the one that sounds like a giant kazoo (now is that the rebec?)

Players not only identify individual instruments, but learn to place them in the correct ensembles and the correct period. Even little kids can play the simplest games— which, as I said, are not that exciting. Part of the problem is that the same instrument always plays the same song on the cassette, thus making it possible to identify instruments by the tunes on the tape without really knowing which instrument makes which sound.

As a teaching tool, Music Maestro is worth the money. But a barrel of laughs it ain't.

Christian Curriculum Project
$50/year plus $2.50 shipping.

Here's something perfectly delightful for music fans. Christian Curriculum Project's Music & Moments with the Masters series is a four-year music curriculum. Year 1 features J.S. Bach, Handel, Haydn, and Mozart. Year 2 has Beethoven, Schubert, Berlioz, and Mendelssohn. Year 3 it's Schumann, Chopin, Verdi, and Grieg. Year 4 you get Wagner, Brahms, Tchaikovsky, and Dvorak. For each musician you get one professionally-narrated cassette tape that tells the story of the man's life interspersed with excerpts from pieces he composed during the period being narrated. You also get a second tape of the master's "Greatest Hits." Each year, then, has eight tapes in all, plus a small booklet giving background information and a valuable resource list for further reading and study. *The Gift of Music: Great Composers and Their Influence* (Crossway Books) also now accompanies this series.

CCP is using cassettes published by Allegro and CBS Records. The quality is superb and they have great kid-appeal.

EDC
The Story of Music, $4.95. Combined hardbound volume, *Music & Painting,* that also includes *The Story of Painting,* $12.95.

Lively, colorful book that introduces

musical techniques, instruments, and great composers, from the first instruments to the age of electronic music. You won't find a simpler, more fascinating introduction to music history anywhere.

ESP
   Worksheets, $5/set. *The Orchestra,* **$80.** *What's Music All About?,* **$80. Each of the latter is 24 15-minute lessons on 12 cassettes plus 24 spirit masters.**

ESP, a public school supplier, has a line of spirit master worksheet exercises that cover such things as Introducing the Treble Clef; Music Signs; Music Notation; and so on. More ambitious are there two twelve-cassette-plus-spirit-master-workbook sets, *The Orchestra* and *What's Music All About.*

The Orchestra covers: • What Is an Orchestra? • The Symphony Orchestra • History of the Symphony Orchestra • Players in a Symphony Orchestra • The Conductor • Music Played by a Symphony Orchestra • Who Supports the Symphony Orchestra? [Good question!] • Instrumental Families of the Symphony Orchestra • The String Family • The Woodwind Family • The Brass Family • The Percussion Family • The Concert Hall • Enjoying a Concert • Other Kinds of Orchestras • Dance Orchestras and Jazz Bands • Bands • Small Orchestral Groups • Pop & Rock Groups • Accompanying Orchestras • Unusual Orchestras • Unusual Instruments in the Orchestra • How You Can Join an Orchestra • Future of the Orchestra in America.

What's Music All About? covers: • Origin of Music • Early Musical Instruments • Basic Music Notation • Musical Notation Drill • Major and Minor Scales • The Chromatic Scale and Others • What Is a Melody? • Characteristics of Melody • What is Rhythm? • Characteristics of Rhythm • What is Harmony? • Characteristics of Harmony • Forms Used in Music • Common Terms • Identify Instruments— Visually • Identify Instruments— Audibly • Vocal Skills •

Famous Composers • Classical Music • Music of the Opera • The World of Marches • Jazz • Music from Other Lands • Modern or Popular Music.

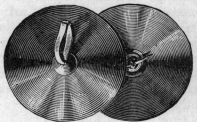

Konos
   Artists and Composers Timeline, **$25. Timeline lines, $9.95. Add 4% shipping.**

Timelines are one of the best ways to learn history. Now your child can get a real feel for art and music history, with the *Konos Artists and Composers Timeline.* You get five laminated blue sheets of figures to cut out and attach to a time line. Each painter holds a major work; each composer holds a major composition. Artists and musicians included range from Renaissance to modern, with most concentrated in between. A fun, hands-on way to study art history, and a natural taking-off point for study of individual musicians and schools of music.

Laissez-Faire Books
   Music: Theory, History, and Performance **(12 cassettes), $129.50 plus $1.50 postage or $2.50 UPS. Includes free brochure, The Fine Arts in America.**

Twelve-part series of lectures of Allan and Joan Mitchell Blumenthal, delivered in 1974 under the auspices of Ayn Rand. Set includes: • The Nature of Music • The Birth of Western Music • The Beginning of the Modern Era • The Pace Accelerates (late Baroque and Rococo) • Consolidation (classical period) • The Climax of Musical Development (Romanticism seen as the climax) • Romanticism explored • The Later Romantics (nationalist composers, post-romantics, impressionism) • Music as the Reflection of a Culture (with particular reference to the parallel disintegration of Western music and culture) • The Identification of Composers Through Style • The Role of the Performing Artist • Landmarks (recorded performances of great artists from Caruso through Segovia and Horowitz), • The Role of the Conductor • and Greatness in Music (a comparison of great and not-so-great music, and outline of the listener's role). This series, reflecting the pragmatist, libertarian viewpoint of Rand and her followers, is available exclusively from Laissez-Faire Books.

Price/Stern/Sloan
   Wee Sing book/cassette sets, $8.95 each. Wee Sing video, $29.95 (VHS or Beta). Wee Color Wee Sing coloring book/cassette/marker sets, $6.95. All prices postpaid.

Music history includes the history of children's music. Wee Sing authors Pam Beall and Susan Nipp performed the formidable task of collecting the best classic children's music, arranging it into sensible order, and producing it with panache. The Wee Sing line now includes the original *Wee Sing, Wee Sing and Play, Wee Sing Silly Songs, We Sing Around the Campfire* (this includes a section of campfire Gospel songs), *Wee Sing Nursery Rhymes and Lullabies* (a story motif holds the songs together), and their latest production, *Wee Sing Bible Songs*. Each cassette comes with an illustrated songbook containing all the songs on cassette, plus some extra. The presentation is so varied and excellent and the price so right that these are the best-selling children's cassettes today.

New from Price/Stern/Sloan Publishers, the *Wee Color Wee Sing* series trades the songbook for a coloring book with pictures illustrating the songs and markers to color the pictures. The cassettes in this series provide music and instructions for creative activities including in the coloring book. Also, the new *Wee Sing Together* video includes 21 songs from the series embedded in a fantasy plot about a little girl's birthday party.

Toys to Grow On
   Introductory Set, $29. Complete set, $75. Shipping extra.

Toys to Grow On sells some of the same musical biographies as Christian Curriculum Project, without the accompanying straight-music cassette or teachers' guides. Their Introductory Set includes Bach, Mozart, Chopin, Beethoven, Tchaikovsky, and Brahms. The complete set of 18 includes the above plus: Handel, Mendelssohn, Strauss, Foster & Sousa, Schubert, Berlioz, Haydn, Schumann & Grieg, Verdi, Wagner & Corelli, and Dvorak. Toys to Grow On also has a small selection of other music materials.

SHEET MUSIC

Ability Development
Birch Tree Group Ltd.
Dover Publications
Mandolin Brothers
Shar Products
   These are all sources for a wide variety of sheet music. Ability Development and Shar carry classical and Suzuki sheet music. Mandolin Brothers has mostly folk and pop sheet music for fretted instruments, and Dover carries over 150 classic and pop music scores, at possibly the lowest prices in music publishing today.

Warren Publishing House/Totline Press
   Piggyback Songs series, $6.95 each. Shipping extra.

Sheet music for every child. No notes to read, no tunes to forget. What you get are new songs to sing to familiar old tunes. Example: (to the tune of Farmer in the Dell)

Christmas time is near.
Christmas time is near
Merry Christmas everyone.
Christmas time is near.

It's time to trim the tree.
It's time to trim the tree.
Merry Christmas everyone.
It's time to trim the tree.

Each song has chord names above it (F, C, C7, and so on), so you can play along with an autoharp, guitar, or other chorded instrument.

The series so far includes: *Piggyback Songs, More Piggyback Songs, Piggyback Songs for Infants and Toddlers, Piggyback Songs in Praise of God*, and *Piggyback Songs in Praise of Jesus*. Each book is organized into categories of songs (e.g., *More Piggyback Songs* includes Songs About Winter, About Spring, About Summer, About Fall, About School, About Me, About Animals, and Just For Fun). All books are a large $8\frac{1}{2}$ x 11 inches and contain between 64 and 96 pages.

MUSIC SOFTWARE

Once upon a time the Commodore was *the* computer for music-makers. It had music keyboards and programs that would do everything your musical little heart desired.

Then some clever folks took something called the MIDI interface and made it accessible to personal computers. They also invented digitizers (so now you can *hum* your compositions into an Apple), and great programs that let you play your Macintosh masterpieces on a synthesizer. Even better, with a sound chip upgrade to your old Apple or the gorgeous synthesized sound of the new Apple IIGS, you could make some real nice four-part harmony. Apple's commitment to leading the pack in the sound department means that Macintoshes also output great sound these days, although to be really impressive you had better run it into some bigger speakers. Amiga, Commodore, IBM, Atari, and so on at this moment are no-shows compared to the new Apple and Macintosh line

when it comes to sound.

Here, then, are some of the latest and greatest programs for teaching and playing music on the Apple and Macintosh— and, oh yeah, on those other Brand X machines as well.

One-Stop Shopping for Music Software

Wenger Corporation/Music Learning Division
Coda catalog, $4. Worth it.

Don't waste your time wandering all over the woods looking for music software, MIDI interfaces, books, and accessories. The gorgeous Coda catalog from Wenger has it all. Really. for Apple II family, Commodore 64 and 128, Macintoshes of all sorts, IBM PC (and PCjr, XT, AT, and compatibles), Atari 8-Bit and ST, and Amiga. Did we forget anyone? I don't think so.

What you see is more than you expect to get. The catalog is a work of art. Printed on highest quality paper, illumined like a cross between a medieval manuscript and an Art Nouveau clip-art book. Colorful. Beautiful. Thorough product descriptions. Everything I review below, plus about a thousand music items I don't review, is in this catalog. Really.

Now, Some Music Software

EduSoft
Magic Piano, Apple II family, $49.95.

A year or so ago I said, "It's about time some decent music software came out for something besides Commodore!" This is the decent music software in question: *Magic Piano.*

With *Magic Piano*, you can play, record, and play back songs in any rhythm you choose. Not only that, you can print your masterpieces, and they will come out in beautiful standard music notation. More: *Magic Piano's* "Simon Says" game helps you develop your musical ear. The computer plays a tune (you pick how many notes long), and you try to reproduce it. If you miss any notes, the computer tells you if you were too high or too low, and replays the song. If you absolutely can't figure it out, you can beg to see the tune displayed. Anyone from kids to symphony orchestra players can enjoy this game, as the two-note selections are very easy and the long pieces are very hard.

And to top it all off is a little number called the "Rhythm Game." This is Simon Says with rhythm: the computer belts out a rhythm and you try to duplicate it by hitting the spacebar in exactly the same rhythm. Again, you can choose your difficulty level. Not only can you pick easier or tougher rhythms, but you can decide whether the computer will be lenient and let a close try through, or persnickety and demand rhythmical perfection.

You "play" the computer by tapping the number keys. Easy as Do-Re-Mi!

Electronic Arts

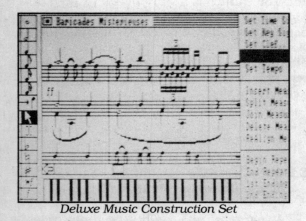
Deluxe Music Construction Set

Deluxe Music Construction Set, $99.95, Macintosh family . Music Construction Set: Apple II family; Commodore 64 or 128; IBM PC, PCjr, XT, or Compaq; Atari 8-bit; $19.95 each. New version available for Apple IIGS features 15 all-new digitized instruments.

Comes with detailed manual, program disk, and instrument and music disk. This program is copy protected, but can be installed onto a hard disk.

Deluxe Music Construction Set is a serious

music processor. You enter notes by clicking on a graphics keyboard or on the display of the music. If you miss where you want to put the note, just drag it to where you want it. The program gives you full editing capability: select multiple notes, cut and paste, etc. You can produce perfectly detailed sheet music. The program prints the score beautifully on the ImageWriter, and typeset quality on the LaserWriter using Adobe's *Sonata* font. You can play your composition on the internal speaker or hook the computer to an amplifier. A full range of keyboard commands has been provided for those who do not like using the mouse.

Some features of this powerful program: • guitar chords supported • takes real-time MIDI music input • capability to change instruments and play styles within each staff • variable volume range and playback speed • full four voice Macintosh sound capable of playback through sixteen different MIDI channels • staccato • smooth • vibrato • dots • triplets • quintuplets • ties • raise or lower an octave • multiple time, key, and tempo choices within one piece • repeats • transposes • more!

The manual for *Deluxe Music Construction Set* is clearly written and easy to follow. Included are an overview, tutorials, and a reference with helpful hints and glossaries of computer and musical terms.

For the professional electronic musician/composer, *Deluxe Music Construction Set* has a complete MIDI software support. Also, a voice editing feature comes with this package which allows you to design your own instrument by custom designing its waveform. The instructions for this feature are a good education in what makes up the sound of an instrument.

Music Construction Set, now available for the new Apple IIGS, is the best-selling music composition program ever written for a personal computer. Over 175,000 copies sold in the USA alone! The Apple IIGS version of *Music Construction Set* features 15 all-new digitized instruments— saxophone, guitar, banjo, piano, snare drum, and many more. No other computer can match this sound quality or variety. The Apple IIGS version also uses a mouse-and-windows interface. Onscreen music looks like real sheet music, and compositions are printed in standard music format. You get the notation options listed above under *Deluxe Music Construction Set*.

Music Construction Set for the other Apple II family computers does not have all the neat features of the IIGS version, but still has plenty going for it.

So now you have a reason to buy a Mac or Apple IIGS!

Great Wave Software

ConcertWare+, **Macintosh, $69.96. Fifty page manual, one non-copy protected disk. Also available:** *ConcertWare+ MIDI* **($139.95) and** *ConcertWare+* **Music Disks ($15 each).** *KidsTime*, **Macintosh, $49.95.** *KidsTime II* **(Apple IIGS) includes only ABKey and KidsNotes: $39.95.**

Concert Ware+ is actually three programs: Music Writer, Instrument Maker, and Music Player.

Music Writer allows you to enter and edit musical compositions. You enter notes by clicking the kind of note and pitch you want with the mouse, or by using the computer keyboard. Without a MIDI interface, you can play up to four notes at once. You can enter one line of notes at a time, or you can enter the music in chords.

The program gives you little control over the appearance of the finished score. It puts the notes on the staff it thinks appropriate. This does not at all limit the musical selections you can enter into this program. The program allows you to enter any piece of music accurately. You can play back the music in Music Writer to hear what you have written.

Music Player can be used to play a selection or sequence of selections once, or repeatedly. You can select which electronic instrument to use for each of the four voices.

Instrument Maker lets you design your own instruments. You design the wave form,

envelope, and, most importantly, the icon to represent your instrument.

ConcertWare+ gets inside the process of music-making more than the *Music Construction Set* family. It is more educational and less of a music processor.

For a really inexpensive taste of computer music practice, try *Kids Notes* from the award-winning *KidsTime* program disk, also from Great Wave Software. *KidsTime* includes, besides *Kid Notes*, *ABKey* (letter recognition skills), *Match-It*, *Dot-to-Dot*, and *StoryWriter* (simple typing and story skills).

Kid Notes is a very simple music processor. When you enter the program, the screen contains boxes for the note value, key signature, and time signature you want, a keyboard, and a display of the notes being entered. You enter notes by selecting the type of note you want and clicking on the key of the keyboard you want to play. The computer sounds the notes as you "play" the keyboard.

The program comes with several favorite children's songs and, for parents, "Notes to the Musically Unsure" with simple music and notation explanations.

Imaja

Listen. **Macintosh family, all models, $69. Not copy-protected.**

An full-featured ear training program for the beginning to advanced musician who owns a Macintosh. *Listen* is an appropriate name for this excursion into melodic and harmonic ear training, designed to complement more traditional music theory studies.

Listen plays the exercise, you play it back on an onscreen piano keyboard or guitar fretboard. Exercises include single note, two note, melody, interval, triad, and chord recognition, among others. Exercises you miss are redrilled (this can be tedious).

What you get is a lot of onscreen control. Pick your volume, pace, duration, vibrato depth, and voice. Choose melodic range, key, and scale (pentatonic, diatonic, chromatic, Ionian, Jazz Altered . . .). Pick the chords and inversions you want to drill. *Listen* does not include rhythmic training, although this is planned for a future update.

Listen keeps track of your right and wrong answers, and even provides graphic hints upon request to tell you if the note you picked was too high or too low.

Listen also supports MIDI. You can select the interface clock rate, Macintosh port, and MIDI channel.

All in all, *Listen* is a really friendly and fun way to brush up your music listening skills.

Wenger Corporation
The Music Class. Apple II Family, 64K or more required. Optional: ALF 3-voice synthesizer card. Fundamentals, Music Symbols, $39 each. Rhythm, Ear Training, Note Reading, $49 each. Shipping extra (about 3%).

This five-volume set teaches the basics of music. The five units are: • *Fundamentals*— teaches note reading and major and minor scales • *Rhythm*— beat out the rhythm of a given sequence of notes • *Ear Training*— recreate a sequence of notes played by the computer • *Music Symbols* — learn what all those blotches and squiggles are all about • *Note Reading*— learn what letter goes with what line or space on the keyboard and treble and bass clefs.

Each disk has a tutorial and interactive tests. Example: *Fundamentals* follow the interval-spanning steps of an animated cat.

Rhythm is taught by the foot-tapping Mr. Metro Gnome.

Ear Training is broken down into three sections: Aural Interval Recognition, Melodic Error Correction and Detection (point out the difference between onscreen music and what you hear), and Melodic Rhythmic Dictation. This is by far the most complete ear training software available.

Work against the clock to identify sixteenth notes, repeats, sforzandos, and so on in *Music Symbols*. Speed is automatically adjusted to your performance, or you can compete with a friend in the Game Show option. Or draw up to 80 symbols of your choice in the Music Box Tool Kit.

Mr. Metro Gnome returns to help you with *Note Reading*. You'll work on Staff Note Reading and Keyboard Note Reading, then face the ultimate test: Rhythms Round Two.

Wenger provides a manager utility with each disk so you can keep track of student scores. There is room for up to 125 students. This ought to be enough for any home school!

You can enter student names and assign each a password. The program keeps records of each student's performance and maintains a Hall of Fame for the best students.

The tutorials teach the students step by step and are very easy to follow. I thought the pacing was somewhat slow due to the computer having to load a new frame from the disk each time the program moves on, but our kids didn't mind. They thought it was great!

PART VII

EXTRAS

CHAPTER TWENTY-TWO

ENRICHMENT AND ACTIVITIES

A treasure chest of all that's neat and nifty, but is not intended to be the primary teaching tool for a subject— that's this chapter. Here you can find the fun and the freaky, your kits and accessories for practicing concepts taught elsewhere. Afterschoolers should find this section especially useful, as should home schoolers who are looking for ways to expand their horizons

The following companies specialize in enrichment materials covering many subject areas. Jazz up your home program with their clever ideas!

ALL-PURPOSE ENRICHMENT AND ACTIVITY CATALOGS

The following catalogs fall into two categories:

(1) Retailers like Brook Farm Books, Holt Associates, Shekinah Curriculum Cellar, and Sycamore Tree. These catalogs collect materials from many sources, organize it, and make it easy to look over and buy.

(2) Producers like Dover, EDC, and Educational Insights. These companies' products are often carried in other catalogs, but nobody carries *all* of their product line. To see everything these companies have to offer, you need their own catalogs.

Brook Farm Books
First Home-School Catalogue, revised edition, $8 US or $10 Canadian postpaid.

Absolutely scads of unusual items, freebies, and fascinating information about home schooling. You can order more than 1,000 of the 2,000-plus listed items directly from Brook Farm Books.

Categories: • Activities • Adolescence (the selection proves it's better to skip the pimpled stage and go straight from diapers to college) • Art (includes sources for art reproductions) •

Baby & Birth (supports natural family life) •
Badges (buy 'em from Brook Farm Books) •
Beginning to Read (Richard Scarry, Dr. Seuss,
and other easy readers) • Biographies • Book
Clubs • Books, Discount • Books, Technical •
Brown Paper school books • Cards (game rules)
• Classics (nice large selection from different
publishers, including illustrated classics and
classics in beautiful bindings) • Coloring
Books • Crafts • Dictionaries •
Education Books and Cassettes • Games •
Geography • Gifted • Global Education (Donn
Reed's for it) • High School Subjects Self
Taught • History (posters, activity units,
American and Canadian) • Ladybird Books
• Languages • Literature (includes Marguerite
Henry, Tintin, and the Tarzan series) • Logic
(two books) • Made Simple books • Math
(includes Saxon math) • Music • Parenting
• Radio and Recorded books (hundreds of
hours of cassettes) • Religion (liberal)
• Resources and Teaching Aids (includes pages
of freebies) • Science (cosmic, fun stuff)
• Vocational Education (Exploring Careers
series) • Writing (the three best books on the
subject). I left out a few of the minor
categories— hope you don't mind! All is indexed
for easy use.

The First Home-School Catalogue stresses
challenging, constructive, informative, fun, and
worthwhile items. You won't find much regular
curriculum stuff here, due to the Reeds'
unschooling philosophy. Think of it as a Whole
Enrichment Catalog.

Dover Publications

Over three thousand paperbacks in all
fields of interest, most priced between $2 and
$5, many specially suited for home study and
instruction. For those who want to enrich their
own and their children's education, but who
aren't rich themselves.

EDC

Hundreds of cleverly illustrated, colorful,
mostly oversized (but not overthick) books from
England that enrich every area of human

knowledge. Every one a bargain. Every one
delightful. Turn your kids loose with these
books and you won't have to teach them a
thing except the Three R's.

Educational Insights

Funthinkers, prices average $12-$15.
Charlie battery model, $45. A.C. model,
$70. *Rainbow*, $169.95. Drill packs of 20
cards, $10.95 each.

Huge assortment of some of the niftiest
enrichment materials around. Every
Educational Insights product has dash and
flair. Prices are better than reasonable, in my
opinion. A few examples from the enormous
number of possibilities:

The *Funthinker* activity kits enrich your
teaching of basic skills. Each comes in a plastic
carrying case, and contains all sorts of goodies
such as sing-along cassettes, stencils for
tracing, storybooks, games, and even supplies
such as scissors and crayons. The series
presently includes *First Steps to Reading*
(prereading exercises), *Learning My Alphabet*,
Understanding Numbers, *Learning Values* (with
Aesop's fables), *Beginning to Add and Subtract*,
Mysteries of Light (an intriguing kit that
contains a prism, a magnifier, and four color
filters among many other things), and
Learning to Draw.

For drill, Educational Insights has several
different electronic tutors. Stick in a card and
press the probe into the hole next to the
answer you hope is right. Flashing lights and a
space-age sounds come from Charlie to let you
know if you got it right or if you blew it.
Rainbow, the more expensive model, has a
touch-sensitive keyboard. Maxx, the most
affordable of them all, is a barrel of fun for
preschoolers. If you'd like to add some zip to
your drill, but can't afford a computer, one of

these might be an acceptable compromise.

I have not begun to even skim the surface of the varied and imaginative product line. See any school supply catalog, or send for Educational Insight's own, and be overwhelmed!

Gifted Child Today

"Reasonably priced, educationally effective materials for gifted youngsters of all ages." Guaranteed lowest price policy. Unconditional return policy. Quantity purchase discount. Toll-free ordering.

OK. So what do they offer? Activities Materials • Affective Education • Audio Tapes for Professionals • Computer Books • Computer Software • Creative and Productive Thinking Materials (some iffy) • Dungeons and Dragons • Economics • Futurism (secular prophecy) • Language Arts • Little Thinker Tapes • Logic (includes Wff 'n Proof games) • Math • Philosophy (modern secular) • Professional Books • Psychology (a series developed by the American Psychological Association) • Science • Study Skills Activities • Trivial Pursuit • Values (á là values clarification). The newsprint catalog would be much more fun to read without the educational jargon.

Holt Associates

John Holt's associates carry on his work, including not only *Growing Without Schooling* but the Holt Associates mail order catalog.

Holt Associates merchandise is chosen with an eye for beauty, imagination, and simplicity. The resulting assortment is unique.

Holt Associates' literature selections are quite good, ranging from *The Bat Poet* to old favorites like the Grimms' fairy tales. For math, there is *Anno's Counting Book* and the indispensable *How to Lie with Statistics.* For science, there is *Powers of Ten,* a mind-boggling book that exponentiates sizes in jumps of ten (how many jumps do you think it takes to go from "people size" to the Solar System)? For music, there is *How to Play the Piano Despite Years of Lessons.* The catalog of

course contains hundreds more books than these, but I wanted to give you a taste of the sassiness and originality of the selections. It's worth sending away for this brochure just to read the names of the books!

Holt Associates also sells some art and music equipment, again with an eye to the gorgeous and/or unusual. We bought our Aulos recorders here, and several boxes of Cray-Pas. Holt Associates sells some expensive equipment too— violins and cellos and (on the more mundane side) pianicas and metronomes.

The emphasis on beauty makes this catalog a joy to read.

Michael Olaf

More than Montessori. Michael Olaf offers a good selection of creative materials for young children from preschool to preteens in all subject areas. Many of their items are imported. The catalog is easy to use and simple in an elegant way. All catalog items are carefully described and most are pictured. Categories: • Plants (leaf presses, identification cards, redwood seeds . . .) • Animals (bird song cassette, ant farm, shell collections, ostrich feathers . . .) • Dinosaurs (postcards, models, games . . .) • Physical Science (mineral collection, fossil cards, games . . .) • Geography (flags of the world, Dymaxion World Puzzle, atlases . . .) • History of Man (lots of Usborne books) • Cooperative Games • Prepared Environment (children's household tools, posters, pictures) • Music (games, instruments, books, composer cards . . .) • Art Appreciation (art postcards, Mommy, It's a Renoir! . . .) • Early Language • Literature • Foreign Language • Writing (Montessori materials, calligraphy, bookmaking) • Reading (Ladybird books) • Math (manipulatives) • Parent and Teacher Books • Montessori Books • and a small list of Montessori sources.

Playing for Knowledge

PFK distributes enrichment materials from more than 30 publishers. The newsprint catalog is not the easiest to find things in, but it contains some gems. Examples: *Eight Ate: A Feast of Homonym Riddles. It's Easy to Have a Snail Visit You,* one in a series that tells you how to catch and house and care for the critters. Can you make a silk purse out of a sow's ear? The *Recyclopedia* has all kinds of projects you can make from trash. Lots of books for "gifted" children. How-to-draw books, books on dinosaurs, David Macaulay's marvelous series on how great buildings are made, more. Some of the standard messing about with students' feelings and values, but these selections are swallowed up in the large number of truly valuable ones.

Rhamphorhynchus.

Playthinks
Prices range from $2.95 to $40. Kit components now offered separately.

Bill and I had an idea once upon a time. We'd put together some of the best materials from different manufacturers into kits to teach individual skills, such as handwriting or beginning art.

Well, Playthinks beat us to it. Their colorful, yuppy-oriented catalog has kit after learning kit for all ages and stages, plus books for the parents.

Kits are divided into three categories: Concept Kits, Speciality Kits, and Library Kits. Each Concept Kit is for a different developmental level (from birth to age five) and includes a number of colorful, multi-sensory learning tools, which you might recognize as games and toys. Specialty Kits include such topics as The Creative Cook, Abracadabra, a kit

for handmaking Christmas presents and a Hanukkah kit. Library Kits are collections of books like *Biographies of the Great* (Einstein, Mozart, and Da Vinci), *Science Information and Experiments, Timeless Classics, the Early Reader's Shelf, Shaping Values and Manners,* and so on.

Kit prices range from $20 to $40. You will find a lot of tempting sets . . . like *Tick, Tock, My Friend the Clock, A Child's Flight With Nature, How Do Things Grow?, Choo-Choose This For Your Train Lover, Around the World . . .* If the kit price is too steep, you can purchase the individual items you want separately.

I notice some of the identical items in these kits that we would have put in ours, so Playthinks must have good taste. Right?

Shekinah Curriculum Cellar

All-purpose home schoolers' catalog. Thousands of items. Categories: Parent Helps • Bible • Devotional • Character Training • Phonics • Reading Skills • Literature (biography, Christian and non-Christian fiction, nonfiction, adventure and mystery, poetry) • English and Creative Writing • Spelling and Vocabulary • Penmanship • Arithmetic • Science (including Creation Science) • Health, Safety, and Manners • History and Geography • Critical Thinking Skills • Art, Drawing, and Crafts • Music • Integrated Curriculum • and Miscellaneous. Every item chosen for simplicity of use, every item described. Many unusual or hard-to-find items.

Sycamore Tree

Another all-purpose home schoolers' catalog. Sycamore Tree has been around longer than Shekinah Curriculum Cellar and has an even wider selection. Categories: • Bible

• Character Development • Reading • Math
• Penmanship • Grammar and Composition
• Spelling • Social Studies • Science • Foreign
Language • Sex Education • Physical
Education • Arts and Crafts • Music • Cooking
and Nutrition • Games and Puzzles • Felts •
Toys • Videos • Travel • Reference Materials •
Resource Materials • Parent Helps • and
Curriculum (wide selection includes Weavers,
Little Patriots, Konos, and Alpha Omega,
among others). Sycamore Tree carries different
materials than Shekinah in many areas.
Emphasis is on creativity, simplicity,
educational excellence, and fun.

ACTIVITY CALENDARS AND ALMANACS

Center for Applied Research in Education
Early Childhood Teacher's Almanack,
$17.95. *The New Teacher's Almanack*,
$18.95. Shipping extra.

Two school-year almanacs designed for
classroom teachers. Something for every day of
the year.

The Early Childhood Teacher's Almanack
is an oversized 11 x 8½" full of monthly
celebrations, natural science activities, recipes
the kids can make, field trip ideas, enrichment
explorations, arts and crafts, and projects.
Some samples: • Make finger paint • Take
nature walks • Sun-dry fruit leather • Bake
Doggie Crackers • Measure air pressure with a
homemade barometer • Sprout seeds • Make a
wind roarer • Create sand paintings • Bake
natural pizza • Identify animal sounds • Walk
on homemade stilts. Illustrated in old-timey
style, 10 chapters from September to Summer.

The NEW Teacher's Almanack is an
illustrated 395 oversized pages including • an
annotated calendar of famous people's
birthdays, holidays, special weeks, and
historical events • sayings of famous people
• historical facts • unusual teaching tips
• biographical material written in controlled

vocabulary • bulletin board ideas • special
activities and projects • sources of free or
inexpensive materials • recipes for art supplies
• recipes for kid-made food • games • writing
sparkers • more. Same 10 chapter September-
to-Summer format. Hardbound.

Every Day is Special
Activity calendar, $15/12 months, $2
for sample month. U.S. funds only.

Tender loving care went into this home
schooling calendar, the product of a home
school mother.

Every Day is Special has 12 months of daily
activities and neat historical facts in a calendar
format. Did you know June 1 was Roquefort
Cheese Day? (The day's activity suggestion:
"Have a cheese-tasting party!") June 3,
likewise, is Chicken Bone Day, a chance to put
ye olde dry bones to use.

Activities include discussion and writing
sparkers, puzzles and riddles of all kinds,
activities with food (have a "rainbow lunch"),
art and crafts, and on and on. The author is
widely read, knowledgeable about many fields,
and incredibly creative.

Families that like discovery learning will
find *Every Day is Special* a great resource for
project ideas. Everyone will find it brightens up
the day. Who can be dull anticipating a
Rainbow Lunch, or cheese-tasting party, or
bone-cracking spree, or . . . ?

Gospel Publications

Children's Calendar, $6. Sponsored *Calendar,* includes gift wrap, card, newsletters, and birthday card with small gift, $10. *Make Your Own Calendar,* $1 or 12 for $5. Free newsletter with funstuff, quiz, prizes. Materials for telephone ministries, balloon stories. Free lending library of children's Christian books.

Children's Calendar for Christian children. Each tear-off day has a poem, story, or simple activity, as well as a Bible verse for the day. Example: The story of Jenny Lind. A poem about a sick boy who printed Bible verses on balloons and floated them out his window. How to make a scrap book of Bible Bees (e.g., "Never BEE angry."). Durable bright plastic cover, colored pages.

You can also sponsor a grandchild, neighbor child, missionary child, or underprivileged child with a *Children's Calendar.* Your $10 includes, besides a gift-wrapped calendar, a gift card with your name and address, newsletters for the child, and a birthday card with a small gift inside.

Other calendars available from this address. Write for details.

CE Software

CalendarMaker, a computer calendar program, is reviewed below in the Activity Software section.

ACTIVITY MAGAZINES AND SERVICES

Educational Services

Homeschooling At Its Best, $20/year September-May (9 issues). Back issues available: 1986-87, $15; 1985-86, $10.

Homeschooling At Its Best is a home schoolers' enrichment magazine. Each year's subscription covers music, art, oral speech, writing, physical education, and so on. The 1986-87 school year's issues were tied together with a history theme. Each issue covered a section of American history, with a time line, history trivia and facts, quotes from those times, Inventors of the Times, Artists of the Times, Musicians of the Times, Authors of the Times, People of the Times, and so on. Enrichment activities grew out of these features, as for example "Design a brochure for the Tuskegee Institute" alongside a biography of Booker T. Washington. Fascinating reading, great research questions and idea sparkers. Sports activities and a Resources bulletin round this out.

Kathy Means, the editor of *Homeschooling At Its Best,* has studied under Dr. Madeline Hunter and is available for home education consultation and presentations at reasonable rates. She is also the sister of Kim Solga, the artist who produces *KidsArt News* (small world!). Kim does the graphics and the magazine is produced on an Apple Laserwriter. Looks great!

74 Brand-new FREEBIES

Freebies

One year (6 issues), $9.97. Single copy, $2. Cancellation privilege within ten days of receipt of first issue.

This "Magazine with Something for Nothing" has tons of legitimate, up-to-date free and almost-free offers. Each offer has been researched to make sure the supplier has enough stock on hand to satisfy Freebie subscribers. The offers are written up in a style similar to mine; all ordering info is neatly appended. Example:

NO MUSS, NO FUSS
Digging in rich, brown earth gives you a satisfying feeling. But finding dirt from your indoor planting trays tracked all over your carpets makes you feel less gratified.
This gardening season, send for a **sample Jiffy-7 plant starter pellet** and help prevent dirty floors . . .

The review then explains the virtues of these pellets and the accompanying free brochure, and winds up with:

Send:
A Long SASE with 39¢ postage affixed
Ask For:
Jiffy-7 plant starter pellet
Mail To:
Jiffy Products of America, Inc.
Attn: Free Jiffy-7 Offer
P.O. Box 338
West Chicago, IL 60185

Each issue contains the following departments: • Food & Drink • Garden Plot • Freebies Report • Craft Cupboard • Kid Stuff

• Free & Easy (simple how-to project using on-hand household items) • Easter Parade • Catalog Quest (the issue I saw listed the HearthSong catalog, among others) • Money Matters • Home Help • Teacher's Edition (classroom freebies) • Big Spenders ("freebies" that cost up to $2 for the postage and handling) • Grab Bag • Feeling Good (health freebies) • Bulletin Board (a classified section) • and Freebie Finders (readers ask where to find things and the *Freebies* staff answers).

Are these freebies any good? Surprisingly, yes. One Jiffy-7 pellet might not seem too exciting, but most of the offers are really useful items. Examples: A free packet of Water-Less Crystals, enough for fifteen to thirty house plants (and the crystals stay active for up to six years!). Two product samples (buttermilk powder and baking cocoa), five coupons, and 26 recipes for 75¢. Sample of concentrated liquid wax for $1. Two plan sheets for build-and-stack storage units and understair storage for 50¢. Three pairs of plastic bunny scissors for 75¢. A teddy-bear catalog for $1. How to make a lacy Easter basket with a balloon, some yarn, water, lace, glue, and a few other fixin's (this one was on the house). A beaded bracelet kit for $1. Faux pearl jewelry set (necklace, bracelet, and earrings), $2. Zan-y-mals sewing projects for children, $2. Set of three puzzletters for you to write on and give for presents: $2. Genuine Sports Shooter eight-foot balloon, plastic air top, and mini paratrooper for $1. Keep in mind these prices are just postage and handling: the items themselves are absolutely free.

Freebies is two-color and very attractive, with lots of graphics and zippy writing. And now that I've finished writing the review, I can finally start sending away for the dozen or so neat items that have caught my eye in this issue . . .

Instructor Books
Big Book of Absolutely Everything, $18.95. *Page-a-Day Pursuits,* $19.95. *Holiday Word Puzzles,* $12.95. *Artfully Easy,* $12.95. All oversized books, spiral-bound. Add 10% shipping.

Instructor magazine's *Big Book of Absolutely Everything* is over 250 pages of easy-do activities and projects for classroom teachers. *Page-A-Day Pursuits* is a classroom activity calendar with over three hundred reproducible worksheets. *Holiday Word Puzzles* is a particularly nifty activity book with crossword puzzles, riddles, and lots of other brainteasers based on holidays of all religions and nations. *Instructor's Artfully Easy* has over 300 quick classroom art projects.

All *Instructor* books are oversized, spiral-bound (neat!), with a nice clean layout and lots of appealing graphics.

You will have to adapt these books, and the others in *Instructor's* bookshelf, to your home situation if you decide to use them. It won't be hard: most are seatwork for one child. Siphon off any controversial material (these *were* designed for public school classrooms) and use the rest!

kinds of paper is followed by, "Make a paper airplane from construction paper and one from typing paper. Did one fly better than the other?" That issue, on Paper Crafts, also included • a brief history of paper • a step-by-step recipe for making paper • science report suggestions on wasp nests (wasp nests are made out of paper) • the game Paper Bag Kickball • how to put on a family puppet show • how to make paper fans, newspaper hats, and paper dolls • paper maché activities • tissue paper activities • field trip suggestions (starring a paper factory) • how a book is made • and paper craft book reviews. Actually, there were more paper activities than I have room to mention! Plus a list of special days for the month to mark on your calendar, a kids' contribution page, book reviews, resource listings, and so on. The repro of this magazine is not up to professional standards, but it's lots of info in a small space at a small price.

Oak Heritage Press
One year (10 issues) of *Creative Learning Magazine,* $9, $13 outside North America. Sample issue, $1. Back issue, $1. All 10 1986 issues, $9.

Home schooling enrichment and activity magazine. Each small 5½ x 8½ issue of *Creative Learning Magazine* has a particular theme, e.g., Physical Fitness or Animal Babies. Inside are a variety of short information articles and activity starters covering all subject areas. Examples: A paragraph about the different

Shining Star
One year (four issues), $15. Sample issue, $4 USA, $5.95 Canadian.

Christian education magazine loaded with almost a hundred pages of reproducible puzzles, games, and work sheets, plus teacher tips, stories, and an three-month Activity Calendar. The merciful editors include an Answer Key in the back in case you or your little ones can't figure out the puzzles.

Sample Scripture of the Week postcard

Peter Wannemacher
    Scripture of the Week. Make checks out to Peter Wannemacher. $12.50 for a year, $6.50 for 6 months, $3.50 for 3 months, 50¢ for sample. The perfect Christmas or birthday gift (don't wait until Christmas to give it!).

    This is fun. You're going to like Peter Wannemacher's "Scripture of the Week."
    Mr. Wannemacher, an expert calligrapher, artistically letters a different Bible verse every week, prints it up beautifully onto postcards with a variety of colored inks (the result looks engraved), and will send you or some loved one a postcard every week for the insignificant sum mentioned above. A sample is only 50¢.
    I'm warning you— prepare to be blown away by Mr. Wannemacher's spectacular effects! We have received cards with the Scripture done in rainbow colors or in metallic ink— to name just two of his more memorable efforts.
    Why is this listed under Activity Magazines and Services? Because this is an ideal way to start your week— or to lighten up someone else's. And cheering up our friends and neighbors is the ultimate enrichment activity.

Personification of the days of the week.

ACTIVITY SOFTWARE

CE Software
    CalendarMaker, **Macintosh family, $35. Not copy protected— hard disk and LaserWriter compatible.**

    One of thea best original shareware programs (you try and pay only if you decide to keep), *CalendarMaker* is now sold directly for a low price.
    On the surface, this is a make-your-own-calendar program. What it really is is an invitation to creativity!

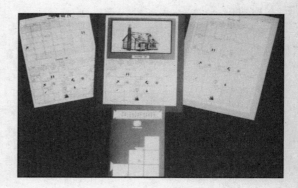

    You choose one of three calendar styles: month-with-a-picture; month without a picture, but with bigger date boxes; or double-months-per-page. Choose Sunday-Monday or Monday-Sunday format. Use icons (little pictures) to highlight your special dates. (The program comes with its own icons and you can import icons from other programs, scrounge icons by capturing graphics from Paint or programs files, or design your own.) Write up to 255 characters' worth of info in any date you like. Add picture backgrounds, read in information from other calendar programs if desired, and save your calendar. Next you can print it, reduce it, print to disk, or print to a draw (PICT) file for further massaging by other progams (notably, *MacDraw™, MacPublisher™,* or *PageMaker™*).
    Now, the improvements. *CalendarMaker* now can print in color on the ImageWriter II. Every date can have a different color! You can pick fonts, size, style, and justification for every date. Custom paper sizing is now available.

Print current month only or print a range of months.

And, even more, Davka Corporation's *Hebrew CalendarMaker* lets you add Hebrew dates, Torah portions, and Jewish holidays to *CalendarMaker* if you are so inclined. See the Davka listing in the Classical Languages chapter.

Now, the $64,000 question: Why am I reviewing *CalendarMaker* in this chapter? The answer: because, with *CalendarMaker, you can make your own activity calendars.* Give your kids some real hands-on experience with time and seasons. Plan your home school projects and field trips. Save all those neat ideas you've been clipping from magazines somewhere where they not only won't get lost, but might get done. Or just produce a never-failing supply of birthday and Christmas presents, personalized to fit the recipient. And, since CE Software always goes the extra mile to serve their customers, who knows what terrific free-or-cheap upgrades they may have in store for future editions of *CalendarMaker?*

TRAVEL WITH YOUR FAMILY

Travel, like pasta, is a broadening experience. It's enlightening. Educational. But some might question a chapter about family travel in a book on home learning. "What's with this on-the-road stuff?" I can just hear someone ask. "Granted that travel is educational, what does it have to do with learning at home?"

My answer is that home and travel do mix. Whether your *house* is an apartment, a mobile home, or a two-story Colonial overlooking the Cape Cod surf, your *home* is where your family is. Home can temporarily be a tent in Yellowstone National Park or a Howard Johnson motel room, as long as the rest of the family shares it.

So if you pack up your family in your old RV and hit the road, you are still learning at home. And what an education! It may not extend quite from the halls of Montezuma to the shores of Tripoli, but however short the foray, travel expands the mind. Reading about Gettysburg is not the same as visiting the very battlefield on which the Blue and the Grey so valiantly contended. All the study units on Hispanic culture can never mean as much as a simple trip to a Mexican village. Even the great

scenes of nature vary from location to location. To a prairie dweller, the Rockies loom quite differently in person than they did in the imagination. To a mountain or city dweller, the open miles of Big Sky country literally open new vistas.

PLEASE WALK ON THE GRASS

Anyone can circle the earth a never see a thing. Hopping from airport to airport and hotel to hotel; "doing" Paris on a whirlwind tour of all the stock tourist attractions; spending your precious hours overseas shopping in a Spanish or English or American mall: this is not the way to make the most of travel.

Especially *family* travel! Hear the children complaining loudly and often when the fun family trip turns into eternity in the back seat of a car or a mere exercise in pavement-pounding. "So who cares if we get to see some famous building or natural wonder?" they will demand. "We already saw it on TV." What they are really saying is, "We are not interested in spending all day looking at things from afar. Please give us something to *do*."

The most successful family travel aims for a destination where children can *do* something: go deep sea fishing, get art lessons from a landscape painter in the great outdoors, track beavers to their dam, feed the chickens, hike up a mountain and down again. And just possibly you, the mature adult, might enjoy some of this too!

MAGAZINES

Travel With Your Children
   Family Travel Times, **one year (11 issues, including one double issue). $35 USA, Mexico, U.S. Virgin Islands, Puerto Rico (all US funds only). $39 Canadian (US funds) or $54 (Canadian funds). Outside North America, $48 (air mail). Sample issue $1.**

Travel-loving families get not only a family travel newsletter, but free phone travel consultations, with their subscriptions to *Family Travel Times.* Founded by family travel expert Dorothy Jordon, *Family Travel Times* covers

   • Planning for your vacation. For each destination covered, *FTT* gives you the needed details, including availability of cribs, highchairs, airline infant seats, and so on.
   • Time together/time apart. *FTT* believes strongly in planned children's programs for children so that parents can have "adult" vacation time alone. Destination writeups describe what programs are available for each site.
   • Warm welcomes. As *FTT* says, "It's not enough to be tolerated and not welcomed." *FTT* searches out hotels, resorts, and vacation sites that truly enjoy having families and are prepared to serve them.
   • Sightseeing everyone enjoys. Detailed, "tried and true" advice on activities and places all family members can enjoy.

A sampling of some *FTT* articles: Adventure vacations. London/Paris update. Europe. Philadelphia. Tennis and golf vacations. San Francisco. The Babysitter Dilemma (no problem for those of us who manage without!). Take-along toys and games. Book reviews.

When *FTT* profiles a city (say, Chicago) they go all out. You get listings of Tours and Overviews, Views From the Top (high places where you can see the whole city), Festivals, Family Sightseeing (zoos, planetariums, parks, and so on). Each listing gives you a phone number to call or an address to write, plus date and time information on special events in that locale.

PLACES TO STAY

You can travel for its own sake, jetting about here and there. Or you can pick a destination you want to visit, go there, and stay there.

The following listings provide places to stay, mostly with a rural flavor, and people to meet, likewise.

Christian Life Workshops
   Bed and Breakfast Directory, **$9.35 postpaid.**

Listing of Christian families around the USA who are willing to put up traveling families overnight. Hosts charge small fee, provide breakfast, bed, and tourist advice. Also includes tips on how to be a better host or guest.

***Home Education* Magazine**
   GWS Travel Directory. **Write for price.**

Helen and Mark Hegener, editors of *Home Education* magazine, have taken over responsibility for running the *Growing Without Schooling* Travel Directory. This is a listing of alternative-education-minded folk interested in hosting home education families.

Michel Farm Vacations

Room and 2 meals ("Mulligan" breakfast and evening meal): per week, $265/person; per weekday, $40/person; per weekend day, $55/person. Lunch on farm or box lunch for tour, add $5. House with kitchen facilities: per week, $150/person; per weekday, $23/person; per weekend day, $30/person. Room only with Continental breakfast: per week, $100/person; per weekday, $15/person; per weekend day, $20/person. Under-4's, free. 30% discount on children aged 4-12. Single occupancies, add 20%.

Central booking agent for farm vacations in the Harmony, Minnesota, area. Over 20 host farms available. Wide variety of winter and summer sports nearby. "Among the many leisure activities available is our guided tour of the Midwest's largest Amish colony." You get room and board on the host farm, including lots of homemade bread, homemade soups, homemade sausage. Lounge around in peace and quiet or watch the actual operation of the farm. Treat your kids to the sight of cows being milked and machinery at work, or spend some time feeding and getting to know a calf, a sow and her piglets, chickens, or other animals which will be penned in small enclosures for your convenience.

Choose from 14 vacation tours in advance:
• Guided driving tour of the Harmony area Amish settlement, with time for shopping for Amish furniture and crafts (guide rides in your car— $30/car) • Niagara Cave Tour • Historic Lanesboro, with special dinner in town • Ernie Tuff Museum • Scenic drive includes visits to museum, cave, and park • Rochester, including the Mayo Clinic • Lake City, including a possible ride and dinner on the paddlewheeler "Hiawatha" • Shopping or skiing in the Red Wing area • Northeast Iowa tour, with visit to Bily Clocks and the house where Antonin Dvorak composed the *New World Symphony* • Norwegian-American museum in Decorah • Golfing on one of seven courses • Hiking, biking, or cross-country skiing (this is free) • Trout fishing • Canoeing • Deer hunting on several of the host farms.

Oak Leaf Bread and Breakfast

With bed & breakfast: $30/two people, $8/each additional person (up to six), $5 for each additional person (up to 12). $250/five days of family reunion or retreat without breakfast. Children under 5 free. Traveling animals stay in the barn.

Southeastern Kansas is the place for this working ranch operation with registered cattle and a "marvelous hog operation." Oak Leaf B&B has "all the stuff of which farms are made: chickens, milk cows, garden, barns, hay lofts, mud, and dogs." Pet the buffalo. Gather the eggs. Help milk the cow. Work in the special kids' garden, or play volleyball, badminton, croquet, and horseshoes. Visit the on-site country art gallery with offerings from local artists and craftspeople, or try your hand at a variety of herb and flower crafts.

Your hosts, a Mennonite couple, provide gracious service and "the best cinnamon rolls in three counties, maybe four," according to their employers. Not to mention the homemade sausage with good coffee and cabbage, for the non-German palate.

Three state parks and reservoirs are within driving distance, if you just absolutely can't bear to stay out of the car.

Stay in the house, or in the completely furnished guest house that can sleep up to 12 people.

Oak Leaf recommends that you plan a longer stay if you really want to see the ranch in operation. Unscheduled and spontaneous people will enjoy it best.

PLACES TO GO

Adventure time! What we have here is jumping-off places and the means to get there. You arrive and then go on a quest instead of rusticating in some peaceful backwater.

Cruise Vacations

It may not be too late to sign up for a "Cruise With a Purpose," with hosts Dr. and Mrs. Raymond Moore and attorney John Eidsmoe. Salt air, food, fun, and fellowship! Call for details.

F & W Publications
Adventure Holidays, **$9.95.**

Looking for something spicy, something out of the ordinary, for your family vacation? *Adventure Holidays*, another annual directory from F & W Publications, lists hundreds of far-out vacations. Prices, dates, special equipment or experience required, and other essential information is provided about every adventure holiday. How about windsurfing . . . canoeing . . . hiking . . . riding . . . sailing? Too tame? All right, consider deep sea diving or gorilla tracking, if you prefer. All this and more in the perfect resource for armchair adventurers.

Nature Expeditions International

Adventure travel vacations led by highly-credentialed faculty: anthropologists, naturalists, and biologists. The expedition groups are kept small— usually about a dozen people, although Nature Expeditions guarantees most expedition departures with a minimum of six members.

Every NEI trip leader is required to have an M.A., Ph.D., or equivalent professional training, in addition to teaching experience on the college level. They must have lived or traveled extensively in the host country. Most speak the host language.

More than 30 itineraries available. Example: Australian Natural History

Expedition. Departures in 1988 on April 9, July 16, August 13, September 10, October 15, November 19. Trip fee of $2690 (11-16 members) or $2990 (6-10 members) does not include airfare of $1811 from San Francisco. The trip lasts for 23 days and includes a lot more than mall shopping. For instance: • Outback and Red Center • Aboriginal cave paintings of the Northern Territory • Sub-tropical rainforests in Lamington National Park • World's largest coral reef • Wildflowers in the Grampions • Drive in four-wheeled vehicle and camp in the "magnificent Olgas" • Stay in a historic sheep station near Hamilton • Much wildlife observation.

Other NEI tours include: Ancient Mexico. Burma & Thailand. Easter Island. Galapagos/Machu Picchu (evolutionary). Hawaiian Natural History. India Wildlife. Kenya & Tanzania Wildlife. Nepal Discovery. New Zealand Walking. Sea of Cortez. West Indies Natural History. South Pacific Discovery. Great Whales. Himalayan Kingdoms. Oregon Country. Amazon Expedition. Many more.

PLACES TO WORK

F & W Publications
Work Your Way Around the World, **$10.95.** *Directory of Overseas Summer Jobs, Summer Jobs in Britain, Summer Employment Directory of the United States*, **$9.95 each.** *Kibbutz Volunteer*, **$8.95.**

Have you ever wanted to sail around the world on a yacht? How about living at a ski resort with unlimited free skiing? Or getting a great tan in the Australian Outback?

If you are a flexible single person or enjoy an especially flexible family life, all this is possible. *Work Your Way Around the World* gives you all you need to find fascinating work overseas or at home, including ways to scrounge free transportation to and fro. Some of the more memorable sections:

• Working a Passage includes how to get work on freighters, inland boating, and the invaluable How To Win Friends & Influence Captains, plus salty details on crewing in waters around the world (beware of Caribbean pirates!)

• Travel Ways and Means covers every continent and provides tips for border-passing

• Enterprise presents local entrepreneurship possibilities, some shady (gambling), most not

• Work Your Way lays out the possibilities in Tourism, Picking (fruit), Farming, Teaching English, Domestic Work, Business and Industry, and Voluntary Work

Plus over 170 pages on how to work you way in Europe, country by country, and another 110 pages on how to work your way worldwide, continent by continent. Fascinating personal stories from those who have done it intermingle with practical tips on how to do it.

Then, to make it even easier, F & W Publications provides annual Summer Employment Directories. The *1988 Directory of Overseas Summer Jobs* has more than 50,000 listings. *1988 Summer Jobs in Britain* lists 30,000 jobs in Scotland, Wales, and England. *Kibbutz Volunteer* has details on more than 200 Israeli Kibbutzim. *1988 Summer Employment Directory of the United States* lists 50,000 summer job opportunities in the USA. Bonus: all these books give tips on applications, legal matters, and other helpful extras. This may not be the ultimate answer for large families (though again it might if your spirit is sufficiently adventurous), but let no wide-awake home schooled teenager now moan, "I can't think of a thing to do"!

HOW TO GET THERE

Market Dynamics Consultants
Sophisticated Traveler's Pocket Guide to Airport Facilities and Ground Services, **$16.95 postpaid.**

Stress! That's what flying means to me. Beside the fact that airplane smell makes me queasy, there's the little matter of finding your gate and getting there in time.

The last time we flew I turned to Bill and asked, "Why isn't there a map of this airport somewhere so I could know where we're going?" At the time we were lost, searching for a way to get from Point A (somewhere in the bowels of the airport) to Point B (our car parked somewhere in a hundred-acre lot). Good question. Now here is what appears to be the good answer.

The *Sophisticated Traveler's Pocket Guide to Airport Facilities and Ground Services* has
• layout diagrams with airline and gate locations
• available modes of ground transportation
• airport shops and services
• intra-airport transit times,
for 36 major airports. This means that while you are wandering through the airport maze, or even while you're still on the plane, you can be figuring out where to go next and how to speedily get there.
The ad says the Guide is "compact enough to carry in your briefcase," which would help. And if it saves you even one headache or one missed connection, it's worth it.

Stand-Buys Ltd.
    Annual membership, $45, includes all household members.

Carefree types who like to save money might benefit from this discount travel strategy. Stand-Buys is a clearing house for major tour operators and travel suppliers. The seats these big players can't sell, Stand-Buys picks up between three and eight weeks before the trip leaves. Call the members-only hotline as often as you like to find out what is available. When you find a trip you like, call stand-buys' reservation desk and book a confirmed seat. These are not wait-at-the-airport-with-packed-bags-and-wait-for-a-cancellation seats, but full-status confirmed bookings.

Stand-Buys' quarterly *Travelwatch* newsletter also includes tours you can book in the normal way— up to one year in advance.

Club membership also includes free second nights at Holiday Inn, Hilton, Marriott, Sheraton, Stouffer, Ramada Inn, or Days Inn, plus $100,000 free travel insurance on every club trip, plus discount auto rentals.

In a recent year Stand-Buys offered over 3,000 different trips, at discounts of up to 67 percent off the regular price. More than 40,000 travelers have taken advantage of Stand-Buys.

TRAVEL PREPARATION AND ASSISTANCE

EDC
    ***Car Travel Games, Air Travel Games,* $3.95 each.**

Clever books of things-to-do for children aged seven and over. The games and puzzles, etc., all depend on close attention to the colorful pages, so these are not good choices for the car- or air-sick child. Many of the games included could be played just as well at home.
Gazelle

***Fun for the Road,* $1.75 postpaid.**

World's most inexpensive book of travel games. Games do not depend on looking at the book's pages— a plus for those prone to motion sickness.

Jeffrey Norton Publishers

New from Jeffrey Norton: Travel Tips videos present the tourist's side of several European countries. You get a look at the major attractions (landmarks, museums, natural wonders) and tips on how best to plan your itinerary, along with suggestions on housing and shopping.

Travel With Your Children
    ***TWYCH's Airline Guide,* $5. *Skiing With Children,* entire guide $54; guide to USA only or Europe and Canada only, $29 each. Individual resort sheets, $1 each ($5 minimum). *Cruising With Children,* entire guide $34, individual sheets $1. Make checks payable to Travel With Your Children.**

TWYCH's *Airline Guide* (updated annually) packs all you need to know about air travel with children into just four large pages. A chart of all 60 major national and international airlines tells you at a glance if car seats are OK: if the airline provides children's meals, diapers, or bibs: if families with children get special seating: and other essential information.

There's more! TWYCH's *Skiing with Children* and *Cruising with Children* guides tell you all about the specific services and family amenities of (respectively) 140 ski resorts in the US, Canada, and Europe and more than ninety ships representing over thirty cruise lines. This is extremely detailed, helpful information presented in report sheets which you may purchase separately or together.

Finally, a newsflash: Dorothy Jordan has just collaborated with Marjorie Cohen to produce *Great Vacations With Your Kids. Great Vacations,* projected to come out about the same time as this book, will focus on US

Vacations, projected to come out about the same time as this book, will focus on US vacations, and can be ordered through TWYCH. Write for details.

ARMCHAIR TRAVEL

Blue Lion Software
    Ticket to London, Ticket to Paris: **IBM PC and compatibles (requires 128K and Color Graphics Card), PCjr, Tandy 1000, Apple IIe/IIc (128K), each $39.95; Commodore 64/128, $29.95.**

Ticket to London and *Ticket to Paris* are computer adventure tours of the cities in question. Superb, realistic graphics and authentic details provide educational value, while you follow clues about the city trying to solve a mysterious puzzle. You explore famous attractions and side trips while you learn to answer questions about life in London or Paris. Extra bonus: *Ticket to Paris* allows you to use English or French in your dialogs, and even provides an onscreen dictionary to help you with any tricky words.

Each game is a tremendous amount of fun, and the amount of detail is quite impressive. You have to contend with normal opening and closing times as you plan your day, and figure out the proper routes across town. The interactive format makes this much more entertaining than a straight video tour, and you pick up as much travel trivia as if you had struggled through a guidebook. Excellent for dispelling fear of travel to those cities and for beating the high price of airfare. We hope Blue Lion will add many more *Tickets* to this line.

Worldwide Slides
    Most View-Master packets, $3 apiece. Battery-operated projector, $19.95. Deluxe Viewer, $6.95. 3-D Viewer, $3.95. Add 10% shipping.

Do you remember that Christmas you got your first View-Master? Sure you do. Wasn't it fun to click the switch, advance the reel, and see the beautiful color display?

Most of us ended up with packs of cartoon reels as children. But View-Master also developed hundreds of packets of travel reels to go with their viewers. These are now available from Worldwide Slides.

The typical three-reel package includes 21 3-D images, all lovely pictures of famous or important sights. Some packages available: • Scenic USA • Alaska • Eskimos of Alaska • Alabama • Grand Canyon • Tour of Canada • Maritime Provinces • Library of Congress • Paris, France • Castles in Europe • Puerto Rico • Luxembourg • Athens • Norway • Disneyland. This is just the tip of the iceberg.

With a View-Master projector, the whole family can travel from your living room. Or get the inexpensive standard viewers, point at a light source, and travel!

FUN

CHAPTER TWENTY-FOUR

FUN LITERATURE AND TAPES

One of my favorite books is *Words That Sell* (Caddylak Systems, $21.95), a thickish oversized paperback crammed with advertising terms and slogans. Late last night we were reading this book, filling in the blanks left for a product name with our family name, and laughing our heads off.

> Switch to . . . *Pride.*
> Success starts with . . . *Pride.*
> *Pride* spoken here!
> *Pride* means business.
> A little *Pride* can go a long way.
> The *Pride* advantage.
> They don't call us *Pride* for nothing!
> A major breakthrough in . . . *Pride*
> *Pride* is our middle name!
> Nothing's built like a *Pride.*
> *Pride* is our business.

I was smothering my giggles on Bill's shoulder in an attempt to avoid waking up our little Prides who do, indeed, go a long way every time my back is turned on them. It just goes to show that you can find fun in the most unexpected literature.

But *Words that Sell* also comes in handy for its primary function. I was struggling to find a good word that meant "not classic but good anyway," to sum up the kind of children's media reviewed in this chapter. So rest assured that the works in this chapter are

> not legendary
> not historic
> not antique
> not from the storied past
> not in the rich tradition of anything
> not redolent of another age
> not limited editions
> not quaint
> not hallmarks of anything
> not timeless or immortal.

They are, however, fun . . . amusing . . . entertaining . . . diverting . . . sunny . . . convivial and so on through another several dozen useful synonyms. So relax! Put your mind at ease. Take it easy! And enjoy! Laugh it up! Get away from it all. Have some good times! (Help! I can't stop!)

MAGAZINES

Cricket
One year (12 issues), $22.50 U.S.A., $26.50 Canadian and foreign. Single copy $1.95.

Cricket has been called "the New Yorker of kiddie lit." Each issue is a work of art: beautiful illustrations and stories written by top writers. *Cricket's* editor, Marianne Carus, is very, very picky about what goes in to the magazine. She has been known to turn down stories offered by the likes of world-famous writer William Saroyan. (Saroyan later tried again with a better story, which she accepted.)

Let's talk about awards and endorsements. What other magazine comes with a personal recommendation from Isaac Bashevis Singer? *Cricket* has won many awards for excellence, including finalist status in the National Magazine Awards competition— the only children's magazine so selected.

Of interest to home schoolers: Nancy Wallace's son Ishmael once "placed" in a *Cricket* writing competition.

The magazine's mascot is (surprise!) a cricket, who with his buggy friends, collectively known as Everybuggy, cavorts around the margins helping readers better understand the stories. Cricket also has his own adventures and his own comic strip in the back of each issue.

Stories range from Sid Fleischmann's howlingly funny McBroom tall tales to true tales about volcanic eruptions (remember Krakatoa?) and "realistic" stories about kids and their relationships, with everything in between. Many stories have fantasy themes (friendly ghosts, brave mother dragons, and the like).

God's World Publications
God's Big World (K), *Sharing God's World* (grade 1), *Exploring God's World* (grade 2), each $8.50 (includes teacher's guide). *It's God's World* (grades 4-6), *God's World Today* (junior high), $9.50 (includes teacher's guide). *World* (senior high and adult), $18. Bulk orders get discount. Each paper 30 issues, September to May, except *World* (40 issues).

An idea whose time has come. News for kids from a Christian viewpoint. Professionally produced, entertaining but not superficial.

GWP has papers for all different reading levels from kindergarten to adult. The papers for children are carefully matched to their interests and abilities. Following a newspaper format, you get feature stories, reports on hot news items, editorials, cartoons, and letters-to-the-editor. Papers for the kindergarten through junior high set also include activities for kids. A teacher's guide is included with each edition.

Young Companion
$4/year, monthly issues.

This magazine charms others as well as myself. One reader wrote to share how delighted she was with the innocent stories designed for *older* children.

Young Companion is perhaps the only magazine for preteens and teens that does not assume the readers are into drugs and sex and rock. Style is down-to-earth and pious rather than sentimental (another plus).

A Mennonite production, *Young Companion* projects the Christian culture of our past into the graceless confusion of the present.

Young Pilot
$9/year U.S. $11 Canada.

Young Pilot, a professional, rather sentimental magazine for Christian children, is loaded with tear-jerking stories, cartoons and stories about courageous Christians, activity pages, silly riddles kids love, letters to the editor, and even a nature centerfold.

Each issue has a character theme, such as obedience. Heavy emphasis on missions and witnessing, stewardship, obedience to parents and teachers, and so on. Not confrontational on cultural issues.

READING LISTS

Foundation for American Christian Education

Do you love America and want a family reading program that reflects this? The Foundation for American Christian Education's *Family Program for Reading Aloud* contains discussions of more than 100 patriotic books. Three chapters introduce reading aloud and the listening-learning skills. Three more suggest books to read to the youngest (FACE is pro-Mother Goose). Six chapters introduce American themes, including immigrants and ethnic groups, pioneers and Indians, and even American horses! The last two chapters help you evaluate your family reading program.

Home Life
***Books Children Love**, $12.95. **For the Children's Sake**, $6.95. Susan Schaeffer Macaulay tape set, $19. Add 10% shipping.*

More than reading lists. *For the Children's Sake* is a wonderful book about how children learn which, among other things, shares the idea of learning through "living books"— real masterpieces— rather than committee-written textbooks. Based on the writings of British educator Charlotte Mason, *For the Children's Sake* presents a natural, rich style of learning founded on Christian principles and suited to all times and cultures. Author Susan Schaeffer Macaulay has followed this up with a four-tape set in which she and colleague Diane Lopez share further insights into the Charlotte Mason educational method, also available through Home Life.

From the same publisher (Crossway Books), *Books Children Love: A Guide to the Best Children's Literature* goes far beyond a reading-list approach. Most reading lists deal exclusively with fiction, but *Books Children Love* lists hundreds of books from more than two dozen subject areas, with comments on each one. Author Elizabeth Wilson has selected "excellently written, interest-holding books on as wide a range of topics as possible— books that also embody ideas and ideals in harmony with traditional values and a Christian worldview." Susan Schaeffer Macaulay wrote the foreword to this lovely thick book.

Mel Gablers—Educational Analysts
Recommended Reading/Literature, $5 donation. Shipping extra. It doesn't hurt to tuck in a little something to support the Gablers' research.

A treasure trove of information on books good or otherwise. The Gablers' *Recommended Reading/Literature* handbook, one of several dozen dealing with the subject of books and textbooks, consists of recommended reading lists for different age levels, articles from different sources on the benefits of reading great books, and incisive analysis of what is wrong with much children's literature today.

Zondervan Books
    Honey for a Child's Heart, $5.95. At
your Christian bookstore.

Have I got a book for you! Zondervan's
Honey for a Child's Heart, subtitled *The
Imaginative Use of Books in Family Life,* is the
most fantastic, inspiring book about books that
I have ever read. Gladys Hunt, the author,
expertly deals with the questions of what
makes a good book a good book and explains
how to make family reading a rich part of your
life, as well as providing 58 pages of suggested
reading for different age levels. The book is
illustrated with pictures from recommended
books and is an absolute delight to read.
Gladys Hunt says everything I wanted to say
about literature, and says it better. I'd put this
book in my own mail-order catalog in a minute
if Zondervan would quit insisting that they sell
"only to established bookstores." Your best bet
is to hop down to the bookstore and hunt it up.

BOOKS

A Beka Books
    Reading for Fun summer library (K),
$19.95. *Treasure Chest* summer library
(grade 1), $16.95. Add $3.50 shipping.

I know your children are going to like this,
if they're anything like our kids! A Beka has
come up with two summer reading
libraries— one for kindergartners, the other for
first graders. Both come with oodles of books.
Reading for Fun, the summer library for
kindergartners, has 55 (count 'em!) colorful
little books, all packaged in an attractive case.

Starting with truly tiny little phonics readers,
the books get bigger and the stories get longer.
Every book is short enough to be read in a
single sitting, a big plus with littlest readers.
    Treasure Chest, the summer library for first
graders, comes packed in (you guessed it) a
treasure chest. Twelve books with full-color
covers carry on the "treasure" theme with
classic tales intermixed with new stories.
    Both summer libraries have great kid
appeal and are guaranteed to banish the
reading blahs any time of the year.

Capper's Books

Capper's has been around for awhile; Laura
Ingalls Wilder was reading *Capper's Weekly*
before the turn of the century.
    According to Capper's, "our true specialty is
in our strong selection of popular children's
classics." These include such titles as *Mrs.
Wiggs of the Cabbage Patch,* which we are glad
to report has nothing to do with Cabbage Patch
dolls, *A Girl of the Limberlost,* and nature-lover
Thornton W. Burgess's 1909 classic, *Old
Mother West Wind.* These gentle stories
contrast sharply with the selfishness,
nastiness, and flippishness of much of what
now passes for children's literature.

Children's Book and Music Center

This enormous newsprint catalog is "the
largest supply of children's books, records, and
cassettes in the country." Many topics,
including basic school subjects like math and
reading readiness, creative arts, and physical
education. The Children's Book and Music
Center literature collection is three jam-packed
pages of contemporary favorites. Here's where
to get the compete Babar collection, or piles of
books by Bill Peet, Ezra Jack Keats, Maurice
Sendak, Richard Scarry, Dr. Seuss, Peter
Spier, and Shel Silverstein. Also fairytales,
poetry (from Robert Louis Stevenson to Shel
Silverstein), and several literature anthologies.

Apparently Children's Book and Music Center stocks more items than they list in the catalog, as a little box on the page says, "We stock thousands of paperbacks including fiction and nonfiction for all ages. Call with your special request."

Children's Small Press Collection

The Children's Small Press Collection represents nearly 100 small progressive children's publishers. The Collection includes a wide selection of books "on the forefront of children's issues." Topics include: • Activities (cookbooks, early childhood activity books, a children's organizer . . .) • Family and Human Relations (lots about divorce, fighting, and single parents) • Feelings • Fantasy and Fun • Fiction for Young Readers (all contemporary) • For the Middle Young • Resources for the Gifted (that's their title for this section, not to be confused with the company by that name) • Teen Guidance • Safety Issues • Parenting • Health and Sexuality • Science and the Environment • Teacher Resources • Nursery Rhymes and Poetry (includes *Black Mother Goose* and *Father Gander*) • Child Authors (only two books in this category) • Puppetry and Storytelling • Multicultural, Historical, and Bilingual • Conflict Resolution, Problem Solving (pacifist). Member publishers include New Seed Press, Parenting Press, Shameless Hussy Press, Women's Press, Feminist Press, Rainbow Press, and even Garlic Press (we kid you not!).

CHINABERRY
BOOK
SERVICE

Books and music
for children and families

Chinaberry Book Service

Warm, inviting, supremely helpful catalog of literature for children from birth through the late teens. This is a real book service, not just a glitzy pictures-with-minimal-description catalog. Each and every book is lovingly described by a mother who has read it and used it with her own children. Very large selection (the current catalog has over 80 newsprint pages), ranging from classics like *Charlotte's Web* to brand-new books. Just one example, from the writeup of *If You Give a Mouse a Cookie:*

> I'm getting tired of special ordering this book! No longer do I wonder if the fact that it is available only in hardcover is enough to turn everyone off . . . EVERYONE to whom I've shown this book (and obviously those special orders) thinks this book is irresistible. It seems to be one of those books you can read a million times and never feel like hiding it from your child so you won't have to read it yet AGAIN.
>
> It is the story of a boy who makes the mistake of giving a mouse a cookie. (The mouse is quite adorable.) Now, if you give a mouse a cookie, he's going to need some milk. (We see the boy getting the mouse a glass of milk.) But then, the mouse will probably ask for a straw. (The boy gets a straw.) Then he'll want to look at himself in the mirror to make sure he doesn't have a milk moustache. (The boy gets a napkin and holds the mouse up to the bathroom mirror so he can see himself.) . . . Eventually, the story comes full circle and the endearing mouse, who is thirsty, needs a drink of milk. And, of course, if he asks for a glass of milk, he's going to want a cookie to go with it. (By this time, the boy is completely wiped out, and the kitchen is a mess.)
>
> Text is sparse. The colored illustrations are uncluttered, but with enough detail to keep you looking for more tidbits to chuckle over.

Chinaberry has everything from board books to Newberry award-winners to fabric-covered scrapbooks to Please Packs. Some New Age, some Christian, some secular, chosen not so much for ideology (although Chinaberry has New Age leanings) as for beauty, serenity, cleverness, and fun.

Christian Light Publications

Christian Light offers literature they consider suitable for young children, chosen in conformity with Mennonite moral standards. Each work offered comes with a code that explains just how good they think the book is and if they recommend it with any reservations.

Discover and Learn Reading Resources

Christian and secular literature for all ages. Small catalog includes • Four books for young children • Books for Preteens section introducing the "Childhood of Famous Americans" series • Adventures and Mysteries • Devotionals • Fantasy/Science Fiction (all Christian) • Books for Teens and Adults (Margo mysteries, Peggy books, Anne of Green Gables series, Jeanette Oke love stories, and so on) • Informed Reading. Two great books in the last section: *Honey for a Child's Heart* (I've been looking all over for this!) and *401 Ways to Get Your Kids to Work at Home*. The line will expand if you support it.

EDC

Find It board books, $2.95 each. What's Happening series, $3.95 each. Picture Word books, $2.95 each paperback, $6.95 each hardbound, $11.96 library bound, or $12.95 for hardbound combined volume *Words to Read* (contains all three books). First Experiences series, $2.95 each or $8.95 for hardbound combined volume. Children's Picture Bible series, $4.95 each of $12.95

for combined hardbound volume, *The Story of Jesus*. Slot books, $8.95 each. Michael and Mandy series, $3.95 each. Story Books, $2.95 each or two hardbound combined volumes, *Dragons, Giants, and Witches* and *Princes, Wizards, and Gnomes*, $10.95 each. Upside Down books, $4.95 each. Picture Classics, $2.95 or $10.95 for hardbound combined volume, *Children's Classics*.

Immense array of all sorts of educational and fun reading matter for children. EDC publishes the Usborne Books line, originally produced in the United Kingdom.

Elsewhere in this book I have mentioned a dozen or so of the more overtly educational series; now let's look at what reading matter Usborne has to offer.

Find It board books for youngest children (six months on up) are twelve thick pages apiece. Your youngster searches for the hidden animal in every picture. Stephen Cartwright's charming art illustrates this series. Included: *Find the Duck, Teddy, Piglet, Puppy, Kitten, Bird*.

Also illustrated by Stephen Cartwright, the What's Happening series for two- to six-year-olds presents common situations (*On the Farm, The Seaside, At the Zoo*) with an amusing difference. Look for hidden objects, recognize details of color and shape.

Picture Word books (*The House, The Shop, The Town*) are pages of colorful scenes containing dozens of labeled objects. Similar to the Richard Scarry approach, but with real people, not cartoon animals.

The First Experiences series, again illustrated by the inimitable Stephen Cartwright, covers *Going to the Dentist, Going to a Party* (monster costumes in this one), *Going to the Hospital, The New Baby* (a very gentle, pro-baby story), *Going to School, and Moving House*. Gentle story lines accompany the amusing art. Suitable for three years old on up.

The Children's Picture Bible series only covers parts of the life of Christ: *The Childhood of Jesus*, *Miracles of Jesus*, *Stories Jesus Told*. Realistic art. Ages eight on up.

Slot Books are something different. These fantasy stories are not illustrated quite as beautifully as the other Usborne books, but they are more interactive. You remove the magic carpet, space ship, or whatever from the pocket. Place it one the first page, follow the dotted line, and pop it through the slot to follow the story line. Includes: *There's a Mouse About the House*, *A Squirrel's Tale*, *The Amazing Journey of Space Ship H-20*, *Ted and Dolly's Magic Carpet Ride*, and *Ted and Dolly's Fairytale Flight*.

The Michael and Mandy series is another learn-to-cope-with-scary-experiences series, of which we have plenty in the USA. Covered: *Mandy and the Hospital*, *Mandy and the Dentist*, *Michael's First Day at School*, *Michael in the Dark*, *Michael and the Sea*.

The Usborne Story Books series for ages six and up is all that fairytale stuff: *Dragons*, *Giants*, *Witches* (available separately or as a combined volume), and *Princes and Princesses*, *Wizards*, and *Gnomes* (also available separately or combined). Stephen Cartwright illustrations.

Upside Down books, yet another innovative Usborne product, each contain two stories. Read one, flip the book over, and read another. These are familiar fairy tales: *King Midas* and *The Emperor's New Clothes*; *The Three Bears* and *The Little Match Girl*; *Cinderella* and *How the Elephant Got Its Trunk*; *The Frog Prince* and *The Pear Tree*; *The Pancake that Ran Away* and *Toads and Diamonds*; and *Sleeping Beauty* and *The Soldier and the Seven Giants*. All freshly retold versions of the original tales.

Lastly, besides the myths and legends, animal stories, and others such that I just don't have room to write up, are the Picture Classics. See these described in the Classical Literature chapter.

First Words

Here's a neat concept— a whole catalog of books for babies! Well, not just babies. Toddlers will like them, too. Delightful selection includes some surprises. *The Rebus Treasury* is 40 best-loved songs and rhymes "told" with rebuses— drawings that, put together, make the sounds of the words. Janet and Alan Ahlberg's winsome *Peek-A-Boo* book shows a baby's world from breakfast to bedtime, with cutouts to peek through. *My Play-a-Tune Book* contains its own electronic keyboard. *Jigsaw Puzzle Board Books* sound . . . unusual (would you believe four odd-shaped board books that fit together as a puzzle?) Many Mother Goose books (and updated versions), just enough ABC books. Photo books. Poetry. Baby albums. Toy books (pop-ups, slot books, flip books, and so on). Picture books. Counting books. Bedtime books. Activity books. Books on reading. Very easy-to-follow format includes small book pictures, pithy descriptions.

Gospel Mission

Wholesale Christian book outlet. Their Children's Heritage line of classic Christian tales from the nineteenth century has a whole different outlook on life than modern children's literature. Personal piety and care for the poor are stressed. Lovers of Louisa May Alcott's *Little Women* series will find that warmly pious atmosphere recreated here.

Hewitt Research Foundation

Dr. Raymond Moore's organization, founded to help home schoolers, carries a long list of Christian literature, including their own character-building books and the *Godly Heroes* biography series, among many other clever and useful educational items.

High Noon Books (division of Academic Therapy Publications)

Really interesting high-lo books (high interest, low reading level) designed for preteens and teens, but also usable by any young child who can read. The books are inexpensive, and the mystery/adventure format keeps interest high. High Noon books all foster morals without being preachy— the heroes are good and the bad guys are bad. Son Ted's opinion: "I like them because they're exciting."

Open Court Publishing Company
Lit Kit prices between $40 and $70. From 8 to 18 books per Kit.

Open Court's Lit Kits are, according to the publisher, "The best in children's books grouped by grade and interest level." I really like most of their selections, but as a Christian I have trouble with the witch/dragon stories that make it into many of the Kits. Sheerly from the viewpoint of literary quality, each Kit's selections are well chosen.

An example of one Kit (for second grade): *Make Way for Ducklings; Pickles and Jake; Madeline and the Bad Hat; Madeline and the Gypsies; Jack Jouett's Ride; Dandelion; Stone Cutter; Magic Michael; Hildilid's Night; The Shy Little Girl; Blaze and the Forest Fire; Frederick; Swimmy; Bearymore; Bedtime for Frances; Moon Mouse.* You can see you get your $51.75 worth. You can also see that not all Kits contain occult lit. When you consider how popular that genre is nowadays, Open Court is actually very conservative in the amount

included.

The books are paperback, and per book the price is certainly right. The Lit Kit is certainly an easy way to build a home library.

Orange Cat Goes to Market

Helen Hegener of *Home Education* magazine strongly recommends this catalog of children's literature. At press time, I had not yet got my hands on a copy. My guess, based on Helen's recommendation, is that those who like Chinaberry Book Service will like this one.

PermaBound

Enormous catalog of all sorts of books bound with the special PermaBound process. PermaBound promises to make paperbacks far more durable, for far less than the price of hardbound. Much modern children's literature, some classics. Minimum order policy means you might want to co-op with other families.

Telltales
Ambitious, mostly color catalog of children's books. Some old friends you might recognize: *Black Beauty, Little House* series, *Blueberries for Sal, The Secret Garden.* Unusual books: *Father Fox's Feast of Songs*, Peter Spier's *Dreams* (cloud castles in the air), *Piggins* (the pig butler), *Sailing Ships* pop-up book. Special features: short biographies of selected author and illustrator, autographed copies available of some works, yuppy accessories (totebags and T-shirts). Large selection.

CHILDREN'S BOOK CLUBS

God's World Publications
     Many titles in the $1-$2 range. Mostly paperbacks.

New in 1987— the God's World Book Club. All subscribers to any God's World publication are automatically in the Club. Others may join simply by writing and asking to be added to the mailing list.

What you get are children's classics and Christian books for ages kindergarten through senior high, all at substantial discounts. Some items, like a slipcased set of the *Little House* books for $19.95, remain available at all times. On other items, old inventory disappears as new titles are added— so don't hang on to your order too long before sending it in! At present, about 70 titles are offered, with many more to be added.

The God's World Book Club should help Christian parents answer the perennial question, "Whatever *shall* I find for my children to read?"

Grolier Enterprises

One morning you unwittingly open your mailbox and there it is, lurking inside. It looks innocuous enough— an ad for a children's book club. The one I got most recently said "Your child's lifelong love of reading begins with . . . 4 books for only $1.95, Plus A FREE Tote Bag."

So what's so dangerous, you ask? Grolier Enterprises' Beginning Readers' Program may do exactly what it says! Are you *ready* for a lifelong love of reading? Are you ready to have your arm jerked off every time you try to walk your children past a bookstore or a library? Reading can get to be a *habit*, you know!

The initial four books, at $1.95 for all four plus shipping and handling, are just to hook you on the program. Thereafter, every four weeks, you will be sent two more books. If you want to keep them, you will pay $3.99 each plus shipping and handling. If you don't want to keep them, you will have to repack them, drive to the post office, and return them. This must be done within 10 days. It is, in short, a lot of effort to return the books. Keep that in mind when considering enrollment.

The Beginning Readers' Program features the likes of Dr. Seuss and the Berenstain Bears. How do I know you can get hooked on Seuss? Because those are the books my father used to teach me to read, and I wore out three library cards before I turned 15!

Grolier has a similar program, entitled Disney's Wonderful World of Reading. The ad for this one offered two free books and a bookrack, plus a chance to win a sweepstakes. Terms are the same as for the Beginning Readers' Program. The books are, you guessed it, Walt Disney productions like *Pinocchio* and *Cinderella.* You know as much about Walt Disney as I do, so I leave this offer to your judgment.

CHILDREN'S SPOKEN-WORD CASSETTES

Caedmon Tapes
     Most cassettes and records, $8.98 each. Sets cost less per recording.

Caedmon has a vast collection of spoken-word recordings of literature— modern, classical, ancient, British, American, European and other, for people both young and old. Some recordings, like Carol Channing's performance of *Winnie-the-Pooh*, have music as well, and this is indicated by a little black musical note in the margin. Many are abridged, the better to fit on a C-60 cassette. The selection includes novels, fairytales, poems, and legends, science fiction and fantasy. Many works are read by the authors. Some *poseurs* are included here also, but the good outweighs the bad.

Caedmon cassettes are not narrated but "performed" by the likes of W.H. Auden, Dylan Thomas, Carol Channing, and Michael Bond (of Paddington Bear fame). The recordings are not all entertainment, though. You can get several "Great Speeches" sets featuring speeches that changed history, Studs Terkel's story of the Depression in the words of those who lived it, Camus reading his own novels (in French, naturally). Eggheads, in short, are in for a feast.

Caedmon's catalog is prosaic and prices are not cheap. For diehard cassette fans, there is a way around the price boondoggle: sign up for the Library Subscription Plan. Of the four options, the one most likely to interest home schoolers is the Small Budget Children's Plan. You agree to buy each new Caedmon release in that category at a reduced rate, for a maximum investment of $55/year for 10 cassettes. In return, you get 40 percent off on all Caedmon recordings and all Arabesque recordings (classical music and opera).

Mind's Eye
Most cassettes $5.95 each, including *Color Book Theater*. Sets are less per cassette.

Tremendous selection of stories both classical and just plain fun. Will Rogers and other humorists, *Color Book Theater* (reviewed in the Classical Literature chapter), mystery, science fiction, history— you name it, The Mind's Eye has it. Lovely catalog for browsers.

CHILDREN'S MUSIC

Children's Book and Music Center

Immense variety of children's recordings. Includes: • Mother Goose & Nursery Rhymes • Lullaby & Rest Time • Read-Alongs • Great Books Dramatized • Lots of favorite (but not classic) books on record or cassette. Plus • Movement Recordings • Foreign Language Recordings • Folks Songs. Also books, videos, school helps, and so on.

Children's Recordings

Almost everything applauded today in children's music and stories. Categories in this large newsprint catalog include: • What's New • Stories, Tales, Yarns (from *Wind in the Willows* to *Charlie and the Chocolate Factory*) • *Chronicles of Narnia* • Readalongs • Music and Song (Burl Ives, Sesame Street, and *Earth Mother Lullabies*, among dozens of other recordings— quite an eclectic selection!) • Other Lands • Elephant Records • Raffi! and Other Canadians • Soundtracks • Disneyland • Sound Effects • Barry Polisar • Hap Palmer • Tom Glazer • Holiday • Mr. Rogers • Activity • Nostalgia • Ella Jenkins • Poetry • Lullabies. The catalog also contains a Preschool Guide list of suggested recordings for this age group, a Title Index, and a list of the A.L.A. Notable Recordings carried by Children's Recordings.

A Gentle Wind
Tapes, $6.95 each; Samplers, $4.95 reach. Add $1.75 shipping for snail mail or an extra 50¢ per item for first class.

Some of the most original music cassettes for kids around. You can buy a variety of Sampler cassettes for a small sum, each containing one song from a number of their cassettes. This gives you an accurate idea of what you would like to order. Choice selections: Paul Tracey's *Rainbow Kingdom*, Tom Smith's *Chip Off the New Block*, Chris Holder's *Storysinger*, and every Sampler (at the moment, there are four). New Age flavor to some cassettes, old-timey flavor to others, uniformly gentle presentation (no rock-you-out-of-your-socks screaming hype). All cassettes are high quality and easy to listen to over and over and over again.

Golden Glow Recordings
$9.70 each tape postpaid.

Good Morning Sunshine: Songs for a Day Full of Wonder and *Nitey-Night: Tender Melodies for a Beautiful Bedtime* both feature a wide variety of instrumentals (hammer dulcimer, recorder, oboe, harp, guitar, banjo, piano, sax, trombone, flute) each accompanying different songs. The tunes are classic children's favorites (Hokey Pokey, nursery rhymes) sung in an ethereal style. Harmonies change with each verse, in accordance with Golden Glow's philosophy that children's recordings should be "rich and thick with music." This attention to detail is paying off: Golden Glow has sold thousands of these tapes already.

Kimbo Educational

Kimbo has one of the largest collections of children's music. Nursery favorites, folk songs, sing-alongs, and so on. Hap Palmer, Raffi, Slim Goodbody, wakeup songs, parachute music, anything you can think of.

Music for Little People

Yet another source for lots of contemporary children's music and family listening, as well as musical instruments galore for those who would rather make it themselves. Lovely catalog, New Age flavor.

VIDEO

Christian Family Video Club
$150 annual subscription fee entitles you to video rentals from list of over 300 Christian videos.

Pricey membership for serious video buffs. The promo I saw offered *Pilgrim's Progress* free to paid subscribers. I'd want to know if it was the (good) cartoon version or the (bad) version with human actors.

Entertainment Plus Family Video Club

Up to 50 percent discounts on "over 1,000 wholesome titles." Examples: Sandi Patti in concert. Disney movies. National Geographic specials. Send for brochure explaining how the club works.

Music for Little People

Middle-sized selection of videos with "educational value." Beyond the usual Sesame Street choices, this includes such offerings as • *Making Music With Eric* (fiddle up a cornstalk, play the spoons, tin can bongos, and other down-home oddments) • *Raffi In Concert* • *Baby Animals Just Want to Have Fun* (real animals at play) • and *Lorax* (the Dr. Seuss antipollution video).

Omega Entertainment

I didn't believe it until I saw it— a *good* cartoon version of *Pilgrim's Progress!* Yes, Omega Entertainment really has this classic story as a professional full-color cartoon in the old Disneyesque style. I hated to send it back after reviewing it, since the children continued to clamor for it for weeks. Omega also has a line of Christian sports videos that combine athletes' testimonies with sports tips, hilarious bloopers, and great moments in the games. Plus evangelistic films, Christian issue films, and a whole lot more.

White Lion Media

"The best new Christian and family videos for as little as $19.95 each." Popular titles, special offers.

CHAPTER TWENTY-FIVE

TOYS AND GAMES

Q. What do you get when you cross a horse with a donkey?

A. *A mule, which is neither horse nor donkey.*

Q. So what do you get when you cross an educational product with a toy or game?

A. *A whale of a good time!*

Now that educational toys and games are in such hot demand, everyone wants to be educational. In one sense, it is true that all experience is educational. On the other hand, this can be carried too far. Consider this ad for an Interactive Posterior Stimulus Module: "Your children will have hours of fun learning from our IPSM. They can manipulate the circular shape and learn about density. (Don't forget, the IPSM can be used as a very large stencil!) Aural development is enhanced by rapping the IPSM smartly against its base and observing the variations in sound. Gross motor skills are fostered by lowering and raising the IPSM. The IPSM can also be used for values education. Remembering to always lower the IPSM at the end of an educational session is not only good exercise but also demonstrates kindness to others." I could go on and on. But why waste more space describing a toilet seat?

Beware, beware, beware! Get to know what the ad jargon really means. "The product develops gross motor skills," could refer to a eating or a Ring Toss game. "Your children's perceptual ability will be enhanced" could be said of a nature walk or a comic book.

"Children will have hours of fun playing with it" is a cheap shot aimed at your supposed desire to be rid of your kids' company.

In real life, virtually *anything* can be touched, tasted, smelled, and looked at, and most things can be shaken and listened to as well. Just because my baby daughter tries to teethe on my shoe as she plays about the floor does not mean shoes should be sold as a "tactile stimulus experience." Every house, except those of the desperately poor, has things to look at and listen to and taste and smell and feel. Good toys and games aren't "experiences": they are something to *do*.

TOYS, PRO AND CON

At the same time as the educational toy market is swelling to eight times its previous size, a movement is afoot to talk parents out of buying any toys at all. "Toys are childish!" voices cry. (True, of course.) "Children should use *real* tools and do *real* work instead of all this fooling around with expensive gewgaws."

It's bad enough that toys cost so much, and even worse if you have to feel guilty about buying them. Should we feel guilty about buying toys, or (more consistently) stop buying them altogether? Are Junior's Lego bricks a harmful influence?

After giving the matter deep thought, and riffling through more toy catalogs than I care to mention, I think I've found some helpful guidelines.

Passive toys, toys that do things without having anything much done to them, are worthless. In this category put talking dolls, battery-operated miniature cars, and the TV set, as long as these items are used as designed. If the talking doll is used as a regular doll and not limited by the extent of her built-in vocabulary; if the minicar's battery falls out and it can be propelled about the floor on pretend journeys to Alaska; if the TV is turned into an aquarium; then they become useful.

Toys that duplicate adult tools are only useful if it will be years and years before your children are ready for the real thing. What is the sense of buying Junior a toy typewriter when, for the same price, you could get a real used typewriter that he could really learn to type on? Why get Suzy her own tiny set of breadpans and mixing bowls when she can help you with your real baking? Our seven-year-old son, Teddy, washes the (real) dishes in our (real) kitchen sink for $5 a week, and is saving up for his own used IBM Selectric typewriter. Joseph, our six-year-old, figured out how to run our laser printer before I did! Sarah, our three-year-old, has already figured out how to install and remove drill bits from Dad's manual drill. Magda, our two-year-old, *loves* tools and is always hovering over the tool caddy every time we have a project. Both boys, and now Sarah, help Dad screw together bookcases and do other carpenter work. It would be too much for a seven-year-old to wield an adult-sized hammer, though, so we bought Ted a good set of children's tools, and Joe will soon get one also.

Open-ended construction toys and art materials are good for fantasy play. Under this heading come all sorts of building blocks and construction kits: Legos, Duplos, Tinker Toys, Erector sets, Lincoln logs, and so on. These are the products that really will give Junior "hours of fun," since they are limited only by his

imagination. I do not include kits that only build one particular item, like a castle or a Frontier Town, in this category. These are fun only while the project lasts, and then you have to either store them for years or throw away hours of Junior's work.

Board games and other family games are great relaxers. This does not apply to the "wipe out your opponent" sort. Competitive games have their place, but I have never seen any happy results from families playing them. You can change a competitive game into a cooperative game by making the goal to have everyone win, which is how we do it. We don't stop playing until everyone is "home." Games whose only purpose is to produce one "winner" and many "losers" and that teach you nothing along the way belong in the trash.

For children, play is learning. For adults, play is relaxation. If you relax too much, you get limp and sloppy. If you never relax, you get ulcers. The proper balance of play and work produces healthy bodies and minds. "A cheerful heart doeth good like a medicine" (Prov 17:22).

ALL-PURPOSE TOY AND GAME COMPANIES

These are the stuff-it-all-into-one-big-catalog folks. Lovers of one-stop shopping will be pleased by these companies.

Animal Town Game Company

Cooperative board games, classic games from around the world, books about games, books for children, rubber stamps, "old-time radio" shows on cassette, lullabies, songs, and stories. When we want to retreat far from the madding crowd, instead of hopping into the car and burning oil for hours we play their *Back to the Farm* game ($21 plus shipping).

Animal Town's philosophy is pro-family and Mother Earthish, somewhat sentimental for the olden days and with a California flavor. The board games are beautiful, and Animal Town encourages you to change the rules to fit your family's needs, which we have done. Their own family-designed games are not cheap, but are very well made. Catalog items are fairly priced.

Childcraft

Childcraft's motto is "Toys That Teach." Their Catalog is big, bright, and filled with an assortment of educational toys, equipment, and books in all subjects. Childcraft has lots and lots of play equipment and giant building materials: Big Waffle Blocks, giant cardboard blocks, a Combi Kit that can make toys big enough to ride on, the Quadro construction kit that makes a gym, and lots more. There's something in every price range, but yuppies will feel more comfortable with the prices than bargain-hunters. The selections have good educational and play value.

Constructive Playthings

Constructive Playthings has two catalogs: a school catalog, loaded with institutional playground equipment and heavy-duty playthings, and a Home Edition. The latter has hands-on stuff only (no books or workbooks). I've seen a lot of catalogs, but this one has several unique crafts that tempted me: a shellcraft kit for my son who loves seashells by the seashore, and a early knitting kit that I'll try to give to my daughter if the boys don't get their hands on it first! The no-spill tempera markers also are a good idea. We struggled with a set from another company that had paintbrush tops attached to bottles, out of which the paint stubbornly refused to flow. Constructive Playthings tests all its products to avoid lemons like that. You may also be interested in the large selection of family games, the free toy guide, or Constructive Plaything's Jewish Education catalog. Lots of reasonably-priced items for ages birth to eight, many under $5.

Developmental Learning Materials (DLM)

DLM, a public school supplier, carries a large selection of their own educational games. These colorful games are reasonably priced and easy to play. DLM has games in many subject areas.

Lane Nemeth, Discovery Toys® president

Discovery Toys®, Inc.
Eighty percent of toys cost less than $8.

Discovery Toys® sells *only* through home demonstrations.Their product line is constantly changing to reflect the best available in the toy market. Discovery Toys® are imported from all over the world, and the country of origin is mentioned in each of the catalog entries which your local home sales lady shows you. In case you're not quite sure about what a particular toy is good for, each item is described in terms of its "Educational Play Value." Every item is beautiful, every item is educational, and many are not to be found anywhere else.

Discovery Toys® does *not* send their catalog to the general public, preferring to deal only through local representatives. You may buy toys at a toy party, or order through your rep's catalog.

By hosting a Discovery Toys® demonstration, you can get a commission on the toys sold and perhaps even half off one of the most-wanted items (Microscope, Children's Encyclopedia, several neat and expensive construction sets . . .). Discovery Toys® is also looking for people to do the selling at their home demos.

Growing Child

Would you like to bridge the generation gap? Growing Child offers a large selection of classy playthings, with an emphasis on classic toys that you might have played with and that can be handed down to your grandchildren. This is not another yuppy catalog: the prices are reasonable. All catalog items are age-graded and developmental.

Growing Child is not a bunch of aging nostalgia buffs, either. You can find many of today's best toys along with the old-time favorites like nesting blocks and counting frames. Goodies like Dr. Drew's blocks, a Noah's Ark puzzle with interchangeable pieces, and Lauri puzzles are scattered throughout the catalog. And Growing Child has a large selection of children's literature, including several pages of award-winners.

HearthSong

"A Catalog for Families." Natural fabric kidstuff, books on parenthood, wool-stuffed dolls, art supplies, cookbooks, knitting 'n' sewing stuff, books, seasonal gifts. Everything beautiful, no schlock.

Just For Kids

Definitely yuppy catalog of toys and clothing. Colorful, many pages, rather more frivolous and decorative items than other catalogs. No bargains here: some expensive toys like the Rocking Kitten ($139.95) or the Emigrant Doll Family ($149.95). Good service.

Legacy (a division of Anthony Paul, Inc.)

Ambitious venture with a format similar to Discovery Toys®. These are the people who sell the Agapeland series. They have now branched out into toys, playing on the "character development" theme. However, the toys are just that—toys—not character lessons in disguise. Categories include • Good Old-Fashioned Toys (replicas and updated versions of classic toys) • Creative Play Toys • Outdoor Games (sand play, etc.) • Preschool Toys • The Land of Pleasant Dreams (cartoon fantasy books/cassettes with plaid animals preaching character lessons) • Agapeland material • Musical Instruments (didn't I see most of these in the Rhythm Band catalog?) • Science and Discovery (water clock, dinosaur model, etc.) • Games and Puzzles. Pricey items strongly hyped. Example: a sand castle play set is said to "Stimulate creativity and imagination, encourages social interaction." Really, now. The toys are probably good, but this catalog would benefit from (1) more mellow salesmanship, and (2) more believable lists of "what this will do for your child."

The Toy Factory

A family-owned business established in 1972, The Toy Factory carries toys from around the world, folk toys, make-your-own-toy kits and parts, and a large selection of children's books. The newsprint catalog appears geared to the better-off *Mother Earth News* subscriber. Lots of nature study and environmental stuff; lots of expensive toys made out of natural hardwoods. The children's books include series of Caldecott and Newbery Award winners, plus Mrs. Piggle-Wiggle, Curious George in all his misadventures, and other children's standards. Interspersed throughout the catalog are "parenting" tips from a secular standpoint.

Toys to Grow On

This one is a doozie. Toys to Grow On has a big, beautiful color catalog. So do lots of other companies. Ah, but who else sells kits designed to provide 99 hours of fun for . . . Babies, Toddlers, Preschoolers, and School-Age Kids? Each kit is $44.95, thus putting it out of *my* reach, but perhaps not out of yours. And there are such items as a Hermit Crab Lab (including two crabs and extra shells), a build-it-yourself roller coaster for marbles, minigolf with marbles, *Tot Trivia,* etc. etc.

But that is not what makes Toys to Grow On so amazing. Their hustle is what amazes me. Who else has a Never Forget Birthday Club? Who else gives away a No-Choke Testing Tube (it lets you know whether any given object is small enough to be swallowed by a young child) *free* with any order? Who else has a chatty company newsletter bound into their catalog, with enticing article titles like, "Why Is This Man Skating Away With Your Toys?" Who else gives away $50 gift certificates to customers who send in interesting tidbits that get published in the catalog? Who else tells you how to gather a variety of insects in next to no time (hold an open umbrella underneath a low branch of a bush and *shake!*)? Hustle isn't everything, but in a country where people dress for success it's bound to help.

CHRISTIAN TOYS

In a reaction against the increasing brutality and amorality of children's toys, several Christian companies are now coming out with their own line of toys.

Praise Unlimited
Praise Dolls, $37-$40 each. Scented 6 inch Praise Dolls, $5.50 each. Judah action figure, $7. Other action figures, $7-$14. Full Armour of God 7-piece plastic armour set, $24. B-I-B-L-E Bear, $32. Praise Phone, $19.50. Fruit of the Spirit Toy, $14.

Praise Unlimited is a company on crusade. Listen to their brochure:

> In the last few years changes have been occurring in the toy industry. These changes have shown movement away from traditional toys into a new era of violence-related, humanistic-type toys.
> The innocence of tea sets, baby dolls, train sets and simple board games has been replaced

with violent video games, voluptuously endowed fashion dolls, figurines encouraging destruction and fantasy role-playing that many times leads to an inability and lack of desire to cope with a real world.

The answer? "God-inspired" Christian toys. First come the Praise Dolls: Joy, Hope, and Faith. Just like the typical trademarked dolls, the Praise Dolls come in several sizes, and have all sorts of trademarked accessories. Unlike the Rainbow Brites and Strawberry Shortcakes, Praise dolls make Christian comments when you squeeze them. Example: "Did you know that Jesus loves you and He is Lord!" Also, purchasers of the large 21 inch model receive a certificate which, if once sent in and forwarded to Praise Unlimited, gets placed in a 16 inch Friendship Praise Doll box, and the whole kit and caboodle gets sent to an underprivileged child free of charge.

In the same line, Praise Unlimited has come out with a "Judah the Christian Soldier" doll for boys. Judah wears the Full Armor of God, which is completely removable except for the shin-guards. Price includes the gift of a second Judah to a needy child, when a Friendship Card is returned by the purchasing child.

The Full Armor of God is also available separately in kid-size.

Praise Unlimited also sells a Noah's Ark kit. Again, a small Noah's Ark goes to a needy child when a purchaser of the large set returns a card.

New from Praise: • Christian, the Praise Kid, a 16 inch talking doll • B-I-B-L-E Bear (he sings guess what?) • Fruit of the Spirit Toy (a shape sorter with fruit inscribed with Christian character traits) • The Praise Phone (toy telephone with three Messages of Love disks) • All sorts of school totes, lunchboxes, etc.

Judging from the pictures, all products seem carefully and professionally made. The brochure informs us that Praise Unlimited products meet all consumer safety regulations.

Praise Unlimited toys are sold through local distributors.

Rainfall Toys
    Bible Greats action figures, $6.99 each. Bible Play-alongs, $3.99 each. Bible Peel &

Play, $5.99 each. Read 'n Play sets, $6.99 each. Color 'n Dial, $9.99. Refills, $5.99 each. Piano Play-Book, $14.99. Choices, Children's Choices, $14.99 each. Kingdom Critter Jrs, $14.99 each. More toys available.

Rainfall Toys has "Refreshing!" as their motto. The Rainfall lineup includes toys and games priced lower than the competition.

Bible Greats action figures are seven- to eleven-plus-inch-tall fully poseable figures with authentic costumes, accessories, and a full-color story booklet. Now available: Noah, Daniel, Joseph, Moses, Samson, Ruth, Deborah, Esther, Gideon, Joshua, and David & Goliath (the latter costs extra). These figures are not durable enough to take severe handling, so are recommended for ages four and up.

Bible Play-Alongs are fully-dramatized and orchestrated Bible stories on cassette. Each comes with the same full-color booklet accompanying the Bible Greats sets.

Bible Peel & Play sets each include two background scenes, play boards that set up as an easel, 30 full-color reusable, washable vinyl pieces to stick hither and yon, instructions, and Bible story sheet. Presently available: Noah, Joseph, and Jonah.

Read 'n Play is something different— Kurt Mitchell's cartooned full-color storybooks with accompanying character play figure. Jonah is presented as a sober mouse in a purple robe, while Esther is a lovely white mouse. Stories are adapted from the New International Version Bible.

Color 'n Dial lets you crank the 22-foot roll of stories to color, presenting one scene at a time. This refillable rugged plastic case also includes molded crayon tray, eight crayons, crayon sharpener, and crayon storage box. Refill scenes available are The Prodigal Son, Jesus' Miracles and Parables, They Came Two by Two, A-Z Things We Know, Count and Color, and Color Things that Go.

Kingdom Critters Jrs are your basic stuffed plush animals, only this time each is accessorized like a Bible figure and sports both a character trait name (e.g., Loyal Collie) and a fantasy story booklet. Very soft and cuddly and long-lasting.

Rainfall's two Choices games are reviewed in the Character Education chapter, and the Piano Play-Book in the Music chapter. Love that Piano Play-Book!

ACTION GAMES

Here's stuff for the sweat set. Run! Jump! Shoot little disks back and forth!

"Seaweed" and "Royal Majesty"

Clark County Crafts
   Carrousel riding horses, $18 each. Quantity discounts. Custom buttons, 75¢ each (minimum of 4 buttons).

Looking for an old-fashioned stick riding horse with personality and pizzazz? Clark County Crafts, an Oregon home business, may have what you're looking for. What you get is a hardwood dowel with a stuffed "horse head"

mounted on it. Each horse is crafted from different combinations of fabric and uniquely accessorized. Face fabric may be corduroy, calico, flannel, satin, plush fur, velvet, velveteen, or fleece. The mane might be wool yarn, worsted acrylic, cotton, silk, or fringe. Eyes can be felt circles or acrylic "glass"; the essential halter could be lace, ribbon, leather, crocheted yarns, fringe, or cording. All this in any of a rainbow of color combinations, and each with its own name. "Seaweed," for example, is a lovely green with silk ears and ball fringe for a halter.

Clark County Crafts also makes "Pup-Pets" to order. Send a picture of your pet, or pick any animal you want, and Donna Salmonson will present you with a plush, stuffed version of the same. Her specialty is cats, bears, and dogs, but she's willing to tackle penguins and aardvarks if need be.

Also available is a custom flag/banner service. Send a picture or drawing of what you want, including outside dimensions, and they'll give you a free estimate. Banners are one-sided, but flags are two-sided and can have different designs on each side.

Last of all from Clark County Crafts— an interactive craft project for your kids. They send you materials so you can draw, paste, paint, or whatever moves you, a button face. Send back these artworks and they turn them into buttons.

Family Pastimes

Cooperative games and books about same, educational puzzles, game plan kits. Also wholesales to home businesses (take note!) Some action games (a la table hockey) and plans to construct same. Example: Huff 'n' Puff game is won by puffing ball across table without dropping it into trap. Non-macho types use the little squeezers provided. New Age flavor to some games.

Into the Wind Kites

A kite of beauty is a toy forever . . . Kites, I daresay, are one of the few fun things left that haven't been packaged as "educational." However, kiteflying is no longer sheer frivolity, either. Men with muscles of steel now spend their free time hauling stunt kites about, or being hauled about by same, as a sport. Two new string stunt kites have been clocked at speeds in excess of 90 mph while still going through precise maneuvers.

Gentler sorts can still laze about in the grass watching their kites float about in the bonny blue. New kite materials make the devices both compact and lightweight, so you can stuff them in a bag and take them along for your family picnic.

Into the Wind has a selection of kites that range from elegant simplicity to downright weird. Some kites are shaped like stars, some like manta rays, some like shoeboxes. You can get a Sky Shark (it looks like Jaws aloft), an eagle, or butterflies, dragonflies, peacocks, goldfish, and other extravagant, colorful creatures. Dragon kites have long, long tails and Precision Star Cruisers have each other (you can stack six on a line). Airfoils! Amazing Flying Bird that winds up and flaps his wings! Windsocks! Airplane Kites! Wind Fish! Fighter Kites! Kitemaking materials and accessories! A little further afield in the field of flight, Into the Wind also has a pile of boomerangs.

Don't think this all means lots of money, either. A silk Oriental Dragonfly kite costs only $18, and a Rainbow Octopus kite is just $5. Well-heeled types can manage to spend $100 or more on a single kite, but most offerings in this catalog are in range of the average kite fanatic.

Into The Wind's Pocket Guide to Kiteflying sells for a mere 25¢ and can help you pick the kite you want to buy . . . or make. Into The Wind has materials for kitemaking, too.

Warren Pub Co/Totline Press
1•2•3 Games, $6.95. Add $1.50 shipping.

Subtitled "No-Lose Games for Young Children," *1•2•3 Games* is a collection of non-competitive games for groups. Charming format, easy instructions.

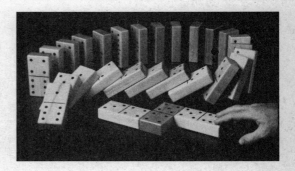

World Wide Games
Marble roller, $41.95. Table cricket and box hockey, $99.95 each. British ring toss, $23.95. Shoot-the-moon, $20.95. Maori Sticks, $4.95. Pommawonga, $8.95. Pic-E-U-Nee, $9.95. Backgammon, $49.95. Blocks, $75. Large Dominoes, $49. Hindu Pyramid, $9.95. Sponge Polo, $79.95. Wykersham, $42.95. *New Fun Encyclopedia*, $10.50 each volume.

If you like wood, you'll love WWG's games. They have marble mazes and table cricket and box hockey and British Ring Toss (toss rubber rings at hooks on a board). They have Shoot-the-Moon and Maori Sticks and Pommawonga and Pic-E-U-Nee (one-handed Ping-Pong). Backgammon. Building blocks. Solid cherry wooden toys. Large Dominoes. Hindu Pyramid. Sponge Polo. Wykersham. Etc.

WWG also has books about games, such as the *New Fun Encyclopedia*. And for people who like to play in huge swarms, there are six-foot Earthballs and the ever-silly Parachutes.

WWG's Warren and Mary Lea Bailey stand ready to lead workshops on games and games playing. Warren can teach you how to make and fly a kite, and Mary Lea can unravel the intricacies of folk dancing.

BOARD GAMES/FILE FOLDER GAMES/CARD GAMES/BLOCKS

Take it easy! Flop on the floor and push a little token around the board. No commercials, no raucous hucksterism, just a fun family time.

Ampersand Press

Inexpensive, clever card games that teach about the food chain (*Predator* and *Krill),* flower lifestyle (*Pollination),* electricity (*AC/DC),* comets (*Good Heavens!),* and so on. Their Science Participoster has lots of clever puzzles to fill in and people have been raving to me about it. Rumor: Look for a weather game or sea game from these people soon.

Animal Town Game Company

Animal Town has the largest selection of board games I've seen. Animal Town has games from around the world, including some that have been classics from century. A family-owned and operated business, Animal Town also develops their own extremely beautiful and slightly preachy board games. Lots of other browsing stuff in this catalog!

Aristoplay

Educationally appealing, gorgeous board games loaded with extras. Versatile (most can be played on many different levels of difficulty). Fun. Challenging. Reviews of these games are scattered throughout this book and *The NEW Big Book of Home Learning.* Aristoplay's lineup includes • *Music Maestro* (recognizing modern, classical and medieval instruments, orchestra readiness) • *Made for Trade* (Early American history game that teaches economic principles) • *By Jove!* (mythology game) • *Artdeck* (learn to recognize modern masters) • *Where in the World?* (geography) • *Dinosaurs and Things* (evolutionary look at the Big and the Ugly) • *Good Old Houses* (architecture game) • *Main Street* (commercial architecture) • More!

Dr. Drew's Blocks
Set of 72 blocks and bag, $34.95 plus $4 shipping; set of 32 blocks, $17.95 plus $2.50 shipping; set of 18 blocks, $12.95 plus $1.50 shipping.

I never thought I'd be caught dead writing an entire review about a set of wooden blocks. Blocks are blocks are blocks, right? Wrong!

For one thing, Dr. Drew's blocks are made out of hardwood, not your typical soft pine. This means they clack together in a satisfying fashion and that they don't immediately develop a leprosy of dings and dents like common blocks. Dr. Drew's blocks are also slim and rectangular (3 x 2 x 1/2), so even babies can grasp them easily and adults can build terrific constructions (see the accompanying photo). The blocks come in a natural, splinter-free finish that go with any decor except Recent Plastic. They are truly a "discovery" toy, limited only by your imagination and the size of the set you purchase. The whole kit and caboodle comes with a durable and attractive canvas bag, so you have someplace to put them (most other sets come with a cardboard box that immediately generates into a ragged eyesore). Now you know why Dr. Drew's Blocks received the 1982 "toy of the year" award from the Parents Choice Foundation.

Oh yes: the inventor, Walter F. Drew, is a for-real Ph.D. and early childhood educator. He would say that the simplicity and uniformity of his blocks make it easy for children to discover number relationships and basic geometric patterns and to develop their creativity through construction and free play. He would also point out that all ages can play with the blocks together. I will just say that these blocks are *fun* (we own both the biggest and the smallest set) and that you will kick yourself if you don't buy the large set.

Educational Insights
Listening Lotto-ry: $12.95 each for Set A (basic sounds) or Set B (more complex sounds). Kitty Kat Card Games, $4.95 each. Kitty Kat Bingo games, $10.95 each (includes 65 cute little Kitty Kat counters). Primary Math Games, Intermediate Math Games, each $14.95/set of 3 included games. Plus 'n Minus Games, $9.95. *Thinkfast!, Gotcha!, Capture the Flags,* $4.95 each. *Presto Change-O,* $14.95.

Send for this catalog! Educational Insights is the most innovative, creative manufacturer of school learning materials around. Board games galore. Phonics and math records. Puzzles. Trace 'n Write Handwriting. Science kits. BrainBoosters™. Human Body Kits. Electronic tutors. All priced ridiculously low, all colorful, all fun. Completely wipes out the competition.

Now, what does Educational Insights have in board or card games? How about Listening Lotto-ry, in which students match the sounds they hear to the objects on the picture cards? Kitty Kat Card Games teach upper/lowercase alphabet recognition (*Katnip!*), beginning consonant sounds (*Meow!*), and numeral/set recognition (*Whiskers!*). Kitty Kat Bingo games cover color and shapes, numbers, or the alphabet. Or how about a nice math game? Primary Math Games is a set of three games— *Sum Buddies* for basic addition, *Minus Maze* for subtraction, and *Time Out* for time-telling— all colorful and actually fun to play. Plus 'n Minus Games is math drill made

painless as students must add and subtract to find their way around the gameboard. The double-sided board (one for addition, one for subtraction) comes with a reproducible activity workbook. Intermediate Math Games consists of *Prehistoric Times* (multiplication), *Dinosaur Division* (division), and *Ballpark Figures* (estimating skills).*Thinkfast!*, *Gotcha!*, and *Capture the Flags* are high-speed math competition using all four basic arithmetic processes: addition, subtraction, multiplication, and division. *Presto Change-O* helps kids learn to make change as they collect an allowance, do chores for cash, and blow their stash on treats.

Educational Insights is always coming out with something new, so send for their latest catalog and stay on top!

Jeffrey Norton

Deal Me In, subtitled *The Use of Playing Cards in Teaching and Learning*, is more than directions for a slew of card games. The author, Dr. Margie Golick, contends that playing cards are a high-interest educational tool as well as a means of social entry for children who lack physical prowess or social skill. Some skills she claims card games can develop: rhythm, motor skills, sequencing, sense of direction, visual skills, number concepts, verbal skills, intellectual skills, and social skills. After a lengthy introduction presenting her case for card games, she gets down to cases with more than five dozen games, plus card tricks and logic games. Every card game is summarized, learning skills enhanced by the game are summarized, and then you get the rules: rank of cards, basic overview of the game, bidding (if appropriate), object of the game, rules of play and scoring, comments, and necessary vocabulary for play.

The book includes several indexes to help you find the game you want, and some psychotherapeutic moralizing by the author. She approves of gambling and swearing, and although her comments on these subjects do not take up any significant part of the book, I didn't want you to buy it and then accuse me of not warning you! By and large, a helpful

resource that could use some light editing in the next edition.

Rainfall Toys
Bible Challenge, $19.99. Choices (children's or adult's version), $14.99 each.

Bible Challenge is a Scripture knowledge game based on Scripture itself, not on trivia like, "What is the shortest verse in the Bible?" The two *Choices* games both present ethical problems for the players to answer with the help of Scripture. Unusual, thought-provoking format. Kids' version has a colorful gameboard and less "heavy" questions.

Shakean Stations
Twelve-game sets, $14.95 each. Twenty-Four-game set, $21.95. Seven-game sets, $13.95 each. Puzzle games, $5.95. Twenty manila file folders, $1.50. Twelve string tie envelopes, $1.50.

Delightful, inexpensive "file folder" games. You cut out the colorful game board portion and mount it on a legal-size file folder, then laminate or cover with clear contact paper (this last step is not essential but it does help the game last longer). Play pieces are stored in a string tie manila envelope that you mount on the back of the file folder. The whole process takes next to no time, and you end up with a long-lasting game for under $2, and in some cases less than a dollar.

Shakean games are sold in sets of 5, 7, 12, or 24. *Reading Unlimited*, the only set of 24 games, covers phonics from alphabet recognition through syllabication. Games sold in sets of 12 include: • *Smart Start*, a set of reading readiness games • *Sports of Sorts*, vocabulary and word-building skill games with a sports theme • *Number the Big Top*, arithmetic practice and drill with circus-theme games • *Play the Numbers*, intermediate arithmetic (including division, decimals, and other tougher operations) • and *The Space Place*, math concept games.

Classroom games (which can be played with as few at two or as many as 36 players) come in sets of seven, for grades 1-4. These are *Everybody Plays* and *Play It Again*. Both these sets concentrate on phonics and language arts.

Shakean Stations' *Puzzle Games* set comes with five gameboards and 22 word lists for practicing specialized skills, such as matching states and their capitals or working on antonyms and homonyms or drilling math facts. You pick the list you want to work on, and write each word twice, once on the puzzle square and once on the corresponding gameboard. Players put the puzzle together by matching the problem (like the capital of Alaska) to the solution (Juneau). Each puzzle is self-correcting, and if you cover it with contact paper (available in any school supply catalog) it should last and last.

Look at the prices Shakean Stations charges for their teacher-made games, and you will (1) agree that we still are blessed with some kind-hearted teachers and (2) send for their free catalog.

BABY'S PLAY

Bear Creek Pubs
  No Bored Babies, $4.50 postpaid.

No Bored Babies is a delightful book on how and why to make toys for your baby. The "why"— because department-store toys entertain adults more than babies. The "how"— it's simpler than you think! Follow the simple directions in this graphically appealing, not at all overwhelming book and you will be zapping out dozens of toys in next to no time. Sections include: • Why Make Your Own Toys • Setting Up Your Toy Workshop (materials to save or collect) • Safety • The Visual Crib (birth to six weeks) • Batting Practice Time (six weeks to three months) • Reaching Grasping, Chewing and Kicking (three months to six months) • The Mover and Shaker (six to nine months) • The Explorer (nine to fourteen months) • Challenge (fourteen to twenty-four months) • and Household Objects as Playthings. A sampling of the fantastic ideas (all illustrated with line drawings): Make a Feelie Mural of different fabric pieces glued to cardboard to hang on the wall next to the changing table. Make soft blocks (your choice of hidden jingles tucked in a plastic film canister or straight polyester fiber stuffing). Chewable books! Caterpillar pull toy! Shape sorter! Sponge puzzle! The directions are absurdly simple and easy to follow. In fact, a wideawake six-year-old could make many of these toys. And thus, an idea: why not get double duty from *No Bored Babies* by letting your other children make them? Eureka! No bored older children, either!

EDC
  Parents' Guides to Entertaining and Educating Young Children, Babies & Toddlers, $5.95 each.

Two books, each 48 pages of colorful illustrations, encouraging advice, and creative suggestions on how to entertain and educate your little one from birth to the preteen years. Like all the other Usborne books from England, the Parents' Guides feature colorful cartoon graphics that teach along with the text.

Entertaining and Educating Babies & Toddlers has • an introductory advice and how-to-use-this-book section • Three toys-you-can-make sections: Things to Look At, Things to

Listen To, Things to Feel and Hold • Learning to Talk • Books, Pictures, and Stories • Energetic Play • Messy Play • Imitating and Pretending • Things to Fit Together and Take Apart • Walks and Trips • Going Swimming • Music, Songs, and Rhymes • Guide to Stages of Development • and a handy index. All sections include make-it-yourself suggestions, in keeping with the strained financial situation of young British couples.

Entertaining and Educating Young Children also has a wealth of clever suggestions. Notice the book's philosophy—

> Children will play, provided they are not actually prevented from doing so, whether or not they have help from adults but there is no doubt that the learning quality of their play can be greatly influenced by the adults around them. Adults can provide materials, suggest directions, give advice and encouragement and open the door to new activities.
>
> The emphasis in this book is on activities for adults and children to share together.

Those activities include: • Drawing and Coloring • Painting and Printing • Cutting and Sticking • Modelling and building • Books, Pictures, and Stories • Fun with Words and Letters • Fun with Numbers • Listening to and Making Music • Playing with Sand and Water • Dressing Up and Pretending • In the Kitchen • Growing Things • Learning About Animals • Collecting Things • Getting Exercise • Going Swimming • Outings and Journeys • Parties. There also are sections on wet afternoons and other difficult times and the study of play, as well as an index.

MAGIC AND FANTASY

No, we're not looking at a collection of occult material here! This is trick magic,

puppeteering, ventriloquism and other fantasy fun completely unrelated to witches and goblins. Christian street preachers use these materials to get the crowd's attention, and you can try them at home to charm the kids and develop your own dexterity.

Hank Lee's Magic Factory
Catalog, 270-plus oversized pages, $5, or $8.95 with binder. Magic of the Month Club, $12/year.

What workshop is full of magical things and populated by elves? You're thinking of Santa's, right? Well, the mythical Mr. Claus has real-life competition. Hank Lee's Magic Factory in good old Boston (love that dirty water!) is staffed by such imps as Elmo, Joe-O, Bob-O, Phono ("Still answers the phone at night and on weekends"), and Byte-O ("The computer elf"). Hank Lee's catalog has an immense selection of magic tricks, equipment, props, and books. I find it easier to follow than Tannen's (see below). Let me warn you, though, once you pick it up you will have trouble putting it down! The descriptions of the magic tricks make fascinating reading, and the layout makes browsing a delight. Now who wants a pair of soft dice that change colors and produce baby dice . . .

To make it even easier for you to blow all your hard-earned shekels on magic, Hank Lee has invented a Magic of the Month Club. Members get a membership card, "Noosletter" subscription, and discounts of 10 to 40 percent off selected books and magic, plus previews of the hottest new stuff.

And for the really dedicated magic fan who also owns a computer, Hank Lee has set up a magic bulletin board. Call (617) 484-8750 between 5 PM and 8 AM Eastern time. The password is HANKLEE. You can leave orders using your credit cards, leave questions and messages (questions will be answered as EMAIL for the next day), check out the latest magical goodies, and so on.
Maher

It's enthusiasm time again! Anyone who is the slightest bit interested in visual teaching will love Maher's free catalog of ventriloquist dolls, puppets, and visual instruction (balloon, chalk talk, clowning, etc.) For the novice Maher has a unconditionally-guaranteed home-study ventriloquist course (30 lessons for $79.95). Maher's selection also includes dialogues, scripts, cassette tapes, books, and novelties. But best of all is the Christian emphasis of Maher's inventory. It seems that a goodly chunk of the world's practicing "vents" are Christians engaged in it as a ministry, and they've written all sorts of books of Gospel dialogues and how-to's for Christian ventriloquism.

Maher also offers deluxe vent figures that they rebuild from commercially produced dolls. These have a lot of features for a base price of less than $190. Add-on features, such as winkers, raising eyebrows, and spitting (some people want that!), cost extra. For young folks Maher has some animal characters (Eagle, Buzzard, Sheep Dog . . . and Grumlett!) for $39.95 each, or rebuilt commercial figures for $59.95. Catalog of "Knee Pal" professional dolls costs $2 (refunded with order). Prices of these dolls start at $260.

Maher Workshop

A Chuck Jackson/Maher Workshop character

Once you have learned to amaze your friends with ventriloquism, it's time to think about investing in a deluxe dummy of your very own. Maher Workshop, a business completely unrelated to the Maher Studios (see above) in spite of the identical name and similar interest in ventriloquism, has "the most complete selection anywhere of figures with Personality and Audience Appeal." Chuck

Jackson hand carves his basswood figures and adds a lot of quality touches, which is why the Junior Series starts at $469 and the Standard Professional Series starts at $599. Special effects can be added to the "Pro" figures, such as raising eyebrows, winking, and shaking hands. Fifteen-year warranty, 100 percent satisfaction or money back within first two weeks. Recommended by missionaries and pastors. Figures available in all colors, both sexes, and all ages. Catalog, $2.

Son Shine Puppet Company
    Puppets from $15 to $99. Teaching materials and dialogs, many under $5. *Son Shine Gazette,* **monthly newsletter, free sample copy.**

Everything you can imagine having to do with puppets, all designed for use in puppet ministries. Patterns for creating your own muppet-style puppet with a changeable face! Stage plans! Dialogs! How-to books! Pre-recorded puppet music and soundtracks! Larger than lifesized costumes! Children's church lesson units! And, of course, lots and lots of puppets.

Extremely affordable and fun for kids are Son Shine's new patterns and precuts kits for making Almost Anything Puppets. The materials packet includes precut fake fur for one long-mouth puppet and one wide mouth puppet, each 12 inches tall, plus extra fur for the ears, etc. If I understand the catalog listing right, you can get both pattern and materials for only $5.99. And, unlike most puppet projects, Almost Anything Puppets can become almost anything your child imagines. See the photo on the previous page for some examples!

Also available from Son Shine: The Son Shine Gazette. This bimonthly newspaper is a {children's ministry resource shopping guide." A typical issue includes scripts and ideas for puppetry, dramas, object lessons, and teaching tips as well as updates on Son Shine's speakers' schedule and their puppet lineup.

Son Shine conducts puppet training seminars for beginning and advanced puppeteers, as well as teachers interested in learning new techniques and teaching ideas. Contact Randy and Glenda Hoyle at Son Shine for more info.

Louis Tannen

850-plus-page hardbound catalog, $8 postpaid USA, $10 foreign. Summer Magic Camp, $350. *Magic Manuscript* magazine, $18/year (6 issues), $3.50 for sample copy. Foreign and Canada, add $7/year for surface mail, $34/year airmail.

Another fabulous magic catalog: typeset, indexed, and illustrated. Tannen's catalog includes close-up magic, magic for kids, stage magic, silk magic, card magic, coin magic, and some heavy-duty illusions for professional magicians. The book section is huge. Tannen's fifteenth catalog was the 1985-87 edition, so you know they've been around for a while.

Tannen also runs a Summer Magic Camp for boys and girls ages 9 to 18. Held on the grounds of LaSalle Academy (which I *think* is in New York State), the camp fee includes a Magic Supply Kit (retail value $50) as well as the magic instruction. Campers get "a rigorous schedule of evening shows, celebrity performers, and finale appearances by the campers." Well-known magicians serve as guest teachers and lecturers. You've got to admit that this camp sounds like a serious-minded prankster could get something out of it.

And if you should be looking for a full-color magic magazine, Tannen publishes the world's only. *Magic Manuscript* has news, reviews, interviews with the pros, and pictures of people

making rings of fire or chopping lovely ladies asunder (temporarily, of course).

HOBBIES AND PUZZLES

All Night Media

Delightful, whimsical, strange, beautiful, educational, rococo— what is all the above? The All Night Media collection of rubber stamps and accessories. Lots of • teddy bears • slogans ("I'd rather be eating chocolate") • Alphabeasts™ (alphabet of beasties whose bodies form the letters) • other alphabet sets • bookplates • bunnies • business stamps • cats 'n dogs • celebration and holiday stamps • nature stamps • country stamps • custom stamps • fantasy stamps • food • romance • designer stamps • message bearers • tons more. Lovely glossy catalog. If you can't find what you're looking for, it must not exist.

Oh, yes— strange kids can join All Night Media's Stamp Cadets. Your $4 membership entitles you to • the catalog • a $2 credit towards any purchase • Official Stamp Cadet membership card • Stamp Cadet Mask "to conceal your secret identity and protect against flying space debris" • Stamp Cadet Rubber Seal • One copy of "101 Ways to Stamp Your Art Out," a 28 page booklet of tips, tricks, projects, and inspiration for rubber stamp fanatics.

Official Publications

Children's Fun Puzzles, $5/year (6 issues). Add $2.75 postage outside USA.

I don't know how they do it. Official Publications publishes all sorts of puzzle magazines, including *Children's Fun Puzzles*. Now, how do they come out six times a year with dozens of • crosswords • mazes • find the twins • connect the dots • picture puzzles • mysteries • memory quizzes • and even a puzzle on the cover, for less than $1 per issue?

This is the *only* puzzle magazine that readers have raved to me about. Large, easy-to-read format, challenging puzzles (including some of the same sort adults delight to solve), all designed for the 7- to 12-year-old set.

Pacific Puzzle Company
    United States puzzle: Small $20, medium $32, large $45. Nameshape™ Continental US, $38. Continents: Europe, Asia $18 each; Africa $19; North, South America $15 each; set of 5 continents, $73. Dymaxion World puzzles: small $18, large $29. Bible Map puzzles: Early Bible Lands, New Testament Palestine, $17 each; Old Testament Palestine $18; Roman World, $20; complete set of 4, $64. Alphabet puzzles (uppercase, lowercase), $22 each. Number puzzle, $12. Geometric shapes puzzle, $16. Marbled paper puzzles: small $5, large $10, jumbo $45. Stenciled animal puzzles: $4.50 each. Animal puzzles, $16-$19. People puzzles™, $10-$16. Other puzzles available. Shipping: $3 first puzzle, $1 additionals. Canada, AK, HI add 50% more shipping. Inquire for foreign shipping rates.

Exceptionally high-quality line of geographical, educational, and novelty puzzles. Pacific Puzzle Company uses the best materials available, including imported birch plywood, and (for their geographical puzzles) the nicest full-color maps they can find. Puzzle shapes are carefully cut to truly represent the shape of the state, country, letter, or whatever.

Now, let me tell you about what exactly Pacific Puzzle Company has to offer. Beyond the usual United States, world, and continent maps (all impressively crafted and really solid), you can get the Nameshape™ map of the continental US. In this striking puzzle, each state shape is formed by the letters of its name. The smaller states are abbreviated, in case you were wondering how big this would have to be for Rhode Island to be spelled out. Educational value of the Nameshape™ map is obvious. And then there's the Dymaxion™ puzzles. Designed by Buckminster Fuller, these 20 triangular shapes put together to present the world. However, unlike other map puzzles, you can put it together correctly dozens of different ways, depending on which viewing angle you choose to highlight.

Pacific Puzzle Company's solid wood alphabet and number puzzles use the contrasting colors of natural birch and mahogany to spotlight letters and numerals. Unlike crepe rubber puzzles I have seen, these leave the center holes of the characters empty (e.g., the two holes in the letter "B" and the middle of the "O"), making them safe for young children. A knobbed geometric shape puzzle is also available.

Now, back to the unusual. PPC's People Puzzles are stylized person-shaped cutouts in a drawstring bag. There's a catch: the pieces only fit together *one* way, making it a popular challenge for adults and older children. You get a choice of the children's People Puzzle™ (24 pieces), the Natural People Puzzle™ (50 pieces, birch and mahogany) and a Four-Color People Puzzle™ (50 pieces colored red, brown, yellow, and natural that make a statement about universal brotherhood).

Marbled paper puzzles are marbled sheets laminated to hardwood and cut into fine-piece interlocking jigsaw puzzles. Inexpensive in the small size, agonizingly difficult in the large, and beautiful in all. Stenciled animal puzzles are just that: country-style stencils on natural birch. Only 12 pieces apiece, these lovely designs are for younger children.

There's more, but I'm sure you get the idea. Now, price. Some of Pacific Puzzle Company's offerings seemed pricey to me at first blush. After all, $20-$45 is a lot to pay for a map puzzle when you can get a cardboard puzzle for $1.29. Ah, but these are more than puzzles— they are *artwork!* Develop your children's artistic taste and respect for beauty at the same time as their puzzling ability with these elegant puzzles.

Rubberstampede

Beautiful rubber stamps. The selection is eclectic, with offerings ranging from a mother bunny trundling her baby rabbits in a carriage to a piece of pizza to aid in teaching fractions.

Cartoons and animals are intermixed with serious art. The catalog is large and contains every stamping accessory your little heart could desire. You can get personalized stamps and custom stamps and Rainbow Pads and un-inked pads and metallic inks and stamp holders and stamp sets (Betty Boop or Teddy Bears, to name just two).

Rubberstampede's Alpha Bears™ set sells for $12.95 and has been a big hit with teachers.

Rubberstampmadness
One year (6 issues) $10, sample issue $2.

Introducing the one . . . the only . . . magazine for rubber stamp artists! Large newsprint magazine has news, tips, and some positively ginchy ads. One back issue tells you all you ever wanted to know about carving stamps from erasers; another covers stamping on fabric. A quick browse through the ads shows that rubberstamping is not only alive and well, but in danger of becoming a recognized art form. Time to get in on the ground floor, right?

Universal Publishing Company

Universal handles promotional activities for several companies specializing in collectibles. For example: send $1 in US funds to JOLIE COINS, Box 399C, Roslyn Heights, NY 11577-0399 for 12 different pieces of genuine foreign coins/paper money from around the world, a free 32-page catalog, and a $1 credit slip good towards any catalog purchase of $10 or more. For the same amount you can get 50 different cat or dog stamps from around the world and a 32-page catalog from CAT & DOG STAMPS, P.O. Box 466F, Port Washington, NY 11050. Or, if you'd prefer eight different full gum old mint US commemorative stamps (including 3, 4, 5, 6, and 8¢ denominations), send another $1 to JOAN ALEXANDER, P.O. Box 7K, Roslyn, NY 11576. Universal says, "These offers are excellent collection starters, party favors, treats, and educational materials for both young and old."

None of these companies sends approvals or sells the names and addresses they receive.

UNUSUAL GIFTS

Many of the products mentioned in this chapter are unusual, but the following companies are really unusual. I very much doubt if your nephew Sidney will get two ecological card games or two logic games this birthday. Niece Brunnhilde is also unlikely to receive two corn cob dolls or two sets of teddy bear stamps. These products are authentic, inexpensive, fun, and unique. What more could Sidney or Brunnhilde want?

Archie McPhee and Co.

These people are CRAZY! Archie McPhee and Company are the Jerryco of novelties—not because they remainder novelties (which they don't), but because of the . . . um . . . special brand of humor displayed in their catalog. Where else can you find the world's most lovely rubber bugs, or rubber ants for everyday use? How about a Flamingo Snowball (turn it upside down, shake, and watch the snow)? Need a life-size animated statue of Bozo the Clown (that one may already be sold)? Something gruesome or strange for every occasion, lovingly described with tongue in cheek.

Jonson Specialties

Did I say "unusual"? Jonson Specialties has it all: stick-ons, balloons, lollipops, giveaway toys, games, rings, flag picks, pens, pencils, pencil tops, toys animals, treasure chests, and even vending machines and capsules. Short-lived but inexpensive yo-yo's. Twist balloons. Eraser collections. Most items come in packages of a dozen to a hundred, so are well suited for party gifts.

Mountain Craft Shop

One-stop shopping for hundreds of American folk toys. Mountain craftsmen make these authentic reproductions. It's a little bit of history at a very reasonable price.

Paper Soldier

This, my spies assure me, is a source for wonderful antique pop-up books, paper dolls and soldiers, and all sorts of other neat things. Are they? I'll have to write again and see if they answer this time.

Pleasant Company

Very fancy collection of storybooks, associated dolls, and accessories for same. The American Girl collection features three doll characters: a Victorian girl, a Swedish immigrant girl, and a girl of the Forties. Each has a set of three hardbound storybooks about her adventures and accessories that reflect her historical period. *Not* cheap— the catalog bills these playthings as "keepsake quality."

Wff 'n Proof Learning Games

What company has managed to integrate Chicago schoolchildren where the Federal, state, and local governments failed? Answer: Wff 'n Proof Learning Games Associates. It seems that some of our university profs are actually producing something useful— a series of educational games that really gets kids involved.

The game that got dozens of Chicago schoolkids, black and white, to voluntarily board buses and spend their Saturday mornings nerding math is *Equations*. This deceptively simple pre-algebra game consists of a set of numerals and operations. One player sets a goal. Then everyone in turn tries to pick a resource from the remaining pool that will (1) not allow the goal to be reached in one or less steps and (2) not make reaching the goal impossible with the remaining resources. From here the description gets more complicated. Suffice it to say that it takes only 15 minutes to learn to play *Equations*, but a math major like me or my M.I.T.-graduate husband Bill could spend weeks playing it without getting bored. In Chicago kids play *Equations* in the Academic Games League. At home, they can play it with you, or (thanks to the folks at Wff 'n Proof) with the family Apple.

Nobody can play *Equations* without sharpening their thinking and their arithmetic skills. Boys tend to love it more than girls, but everywhere it's been tried the math skills have gone up and the absentee rate down.

Wff 'n Proof has a pile of other games for science, language, grammar, logic, and set theory. All stress abstract thinking. The Wff 'n Proof Game of Modern Logic has been shown to increase I.Q. scores by more than 20 points in avid users.

Wireless

Just plain zany. Catalog put out by the perpetrators of "Prairie Home Companion."

How-to music books mingle with *Swedish Humor and Other Myths* and radio humor cassettes. Lots of Scandinavian ethnic gifts with a humorous twist and educational items. If you're looking for a truly unusual gift for that eccentric someone, you'll find it here.

TOY SOFTWARE

Brøderbund
   The Toy Shop: **Apple II family, Commodore 64/128, $59.95; IBM PC and Macintosh, $64.95. Refill pack, $24.95.**

Brøderbund's *Toy Shop* is the only software that demands to be included in a Toys and Games chapter. You get to make your own toys without worrying about the basic design. Toy Shop presents you with a list of projects, from which you choose the one that tweaks your fancy. You then customize it with patterns, graphics, and even text if desired, and print the precision parts on your printer.

Attach the printout to the self-adhesive cardstock included with the program, cut it out, and put it all together with the wooden dowels, wire, elastic bands, and balloons included with *Toy Shop*. Now, what will it do? Fly in the air! Roll on the floor! (No, not you— the antique truck.) Twirl round and round!

   The mechanical models included are: • Antique Truck • Balancing Jet • Carousel • Equatorial Sundial • Experimental Glider • Flying Propeller • Helicraft • Jet Dragster • Medieval Catapult • Mechanical Bank • Mercer Raceabout • The Oracle • Pennypower Scale • Spirit of St. Louis (an airplane, not a ghost) • Starship • Steam Engine • Steam Oil Pump • Steam Table Saw • Tractor Crane • Zoetrope.

   You can make as many of these action toys as you want, and if you ever run out of materials, just order Brøderbund's *Toy Shop Refill Pack*.

INDEXES

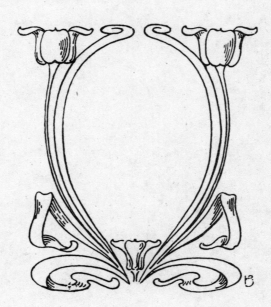

INDEX OF SUPPLIERS

This index was designed both to give you the necessary information to order products and catalogs, and to give you an idea of each company's services. Besides addresses, the index contains telephone numbers, types of payment accepted, price of catalog or brochure (if any), refund policy, a general description of the company, and a listing of the chapters in which the supplier's products are reviewed.

The subject listings are abbreviated as follows:

KEY TO SUBJECT ABBREVIATION

Key	Chapter
Art	Arts and Crafts
Bus	Business Skills
Char	Character Education
Class	Classical Languages
Desk	Desktop Learning
Eng	Engineering and Industrial Arts
Enrich	Enrichment and Activities
Fam	Family Management
Fun	Fun Literature and Tapes
Foreign	Foreign Languages
Gift	Gifted Education
Health	Health Education
Home	Home Skills
Lit	Classical Literature
Logic	Logic and Thinking Skills
Music	Music
Phys	Physical Education
Safety	Safety Education
Sex	Sex Education
Spec	Special Education
T & G	Toys and Games
Travel	Travel With Your Family

HOW TO BE A PERFECT CUSTOMER

First, *please do not call a toll-free number except to order,* unless the index entry specifically says that the supplier is willing to use his toll-free line for inquiries. Each call on a 800 number costs the supplier a substantial amount, and it is frustrating to have callers rack up your phone bill for questions that could have been answered just as well by letter.

It is always wise to get the supplier's catalog or brochure before ordering. Prices change, and so do refund policies. You are less likely to be disappointed if you carefully check these out before ordering.

When requesting information by letter, an SASE (self-addressed stamped envelope) is always appreciated. This does not apply to requests for free catalogs, since these seldom fit in a standard envelope.

Companies that offer free catalogs do so in the hope that we will become interested in their products and buy from them. Catalogs are expensive to print and mail. By all means, send for any catalogs you think might be useful. Just give the supplier a fair chance to sell you something in return!

A Beka Book Publications
Box 18000
Pensacola, FL 32523-9160
(904) 478-8933
Check or cashier's check.
Free order form.
Christian texts and supplies.
Fun, Health.

ABC School Supply
P.O. Box 4750
Norcross, GA 30091
(404) 447-5000 weekdays.
MC, VISA. Free catalog.
Returns within 30 days. 15% service
charge if company not at fault.
School supplies pre-K-6.
Art.

AIMS Education Foundation
P.O. Box 7766
Fresno, CA 93747
(209) 291-1766
Check, M.O., school P.O.
Activities that integrate math, science,
other fields. Newsletter.
Eng.

A.K.A., Inc.
188 Onville Road
Stafford, VA 22554
(703) 659-2196
AIDS booklet.
Quantity discounts available.
No free info. Booklet only costs $2 plus
$.75 shipping.
Sex.

AMR
see Advance Memory Research

AMSCO School Publications
315 Hudson St.
New York, NY 10013
(212) 675-7005
School books.
Class, For, Lit.

A+
P.O. Box 52324
Boulder, CO 80321-2324
MC, Visa, AMEX, or they bill you.
Allow 30 to 60 days for
delivery of first issue.
Computer magazine for Apple II
family users.
Desk.

Ability Development
Box 4260
Athens, OH 45701-4260
1-800-221-9254 OH: (614) 594-3547
VISA, MC. COD. Free catalog.
"The Suzuki Place."
Music.

Academic Therapy Publications
20 Commercial Boulevard
Novato, CA 94947-6191
(415) 883-3314
*Directory of Facilities and Services for
the Learning Disabled.*
Other publications.
Spec.

Achievement Basics
800 South Fenton St.
Denver, CO 80226
(303) 935-6343
Check or M.O. Free brochures.
Junior Business and speaking.
Bus.

Advance Memory Research, Inc. (AMR)
2601 Ulmerton Rd., E.
Suite 101
Largo, FL 33541-3832
1-800-323-2500 FL: 813-539-6555
MC, VISA, AMEX, D Club, C Blanche.
Free brochure. Call toll-free for info.
Foreign language and speaking courses.
For.

Advanced Training Institute of America
Box 1
Oak Brook, IL 60522-3001
Home school program.
Char.

All Night Media, Inc.
Box 2666
130 Greenfield Ave.
San Anselmo, CA 94960
1-800-STAMPED. CA: (415) 459-3013.
Check or M.O. Catalog, $2. Stamp Cadet
Membership, $4, includes catalog,
newsletter, tips booklet, and other
ephemera.
Rubber stamps and accessories.
T & G.

Alpha Omega Publications
P.O. Box 3153
Tempe, AZ 85281
1-800-821-4443. Ask for Home-School
Department.
Free brochure.
Christian curriculum. Home school pro-
gram.
Art, Class, For, Phys.

American Bible Society
1865 Broadway
New York, NY 10023
(212) 581-7400 24hrs., 7 days.
1-800-543-8000 Op. 312. Credit Card
orders only. Visa, MC.
$20 minimum.
Handling charge, credit card orders $1.95.
Foreign language Bibles.
For.

American Classical League
Miami University
Oxford, OH 45056
Check or M.O. US funds only.
Membership organization for teachers of
Latin, Greek, and classical humanities.
Workshops, newsletter, etc.
Class.

American Map Corporation
46-35 54th Rd.
Maspeth, NY 11378
(718) 784-0055 9-5 EST weekdays.
Visa, MC, AMEX. Free catalogs.
30-day money back on language
materials only.
Maps. Language courses.
Anatomy manual.
Health, For.

American Reformation Movement (ARM)
Independence Square, Suite 106, Box 138
7341 Clairmont Mesa Blvd.
San Diego, CA 92111
(619) 298-8607
"On Teaching" newletter.
Char.

Ampersand Press
691 26th St.
Oakland, CA 94612
(415) 832-6669
Check or M.O. Free brochure.
Science games.
Eng, T & G.

The Ancient World
see Ares Publishers, Inc. Also available from Bolchazy-Carducci Publishers.

Animal Town Game Company
P.O. Box 2002
Santa Barbara, CA 93120
(805) 962-8368 for info.
Check or M.O. Free catalog.
Returns accepted.
Creative family entertainment.
Fam, T & G.

Anne Campbell
235 Pasadena
Tustin, CA 92680
(714) 838-5528
Arts in Residence monthly art newsletter for children.
Check or M.O. Make check out to Anne Campbell.
Pro-rated refunds.
Free brochure.
Art.

Apprentice Academics
3805 Mosswood Dr.
Conroe, TX 77302
(409) 273-5175
MC, Visa. Free full-page sized info pak.
Various discount options. No refunds.
The Midwifery Home Study Course.
Health.

Archie McPhee & Company
Box 30852
Seattle, WA 98103
Crazy stuff. jokes, novelties.
T & G.

Ares Publishers, Inc.
7020 N. Western Ave.
Chicago, IL 60645
(312) 743-1907, Ext. 5
The Ancient World. Scholarly journal of antiquity.
Check (U.S. only), M.O., MC, Visa.
Back issues, $5 each.
Class.

Aristoplay, Ltd.
P.O. Box 7028
Ann Arbor, MI 48107
(313) 995-4353
Visa, MC. School P.O.'s net 30.
Free color catalog.
Refund or exchange of damaged or defective games.
Lovely, classy, award-winning educational games.
Art, Lit, Music, T & G.

Art Extension Press
Box 389
Westport, CT 06881
(203) 531-7400
Visa, MC. Free brochure.
Art history and appreciation.
Art.

Art With a Purpose
see Share-A-Care Publications

Arts in Residence
see Anne Campbell

Audio Editions
P.O. Box 998
Burlingame, CA 94011
Business, self-help, classics, etc.Sound recordings on audio tape.
Bus.

Audio Forum
See Jeffrey Norton Publishers, Inc.

Ball-Stick-Bird Publications, Inc.
P.O. Box 592
Stony Brook, NY 11790
(516) 331-9164
Ultimate reading system for labeled children and adults.
Space theme, moral values.
Check, M.O. No returns.
Free color brochure, info.
Spec.

Bear Creek Publications
2507 Minor Ave E.
Seattle, WA 98102
No Bored Babies book $4.50 ppd.
Toys you can make for your baby.
Recommended.
T & G.

Berlitz
866 Third Ave.
New York, NY 10022
1-800-223-1814 NY: (212) 702-2000
Great Britain: 0323-638221
Foreign language courses and accessories.
For.

Bethany House Publishers
6820 Auto Club Road
Minneapolis, MN 55438
(612) 829-2500
Basic Greek in 30 Minutes a Day.
Christian publisher, many other books.
Check or M.O.
Class.

Bible Games, Inc.
see Rainfall Toys

Birch Tree Group Ltd.
Divisions: Suzuki™ Method International
          Summy Birchard Music
Box 2072
Princeton, NJ 08540
Educational music publishers.
Music.

Blue Chip Software
185 Berry Street
San Francisco, CA 94107
1-800-824-9236
CA: (415) 546-1866
Division of Britannica Learning
Corporation
Fantastic business simulations.
Available for most popular personal com-
puters.
Visa, MC. Free catalog.
Bus.

Blue Lion Software
P.O. Box 650
Belmont, MA 02178
(617) 876-2500
Visa, MC, AMEX. Free brochure.
Ticket To… travel software
Travel.

Bluestocking Press
P.O. Box 1014
Dept F
Placerville, CA 95667-1014
Series of books on what to read and
where to find it.
Discounts for quantity purchases.
Check or M.O.
Send large SASE for free info.
Lit.

Bolchazy-Carducci Publishers
44 Lake Street
Oak Park, IL 60302
(312) 386-8360
MC, Visa, AMEX.
Free catalog. Must request buttons cata-
log separately.
Returns: resaleable condition, 30 days.
 Latin and Greek materials—books, film-
strips, music, even buttons!
Class.

Britannica
see Encyclopaedia Britannica, Inc.

Britannica Learning Companies
See Blue Chip Software

Brite Music
Stacy Anne Wells, Home school
Distributor
4402 Bristolwood Dr.
Flint, MI 48507
(313) 238-2953
MC, Visa. Music-by-the-Month plan.
Free color brochures.
Brite Hostess and Distributorships avail-
able.
Children's materials, character emphasis,
also child safety training materials.
Char, Safety.

Brøderbund Software
17 Paul Drive
San Rafael, CA 94903-2101
(415) 479-1700
Award-winning software, all categories,
most computers.
Bus, T & G.

Brook Farm Books
Box 66-BG
Bridgewater, ME 04735
Box BG
or
Glassville, New Brunswick E0J 1L0
CANADA
The First Home-School Catalogue.
Ethics book.
Char, Enrich.

Buck Hill Associates
Box 28
Church St. Extension
Saratoga, NY 12866-2109
Historical reproductions of books,
posters.
Lit.

Burt Harrison & Co.
P.O. Box 732
Weston, MA 02193-0732
(617) 647-0674
Check or M.O. Catalog $2, refundable
with first order.
Math and science manipulatives.
Eng.

**Business Computers of Peterborough,
Inc.**
Upper Union St.
P.O. Box 94
W. Peterborough, NH 03468-0094
1-800-854-3003, orders only.
(603) 924-9406 for inquiries.
MC, Visa, no surcharge.
Personal checks require clearing period.
M.O., bank checks, certified checks pro-
cessed same day.
No sales tax.
Discount software for Apple computers.
Desk.

CE Software
801 73rd Street
Des Moines, IA 50312
(515) 224-1995
Visa, MC. Free brochure.
CalendarMaker for the Mac.
Enrich.

Caddylak Systems, Inc.
201 Montrose Rd.
P.O. Box 1817
Westbury, NY 11590-1768
(516) 333-8221
MC, Visa, AMEX, or they'll bill
your company.
Office organizers, *Words That Sell.*
Bus, Fun.

Caedmon Tapes
1995 Broadway
New York, NY 10023
1-800-223-0420 NY: (212) 580-3400
Visa, MC. Free 94-pp catalog.
Spoken-word recordings, all categories,
including children's recordings
For, Fun.

Cambridge University Press
32 East 57th St.
New York, NY 10022
Latin course for children.
Class.

Capper's Books
616 Jefferson
Topeka, KS 66607
(913) 295-1107
Visa, MC. Free brochure.
Authentic pioneer, old-timey stories.
Fun.

Carolina Biological Supply
2705 York Rd.
Burlington, NC 27215
Visa, MC, AMEX.
Huge color catalog $10.95.
Science teaching supplies and equipment.
Health.

Center for Applied Research in Education, Inc.
P.O. Box 430
West Nyack, NY 10995
Art series, almanacs.
Art, Enrich.

Challenge
Box 299
Carthage, IL 62321-0299
(217) 357-3981
1-800-435-7234
Visa, MC, or school P.O.
Magazine for gifted children.
Gift.

Chasselle, Inc.
9645 Gerwig Lane
Columbia, MD 21046
Free catalog.
School supplies.
Art.

Child Life Play Specialties
55 Whitney St.
Holliston, MA 01746
1-800-462-4445 MA: 1-429-4639
Visa, MC. Free catalog.
Replace transit-damaged parts.
Wood outdoor gyms (swing sets, &c.)
Phys.

Childcraft Education Corp.
20 Kilmer Rd.
Edison, NJ 08818
1-800-631-5657: NJ 1-800-624-0840
9-6 EST M-Fri. Visa, MC, AMEX.
Free color catalog.
Returns w/permission, 30 days unused.
Educational furniture, toys, and games.
Phys, T & G.

Children's Bible Hour
Box 1
Grand Rapids, MI 49501
Christian tapes, mags for kids.
Char.

Children's Book and Music Center
P.O. Box 1130
Santa Monica, CA 90406-1130
1-800-443-1856 M-Sat 9-5:30 PST
CA: (213) 829-0215
Visa, MC. Catalog $1.
You may call the toll-free line for assistance in choosing materials.
"The largest supply of children's books, records, cassettes in the country."
Wide selection of books, thousands of tapes, musical instruments.
Fun.

Children's Recordings
P.O. Box 1343
Eugene, OR 97440
Check, M.O. school P.O.
Free newsprint catalog.
Returns: Defective merchandise or damaged in shipping.
Contemporary children's records and tapes.
Fun.

The Children's Small Press Collection
719 North Fourth Avenue
Ann Arbor, MI 48104
1-800-221-8056 MI: (313) 668-8056
Visa, MC, school P.O. Free catalog.
Children's books, records, and games from almost 100 small publishers.
Fun.

Chinaberry Book Service
3160 Ivy St.
San Diego, CA 92104
(619) 284-0902
Visa, MC. Large newsprint catalog, $2.
Satisfaction guaranteed.
Extremely detailed children's book catalog. New Age flavor.
Fun.

Christian Character Concepts
Rt. 1, Box 36-D
Falls Creek Estates
Flint, TX 75762
(214) 894-6619
Check or M.O. Free brochure.
Please send SASE.
Character curriculum. Spanish.
Char, For.

Christian Computer News
see Christian Computer Users Association,

Christian Computer Users Association, Inc.
1145 Alexander, S.E.
Grand Rapids, MI 49507
(616) 241-0368
Christian Computer News magazine,
Christian Computer Users Sourcebook.
Membership organization, non-profit.
Check or M.O. Free brochure.
Desk.

Christian Curriculum Project
2006 Flat Creek
Richardson, TX 75080
Check or M.O. Free brochure.
Innovative subject curricula.
Music.

Christian Education Music Publishers
2285 West 185th Place
Lansing, IL 60438
(312) 895-3322
Check or M.O. Free catalog.
Refunds only for defective materials.
Music reading course.
Music.

Christian Educational Computing
1035 Dallas SE
Grand Rapids, MI 49507
(616) 245-8376
Check or M.O. US funds only.
Computer users' magazine for
Christian educators.
Desk.

Christian Family Video Club
Christian Audio Visual Specialists, Inc.
910 Hilton Road
Ferndale, MI 48220
Check or M.O. Free brochure.
Club plan, yearly fee.
Christian videos.
Fun.

Christian Life Workshops
182 S.E. Kane
Gresham, OR 97030
(503) 667-3942
Check only. Brochure with SASE.
100% refund, except shipping
and handling.
Home school workshops on tape. Books.
Organizer. Seminars. *Family Restoration
Quarterly. Bed & Breakfast Directory.*
Fam, Home, Travel.

Christian Light Publications
1066 Chicago Ave.
P.O. Box 1126
Harrisonburg, VA 22801-1126
(203) 434-0750
Check or M.O. Free catalog.
Sci equipment for AOP, school supplies,
Mennonite-approved books.
Fun.

Christine Wyrtzen Ministries
P.O. Box 8
Loveland, CA 45140
(513) 575-1177
Visa, MC. Free brochure.
Satisfaction guaranteed.
Critter Country materials.
Char.

Chronicles of Culture
P.O. Box 800
Rockford, IL 61105
(815) 964-5054
Magazine promoting classical values
Lit.

Citizens Against Crime
Melody LeBaron
1509 W. Corvallis Dr.
Greensboro, NC 27408
(919) 275-3465
Safety ed guides.
Safety.

Citizens Commission on Human Rights
5265 Fountain Ave., Suite #2
Los Angeles, CA 90029
(213) 667-2901
Pamphlets warn against "therapeutic"
drugging of children.
Safety, Spec.

Clark County Crafts
1260 NE Seavy Ave.
Corvallis, OR 97330
(503) 754-1847
Check or M.O. Free brochure
(large SASE appreciated).
Carrousel riding horses, custom buttons,
custom banners and flags, Pup-Pets.
Quantity discounts.
T & G.

The Classical Bulletin
Ares Publishers, Inc.
7020 North Western Ave.
Chicago, IL 60645-3426
Check, U.S. funds only, or M.O. payable
to *The Classical Bulletin.*
Class.

Classical Calliope
20 Grove St.
Peterborough, NH 03458
(603) 924-7209
Visa, MC. $10 minimum.
Children's classical humanities magazine.
Lit.

Coda
See Wenger Corporation.

Committee on the Status of Women
1850 E. Ridgewood
Glenview, IL 60025
Check or M.O. Free info packet.
Sex respect curriculum
Sex.

Community Playthings
Route 213
Rifton, NY 12471
(914) 658-3141
Check or M.O. Free catalog.
Returns, 10% handling charge.
Play furniture and equipment.
Phys.

Computer Literacy Bookshops, Inc.
Main store:
2590 N. First St.
San Jose, CA 95131
(408) 435-1118
Original location:
520 Lawrence Expressway
Sunnyvale, CA 94086
(408) 730-9957
Other stores also.
Hours: 9-9 PST M-Fr, 10-6 PST Sat-Sun.
Visa, MC, AMEX, DC.
Computer books.
Desk.

Concordia Publishing House
3558 South Jefferson Avenue
St. Louis, MO 63118-3968
1-800-325-3040
MO: (314) 664-7000
Lutheran sex education series.
Free color brochure.
Sex.

Constructive Playthings
1227 E. 199th St.
Grandview, MO 64030
1-800-255-6124 MO: (816) 761-5900
Visa, MC. Free home catalog.
Play furniture, toys, and school supplies
pre-K-3. Free toy guide for parents.
Free catalog of Jewish Educational mate-
rials.
Char, T & G.

Conversa-Phone Institute, Inc.
One Comac Loop
Ronkonkoma, NY 11779
(516) 467-0600
Check or M.O. Sells through distributors.
Recorded courses, self-help.
For.

Covenant Home Curriculum
3675 N. Calhoun
Brookfield, WI 53005
K-12. Curriculum. quarterly tests. catalog
of educational coloring books.
Art.

Creative Kids
P.O. Box 6448
Mobile, AL 36660-0448
(800) 345-8112
MC, Visa, AMEX, Discover. Free catalog.
Unconditional guarantee.
Mag by/for talented kids.
Gift, Enrich.

Creative Learning Magazine
See Oak Heritage Press

Cricket
Box 300
Peru, IL 61354
1-800-435-6850 IL: 1-800-892-6831
Check or M.O. or they'll bill you.
Magazine for children.
Fun.

Cruise Vacations
2600 Tulare St. #140
Fresno, CA 93721
1-800-344-7100 9-5 PST
CA: 1-800-233-7100
Home educators' cruise.
Travel.

Curriculum Resources
Box 828
Fairfield, CT 06430
1-800-243-2874 CT: (203) 576-0714
Visa, MC. Catalog, $1.
Craft kits and supplies.
Art.

David S. Lake Publishers
19 Davis Drive
Belmont, CA 94002
(415) 592-7810
Visa, MC. Free catalog.
Sells through bookstores.
Art.

Davka Corporation
845 N. Michigan, Suite 843
Chicago, IL 60611
1-800-621-8227 IL: (314) 944-4070
MC, Visa.
Learning to Read Hebrew software
Class.

Developmental Learning Materials (DLM)
Teaching Resources
One DLM Park
Allen, TX 75002
1-800-527-4747 TX: 1-800-442-4711
8-5 Central Time weekdays.
Minimum order $15.
School programs and texts.
T & G.

Dick Blick: 5 mail order addresses.
Send order to the one closest to you.
Dick Blick West
P.O. Box 521
Henderson, NV 89015
Central: P.O. Box 1267
Galesburg, IL 61401
East: P.O. Box 26
Allentown, PA 18105
Georgia: 1117 Alpharetta St.
Roswell, GA 30075
Connecticut: P.O. Box 330
Farmington, CT 06032
1-800-447-8192 IL: 1-800-322-8183
MC, Visa, AmEx, COD.   Catalog $2.
Art and craft supplies.
Art.

DIDAX, Inc.
6 Doulton Place
Peabody, MA 01960
(617) 535-4757/4758
Check or M.O. Free Catalog
Art, Lit.

Discover and Learn Reading Resources
P.O. Box 697
Portage, MI 49081
(616) 375-3959
Check or M.O. Free brochure. Large
SASE appreciated.
Books for Christian kids and adults,
all ages.
Fun.

Discovery Toys
P.O. Box 232008
Pleasant Hill, CA 94523
(415) 827-4663 for referral info only
Home distributors, party plan.
Toys with "educational play value."
T & G.

Donut Records
4518 Ensenada Dr.
Woodland Hills, CA 91364
(818) 884-3447
Check or M.O. Brochure, 25¢.
Bibletoons musical Bible stories.
Char.

Dover Publications
31 East 2nd St.
Mineola, NY 11501
No phone orders.
Check or M.O. Free catalogs.
Return in 10 days for full refund.
Reprint bookseller. Good selection.
Art, Music, Enrich.

Dr. Drew's Toys, Inc.
P.O. Box 1003, Dept. H
Boston, MA 02205
Check or M.O. Free flier.
Thin rectangular hardwood blocks.
T & G.

EDC Publishing
Division of educational development corporation
P.O. Box 470663
Tulsa, OK 74147
1-800-331-4418 OK: (918) 622-4522
Visa, MC. Free color catalog.
Returns after 60 days, less than 12 months, resaleable condition, 15% restocking charge, written authorization.
Quantity orders only. For individual books, order through **Families that Play Together**. Usborne books.
Art, Bus, Desk, Eng, Enrich, For, Fun, Gift, Home, Lit, Music, Phys, T & G, Travel.

EKS Publishing
5336 College Avenue
Oakland, CA 94618
(415) 653-5183
Check, M.O., or COD. Free catalog.
Returns: Up to 6 months if book in perfect condition.
Biblical/prayerbook Hebrew texts, teaching aids, and games for all ages.
Class.

ESP Inc.
1201 E. Johnson
P.O. Drawer 5037
Jonesboro, AR 72403-5037
1-800-643-0280 AR: (501) 935-3533
Visa. Free catalog.
Full refund if not satisfied.
School workbooks, minicourses.
For, Music.

Eagle Systems International
5600 N. University
P.O. Box 508
Provo, UT 84603-0508
(801) 225-9000
Check, M.O., or they bill you.
Subscriptions: P.O. Box 902
Farmingdale, NY 11737-9802
Happy Times kid character mag.
Free sample copy.
Char.

Eaton Press
47 Richards Avenue
Norwalk, CT 06857
Four cassettes every other month on approval.
MC, Visa, or payment in advance.
100 Greatest Books Ever Written on audio cassettes. Many other elite book and tape series.
Lit.

Echos du Monde Classique
see University of Calgary Press.

Education Services
6410 Raleigh
Arvada, CO 80003
Biblical Psychology of Learning (a great book), also guides to reading, math etc.
Fam, Spec.

Educational Insights
19560 Rancho Way
Dominguez Hills, CA 90220
(213) 637-2131, (213) 979-1955, or 1-800-367-5713
Visa, MC. Free color catalog.
School supplies.
Art, Health, Lit, Enrich, T & G.

Educational Services
175 Gladys Ave, #7
Mountain View, CA 94043
(415) 961-4414
Check or M.O. Free brochure with SASE.
Satisfaction guaranteed.
Publisher of *Home Schooling at Its Best*.
Enrich.

Educators Publishing Service
75 Moulton St.
Cambridge, MA 02238-1901
(617) 547-6706
or
66 Scarsdale Rd.
Don Mills, Ontario, Canada M3B 2R7
(416) 449-4547
1-800-435-7728
Visa, MC. Free Brochures.
Indicate grade level you need.
Language arts and parent helps.
Bus, Spec.

EduSoft
P.O. Box 2560
Berkeley, CA 94702
1-800-EDUSOFT
CA,AK,HI: (415) 548-2304
Visa, MC. Free catalog.
Educational software for the Apple II family.
Music.

Electronic Arts
1820 Gateway Drive
San Mateo, CA 94404
(415) 571-7171
Visa, MC. Free catalog.
Music programs, Apple/Mac.
Music.

Encyclopaedia Britannica, Inc.
Britannica Centre
310 S. Michigan Ave.
Chicago, IL 60604
Write above address, or look in telephone book under "Encyclopedias" for your nearest Britannica representative.
No mail order sales.
Lit.

Entertaiment Plus Family Video Club
P.O. Box 450325
Atlanta, GA 30345
Check or M.O. Free brochure.
Family video club.
Fun.

Evangelistic & Faith Enterprises of America
Rt. 2, Popular Creek Road
Oliver Springs, TN 37840
Answering Service: 1-800-424-2733, Ext 9007
Office: (615) 435-6185
Special education services.
Spec.

Evangelizing Today's Child
Warrenton, MO 63383
(314) 456-4321
Visa, MC.
Christian teaching magazine.
Char.

Everett/Edwards Cassette Curriculum
P.O. Box 1060
Deland, FL 32720
(904) 734-7458
Visa, MC. Free newspaper catalog.
Critics on cassette.
Lit.

Every Day is Special
1602 Naco Place
Hacienda Heights, CA 91745
Check or M.O.
Activity calendar for home schoolers.
Enrich.

Executive Business Summaries
See Soundview Executive Business Summaries.

F & W Publications
9933 Alliance Road
Cincinnati, OH 45242
1-800-543-4644
or
Prentice-Hall Canada
1870 Birchmount Rd.
Scarborough, Ont M1P 2J7
CANADA
(416) 293-3621
Visa, MC. Free catalog.
Returns: Within 30 days resaleable.
Publisher.
Bus, Family, Travel.

Families That Play Together
P.O. Box 560
Sarcoxie, MO 64862
(417) 548-3916 7-10 P.M. Central Time.
Check or M.O. Free catalog.
Usborne books retail.
Books for every catagory. See **EDC Publishing Company** listings in each chapter.
Art, Bus, Desk, Eng, Enrich, For, Fun, Gift, Home, Lit, Music, Phys, T & G, Travel.

Family in America
934 N. Main
Rockford, IL 61103
Check or M.O.
Family issues mag.
Excellent writing and research
Published by the Rockford Institute.
Family.

Family Discovery Center
307 West First South
Manti, UT 84642
(801) 835-2762
Visa, MC. Free brochure.
Large SASE appreciated.
Returns: Within 60 days, resaleable condition.
Foreign language materials,
Mortenson Math, lending library.
For.

Family Enrichment Bureau
1615 Ludington Street
Escanaba, MI 49829
(906) 786-7002
Sex education with morals.
Sex.

Family Pastimes Games
RR 4
Perth ONT CANADA K7H 3C6
(613) 267-4819
Check or M.O. New, expanded newsprint catalog $1.
Board and action games.
T & G.

Family Resources
See SMS Publications.

Fast Track (division of Macmillan)
P.O. Box 859
Farmingdale, NY 11737-9759
Check or M.O. Full year's subscription billed in advance.
Business Summaries Series.
Bus.

Fiberfab International, Inc.
6807 Wayzata Blvd.
Minneapolis, MN 55426
Custom car body kits for VW, ,Ford, Chevy chassis. Free brochure.
Eng.

First Words
305 E. Washington
Delavan, WI 53115
(414) 728-6789 9-5 CST, credit card orders only.
Visa, MC. Free catalog.
Satisfaction guaranteed.
Books for littlest kids.
Fun.

fischertechnik Kits
See Timberdoodle.

Foreign Language Through Song and Story
See Family Discovery Center.

Foundation for American Christian Education (FACE)
Box 27035
San Francisco, CA 94127
Check or M.O. or they'll bill you.
Principle Approach to America's Christian history. Reading list, lots of other materials.
Fun.

Freebies
P.O. Box 20283
Santa Barbara, CA 93120
Cash or check only.
Magazine.
Enrich.

Gazelle Publications
5580 Stanley Drive
Auburn, CA 95603
(916) 878-1223
Check or M.O. Free brochure.
Home School Manual, poetry, travel, and
enrichment books for children.
Travel.

A Gentle Wind
Box 3103
Albany, NY 12203
(518) 436-0391 9-5 EST.
Visa, MC. Minimum charge order, $14.
Free replacement of defective tapes
returned within 15 days. Exchange of
undamaged tapes returned within 15
days.
Original children's music.
Fun.

The Gifted Child Today
P.O. Box 6448
Mobile, AL 36660-0448
1-800-824-7888 HI,AK: 1-800-824-7919
Ask for Operator 50, 24 hours.
Visa, MC. No free samples. Free Catalog.
Gift/talent magazines and resources.
Gift, Enrich.

Gifted Children Monthly
P.O. Box 115
Sewell, NJ 08080
SASE for info.
Magazine for gifted children.
Gift.

Global Specialties
P.O. Box 1405
New Haven, CT 06505
Electronic testing and prototyping.
Breadboards.
Eng.

God's World Publications
P.O. Box 2330
Asheville, NC 28802-2330
(704) 253-8063
Check only. Satisfaction guaranteed.
Christian newspapers for K-12.
Ask about their new Kids Book Club.
Char, Fun.

Golden Educational Center
P.O. Box 12
Bothell, WA 98041-0012
(206) 481-1395
Returns: with written permission,
resaleable condition, within 6 months of
purchase.
Line design books, maps.
Enrich.

Golden Glow Recordings
317 Pleasant St.
Yellow Springs, OH 45387
(513) 767-7228
Visa, MC, or check. No cash orders.
Send SASE for brochure.
Defective tapes replaced.
Cassettes for littlest folks.
Fun.

Gospel Mission
Box M
Choteau, MT 59422
(406) 466-2311
Visa, MC. Free catalog.
No returns for properly filled orders.
Wholesale Christian book outlet.
30% off retail.
Char.

Gospel Publications
P.O. Box 184
Jupiter, FL 33468
(305) 747-2461
Check or M.O. Free newsletter for children.
Children's Calendar. Materials for telephone ministries, balloon stories. Free
lending library of children's Christian
books. Free children's correspondence
course (include $1 to help with postage).
Enrich.

Great Wave Software
5533 Scotts Valley Drive
Scotts Valley, CA 95066
(408) 438-1990
Check or M.O. Free brochures.
Music software, kids' software.
Music, Enrich.

Grolier Enterprises
Sherman Turnpike
Danbury, CT 06816
Club plan.
Beginner Books for kids.
Fun.

Growing Child
P.O. Box 620
Lafayette, IN 47902-1100
(317) 423-2624
Visa, MC, AMEX. Catalog $1.
100% satisfaction guaranteed.
Toys, books and records.
T & G.

Growing Without Schooling
729 Boylston St.
Boston, MA 02116
(617) 437-1550
Check or M.O.
Sample issue, $3. Subscription $20.
Home school magazine.
Art.

Hammond, Inc.
515 Valley St.
Maplewood, NJ 07040
1-800-526-4953 NJ: (201) 763-6000
Check or M.O. Returns with permission.
Geography and other school supplies.
For.

Hank Lee's Magic Factory
125 Lincoln St.
Boston, MA 02111
(617) 482-8749 24 hours, 7 days.
Visa, MC, AMEX, Discover. Catalog $5, or
$8.95 with binder.
Professional magic apparatus,
wholesale/retail.
T & G.

Happy Times
Subscriptions: P.O. Box 902
Farmingdale, NY 11737-9802
(801) 225-9000
Check, M.O., or they bill you.
Kids' character mag.
Free sample copy.
Char.

Harrisville Designs
12 Main St.
Harrisville, NH 03450
(603) 827-3333
Visa, MC, school P.O. Free brochure.
Personal looms for children.
Art.

Harvest House Publishers
1075 Arrowsmith
Eugene, OR 97402-9197
1-800-547-8979 OR: (503) 343-0123
Christian publisher.
Char.

Hear An' Tell
320 Bunker Hill
Houston, TX 77024
Check or M.O. Free brochure.
Returns: Resaleable condition.
Christian Spanish and French
language programs.
For.

HearthSong
P.O. Box B
Sebastopol, CA 95472
(707) 829-0900
Visa, MC. Free catalog.
"A catalog for families."
Art, T & G.

Heathkit
Heath Company
Hilltop Road
St. Joseph, MI 49085
1-800-253-0570 MI, AK: (616) 982-3411
Visa, MC, C.O.D. Charge acct.
Electronics courses, items, kits.
Eng.

Herald Press
616 Walnut Avenue
Scottsdale, PA 15683-1999
(412) 887-8500
or
117 King Street West
Kitchener, Ontario, Canada N2G 4M5
(519) 743-2673
or
Metanoia Book Service
14 Shepherds Hill
Highgate, London N6 5AQ
ENGLAND
(01) 340-8775
or
W. A. Buchanan & Company
21 Kyabra Street
Fortitude Valley, Brisbane
Queensland 4006
AUSTRALIA
(07) 52-4052
Mennonite publisher.
Health.

**Hewitt Research Foundation (or Home
Grown Kids)**
P.O. Box 9
Washougal, WA 98671
Check or M.O. Free catalog.
Innovative home school materials.
Fun, Lit.

High Noon Books
20 Commercial Blvd.
Novato, CA 94947-6191
(415) 883-3314
Call or write for address of one
of their Canadian distributors.
Visa, MC, AMEX. Free catalog.
No returns.
Hi-lo mystery stories with
moral principles
Fun.

Holt Associates
729 Boylston St.
Boston, MA 02116
(617) 437-1550
Check or M.O. Catalog w/SASE.
Books of interest to home schoolers.
Music and art supplies.
Art, Enrich, Music, Spec.

Home Education Magazine
P.O. Box 1083
Tonasket, WA 98855
Check or M.O.
Joyful home school magazine.
Travel Directory.
Travel.

**Home Educators of Special Education
Children**
Myrna Vogel and Saunny Scott
1601 Barker St.
Lawrence, KS 66044
(913) 749-1316
Free educational advice
Spec.

Home Life
P.O. Box 1250
Fenton, Mo 63026
Check or M.O. Free catalog.
One-stop shopping for books and tapes
on education, home management, family
productivity, and other areas of home-
based living. Our home business.
Bus, Fam, Fun, Health, Home, Lit, Safety.

Home School Headquarters
P.O. Box 366
Fremont, NE 68025
Resource guide for home schoolers.
Spec.

Homespun Tapes, Ltd.
Box 694
Woodstock, NY 12498
(914) 679-7832
Visa, MC, COD. (USA only)
Catalog $1; free with order.
Musicianship tapes.
Music.

**Hoover Brothers Educational Equipment
and Supplies**
P.O. Box 1009
Kansas City, MO 64141
(816) 472-4848
MC, COD. Catalog $7.50.
School supplies.
Art.

Horne Book
1558 N. Agusta Ave.
Camarillo, CA 93010
Christian classics and ed materials. consultation, guides, seminars.
Principle Approach.
Also PC-XT clones.
Desk.

Housework, Inc.
P.O. Box 39
Pocatello, ID 83204
MC, Visa. Free catalog.
Professional cleaning supplies for your home. Don Aslett's company.
Home.

Hubbard Company
P.O. Box 104
Northbrook, IL 60062
1-800-323-8368 IL: (312) 272-7810
Visa, MC, AMEX. Free catalogs.
Raised relief maps. Science supplies.
Health.

Hugh O'Neill and Associates
Box 1297
Nevada City, CA 95959
Check or M.O. Nice people.
Big yellow drawing book.
Art.

Ideal School Supply Company
11000 S. Lavergne Ave.
Oak Lawn, IL 60453
(312) 425-0800
School supplies, all subject areas.
Order from school suppliers.
Health.

Imaja
P.O. Box 638
Middletown, CT 06457
Check or M.O. Free brochure.
Listen ear-training software—Mac.
Music.

Independent School Press
A Longman Inc. Company
95 Church St.
White Plains, NY 10601
(914) 993-5000
Check or M.O.
Return: 9 months, permission.
Supplementary public school texts.
Class, For.

Instructor Books
P.O. Box 6177
Duluth, MN 55806
(218) 723-9200
Check or M.O. Free brochure.
Teacher's magazine.
Activity and crafts books, plus teacher's idea books to supplement every elementary-school subject.
Art, Enrich.

The Instrument Workshop
8023 Forest Dr. N.E.
Seattle, WA 98115
(206) 523-6129 6-7 AM, 7-9 PM Pacific Time
Visa, MC. Free list of catalogs.
Old time keyboard instrument kits, plans, tools.
Music.

International Linguistics
3505 E Red Bridge Road
Kansas City, MO 64114
(816) 765-8855
Returns: 30 days.
Foreign language courses.
For.

International Montessori Society
912 Thayer Ave.
Silver Spring, MD 20910
(301) 589-1127
Check or M.O. Free brochure.
Montessori books, course, and newsletter.
Managing Misbehavior tapes.
Fam, Music.

Into the Wind Kites
1408 Pearl
Boulder, CO 80302
(303) 449-5356 M-Sat 10-6, for credit card orders only.
Visa, MC, AMEX.
100% refund or exchange.
You return prepaid and insured.
Kites and accessories.
T & G.

IRIS
Rauld Russell
1820 Stock Slough
Coos Bay, OR 97420
Check or M.O. made out to Rauld Russell.
Free info: SASE appreciated.
K-8 wet-on-wet watercolor painting guide.
Art.

Jameson Books
Green Hill Publishers
722 Columbus St.
Ottawa, IL 61350
(815) 434-7905
Publisher.
Phys.

Jeffrey Norton Publishers
On-The-Green
Guilford, CT 06437
(203) 453-9794
1-800-243-1234 CT, AK, HI: (203) 453-9794
Visa, MC, AMEX, DC, CB, institutional P.O. Also various cassette-of-the-month club plans.
Free catalogs.
Returns: 3 weeks, unconditional.
Spoken-word cassettes, videos.Bus, Class, For, Lit, Music, T & G, Travel.

Jerryco
601 Linden Place
Evanston, IL 60202
(312) 475-8440
Visa (Bank Am), MC. Catalog $1.
$10 minimum order.
Refund on saleable stuff except for postage and handling.
The kings of surplus. Tons for tinkerers.
Eng.

Jewish Museum Shop
1109 Fifth Ave.
New York, NY 10028
(212) 860-1895
Visa, MC, AMEX. $20 minimum.
Returns: 30 days, you pay postage.
Jewish supplies.
Char.

Jonson Specialties
Box 357
Cedarhurst, NY 11516-0357
1-800-221-6714
NY: (718) 327-5965 8-5
Visa, MC, AMEX. Free catalog.
Satisfaction guaranteed.
Toys and rewards.
Char, T & G.

Just For Kids
Winterbrook Way
Meredith, NH 03253
Toys and games. Expensive.
T & G.

Kentuckiana Music Supply
138 E. Wellington Ave.
Louisville, KY
Music.

KidsArt
912 Schilling Way
Mt. Shasta, CA 96067
(916) 926-5076
Visa, MC. Free catalog, SASE appreciated.
Satisfaction guaranteed.
Kids' art magazine, *Kid Prints* home program for teaching fine arts. Imaginative art supplies.
Art.

Kimbo Educational
P.O. Box 477
Long Branch, NJ 07740
1-800-631-2187 NJ: (201) 229-4949
Visa, MC. Free color catalog.
Records, cassettes, filmstrips, especially early childhood and movement.
Fun, Health, Phys.

Kolbe Concepts, Inc.
P.O. Box 15050
Phoenix, AZ 85060
(602) 840-9770
Visa, MC. $20 minimum. Distributors.
Resources for gifted children.
Gift.

Konos Curriculum
P.O. Box 1534
Richardson, TX 75083
(214) 669-8337 or 238-1552
Check or M.O. Free brochure.
Curriculum. Time lines.
Art, Char, Music.

Laissez-Faire Books
532 Broadway
New York, NY 10012
1-800-238-2200 X 500 24 hr, 7 day
Visa, MC. Free catalog.
30 day unconditiona guarantee.
Libertarian bookseller.
Music.

Lakeshore Curriculum Material Center
P.O. Box 6261
Carson, CA 90749
1-800-421-5334 CA: 1-800-262-1777
Info: (213) 537-8600
Visa, MC, AMEX. Free catalog.
Returns: 30 days, unused goods.
School supplies pre-K-3, special ed.
Art.

Lark in the Morning
Box 1176
Mendocino, CA 95460
Rare/ unusual instruments, catalog $2.50
Music.

Latebloomers Educational Consulting Svc
Thomas Armstrong, PhD. Founder.
P.O. Box 5435
Santa Rosa, CA 95402
Help for parents with kids labelled learning disabled.
For free brochure send SASE.
Spec.

Latin Skills software
See Office of Instructional Technology.

Learn, Inc.
113 Gaither Dr.
Mt. Laurel, NJ 08054-9987
1-800-845-6000 UT: 1-800-535-2100
orders only.
Inquiries: (609) 234-6100
Visa, MC, AMEX, D Club. Free catalog.
Courses on cassette/video.
Bus.

Learning Advantage
300 Alexander Park
Princeton, NJ 08540
1-800-972-3200 9-9 M-F EST, 12-5 Sat
MC, Visa. Free brochure.
Software magazines, club.
Desk.

Learning at Home
P.O. Box 270
Honaunau, HI 96726
(808) 328-9669
Visa, MC. Free catalog.
Money-back guarantee.
Curriculum guides, reference materials, workbooks, test prep.
Art.

Learning Company
545 Middlefield Rd.
Suite 170
Menlo Park, CA 94025
1-800-852-2255 CA: 1-800-852-7256
or (415) 328-5410
Refunds: 3-day money-back or exchange for another TLC program.
Innovative educational software.
Eng, Logic.

Learning Systems Corporation
P.O. Box 150
Guilford, CT 06437
(203) 453-3538
Visa, MC. Catalog, 50¢.
All sales are final.
Miniworkbooks, Skillforms.
Desk.

Learning Technologies
4225 LBJ Freeway, Suite 131
Dallas, TX 75224
1-800-238-4277 TX: (214) 991-4958
$19.95 educational software
Refunds: one year.
Eng, Logic.

Learning Things, Inc.
P.O. Box 436
Arlington, MA 02174
(617) 646-0093
Check or M.O. Minimum order, $15.
Free catalog.
Science apparatus, cardboard carpentry,
tools and construction kits for kids.
Eng.

Learning to Draw What You See
See Mary Brock

Legacy
1035 Serpentine Lane
Pleasanton, CA 94566
(415) 484-3220
MC, Visa, no cash or COD.
Party plan sales.
Free catalog.
Glitzy toys and character-building materials.
Char, T & G.

Les Editions du Sphinx
C.P. 27
Sillery, Quebec G1T 2P7
CANADA
Classical studies books in French.
Class.

LISTEN ear-training software
See Imaja.

Living Stories
Milford, KS 66514
(913) 463-5427
Visualized Christian stories. Over 40
years.
Char.

Living Word Curriculum
P.O. Box 3875
Ventura, CA 93006
Check, M.O., or they bill you.
Craft books.
Art.

Long Associates, Inc.
17 E. Schaumburg Rd.
Schaumburg, IL 60193
(312) 894-7610
Check or M.O. Free brochure.
Co-op hardware, software purchasing.
Desk.

Louis Tannen Magic, Inc.
6 West 32nd St., Fourth Floor
New York, NY 10001
(212) 239-8383
Visa, MC, AMEX. $15 minimum.
Catalog, $6 plus $5 UPS.
Magic supplies, books, magazine.
T & G.

Love Publishing Co.
1777 S. Bellaire St.
Denver, CO 80222
(303) 757-2579
Check or M.O. Free catalog.
School texts, workbooks, supplies.
Desk, Spec.

Loyola University Press
3441 North Ashland Ave.
Chicago, IL 60657
Large SASE for free info.
Reading course in Homeric Greek.
Class.

Mac Connection
14 Mill St.
Marlow, NJ 03456
1-800-622-5472 9-9 M-Fr 9-5:30 Sat
(603) 446-7711 info 9-5:30 M-Fri
MC, Visa, no surcharge. Card not charged
until your order shipped. Personal and
company checks: allow 1 week to clear.
C.O.D. max $1000. 120 day limited warranty on all products.
Desk.

MacUser
P.O. Box 52461
Boulder, CO 80321-2461
Check, M.O., or they bill you.
Excellent magazine for Macintosh computer users.
Desk.

MacWorld
Subscription Department
P.O. Box 51666
Boulder, CO 80321-1666
Check, M.O., or they bill you.
Bland magazine for Macintosh computer
users.
Desk.

Maher
P.O. Box 420
Littleton, CO 80160
(303) 798-6830
Visa, MC. Free catalog.
Ventriloquism and other
entertainment supplies.
Unrelated to Maher Workshops (below).
T & G.

Maher Workshops
P.O. Box 1466
Cedar Ridge, CA 95924
(916) 273-0176
Check or M.O. $2, info pak.
Ventriloquism and other
entertainment supplies.
Unrelated to Maher (above).
T & G.

Majesty Music
P.O. Box 6524
Greenville, SC 29606
1-800-334-1071 M-F 8:30-5
Visa, MC, school or church P.O.
Minimum P.O., $25.
Free brochure.
Patch the Pirate cassettes, books, scripts.
Char.

Mandolin Brothers, Ltd.
629 Forest Ave.
Staten Island, NY 10310
(718) 981-3226
Visa, MC, AMEX. Free catalog.
Minimum credit card order, $50.
Refund: 3 days, original carton, new condition.
Stringed instruments and books.
Music.

Manna Computing Concepts
Box 527
Woodstock, GA 30188
$1 catalog. Christian and secular academic software.
Desk.

Marilyn Rockett
1025 Tanglewood
Cedar Hill, TX 75104
Home and home school organizer.
Home.

Market Dynamics Consultants
P.O. Box 130
Wilton, CT 06897
(203) 454-3435
Check or M.O. 30 day money-back guarantee.
Sophisticated Travelers Guide.
Travel.

Mary Brock
8236 E. 71st St. #64
Tulsa, OK 74133
Learning to Draw What You See art course.
Check or M.O. Free brochure.
Mention you saw it in the Next Book of Home Learning and get a $20 discount.
Art.

Master Books
P.O. Box 1606
El Cajon, CA 92022
(619) 448-1121
Check, M.O., COD. Free catalog
Christian publisher.
Sex.

Medical Self-Care
P.O. Box 1099
Augusta, ME 04330
(207) 622-5949, credit card orders
or inquiries
7 AM - 11 PM EST, M-Sat
Visa, MC, AMEX. Free catalog.
Refunds: Unconditional, 30 days.
Health resources. New Age.
Health.

Mel Gablers—Educational Analysts
P.O. Box 7518
Longview, TX 75607
(214) 753-5993
Check or M.O. Donations for materials.
Textbook analyses.Reading lists.
Fun.

Merck & Company
P.O. Box 2000
Rahway, NJ 07065
(201) 574-5403
Doctor's diagnostic manual.
Health.

Michael Olaf
5817 College Ave.
Oakland, CA 94618
Check or M.O. Catalog, $1.
"The Montessori Shop"
Enrich.

Michel Farm Vacations
R.R. 1, Box 914
Harmony, MN 55939
(507) 886-5392
Check or M.O. Free color brochure
shows area sights of interest.
20% deposit, balance due 2 days before
arrival at farm. Refunds—cancellation
received 14 days prior to starting date.
Farm vacations.
Travel.

Microzine
P.O. Box 645
Lyndhurst, NJ 07071-9986
Computer magazine. $169/year.
Desk.

Midwest Publications
P.O. Box 448
Pacific Grove, CA 93950
(408) 375-2455
Check or M.O. Free catalog.
Classroom materials for thinking skills.
Gift, Logic.

Milliken Publishing Company
1100 Research Blvd.
St. Louis, MO 63132-0579
(314) 991-4220
or
Encyclopaedia Britannica Publications
175 Holday Drive
Cambridge, Ont. N3C 3N4
CANADA
(also available widely in teacher's stores,
like the "Play & Learn" Teacher's stores
all over Canada)
or
Encyclopaedia Britannica
22 Lambs Road
Artarmon, NSW 2064
AUSTRALIA
or
Gemini Teaching Aids
19, Kirkgate,
Sherburn-in-Element
Leeds LS25 6BH
ENGLAND
Visa, MC, COD. Free catalog.
Home workbooks and software.
Health.

The Mind's Eye
P.O. Box 6727
San Francisco, CA 94120
1-800-227-2020 CA: (415) 883-7701
Visa, MC, AMEX. Free gorgeous catalog.
Stories on tape.
Fun, Lit.

Mindscape
3444 Dundee Road
Northbrook, IL 60062
(312) 480-7667
MC, Visa. Free catalog.
Software.
Bus.

Missionary Vision for Special Ministries
Ruth Shuman, Director
640 West Briar Place
Chicago, IL 60657
(312) 327-0489
Free materials for SASE. Donations
accepted.
Materials, classroom program to promote
understanding of those with handicaps.
Spec.

Montessori Services
816 King St.
Santa Rosa, CA 95404
(707) 579-3003
Visa, MC, COD. Free newsprint catalog.
Montessori supplies and books.
Home, Phys.

Moody Correspondence School
820 N. LaSalle St.
Chicago, IL 60610
1-800-621-7105 IL: (312) 329-4166
Visa, MC. Free catalog.
15-day free trial.
Self-study adult Bible courses.
Dispensational.
Class.

Mother's Bookshelf
P.O. Box 70
Hendersonville, NC 28793
Books to build your self-reliance and
good ol' know-how.
Division of *Mother Earth News*.
Bus, Eng, Health.

Mothering
P.O. Box 15790
Santa Fe, NM 87506
MC, Visa. Sample issue, $1.
Progressive family issues magazine.
Family.

Motivational Art Training
9300 Beecher Rd.
Pittsford, MI 49271
No phone orders. Check or M.O.
Christian Art Manual.
Art.

Mott Media
1000 E. Huron St.
Milford, MI 48042
1-800-348-6688 MI: (313) 685-8773
Visa, MC. Free catalog.
Classic texts, McGuffeys, Christian char-
acter training.
New McGuffey Academy offers full-ser-
vice correspondence program
Write for details.
Lit.

Mountain Craft Shop
American Ridge Rd, Route 1
New Martinsville, WV 26155
(304) 455-3570
Check or M.O. Free catalog.
$15 minimum order.
Returns must be authorized in writing.
Folk toys and reprints of old books.
T & G.

Moving and Learning
109 Berry River Rd.
Rochester, NH 03867
(603) 332-6917
Visa, MC. Free brochure.
Returns: 30 days.
Developmental exercise program.
Phys.

Music for Little People
Star Route
Redway, CA 95560
1-800-443-9990
CA,AK: (707) 923-2040
MC, Visa. Free lovely catalog.
Returns: Full credit or refund within 30
days.
Cassettes, videos, musical instruments
"especially for families."
Fun, Music.

NACD
P.O. Box 280012
Tampa, FL 33682
(813) 972-2025
MC, Visa. Free catalog, brochure.
Satisfaction guaranteed.
Physical therapy/behavior modification
programs, tape sets. On-site evaluations.
Family, Spec.

NAPSAC
P.O. Box 428
Marble Hill, MO 63764
Check or M.O. US funds only.
Membership organization. Supports alter-
natives in childbirth. Publishes *NAPSAC
NEWS* and several excellent works on
childbirth and medicine. Video/audio con-
ference tapes.
Free book catalog for large SASE. Send
request for catalog to
P.O. Box 429
Marble Hill, MO 88784.
Health.

National Academy of Child Development
see NACD

Nature Expeditions International
474 Willamette St.
Eugene, OR 97401
(503) 484-6529
Wildlife and natural history expeditions.
Free brochure.
Travel.

New Families
P.O. Box 41108, Dept JW
Fayetteville, NC 28309
Check or M.O. Sample copy, $3.
U.S. funds only.
New Age advice on combining career
with family in unexpected ways.
Fam.

OWI, Inc.
1160 Mahalo Place
Compton, CA 90220
(213) 638-4732
Electronic robot kits. Free brochure.
Eng.

Oak Heritage Press
P.O. Box 957
Wrightstown, NJ 08562-0957
Check or M.O. Sample issue $2.
Publisher of *Creative Learning Magazine*.
Enrich.

Oak Leaf Bed and Breakfast
Love Agricultural Resources
Rt 1, Box 113
Elk City, KS 67344
(316) 755-2908 or (316) 633-5260
Check or M.O. Free brochure with SASE.
2,000 acre working ranch.
Travel.

Oak Meadow
P.O. Box G
Ojai, CA 93023
Parent Sensitivity Training, Homeopathic
Medicine in Home courses. Also full-ser-
vice home school curriculum supplier.
Fam, Health.

Office of Instructional Technology
University of Delaware
Newark, DE 19716
Latin Skill s computer programs for Apple
II family.
Free brochure.
Class.

Official Publications, Inc.
P.O. Box 937
Fort Washington, PA 19034
Check or M.O. Free brochure.
Puzzle magazines.
T & G.

Omega Entertainment
2045 San Elijo Ave.
Cardiff, CA 92007
Christian films and videos
Fun.

Open Court Publishing Company
P.O. Box 599
315 Fifth Street
Peru, IL 61354
1-800-435-6850 IL: 1-800-892-6831
Inquiries: (815) 223-2520
or
Fitzhery and Whiteside (Distributor)
195 Allstate Parkway
Markham, Ont. L3R 4T8
CANADA
(416) 477-0030

or
David and Natalie Wheeler (Distributors)
Educational Equipment Wholesale, Ltd.
129 Meadowbank Road
Auckland 5
NEW ZEALAND
Visa, MC, AMEX. Free catalog.
Returns: 90 days, resaleable, permission.
Texts for creative learning.
Fun.

Optasia Fine Art Design
P.O. Box 369
Fruitport, MI 49415
(616) 865-3148
Check or M.O.
Beautiful postcards, note cards to color.
Art.

Orange Cat Goes to Market
442 Church St.
Garberville, CA 95440
Books for kids
Fun.

Orton Dyslexia Society
724 York Rd.
Baltimore, MD 21204
(301) 296-0232
Help for dyslexics.
Spec.

Owner-Builder Publications
P.O. Box 550
Oakhurst, CA 93664
Books on how to build your own house,
how to work with or around zoning regu-
lations.
Eng.

Pacific Cascade Records
47534 McKenzie Highway
Vida, OR 97488-9707
(503) 896-3290
Visa, MC. Free catalog.
Returns: Defective materials only.
Music and folksongs for kids.
Phys.

Pacific Puzzle Co.
378 Guemes Island Rd.
Anacortes, WA 98221
(206) 293-7034
Visa, MC. U.S. funds only.
Refund or exchange if dissatisfied.
Free catalog.
Beautiful hardwood puzzles.
T & G.

Paper Soldier
8 McIntosh Lane
Clifton Park, NY 12065
Antique pop-up books.
T & G.

Parent-Child Press
P.O. Box 767
Altoona, PA 16603
(814) 946-5213
Visa, MC. Minimum credit card order
$10.
U.S. funds only.
Montessori philosophy, art materials.
Art.

Parenting
P.O. Box 56847
Boulder, CO 80321-6847
Visa, MC, or they bill you.
Refunds: Full amount .
Magazine for yuppy parents.
Fam.

Parenting Press
Suite 300
7750 31st Ave. NE
Seattle, WA 98115
Kids' first aid book. Publisher.
Health.

Patterned Language
4305 River Rd. N.
Salem, OR 97303
(503) 393-5153
Check or M.O. Possible rental arrange-
ments for home schoolers.
Free brochure.
Voice or TDD training programs
Spec.

Pearl Paint
308 Canal St.
New York, NY 10013
World's largest art and craft discount center. Seven locations (NY, NJ, FL).
Catalog, $1.
Art.

Pecci Educational Publishers
440 Davis Court #405
San Francisco, CA 94111
(415) 391-8579
Check or M.O. Free brochure.
Reading program and Super Seatwork.
Art.

Perma-Bound
Hertzberg-New Method, Inc.
Vandalia Rd.
Jacksonville, IL 62650
Perma-bound books. Over 9,000 titles.
Fun, Lit.

Peter Wannemacher
Rt 19, Box 3510
Conroe, TX 77303
(409) 231-2704
Check or M.O. Free estimates.
Certificates and diplomas for home schoolers and others.
Scripture-of-the-Week postcards.
Calligrapher. Lovely work.
Enrich.

Play 'n Talk
7105 Manzanita St.
Carlsbad, CA 92009
(619) 438-4330 7 AM—10 PM M-Sat PST.
Visa, MC, or post-dated checks for total price.
Total language arts program.
Bus.

Play-Jour, Inc.
200 fifth Ave, Suite 1024
New York, NY 10010
Capsela Scientific kits.
Eng.

Playing for Knowledge, Inc.
4 Poplar Run
East Windsor, NJ 08520
(609) 448-8443
Check or M.O.
Large newsprint catalog $1 refundable on first order.
Distributor of gift/talented materials.
Enrich.

Playthinks
P.O. Box 2628
Setauket, NY 11733
(516) 751-2421
Visa, MC. Color catalog, $2.
Returns: 30 days, intact.
Kits for learning through play.
Enrich.

Pleasant Company
P.O. Box 112
Madison, WI 53701-0112
1-800-845-0005 WI: (608) 255-6410
MC, Visa, AMEX. Free catalog.
Free *The American Girls* newsletter "for any American girl, ages 6-11."
American history dolls, accessories.
T & G.

Pompeiiana, Inc.
6026 Indianola Avenue
Indianapolis, IN 46220
Pompeiiana Newsletter. Current fads translated into classical Latin, plus student activities.
Check or M.O. U.S. funds only.
Class.

Praise Hymn, Inc.
P.O. Box 1080
Taylors, SC 29687
(803) 292-1990
Check or M.O. U.S. funds only.
Returns: Permission only. Prorated.
10% restocking charge.
Christian music courses, band method.
Music.

Praise Unlimited
1747 Cattlemen Rd.
Sarasota, FL 33582
(813) 377-3895
Christian dolls.
T & G.

Price/Stern/Sloan Publishers, Inc.
410 N. La Cienega Blvd.
Los Angeles, CA 90048
Visa, MC. Free brochure.
Widely available in bookstores.
WEE SING series.
Music.

Prism
P.O. Box 030464
Ft. Lauderdale, FL 33303-0464
Check or M.O. Sample copy $4.
Magazine by/for gifted kids.
Gift.

Publishers Central Bureau
One Champion Ave.
P.O. Box 1262
Newark, NJ 07101
Visa, MC, AMEX. $10 minimum.
Discount books, recordings, videos.
Art, Lit.

Puritan-Reformed Discount Book Service
1319 Newport Gap Pike
P.O. Box 3499
Wilmington, DE 19804-2895
(302) 999-8317
Discount Christian books.
Membership $5/year U.S., $8 Canada, $12 overseas.
Class.

R & E Publications
P.O. Box 2008
Saratoga, CA 95070
(408) 866-6303
Visa, MC. Free catalog.
Child abuse books, educational cooking.
Home.

R.S. Publications
P.O. Box 2245
Sedona, AZ 86336
Check or M.O. Free brochures.
Discovery Spanish, social studies.
For.

Rainfall Toys
1534 College, S.E.
Grand Rapids, MI 49507
1-800-437-4337
Visa, MC. No COD. Free brochure,
SASE appreciated.
Sold in Christian bookstores.
Bible games and toys.
Char, Music, T & G.

Raven Images
316 Manzano NE
Albuquerque, NM 87108
(505) 256-3901
Check or M.O. Free catalog.
Please Packs, stationery and other
good stuff.
Fam.

Reade Books Ltd.
P.O. Box 17021
Seattle, WA 98107-0721
(206) 789-1142
Check or M.O.
Hand bookbinding, book repair.
Lit.

Reading Reform Foundation
7054 E. Indian School Road
Scottsdale, AZ 85251
(602) 946-3567
Check or M.O. Free book list.
Books on reading, learning.
Spec.

Recorded Books
P.O. Box 79
Charlotte Hall, MD 20622
1-800-638-1304
Visa, MC. Free catalog.
Current and classic fiction recorded.
Lit.

Reformed Presbyterian Church of North America
Board of Education and Publication
7418 Penn Avenue
Pittsburgh, PA 15208-2531
(412) 241-0436
Check, M.O., or they bill you.
Free catalog.
Quantity discounts for bookstores and
churches.
Psalm books, cassettes.
Music.

Regents Publishing Company
2 Park Avenue
New York, NY 10016
1-800-822-8202
NY: (212) 889-2780 Op 81
Visa, MC. Free catalog.
ESL and foreign languages.
For.

Reliable Corporation
1001 W. Van Buren St.
Chicago, IL 60607
1-800-621-4344. Free catalogs
Visa, MC, AMEX, or open account for
qualified customers. Free delivery on
orders exceeding cutoff amount. No-
strings guarantee.
Discount office supplies.
Home.

Resources for the Gifted, Inc.
3421 N. 44th St.
Phoenix, AZ 85018
Touchtone phone: 950-1088, wait for
tone, then press 664066(toll-free). (602)
840-9770 for inquiries.
Visa, MC. Free catalog.
Returns: 60 days, resaleable, you pay
postage.
Kathy Kolbe Thinkercise materials.
Gift.

Rhythm Band, Inc.
P.O. Box 126
Fort Worth, TX 76101
(817) 335-2561
Visa, MC. Free color catalog.
Musical instruments for children.
Music.

Rifton: Equipment for the Handicapped
Rt 213
Rifton, NY 12471
(914) 658-3141, (914) 658-3143
Check or M.O. Free catalog.
Returns: Allowed on some items. 10%
handling charge.
Exercise equipment for the handicapped.
Phys, Spec.

Rockport
72 Howe St.
Marlboro, MA 01752
Fitness Walking.
Phys.

Rodale Press
33 E. Minor St.
Emmaus, PA 18049
(215) 967-5171
Publisher. Self-help, health, organic.
Eng, Health.

Rubberstampede
P.O. Box 1105
Berkeley, CA 94701
(415) 843-8910 10-4 M-F Pacific Time
Visa, MC. Free catalog.
Rubber stamps, of course!
T & G.

Rubberstampmadness
P.O. Box 6585H
Ithaca, NY 14851
(607) 277-5431
Check or M.O. Sample issue $2.
Rubber stamp magazine.
T & G,

S & S Arts and Crafts
Colchester, CT 06415
Check or M.O. Free catalog.
1-800-243-9232 CT: 537-3451
8 AM—9 PM M-Fr 8-noon EST Sat
Visa, MC, or school P.O. US funds only.
Open account: 3 credit references,
prepay first order.
$25 minimum order. No COD.
Arts and crafts projects.
Art.

SBI Publishers in Sound
Willow St.
South Lee, MA 01260
(413) 243-3235
Visa, MC. Free catalog.
Classics on tape. Some slow-playback.
Lit.

SMM Educational Services
Box 1079
Sunland, CA 91040
Check or M.O. Brochure with SASE.
Workbooks, cassette mini-courses.
For, Music, Enrich.

SMS Publications
701 Main
Evanston, IL 60202
(312) 328-3386
Publisher, *Family Resources*.
Fam.

Scholastic, Inc.
P.O. Box 7502
Jefferson City, MO 65102
1-800-325-6149 MO: 1-800-392-2179
Technical assistance: (314) 636-8890
Visa, MC, or school P.O. Free catalog.
Returns: Resaleable condition/ 30 days.
or
Scholastic-TAB Ltd.
123 Newkirk Road
Richmond HIll, Ont. L4C 3G5
CANADA
(416) 883-5300
Computer texts, courseware.
Desk.

Scholastic Software
Scholastic, Inc.
P.O. Box 645
Lyndhurst, NJ 07071-9986
Microzine computer magazine.
Desk.

Sculpture Associates
40 E. 19th St.
New York, NY 10003
(212) 254-8585
Visa, MC, AMEX. $30 minimum.
Everything for the sculptor.
Art.

S.E.T.
See Society for the Elimination of
Television

Sex Respect
See Committee on the Status of Women.

Shakean Stations, Inc.
P.O. Box 68
Farley, IA 52046
(319) 744-3307
Visa, MC. Free 8-page color brochure.
Inexpensive file folder games.
Enrich.

Shar Products
P.O. Box 1411
Ann Arbor, MI 48106
(313) 665-7711
Visa, MC, COD. Free B & W catalog.
Stringed instruments, accessories, sup-
plies.
Suzuki materials. Huge list of sheet
music for strings.
Music.

Share-A-Care Publications
Rt. 2, Box 77-E
Reinholds, PA 17569
(215) 484-2367 8-4 EST
Check, M.O., or COD. U.S. funds only.
Free brochure. Send large SASE.
Returns: Permission required,
resaleable condition, 30 days.
Grades 1-8 art program
Art.

Shekinah Curriculum Cellar
967 Junipero Drive
Costa Mesa, CA 92626
(714) 751-7767
Check or M.O. Catalog, $1.
Refunds: Resaleable condition, 15 days.
Co-op buying plan. Write for details.
"Quality books and teaching aids for
home educators."
Art, Enrich.

Shining Star
Division of Good Apple
Box 299
Carthage, IL 62321
1-800-435-7234
or
Beacon Distributors, Ltd.
104 Consumers Drive
Whitby, Ont. L1N 5T3
(416) 668-8884
Visa, MC. Free catalog.
Returns: Permission required.
Christian educational materials, maga-
zines.
Enrich.

Shop Talk
5737 64th Street
Lubbock, TX 79424
Check or M.O.
Newsletter by/for parents.
Fam.

Silver Burdett Company
250 James St., CN 1918
Morristown, NJ 07960-1918
1-800-631-8081 NJ: (201) 285-7700 col-
lect.
Returns: 1 year, permission.
Public school materials.
Lit, Music, Phys.

**Society for the Elimination of Television
(S.E.T.)**
Box 1124
Albuquerque, NM 87103
(505) 247-3245
Free subscription. Donations requested.
Newsletter, T-shirts, speaker's bureau.
Educational organization.
Fam.

Software Shuttle
P.O. Box 316
Dayton, OH 45409-0316
(513) 293-2594
Visa, MC. Free catalog.
Discount software.
Desk.

Son Shine Puppet Company
P.O. Box 6203
Rockford, IL 61125
(815) 885-3709
or
Children for Christ
Mike Dunsworth
288-290 King St., 1st floor
Newtown, NSW 2042
AUSTRALIA
Check or M.O. COD to institutions.
Free catalog. Free sample copy of
newsletter.
Returns must be authorized.
Puppets, costumes, accessories, newsletter.
T & G.

Soundview Executive Business Summaries
5 Main Street
Bristol, VT 05443
Business books summarized.
By subscription only.
Bus.

Springboard Software
7807 Creekridge Court
Minneapolis, MN 55435
(612) 944-3912
Software publisher.
Music.

St. Paul's Publishing Co., Inc.
P.O. Box 772
Fort Scott, KS 66701
1-800-523-5562
Visa, MC. Free sample of magazine.
Satisfaction guaranteed.
Classic family magazine, science supplement.
Lit.

Stand-Buys Ltd.
311 West Superior Street, #404
Chicago, IL 60610
1-800-255-0200 IL: 1-800-826-4398
Outside continental US, (312) 943-5737
Visa, MC, AMEX, Diners Club.
Membership discount air travel.
Travel.

Summer Institute of Linguistics
International Linguistics Center
7500 Camp Wisdom Road
Dallas, TX 75236
(214) 298-2436
Check or M.O. No returns without permission.
Resources for linguistics scholars.
For.

Summy-Birchard Co.
See Birch Tree Group Ltd.

Sunburst Communications, Inc.
39 Washington Ave.
Pleasantville, NY 10570
1-800-431-1934
NY: 1-800-221-5912
Canada: 1-800-247-6756
(914) 769-5030 collect.
Call toll-free for free catalog. Specify
Home Market Brochure or school catalog.
Visa, MC, COD.
Customer satisfaction guaranteed.
Lifetime replacement of defective parts.
Free software updates.
Creative educational software.
Eng, Logic.

SyberVision
Fountain Square
6066 Civic Terrace Ave.
Newark, CA 94560-3747
1-800-227-0600
Visa, MC, AMEX. Catalog, $2.
Returns: 60 days. Quantity discounts.
Unique cassette language courses,
sports and self-help videos.
Bus, For, Phys.

Sycamore Tree
2179 Meyer Place
Costa Mesa, CA 92627
(714) 650-4466
Check or M.O.
Catalog $3, comes with $3 coupon good
toward
first purchase.
Full service home school supplier.
Home school program.
Art, Char, Enrich, Health, Home, Phys.

TAFHE
P.O. Box 1138
Glendale Heights, IL 60139
Software/hardware for home schoolers at
school discounts.
Standalone video units for life without TV.
Fam, Desk.

Teaching and Computers
Scholastic Inc.
P.O. Box 2040
Mahopac, NY 10541-9963
Check, M.O., or they bill you.
Education magazine for teachers.
Desk.

Telltales
P.O. Box 614
Bath, ME 04530
(207) 443-3177 9-4:30 M-F EST.
Visa, MC, AMEX. Catalog, $2.
Satisfaction guaranteed.
Children's books, posters, etc.
Fun.

Ten Speed Press
P.O. Box 7123
Berkeley, CA 94707
(415) 845-8414
Check or M.O.
Housebuilding books.
Desk, Eng.

Thoburn Press
Fairfax Christian Bookstore
P.O. Box 6941
Tyler, TX 75711
1-800-962-5432
TX: (214) 581-0677
Check and M.O., or they will bill you.
Free catalog.
Returns discouraged. With permission,
resalable condition.
10% returns charge plus postage, return
UPS, no returns over $35.
Publishes revised McGuffeys.
Also Christian books and texts.
Lit.

Timberdoodle
E. 1610 Spencer Lake Road
Shelton, WA 98584
(206) 426-0672
Check, M.O., or COD. Free catalog.
Returns: 60 days, resaleable condition.
Educational materials. fishertechnik kits.
Art, Eng, Gift, Logic

Time Life Books
Time & Life Building
541 N. Fairbanks Court
Chicago, IL 60672-2058
Home Repair and Improvement Series.
Eng.

Tin Man Press
P.O. Box 219,
Stanwood WA 98292
(206) 387-0459
Visa, MC. Free brochure.
"Discover" card series.
Logic.

Toad's Tools
P.O. Box 173
Oberlin, OH 44074
Visa, MC, COD. Catalog, $1. Applied to
order.
Returns: 30 days.
Topnotch kids' tools.
Eng.

Todd Gastaldo
1348 Commerce Lane #136
Santa Clara, CA 95060
Send $1 plus large SASE for info on rela-
tionship between "chairdwelling" and
degenerative spine disease.
Mr. Gastaldo is a chiropractor.
Health.

Totline Press
See Warren Publishing House.

The Toy Factory
88878 Highway 101
Florence, OR 97439
(503) 997-8604
Visa, MC. SASE for catalog.
Minimum orders: $8 check, $15 charge.
Toys, games, books, toymaking supplies.
T & G.

Toys To Grow On
P.O. Box 17
Long Beach, CA 90801
Visa, MC, AMEX. $10 minimum.
Free catalog.
(213) 603-8890 6-6 M-Sat PST, orders
and questions.
(516) 794-5340 24 hrs, 7 days, orders
only.
Returns: 30 days.
Gift wrap, $2.
Art, Music, T & G.

Travel With Your Children (TWYCH)
Family Travel Times
80 Eighth Avenue
New York, NY 10011
Family travel magazine. *Skiing with
Children, Cruising With Children* annual
directories.
Travel.

Treehouse Publishing Company
P.O. Box 35461
Phoenix, AZ 85069
Check or M.O. Free catalogs.
Publishes variety of school stuff.
Gift.

Trinity Foundation
P.O. Box 169
Jefferson, MD 21755
(301) 371-7155
Check or cash. Free catalog, brochures.
Returns: Only defective books.
Newsletter, books. Publisher.
Logic.

Tutorial Aids for Home Educators see
TAFHE

Universal Publishing Co. of Port, Inc.
P.O. Box 226
Port Washington, NY 11050
(516) 944-6038
SASE for list of hobby offers.
Publisher of *The Sample Sleuth*.
T & G.

University of Calgary Press
Library Tower
2500 University Dr., N.W.
Calgary, Alberta T2N 1N4
CANADA
(403) 220-7578
Canadian bank cheque, micro-encoded
U.S. bank check, postal M.O., or Visa.
Echos du Monde Classique
Scholarly classical magazine.
Class.

**University of Delaware Latin Skills
Program**
see Office of Instructional Technology

Usborne Books
See Families that Play Together (retail) or
EDC Publishing (wholesale).

View-Master™
See Worldwide Slides

Visual Education Association
P.O. Box 1206
Springfield, OH 45501
Check or M.O. Free brochure.
Flash cards.
Bus, Class, For.

Wannemacher
see Peter Wannemacher

Warner Books
75 Rockefeller Plaza
New York, NY 10019
(212) 484-8000
Publisher.
Health.

Warren Publishing House, Inc.
Totline Press
P.O. Box 2255
Everett, WA 98208
1-800-334-GROW
WA, AK: (206) 485-3335 collect 8-5 PST
Visa, MC. Free catalog.
Refunds: 30 days.
Mateerials for preschoolers.
Art, Home, Music, T & G.

WEE SING
See Price/Stern/Sloan Publishers, Inc.

Wenger Corporation
Music Learning Division
P.O. Box 448
Owatonna, MN 55060
1-800-843-1337
MN, AK, HI, and Canada: (507) 451-1951
collect.
Coda catalog, $4 and worth it.
Music software and accessories.
Music.

WFF 'n PROOF Learning Games
1490 South Blvd
Ann Arbor, MI 48104-4699
(313) 665-2269
Visa, MC, COD. Free catalog.
Games for school subjects.
For, Gift, Logic, T & G.

White Lion Media
P.O. Box 120190
San Antonio, TX 78212-9966
1-800-777-LION Free color catalog.
Videos at discount.
Fun.

Wireless
Minnesota Public Radio
P.O. Box 70870
St. Paul, MN 55170-0252
1-800-328-5252 8 AM - 10 PM CST M-Sat
MC, Visa, AMEX. Free catalog.
Returns: 60 days, except for personalized items.
Many strange things.
Music, T & G.

Word DMS Inc.
P.O. Box 2560
Waco, TX 76702-2560
They bill you.
Survival Series: training for kids.
Fam.

World Of The Gifted
See Treehouse Publishing.

World Book Discovery, Inc.
Merchandise Mart Plaza, Station 13
Chicago, IL 60654
1-800-323-6366
Visa, MC. Free brochure.
Returns: 30 days.
Full line of educational software.
Eng, Enrich.

World Wide Games
Box 450 BB
Delaware, OH 43015
(614) 369-9631
Visa, MC, COD. Free catalog.
Satisfaction guaranteed.
Wooden games.
T & G.

Worldwide Slides
727 Washburn Avenue South
Minneapolis, MN 55423
Check or M.O. Minimum 5-packet order.
Free View-Master™ catalog.
View-Master™ slides.
Travel.

Young Companion
Pathway Publishers
Route 4
Aylmer, Ontario, CANADA N5H 2R3
Mennonite kid's mag.
Char, Fun.

Young Pilot
Prairie Bible Institute
Box 9
Three Hills, Alberta
CANADA T0M 2A0
Christian magazine for kids.
Char, Fun.

Zephyr Press
430 South Essex Lane
Tucson, AZ 85711
(602) 745-9199
Free catalog.
Resources promoting thinking skills, whole-brain learning, and giftedness.
New Age flavor.
Gift.

Zondervan Publishing House
1415 Lake Drive, S.E.
Grand Rapids, MI 49506
1-800-253-1309 MI: 1-800-253-4475
Large Christian publisher.
Fun.

GENERAL INDEX

D

G

H

I

J

More Teaching Resources from Crossway Books!

The Big Book of Home Learning

Mary Pride

The Big Book of Home Learning is the first resource of its kind—a Crossway Books bestseller, and winner of both the ECPA Gold Medallion in Education and the Silver Angel Award.

As the companion to *The Next Book of Home Learning*, *The Big Book* provides the basic tools every home schooler needs. Topics include: Styles of teaching • Home School Organizations • Curriculum Buyer's Guide • Reading • Writing • Mathematics • Science • History and all the other traditional subjects, reviewed by Mary Pride in a delightfully non-traditional and witty way.

This comprehensive guide reveals a wealth of learning opportunities for *anyone* of any age who wants to learn more about *anything*. It gives you everything you need to start and succeed at home teaching and learning.

"It is the fruit of an awesome research project, completed with honesty, objectivity, and skill."— *The Home Schooling Workshop*. "It deserves a place on every home schooler's bookshelf."— *Home Education Magazine*.

$17.50/X-large paperback/ISBN 0-89107-374-4

CROSSWAY BOOKS
A DIVISION OF GOOD NEWS PUBLISHERS
WESTCHESTER, ILLINOIS 60153

Available at your local Christian bookstore.
For mail orders write to Crossway Books.
Add $1.00 for postage and handling.

Committed to offering the __best__ resources for home schoolers!

More Teaching Resources from Crossway Books!

Books Children Love
A Guide to the Best Children's Literature

Elizabeth Laraway Wilson

Books Children Love puts quality children's literature into the hands of parents and teachers. It reviews hundreds of books from more than two dozen subject areas, including: Modern and Historical Literature • Fantasies and Fairy Tales • Art and Architecture • Science • Biography • Study Skills • Crafts • and more, all extensively indexed for easy referencing.

Author Elizabeth Wilson has selected, as she says, "excellently written, interest-holding books on as wide a range of topics as possible —books that also embody ideas and ideals in harmony with traditional values and a Christian worldview." Mrs. Wilson cultivated her love of books through her two sons and four grandchildren, and is now retired after working as an editor and a college-level teacher.

Let good books ignite a child's imagination for learning—use *Books Children Love*. Foreword by Susan Schaeffer Macaulay.
$12.95/Large paperback/Illustrated/ISBN 0-89107-441-4

CROSSWAY BOOKS
A DIVISION OF GOOD NEWS PUBLISHERS
WESTCHESTER, ILLINOIS 60153

Available at your local Christian bookstore.
For mail orders write to Crossway Books.
Add $1.00 for postage and handling.

Committed to offering the best resources for home schoolers!

More Teaching Resources from Crossway Books!

The Way Home
Beyond Feminism, Back to Reality

Mary Pride

In the author's words, *The Way Home* is a "mother's manifesto." She also writes, "Feminism... is aimed at rejecting God's role for women. Those who adopt any part of its lifestyle can't help picking up its philosophy... (they) are buying themselves a one-way ticket to social anarchy."

Mary Pride writes as a former radical feminist and career professional whose perspective changed drastically after she became a Christian in 1977. Now, as a Christian wife and mother of five, she presents the biblical pattern of life for married women and exposes the empty religion which feminism has become. Her message is that home is the center of life, and that a woman's highest calling is to bear and nurture children, care for her husband, and carry on a life of creative, fulfilling work within the home.

"This is a provocative book with well-documented facts. It will be a real encouragement to women who have chosen to be 'keepers at home.'"
—*Bookstore Journal*.
$8.95/Large paperback/
ISBN 0-89107-345-0

 **CROSSWAY BOOKS**
A DIVISION OF GOOD NEWS PUBLISHERS
WESTCHESTER, ILLINOIS 60153

Available at your local Christian bookstore.
For mail orders write to Crossway Books.
Add $1.00 for postage and handling.

Committed to offering the *best* resources for home schoolers!

More Teaching Resources from Crossway Books!

The Gift of Music
Great Composers and Their Influence

Jane Stuart Smith and Betty Carlson

"The authors' joyous enthusiasm...should serve to ignite the curiosity of many readers and lure them on to sample more liberally the magnificent sound structures of Bach and Handel, Haydn and Mozart—not to mention both their forerunners and their heirs."—*Christianity Today.* "I look for this book to open the doors to a new affirmation of life in the area of music."—*Francis Schaeffer.*

"Reading about these great composers has been most inspiring to me. This is a book to read and enjoy."—*George Beverly Shea.*

Now in a newly revised and expanded edition, *The Gift of Music* will open up a fascinating new world for students of classical music.

$12.95/Large paperback/ISBN 0-89107-438-4

For the Children's Sake
Foundations of Education for Home and School

Susan Schaeffer Macaulay

For The Children's Sake is full of fresh new ideas for parents and teachers. Susan Macaulay shows how your home can be just as much of a learning center as any classroom—and, so can your community, a nearby city, or the great outdoors.

"The book challenges parents with the exciting potential for awakening the minds of our children to celebrate the joy of living."—*Christian Home* and *School.*

"Macaulay's approach to education is to view it as the sum of all life. With that foundation, one begins to reassess what happens after class and on weekends with different eyes."—*Eternity.*

"Full of common sense and conviction...a substantial book that can be recommended with confidence."—*Bookstore Journal.*

$6.95/Paperback/ISBN 0-89107-290-X

ᏰᏰ CROSSWAY BOOKS
A DIVISION OF GOOD NEWS PUBLISHERS
WESTCHESTER, ILLINOIS 60153

Available at your local Christian bookstore.
For mail orders write to Crossway Books.
Add $1.00 for postage and handling.

Committed to offering the __best__ resources for home schoolers!

More Teaching Resources from Crossway Books!

The Child Abuse Industry

Mary Pride

A network of federal, state, and local agencies is snatching children right out from under their parents' noses. Every year, the child abuse industry threatens more families. How does it work?

It defines abuse so vaguely that all families could be "guilty." It operates hotlines that are open invitations to slander. It denies due process and a fair trial to those accused of child abuse. It grants immunity to hotline callers and welfare bureaucrats. And, it allows parents who <u>really</u> are abusing their kids to keep their children at home if they cooperate and undergo "therapy."

In this astounding, eye-opening study, Mary Pride examines the truth and the danger behind the current obsession with child abuse. Clear examples and specific case studies illustrate the scope of the problem, and practical strategies combat its further growth.

$8.95/Paperback/ISBN 0-89107-401-5

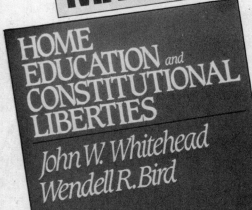

Home Education and Constitutional Liberties

John W. Whitehead and Wendell R. Bird

While SAT scores continue to plummet, reports of violence and disorder in the classroom steadily rise. National studies show that the academic performances of American school-children fall far short of those of their peers in other industrialized countries.

Faced with these problems, as many as one million families may undertake home education this year. If you are one of these, you may face heavy pressures and opposition from state authorities. What rights do you have in the face of this opposition?

Attorneys Whitehead and Bird present the facts in this readable legal study. Legally, many basic constitutional liberties—including the freedoms of speech, belief and religion, as well as the right to privacy—support your right to educate your children yourself.

This practical, thorough analysis will prove invaluable to those considering or conducting home schooling.

$6.95/Paperback/ISBN 0-89107-302-7

Available at your local Christian bookstore.
For mail orders write to Crossway Books.
Add $1.00 for postage and handling.

CROSSWAY BOOKS
A DIVISION OF GOOD NEWS PUBLISHERS
WESTCHESTER, ILLINOIS 60153

Committed to offering the <u>best</u> resources for home schoolers!